THE MONSTROUS BOOK OF SERIAL KILLERS

(SECOND EDITION)

An A-Z encyclopedia of 275 serial killers with 25 research articles, 60 extended case files and photos.

BEN OAKLEY

Published by Twelvetrees Camden

Copyright © Ben Oakley, 2019-2021

THE MONSTROUS BOOK OF SERIAL KILLERS (SECOND EDITION)

An A-Z encyclopedia of 275 serial killers with 25 research articles, 60 extended case files and photos.

by Ben Oakley

2nd edition Independently Published
ISBN: 9798696749570

All rights reserved.
No part of this publication may be reproduced, stored in a retrieval system, or be transmitted in any form or by any means, electronic, mechanical, photocopying, recording or otherwise, without the prior permission of the publishers.

Cover design by Ben Oakley and Marina Luisa. Cover image by Harrison Lake.

Discover more:
www.benoakley.co.uk

The Monstrous Book of Serial Killers (2nd edition)

Also by Ben Oakley

Fiction

Harrison Lake Mysteries
Beyond the Blood Streams
Perfect Twelve

Honeysuckle Goodwillies
Mystery of Grimlow Forest

Subnet Trilogy
Subnet: Unknown Origin
Subnet: Alien Network
Subnet: Final Contact

Non-fiction

True Crime
The Monstrous Book of Serial Killers
The True Crime 365 series.
1978: Year of The Serial Killer.
1987: Year of The Serial Killer (Chapter 2)
1996: Year of The Serial Killer (Chapter 3)

Mental Health
Mentacracy: Living Under the Rule of Mental Illness
Suicide Prevention Handbook (with Supreme Movement)

SECTION LIST

Introduction (2nd Edition) 13
Notes on Research Articles 16
Alcala, Rodney: The Dating Game Killer (Extended Case File) 18
Allen, Howard Arthur 22
Angelo, Richard 23
Amos, Lowell Edwin 24
Andermatt, Roger 25
Acevedo, Francisco 26
Baekuni 27
Balaam, Anthony 28
Barber, Danny 29
Barbosa, Daniel Camargo 30
Barfield, Velma 32
Baumeister, Herb: and the Haunting of Fox Hollow Farm (Extended Case File) ... 33
Berdella, Robert Andrew: The Kansas City Butcher (Extended Case File) 38
(Research Article #1) The Lure of Celebrity Status 42
(Research Article #2) The Lure of Social Media Fame 46
Bergamo, Marco 47
Berkowitz, David: The Son of Sam (Extended Case File) 48
Bible Belt Strangler 52
Biegenwald, Richard 53
Bishop, Arthur Gary 54
Black, Robert: Smelly Bob (Extended Case File) 55
Bonin, William 60
Brandt, Charlie 62
Brashers, Robert Eugene 63
Briley Brothers, The 64
Brown, Vernon 65
Browne, Robert Charles 66
Bunday, Thomas Richard 68
Bundy, Ted (Extended Case File) 68
Bianchi, Kenneth & Buono, Angelo: The Hillside Stranglers (Extended Case File) 73
Burkett, Nathan 75
Burtsev, Roman 76
Butcher of Mons, The. (Extended Case File) 78
Caputo, Richard 82
Catlin, Steven David 84
(Research Article #3) Child Abuse from the 1940s-1960s 85
(Research Article #4) Child Abuse from the 1990s to 2000s 90
Chagas, Francisco Das 92
Chanal, Pierre 94
Chase, Richard Trenton: The Vampire of Sacramento (Extended Case File) 95
Chikatilo, Andrei: The Red Ripper (Extended Case File) 101
Christiansen, Thor Nis 109
Ciudad Juarez Rebels, The 110

Claremont Serial Killer, The 111
Clark, Hadden Irving: The Cross-dressing Cannibal (Extended Case File) 113
Clepper, Gregory 116
Cole, Carroll 117
Colonial Parkway Murders, The. (Extended Case File) 118
Cook, Anthony and Nathaniel 121
Conahan Jr., Daniel Owen 123
Connecticut River Valley Killer, The. (Extended Case File) 125
Constanzo, Adolfo 128
Copeland, Faye and Ray 129
Corwin, Daniel Lee 130
Cottingham, Richard 132
Craine, Louis 133
Crump, Thomas Wayne 134
(Research Article #5) Attitudes towards Women in the 1970s 135
(Research Article #6) Attitudes towards Women in the Noughties 139
Cuellar, Cristopher Chavez 140
Cullen, Charles: The Killer Nurse (Extended Case File) 141
Dahmer, Jeffrey: The Milwaukee Cannibal (Extended Case File) 146
Damergi, Naceur 149
David, Horst 152
DeAngelo, Joseph James: The Golden State Killer (Extended Case File) 153
Dudin, Nikolai Arkadievich 157
Duncan III, Joseph Edward 159
Dutroux, Marc: The Monster of Belgium (Extended Case File) 161
Eckert, Volker 167
Edwards, Edward 168
Eijk, Willem Van 169
Ellis, Walter E. 170
Escalero, Francisco Garcia 171
Evans, Donald Leroy 172
Evans, Gary Charles 173
Evonitz, Richard Marc 174
Ferrari, Werner 175
Fischer, Joseph J. 176
Filho, Pedro Rodriguez 177
Fokin, Victor 179
Fourniret, Michel Paul: The Ogre of the Ardennes (Extended Case File) 180
(Research Article #7) Urban Strangers 184
(Research Article #8) Disconnected Living 188
Fowler, Bobby Jack 189
Francois, Kendall: The Poughkeepsie Killer (Extended Case File) 190
Frankford Slasher, The. (Extended Case File) 197
Franklin, Joseph Paul: The Racist Killer (Extended Case File) 200
Franklin Jr., Lonnie David: The Grim Sleeper (Extended Case File) 202
Fyfe, William Patrick 204
Furlan, Marco and Abel, Wolfgang 205
Gacy, John Wayne: The Killer Clown (Extended Case File) 206
Gallego, Gerald and Charlene: The Love Slave Killers (Extended Case File) ... 212
Garavito, Luis: The Beast (Extended Case File) 215

Gargiulo, Michael Thomas	219
Gary, Carlton: The Stocking Strangler (Extended Case File)	220
Gaskins, Donald Henry	222
Georgiev, Hristo Bogdanov	224
Gilbert, Kristen Heather	225
Gillis, Sean Vincent: The Other Baton Rouge Killer (Extended Case File)	226
(Research Article #9) Highways to Hell	229
(Research Article #10) Project E-Pana: Highway of Tears	232
(Research Article #11) Cheap Travel and Open Borders	236
Gilyard, Lorenzo Jerome	238
Glaze, Billy Richard	239
Graham, Harrison	240
Greba, Alexander	241
Greenwood, Vaughn Orrin	242
Groves, Vincent Darrell	243
Grzesik, Tadeusz	244
Haigh, Paul Steven	245
Hall, Archibald	246
Hance, William Henry	248
Hansen, Robert	249
Hansson, Anders	250
Harding, Donald Eugene	251
Harvey, Donald	252
Hatcher, Charles Ray: One Man Crime Wave (Extended Case File)	253
Heaulme, Francis	258
Heidnik, Gary Michael	261
Hertogs, Jacobus Dirk	262
Hicks, James R.	263
Hojer, Ladislav	264
Holst, Thomas	265
Hubal, Abdullah	266
Hughes, Michael	266
Hwaseong Serial Murders	268
(Research Article #12) Victim Selection in the 1970s	269
(Research Article #13) Victim Selection in the 2010s	272
Ivanov, Yuri	274
Ivanyutina, Tamara	275
Jablonski, Phillip Carl	276
Jackson, Elton Manning	277
Johnson, Martha Ann	278
Jones, Genene	279
Jordan, Gilbert Paul	280
Junco, Francisco del	281
Junni, Ismo Kullervo	282
Kibbe, Roger: The I-5 Strangler (Extended Case File)	283
Kirkland, Anthony	286
Knychala, Jaochim	287
Koltun, Joseph	287
Komin, Alexander: The Vyatka Maniac (Extended Case File)	288
Kraft, Randy: The Scorecard Killer (Extended Case File)	292

(Research Article #14) DNA Evidence Exploded in the 1980s 295
Krajcir, Timothy 297
Kuklinski, Richard 298
Kukula, Henryk 299
Lainz Angels of Death 300
Lee, Bruce George Peter 301
Lee, Derrick Todd 303
Lindholm, Jukka Torsten 304
Lindsey, William Darrell 306
Little, Samuel 307
Lockhart, Michael Lee 308
Long Island Serial Killer: The Craigslist Killer (Extended Case File) 310
Lopez, Pedro: Monster of the Andes (Extended Case File) 314
Louis, Emile 317
Lucas, David Allen 318
Lucas, Henry Lee 319
Luptak, Juraj 320
Maake, Maoupa Cedric 321
Martynov, Sergei 323
(Research Article #15) Toxic Legacy of World War Two 324
(Research Article #16) Toxic Legacy of the Iraq War 327
Mashiane, Johannes 328
Mason, David Edwin 329
Matteucci, Andrea 330
Maudsley, Robert: Hannibal the Cannibal (Extended Case File) 331
Maust, David Edward 334
Maxwell, Bobby Joe 335
McDuff, Kenneth 337
McGown, Richard Gladwell 338
McGray, Michael Wayne 339
McRae, John Rodney 341
Metheny, Joseph Roy 342
Mfeka, Samuel Bongani 343
Mikhasevich, Gennady 344
Minghella, Maurizio: The Valpocevera Strangler (Extended Case File) 345
(Research Article #17) The Macdonald Triad 348
Mmbengwa, David 351
Monster of Florence 352
Moore, Blanche Taylor 352
Morus, Henryk 355
Mulaudzi, Mukosi Freddy 356
Murphy, Donald 357
Nance, Wayne 358
Naso, Joseph 359
Night-time Killers, The 360
Nilsen, Dennis: The Muswell Hill Murderer (Extended Case File) 362
Onoprienki, Anatoly: The Beast of the Ukraine (Extended Case File) 371
Pandy, Andras 375
Parker, Gerald 376
Paulin, Thierry 377

Peiry, Michel 378
Pennell, Steven Brian..379
Pichushkin, Alexander: The Chessboard Killer (Extended Case File) 380
Pickton, Robert: The Pig Farmer Killer (Extended Case File)...............................387
Pintaric, Vinko 392
Popkov, Mikhail: The Werewolf (Extended Case File)..393
(Research Article #18) The Vietnam War Divide..397
(Research Article #19) The Afghanistan War Divide 401
Price, Craig Chandler 402
Profit, Mark Antonio..403
Psicopata, El (The Psychopath)..405
Quansah, Charles 406
Quick, Thomas 407
Radar, Denis: The BTK Killer (Extended Case File)..408
Rand, Andre..413
Randall, James Michael 414
Rasmussen, Terrence Peder...415
Ray, David Parker: The Toy Box Killer (Extended Case File) 417
Recco, Tommy 422
Reddy, Umesh 423
Reinstrom, Lutz 424
Resendiz, Angel Maturino 425
Retunsky, Vladimir 426
(Research Article #20) Exposure to Lead 428
Rhoades, Robert Ben...430
Gary Ridgway: The Green River Killer (Extended Case File)................................432
Robinson, John Edward: The First Internet Serial Killer (Extended Case File) 435
Rogers, Ramon Jay 439
Romanov, Vladimir..440
Rose, Lindsey Robert 441
(Research Article #21) The Renfield Syndrome 442
Rylkov, Oleg..444
Sakharov, Nikolay Alexandrovich...445
Saldivar, Efren...446
Sanchez, Altemio: The Bike Path Killer (Extended Case File) 447
Satish..450
Schaefer, Gary Lee 451
Scheanette, Dale Devon 452
Schiffer, Egidius...454
Seel, Manfred 455
Segundo, Juan...456
Sells, Tommy Lynn 457
Sewage Plant Killer, The..458
(Research Article #22) Movies that Influenced Killers 459
Shankariya, Kampatimar 463
Shawcross, Arthur 464
Shermantine, Wesley & Herzog, Loren: The Speed Freak Killers (Extended Case File)..465
Shemyakov, Eduard 468
Shipilov, Sergey...469

Shipman, Harold: Doctor Death (Extended Case File)	470
Shulman, Robert Yale	474
Sikder, Ershad	476
Silveria Jr., Robert Joseph	477
Simons, Norman: The Station Strangler (Extended Case File)	479
Sinclair, Angus: The World's End Murderer (Extended Case File)	485
Sinclair, Charles Thurman	488
Sleepy Hollow Killer	489
Slivko, Anatoly	490
Slovak, Jozef	491
Smith, Lemuel	492
Smithers, Samuel	493
Snowtown Murders: The Bodies in the Barrels (Extended Case File)	495
Solomon Jr., Morris	499
Spencer, Timothy Wilson: The Southside Strangler (Extended Case File)	500
Spesivtsev, Alexander: The Siberian Ripper (Extended Case File)	503
Stafford, Roger Dale	506
Stano, Gerald Eugene: The Boardwalk Serial Killer (Extended Case File)	507
(Research Article #23) The Rise of True Crime Pornography	510
(Research Article #24) The Rise of Violent Pornography	514
Steinwegs, Kurt-Friedhelm	515
Stoneman, The	516
Storozhenko, Vladimir	517
Suradji, Ahmad: The Black Magic Killer (Extended Case File)	518
Sutcliffe, Peter: The Yorkshire Ripper (Extended Case File)	521
Swango, Joseph Michael	526
Thwala, Sipho	527
Tinning, Marybeth	528
Tkach, Serhiy Fedorovich	528
Tobin, Peter: Bible John (Extended Case File)	530
Trobec, Metod	535
Trudeau, Yves	535
Tuchlin, Pawel	536
Ture, Joseph Donald Jr.	537
Turner, Chester Dewayne	538
Unterweger, Jack	539
Urdiales, Andrew: The Monster in the Desert (Extended Case File)	540
Vakrinos, Dimitris	543
Vega, Jose Antonio Rodriguez	544
Watts, Carl 'Coral'	545
Waxin, Denis	546
West, Fred and Rose: House of Horrors (Extended Case File)	547
Wilken, Stewart	553
Wood, Gwendolyn Graham & Catherine	554
Woodcock, Peter	556
Yapicioglu, Yavuz	556
Yates, Robert Lee	558
(Research Article #25) Active Serial Killers	559
Appendices	563
Bibliography	563

Image Attributions 571
Bonus Content 579

Introduction (2nd Edition)

The 2019 edition of the *Monstrous Book of Serial Killers* went on to become an international bestseller, which was fantastic news when considering the amount of time and work that went into the original encyclopedia's creation. This second edition for 2021 is far superior and has been re-edited, reformatted, and redesigned to make it even more accessible to true crime fans and readers of the macabre.

So what's new?

The first edition listed 250 serial killers along with additional research articles. This second edition lists an additional 25 bringing the total to 275 serial killers, all laid out in an A-Z format. This is on top of the original and newly updated 25 research articles that vary in content from the rise of violent pornography to the effect of war on certain individuals.

87 entries from the first edition have been updated with new information and factual content. This might be for a number of reasons including but not limited to; end of sentences, releases on parole, death notices, end of trials and updates to ongoing investigations. Most have been updated if there has been new research available and new information that has come to light and is relevant for inclusion.

This book remains the culmination of many years of research and data gathering. The aim has always been to put together an ultimate book of serial killers that was more than just a book about serial killers. The listings range in length from one page to ten pages, with the longest going into more depth about each case.

These protracted sections make up the 60 extended case files found throughout these pages. What sets this book apart are the additions of the research articles that provide further knowledge regarding serial killers and can be cited for further publication.

Those articles are between two and nine pages long and provide fully researched and referenced material. There are 12 reasons given as to why serial killers do what they do, these are based on cultural, societal, familial and environmental data.

Read the *Notes on Research Articles* in the next heading to get a better understanding of how they are laid out and the reasons for them.

There is also the addition of over 100 images which were not present in the first edition, making this one of the most complete and accessible serial killer encyclopedia's out there.

Since records began, there have been over 5,000 serial killers that have stained the world with their actions, with over 3,000 in the United States alone. There are 275 of them listed here from all over the world including Russia, Ghana, United Kingdom, France, India and of course the United States. All laid out in an easy-to-read format with bullet-point statistics at the end of each one containing all the vital information you need. Some you would have heard of, others you might not have done.

Due to this new edition being over 700 pages in length, we had to trim down the size of some of the cases. To make space for the kind of case files you want to read, the decision was taken not to list all of the victim names. If we look at Harold Shipman then we have 215 victims; the highest confirmed and convicted victim count in known history. Simply put, to list the names of all 215 victims and the hundreds of others taken by the killers listed here, would have eaten up the space needed for facts and data.

The Monstrous Book of Serial Killers is fully researched and referenced, complete with appendices and a bibliography of all studies and data cited within these pages. There are some ground-breaking revelations and research-backed theories throughout this book. They are provided by cultural understanding, psychological effects, factual evidence, international events and a rising mental health epidemic.

The 2021 edition of this book includes photo collages at various intervals throughout. All photos and images have the correct copyright and usage licenses, which are all listed under the *Image Attribution* section of the *Appendices*. Under or nearby each photo is an attribution number written for example as: *(Attrib 1.)*. This then links to the same attribution number in the appendices for correct citation. Extra care has been taken to ensure that the photos are suitable for all age groups and can be used for publication in this book.

Some other notes that may be important. The book is written in British English, with American English only used in the description of American locations, names, or sayings. Elements of the book, including some research articles have previously been published within the *Year of the Serial Killer* books, also from Twelvetrees Publishing. The names of the killers are laid out in alphabetical order by their surname with research articles intersecting where relevant.

There are no curse words in the book, however some descriptions do include content that may be unsuitable for children or for those of a fragile mindset. This isn't a sugar-coated book on the creation of fluffy toys, this is a book about humans killing other humans and why they do it. Thus a certain level of justifiable content has been included to fully round out the extended case files.

In the digital edition of the book you can jump to any section you wish by clicking on the relevant chapter heading.

All facts and citations are correct as of June 2021.

I fully hope that you enjoy this book as much as I have had putting it together.

Notes on Research Articles

In the build up to *1978: Year of the Serial Killer,* I was tasked with researching the cultural and environmental reasons behind why some people choose to kill. The 1970s and 1980s saw serial killing become an epidemic, especially in larger populated countries and there had to be reasons why those decades saw vast amounts of multiple murderers.

Turns out, there was.

12 reasons were researched and have been laid out in easy-to-read chapters, with each being developed for this book you're holding now. The 1990s and 2000s saw their fair share of serial killers but nothing like in the decades prior to them.

The intricacies of the human mind are incredibly individual so there will always be unique reasons why serial killers kill. The reasons provided in this book reflect cultural, environmental, social and economic factors in the decades before and during the 1970s.

Now that we had reasons leading to the year of the serial killer in 1978, two theoretical questions were put forward.

What if 50 years after 1978 there was another rise in serial killing?

Would the 12 reasons be similar in any way?

Then began the *2028: Rise of the Serial Killer* project, set 50 years after the year of the serial killer and only a few years out from this 2021 edition of the book. The reasons for 2028 were researched in exactly the same manner, trying to find comparable reasons leading up to 2028 that might cause another rise in serial killing.

One could argue that by the mid-1990s, DNA technology had improved so much that serial killers were being caught on their first murder, stopping them before they got going. Yet, in various other cases active as of 2021, there are those that haven't stopped killing and have simply adapted to the ever-changing landscape of technology and surveillance equipment.

Every article from *2028: Rise of the Serial Killer* is here in this book, side by side with the original 12 reasons. The hypothetical articles were first published in my own *1978: Year of the Serial Killer* and provide similar modern factors to show that we might be moving towards a new wave of serial killing. The 2028 research articles directly follow their counterparts, with an example below.

(Research Article #1) The Lure of Celebrity Status

(Research Article #2) The Lure of Social Media Fame

The Lure of Celebrity Status article talks about the rise of the celebrity during the 1960s and 1970s and how so many people wanted fame and recognition. Whilst some sought fame through legal and ethical avenues, others had already given up on all things moral. The article describes those serial killers who sought nothing more than infamy.

Jump forward 40 years and fame has become so much easier to take hold of. Thus, the hypothetical 2028 version of the article is; *The Lure of Social Media Fame*, which becomes the companion piece to *The Lure of Celebrity Status*. You'll notice this research article layout all the way through the book. In addition, there are further individual research articles to be found within these pages.

Now – let's dive in!

Alcala, Rodney: The Dating Game Killer (Extended Case File)

On September 13th 1978, *Rodney Alcala,* AKA*: The Dating Game Killer,* appeared on the national television show; *The Dating Game.* It marked a surreal and defining moment in the history of serial killers.

His total number of victims is unknown but it is suggested to be close to 100. He would generally pose as a fashion photographer to get close to his victims and win their confidence. He would strangle them until they lost consciousness whereupon he would bring them back around and repeat the process many times before ultimately killing them.

Alcala had been compared to *Ted Bundy* numerous times, not least because of his *charming* appearance on The Dating Game TV show. He had a collection of over 1000 photographs of women and young boys, many in sexually explicit poses. It is speculated that some of them could have been other victims as many were not or have not yet been identified.

After a childhood where his father would abandon him and his mother would move them around, he joined the U.S. Army in 1960 at the age of 17-years-old. A few years later he went AWOL and was subsequently diagnosed with borderline personality disorder. He has never spoken of his time in the military.

In 1968, Alcala stalked eight-year-old *Tali Shapiro* as she was walking to school in Hollywood. He told her that he was a friend of her parents and she went with him to his apartment. At the same time a member of the public reported the incident as it had looked suspicious.

When police arrived, Alcala escaped out the back door but not before he had abused, raped and tortured Shapiro. He had beaten her to within an inch of her life with a steel bar. She survived to give a statement but her parents wouldn't allow her to testify against Alcala.

Had they let her do so, she may have stopped a killing spree that some claim could have reached 130 victims. He served only 34 months in prison for raping and beating the eight-year-old girl.

After his release he moved to the East Coast where he went under a new name. He studied film and photography under *Roman Polanski* of all people. He would then approach women and young boys claiming he was a fashion photographer and luring them into posing for him.

One victim he lured in such a manner was a 23-year-old air hostess named *Cornelia Crilley*. In 1971, her body was discovered in her own Manhattan apartment. She had been raped and strangled and was only connected to Alcala 40 years after her death.

Between 1971 and 1979 he had tricked up to 1,000 young men, girls and women into believing that he was a professional photographer. A large majority of the photos were of people in the nude or in sexually explicit poses, including pages and pages of naked girls and boys.

On September 13th 1978, Alcala made his infamous appearance as a contestant on The Dating Game.

"A successful photographer who got his start when his father found him in the darkroom at the age of 13, fully developed! Between takes you might find him skydiving or motorcycling."

Jim Lange, The Dating Game host, introducing Alcala.

In an even more extraordinary twist, he went on to win the show and won a date with the woman looking for love. Alcala had the bizarre tenacity to appear on the show in public to the country after having killed potentially dozens of victims. After his appearance, he would go on to kill at least another three people.

He was arrested in 1979 and has remained in jail ever since as he gets convicted with more and more murders. He has been sentenced to death a number of times, some of which were commuted to life. As of 2021, he remains on death row in California.

It wasn't until March 10th 2010, that the Huntington Beach Police and New York City Police departments officially released 120 of his photographs in order to seek the public's help in identifying them.

There are another 900 photos in Alcala's portfolio that cannot be released due to their sexual content. Some of the 120 have since been recognised by family members as loved ones who had disappeared without a trace and may have been further victims of *The Dating Game Killer*.

Born **August 23rd 1943**.

Active from **1971-1979**.

Arrested on **July 27th 1979**.

Country: **USA (California)**.

Victims: **8-100+**.

AKA: **The Dating Game Killer / John Berger**.

Sentence: **Death penalty**.

Current whereabouts: **Awaiting execution**

The Monstrous Book of Serial Killers (2nd edition)

IMAGE ATTRIBUTIONS
(ATTRIB A1) (ATTRIB 48 TO 53)

PHOTOS ABOVE WERE PUBLICALLY RELEASED FROM ALCALA'S COLLECTION OF PHOTOS. SOME HAVE BEEN IDENTIFIED WHILE OTHERS REMAIN UNIDENTIFIED.

RODNEY ALCALA

Allen, Howard Arthur

American serial killer of elderly women, active between 1974 to 1987. The murder of 73-year-old *Ernestine Griffin* on July 14th 1987 was particularly brutal and resulted in his capture.

The day before her murder, Griffin had contacted her next door neighbour, a dentist named Dr. Seaman. She told him a man had stopped by her house enquiring about a car that Dr. Seaman was selling. The man had left a note with his name and phone number on.

The next morning, the dentist discovered Griffin dead in her home. She had a butcher's knife sticking out of her chest and her face had been smashed in with a toaster. A handwriting expert linked the note to Allen which linked him to the murder. He was quickly arrested and charged.

Allen had previously been sentenced for manslaughter after beating to death 85-year-old Opal Cooper in August of 1974 during a robbery. He was released in January 1985 and committed various robberies until his second murder on May 20th 1985, when he attacked 87-year-old Laverne Hale. Hale would die from her injuries nine days later.

Allen was sentenced to death for all three of his victims but was later commuted to 60 years due to mental incapacity at the time of the murders. He is due to be released in 2035.

Born **August 4th 1949**.

Active from **1974-1987**

Arrested on **February 10th 1987**.

Country: **USA (Indiana)**.

Victims: **3**.

Sentence: **Death penalty, later commuted to life.**

Current whereabouts: **In prison, awaiting 2035 release.**

Angelo, Richard

On November 15th 1987, American medical serial killer *Richard Angelo* was arrested and taken into custody after assaulting a 73-year-old patient of his. By the time of his arrest, Angelo was only 25-years-old and had killed at least eight people.

Sometimes referred to as the *Angel of Death*, Angelo was a nurse at the Good Samaritan Hospital in the Suffolk County area of New York. He used poison to kill and was linked with at least ten deaths and the poisoning of at least 25 others. He poisoned his victims to bring on a cardiac arrest so that he could try and resuscitate them in front of other workers at the hospital. He claimed he did this in order to be seen as a hero.

Angelo was convicted in December of 1989 of two of the murders, one manslaughter, and one criminally negligent homicide. In four other deaths he was convicted of associated assault. It is suspected that he killed at least ten.

Angelo was sentenced to at least 50 years in prison and currently remains incarcerated at the Great Meadow Correctional Facility in Washington County.

Born **April 29th 1962.**

Active during **1987.**

Arrested on **October 12th 1987.**

Country: **USA.**

Victims: **8-26.**

Sentence: **61 years to life in prison.**

Current whereabouts: **In prison.**

Amos, Lowell Edwin

American murderer and possible serial killer, *Lowell Edwin Amos*, is a convicted murderer whose family members died under suspicious circumstances. The deaths of his mother and all three of his wives led him to gain the moniker of the *Black Widower*.

In 1996, he was convicted of the murder of his third wife, *Roberta Mowery Amos*. All the murders looked like accidents. He was convicted of premeditated murder and murder using a toxic substance. One of his wives died after a hair-dryer landed in her bath water as she was in it.

Another died of a cocaine overdose after he injected a large amount of the drug into her vagina. After the death of his mother by apparent natural causes, he inherited over $1million USD. No autopsy was carried out due to her age but it is suspected he used sedatives to drug and kill her.

He is currently serving life without parole at the Muskegon Correctional Facility in Michigan.

Born **January 4th 1943**.

Active from **1979-1994**.

Arrested on **November 8th 1996**.

Country: **United States**.

Victims: **1-4**.

AKA: **Black Widower**.

Sentence: **Life imprisonment**.

Current whereabouts: **In prison**.

Andermatt, Roger

Swiss serial killer *Roger Andermatt, AKA: The Death-Keeper of Lucerne*, killed 22 people over a 16 year period, and remains the most prolific serial killer in the history of Switzerland.

Andermatt was an *'Angel of Death'* killer who murdered elderly people in various retirement homes across the country. All his victims were elderly women aged between 66-years-old to 95-years-old. He used various medicines in order to kill them.

Nursing home staff began to notice the abnormal rise in deaths wherever Andermatt was working and they informed the authorities. In 2001, after his arrest, multiple suspected victims were exhumed and autopsied. It took another four years in a lengthy trial to prove his guilt.

In January of 2005, Andermatt was convicted on 22 charges of murder and sentenced to life in prison. An appeal trial upheld the sentence, when investigators discovered at least another three unlawful deaths in care homes where he had worked.

Andermatt would later claim that he killed out of compassion, and because the nursing homes were overworked.

Born in **1969**.

Active from **1995-2001**.

Arrested in **June 2001**.

Country: **Switzerland**.

Victims: **22-25+**.

AKA: **The Death-Keeper of Lucerne**.

Sentence: **Life imprisonment**.

Current whereabouts: **In prison**.

Acevedo, Francisco

New York serial killer, *Francisco Acevedo*, killed three women over the course of a seven year period. He would only be caught when DNA given from a drink-driving charge in 2010 linked him to the three unsolved murders.

Acevedo had never once been a suspect in the murders until his arrest and the DNA they had on record was never linked to him. His defence team claimed that Acevedo had claimed he did have sex with the women but did not rape and murder them.

He killed 26-year-old prostitute *Maria Ramos* in February of 1989, then 28-year-old prostitute *Tawana Hodges* in 1991. On May 4th 1996, he killed 30-year-old *Kimberly Moore*. She was not known to have been involved in the sex industry. He murdered them all by tying them up, raping them and then strangling them to death.

Moore's body was discovered by a motel clerk in Room 45 of the Trade Winds Motor Court, which is a pay-by-the-hour motel in the Yonkers area. The clerk, *Carlos Gonzalez*, entered the room to inform the guest that it was past checkout time. After she didn't respond, he pulled the sheets off the bed and saw blood on Moore's forehead

Gonzalez became a witness at the trial after being the only person to see Acevedo with one of his victims. In 2012, he was found guilty of all three murders and sentenced to 75 years to life in prison.

Born in **1968**.

Active from **1989-1996**.

Arrested in **April 2010**.

Country: **USA (New York)**.

Victims: **3**.

Sentence: **75 years to life in prison**.

Current whereabouts: **In prison**.

Baekuni

Another one-named criminal, *Baekuni,* AKA: *Babe,* is an Indonesian serial killer who raped and tortured to death 14 young boys. When he was only a youngster, Baekuni ran away from his home in Java and fled to Jakarta. There he was raped on the streets by a gang member.

In 1993, when he was 32-years-old, he began attacking children who were living on the streets. He claimed he did this in retaliation for not being able to fight back against his attacker when he was younger. His victims ranged from the age of four-years-old to 13-years-old and were mostly runaways or homeless children. Because of this, he was able to get away with killing for so long.

Indonesia is home to very few serial killers and Baekuni's case was rare for the country. He was caught in 2010 when he kidnapped a nine-year-old boy, raped him and dismembered his body. His body parts were found on January 8th 2010, and his head was found the day after. The murder led to his arrest.

During his trial, evidence came to light that he had killed at least 14 young boys and attacked another four. Later in 2010, he was sentenced to life imprisonment in a Jakarta prison for the murders of the 14 boys. As of 2021, he remains incarcerated in Jakarta.

Born in **1961**.

Active from **1993-2010**.

Arrested on **January 8th 2010**.

Country: **Indonesia**.

Victims: **14**.

AKA: **Babe**.

Sentence: **Life imprisonment**.

Current whereabouts: **In prison, in Jakarta**.

Balaam, Anthony

Also known as *The Trenton Strangler*, Balaam would be convicted of raping and strangling four prostitutes from 1994 to 1996. He paid in drugs to the prostitutes he didn't kill and would generally kill in the early hours of the morning.

On August 8th 1996, Balaam was arrested after a fifth victim managed to escape and led police to him. All of his murders took place less than two miles from his home and he was convicted because of DNA found on the victims. After his arrest, the rape victim identified him from a line-up, and Balaam was charged with four murders and one rape.

He later claimed that it was the power he gained over women that urged him to kill, the feeling of controlling what happened to them. His final murder was on July 29th 1996, when he murdered 37-year-old prostitute *Debra Ann Walker*.

In 2001, Balaam was sentenced to life in prison, after avoiding the death penalty.

Born **July 9th 1965**.

Active from **1994-1996**.

Arrested on **August 8th 1996**.

Country: **USA (New Jersey)**.

Victims: **4**.

AKA: **The Trenton Strangler**.

Sentence: **Life imprisonment**.

Current whereabouts: **In prison**.

Barber, Danny

An American serial killer who murdered four people between 1978 and 1980. He was convicted of all four murders of women in Texas over a two-year period. He was arrested in 1980 for the murder of 50-year-old *Janice Ingram* in 1979.

Janice's mother *Ruth Clowers* had found her daughter's naked body, she had been beaten with a section of pipe, in a frenzied attack during a burglary. Barber later claimed that it was simply a robbery gone wrong, and when Janice had started screaming he hit her to keep her quiet.

It was upon his arrest that he confessed to three more killings. Barber killed one unnamed victim on June 18th 1978, then 48-year-old *Mercedes Mendez* on January 17th 1979, and finally *Mary Caperton* on April 21st 1980. He was given a life sentence for each of the three aforementioned murders.

For the murder of Janice Ingram, he was sentenced to death, and executed via lethal injection in February of 1999. While he was on death row he created cross-stitch crafts that he sold through a web page.

Born **May 8th 1955**.

Active from **1978-1980**.

Arrested on **May 6th 1980**.

Country: **USA (Texas)**.

Victims: **4**.

Sentence: **Death penalty and three life sentences**.

Current whereabouts: **Executed by lethal injection in February 1999**.

Barbosa, Daniel Camargo

A Columbian serial killer who raped and murdered up to 150 young girls. He was first suspected of raping and killing 72 young girls and was jailed in 1977. Astonishingly, he had escaped in 1984 to Ecuador where he continued his rampage of killing and claimed another 54 lives.

After having studied the ocean currents, he had escaped a primitive prison boat and made it to shore. Prison authorities at the time claimed that he had died at sea, with the media claiming he had been eaten by sharks.

Neither were true, just two weeks after arriving in Ecuador, he abducted and killed a nine-year-old girl, then the next day a 10-year-old. He killed another 52 over a two-year period until 1986. Police at the time believed that the murders were a work of a gang, as they could not comprehend that only one man was responsible.

After raping his victims, he hacked and dismembered the bodies with a machete and disposed of their remains in forests. Barbosa later stated that he liked young girls because he preferred to attack virgins. He claimed it gave him pleasure to see them cry when he raped them.

His sentence of 16 years in prison was the maximum available sentence in Ecuador at the time. He once served time alongside fellow Colombian child serial killer *Pedro Lopez* and was known as the *Sadist of Chanquito*.

Born **January 22nd 1930**.

Active from **1974-1977** and **1984-1986**.

Arrested on **February 26th 1986**.

Country: **Colombia / Ecuador.**

Victims: **72-150.**

AKA: **The Sadist of Chanquito.**

Sentence: **16 years in prison.**

Current whereabouts: **Killed by another inmate on November 13th 1994.**

BAEKUNI

IMAGE ATTRIB. 2

DANNY LEE BARBER

IMAGE ATTRIB. 72

VELMA BARFIELD

IMAGE ATTRIB. 73

Barfield, Velma

On February 3rd 1978, *Velma Barfield*, killed Rowland *Stuart Taylor*. Velma was an American female serial killer who took the lives of six people but was only convicted for the murder of Taylor. She mixed arsenic-based rat poison into Rowland's beer and tea. After her arrest in May 1978, his body was exhumed as evidence of her crime.

As a child, she would steal money from her father to buy things at school that better-off children had. She then stole $80 USD from a neighbour, her father found out and beat her. She claimed she loved her father and after the beatings he would buy her nice things. It has been suggested that Velma and her father were having a sexual relationship.

She married her school friend, *Thomas Burke*, at 17-years-old and had two children with him. After a medically forced hysterectomy she began to feel insecure as a female. Shortly after, Burke became an alcoholic. Velma then took the children out of the house and burned it to the ground, leaving Burke dead inside.

Then she married *Jennings Barfield* who quickly died of a heart attack in 1971. Shortly after, Velma's mother died of arsenic poisoning but it wasn't discovered until later. She would take pleasure in poisoning people under her care and nursing them back to life. An elderly man she was caring for also died under suspicious circumstances.

When her new boyfriend died the same way as the others, Velma's sister told police she had killed a lot of people the same way. After her arrest in 1978 she was convicted and given the death sentence. She was executed in November of 1984, the first woman to be executed in the United States since 1962.

It wasn't until 1998 that the next female would be executed. Her name was *Karla Faye Tucker* and she was sentenced to death for killing two people with a pickaxe.

Born **October 23rd 1932**.

Active from **1969-1978**.

Arrested on **May 13th 1978**.

Country: **USA (North Carolina)**.

Victims: **6**.

AKA: **Death Row Granny**.

Sentence: **Death penalty**.

Current whereabouts: **Executed November 1994**.

Baumeister, Herb: and the Haunting of Fox Hollow Farm (Extended Case File)

In Indiana, American serial killer *Herbert Richard Baumeister*, AKA: *The I-70 Strangler*, killed at least 12 young men from 1980 to 1996. Almost all of the men were last seen at gay bars in the region, before their remains were later discovered at his property on *Fox Hollow Farm*.

Born in 1947, just after World War Two, he was raised in a relatively normal household with three younger siblings. When he reached puberty, something had changed within him. He became antisocial and withdrew from being with friends and family. Some people who knew him as a teenager, claimed that he played with the bodies of dead animals, and was once caught urinating on a teacher's desk.

One former friend said that something wasn't right with Baumeister and recalled a story about a dead crow. One morning on the way to school, Baumeister had picked up a dead crow and shoved it into his pocket. When he got to school, he left it on the teacher's desk in full view of the class.

While a teenager, he was diagnosed by a doctor as having schizophrenia but due to the difference in mental health access we have nowadays compared to then, he was not given any psychiatric treatment for it.

He married when he was 24-years-old, in 1971, and had three children by his wife, Julie Baumeister. By 1988, he had founded and opened the Sav-a-Lot chain shops in Indiana and became a respected member of the business community and local community.

By 1991, after creating a successful business, Baumeister and his family moved to a Tudor-style home and estate in the fashionable Westfield district. The property had a swimming pool, stables and almost 20 acres of land where the family could grow and live in luxury. Inside the house, a tension and a fear was rising, Julie began to believe everything her husband was telling her.

Julie split from him multiple times but always returned to him, in a fashion that some would describe as Baumeister having control over his wife. When colleagues and friends visited the house, they saw messy rooms, unclean surfaces and a complete lack of order. The grounds of the property had been left to overgrow and their land was becoming unusable.

In 1994, their son was playing in the grounds when he found a full human skeleton. They waited for Herb Baumeister to return and he explained it away as being one of his father's fake medical skeletons. He claimed to have found it in the garage one day and decided to bury it. Julie believed her husband but the skeleton belonged to one of his victims.

A year earlier, in 1993, connections in the cases of missing gay men were already being made. A private investigator named *Vergil Vandagriff*, joined forces with an investigator from the Indianapolis Police Department, named *Mary Wilson*. They both believed that the missing men might have been connected in some way and began an investigation to connect the evidence. As the investigation gained media attention, they were approached by a gay man who claimed he knew who killed a friend of his.

He gave them a name but the name didn't show up on any searches. The man mysteriously disappeared for a couple of years until 1995 when he phoned the investigation and gave them the number plate of the man who he suspected to have killed his friend. It is unclear whether he had carried out his own private investigation in order to get the license plate, or whether he had been holding on to it until the right time came around.

The license plate linked to Herb Baumeister, and so Wilson approached Fox Hollow Farm to speak to him. She asked to search the house but he refused. Julie Baumeister also refused police to search the house. Because the only link was a license plate, the investigation couldn't gain a warrant for the house.

By June 1996, Julie Baumeister had finally ended her marriage to Herb, as she had become scared of him. His violent mood swings and weird behaviour had become too much for her to handle. While Herb Baumeister was on a supposed business vacation, Julie called the investigators and allowed them to search the house and the grounds.

The remains of 11 men were unearthed, with only four of them ever being identified. Baumeister found out about the search of the house and eloped over the Canadian border to Ontario. He wrote a suicide note in which he spoke about his failing marriage and dwindling business but didn't mention the murders at all. Shortly after, he shot himself dead in Pinery Provincial Park.

Julie Baumeister went on to tell the investigation that her ex-husband had made over 100 trips to Ohio on apparent business trips. It was then that the investigation linked Baumeister with the murders of nine more men, whose bodies had been discovered along the main highway between Indiana and Ohio; the Interstate 70. Baumeister's body was discovered eight days after he had killed himself.

The Fox Hollow Farm and House was stripped of everything after the bodies had been discovered, and it stood abandoned for many years. Until it was sold cheaply to Rob and Vicky Graves from Indiana. Everything seemed to be going fine until one day Vicky was cleaning the house and the hoover kept coming unplugged at the wall socket for no apparent reason. It scared her and she began to suspect something was wrong with the house.

Then more things began happening.

One day, Vicky came home from work to see Rob painting, and took a good look at his work. She then looked beyond the painting and saw a man outside the window, standing in the grounds of the house. The man turned from her but he had no legs, then he disappeared completely. The family then installed security cameras.

Shortly after, one of Rob's work colleagues named Joe, moved into the spare apartment in the property, with his dog. One night while washing the dishes, there was a knock at the door but no one was there. Then the dog began acting as if someone was in the apartment but no one was there.

A few nights later, Joe was walking his dog in the grounds when he saw a man watching them from the woods. The dog gave chase and Joe followed, to see the man even closer, before running back to the house. After speaking to the Graves, it appeared they had seen the same man.

Another night came and another encounter happened. This time the dog was growling at someone who was trying to open the front door. Joe stood up and the door swung open to a strong wind. He went to the door and looked outside but no one was there. Upon turning to head back into the apartment, a man was running towards him from inside the apartment, screaming for his life.

They then began to research Baumeister's victims and Joe watched some old news footage and was certain he had seen the man in the victim list. On another occasion, Joe's dog uncovered a human bone in the grounds of the estate, in the exact location that he had seen the man in the woods.

Rob Graves then contacted Mary Wilson, the lead investigator on the case. She came out to the estate and showed them where the bodies had been uncovered. They appeared to be in the same vicinity as the locations of the unexplained phenomena.

Suddenly, news of the hauntings grew, and an army of paranormal investigators and demonologists descended on the estate. On one occasion, Joe was in the pool with some others, cleaning the bottom of it, when cold fingers grabbed his neck and pulled him under the water. He escaped and charged out of the pool, screaming at the others to get out before the demon got them to.

Another night brought another haunting. Joe was at the computer working when he heard a knife scratching against the wall, and sure enough he saw a knife on the floor. Using the new experience he had gained from the paranormal investigators, he unplugged all the electrics and used his cell phone to record any unheard noises.

Afterwards, he replayed the recording on the cell phone and a voice crackled through the audio.

"I am the married one."

Because all his victims had been gay men, it was suddenly believed that Herb Baumeister himself had returned to Fox Hollow Farm to haunt those who ventured there.

As of 2021, the Graves no longer live at the property, instead, week in and week out, there are paranormal investigators on site, believing that the property and grounds are amongst the most haunted in Indiana. On one occasion, a large team of investigators arrived at the estate and stayed for six months. The team included a physics expert, a demonologist, EVP and visual specialist, and an army of psychics.

It appeared to them, at least, that evil never dies.

Born **April 7th 1947.**

Active from **1980-1996.**

Country: **USA.**

Victims: **12+.**

AKA: **The I-70 Strangler / Herb.**

Sentence: **Committed suicide before sentencing.**

Current whereabouts: **Suicide by shooting on July 3rd 1996.**

Berdella, Robert Andrew: The Kansas City Butcher (Extended Case File)

On June 23rd 1987, Kansas based serial killer *Robert Andrew Berdella Jr.* dragged a sedated 20-year-old *Larry Wayne Pearson* into his basement. He would then violently torture Pearson for the next six weeks before beheading and dissecting his remains in August of 1987. Pearson was one of six victims to fall foul of one of the evilest killers in the modern era.

Berdella was the eldest son of a deeply religious family, his father was of Italian descent. Raised in Ohio, he was sent on religious education courses and attended the local church for mass. During his childhood he was afflicted with various impediments that saw him bullied in school and beaten by his father.

When he was young, his father rarely allowed him to socialise outside of religious sermons and family chores. As such, Berdella became a loner and was known to have been socially awkward. When he was five-years-old, he was diagnosed with near-sightedness and had to wear thick-rimmed glasses. Combined with a speech-impediment, he withdrew from society at an early age.

In doing so, Berdella didn't follow in his younger brother's footsteps and take up sport, instead becoming lethargic and gaining weight. Because of this lethargy, his father would often compare him to his younger brother, belittling him for not being like his other son.

Although Berdella's father abused his children he would pay particular attention to his eldest son. He emotionally and physically abused them, sometimes beating them with a leather belt. During his school years, he was constantly bullied by other children. Teachers noted later that he was always withdrawn and lost in his own thoughts, rarely mixing with the other children.

As he reached his teenage years, Berdella became confused about his sexuality, which he kept to himself. He finally came out as gay in his late teens. On Christmas Day 1965, when Berdella was 16-years-old, his 39-year-old father died of a heart attack while at home. Berdella turned to religion in the hope that faith would somehow see him through what he described as a difficult time, regardless of his father's abuse towards him. When he didn't find what he needed, he began reading up on other religions and soon started to lose faith in what he had been taught as a youngster.

At around the same time, he had turned his withdrawal into a mask of exaggerated confidence. He became difficult to be around due to his new rudeness and attitude towards others. Then he saw a 1965 film called *The Collector*.

In the case of Berdella, it was one of the first known instances of a movie directly impacting the thought processes of someone who had the potential to kill *and* would go on to kill.

The plot of *The Collector* is about a man who abducts women and holds them captive in his basement. It is a direct correlation to the exact process used by Berdella in his future murders. Except that he chose men instead of women.

Two years later in 1967, Berdella moved to Kansas and went to the *Kansas City Art Institute* where he was known to have become a promising student, but things quickly took a turn for the worst. After falling in with the drug crowd, he started to abuse drugs and alcohol, and even began dealing to other students.

Some serial killers torture small animals in their childhood years, due to being able to overpower small animals where they can't overpower human abusers or carers. Berdella started late and used art as an excuse for torturing animals. As part of his art, he used sedatives on a dog to see the effects, then tortured and cooked a duck in front of other students – for art. After that he left the institute after widespread condemnation.

He was arrested a few months later in possession of Marijuana and LSD. It is unclear whether the LSD was the type known as *Orange Sunshine Acid* which is the type that Charles Manson and other known criminals went on to use. The Orange Sunshine Acid is explained in detail in *1978: Year of the Serial Killer*.

He stayed in Kansas and moved into the now infamous *4315 Charlotte Street*, in the Hyde Park area of Kansas City. He enjoyed using male prostitutes and spent a lot of time in gay bars in the city, openly taking part in casual sexual encounters with other men. He would spend time with drug addicts and homeless people and gain their trust by plying them with drugs.

Ever since his teens, he took pleasure in and saw the benefits of becoming pen-pals with people. He then wrote letters to people all over the world including to Vietnam and Burma, two countries that were very much off-limits to the Western world at the time. In return he would receive photos of ancient sites and small items from those countries, and so his collection began to grow.

In disregarding mainstream religion he had developed a belief and understanding in alternative religions and occult magic. This would lead him to opening a rather unique shop in 1982.

He opened a booth at the *Westport Flea Market* called *Bob's Bazaar Bizarre,* which was an antique and curiosity shop. It sold things like primitive art, Asian artefacts and jewellery. He subsidised his earnings by stealing items for his booth and then started taking lodgers at his home.

He became friends with the son of one of his fellow booth operators, *Jerry Howell*. When Jerry was 19-years-old, on July 5th 1984, he became Berdella's first victim.

Berdella promised to give him a lift to a dance contest but instead drugged him with heavy sedatives, took him home and tied him to his bed. Over the next 24 hours, Berdella raped, tortured and beat Jerry. He died after the drugs stopped his heart and he gagged on his own vomit. Berdella then dragged the body to the basement to try and resuscitate him but instead he suspended the body from the feet.

As Jerry's body was hanging upside down, Berdella cut his throat and other arterial veins in order to drain the blood from the corpse. A day later he returned to his basement and used a chainsaw and knives to dismember the body. He wrapped them in newspapers and put them in several trash bags, which were collected shortly after and taken to the landfill.

We know all this in such great detail because Berdella had been keeping extremely elaborate notes and photographs of his victims and other assaults. His notes detailed each individual act of torture and abuse and outlined the intense physical and mental satisfaction that he took from carrying out the murders in such a way.

He killed another four young men after Howell and his final victim was on June 23rd 1987. *Larry Wayne Pearson* was initially one of Berdella's lodgers and Berdella hadn't planned on killing him. After he bailed Pearson out of jail, he made a crude remark about gay men, and Berdella saw red. Berdella drugged him and dragged him into the basement – where the horror began.

For the following six weeks until August 5th, when he finally killed him, Pearson was tortured and abused in the most horrific of fashions. He would be injected with drain cleaner and had piano wire tightened around his wrists to cause nerve damage. Berdella broke one of Pearson's hands with an iron bar and electrocuted him with an electric transformer.

He kept Pearson in various states of sedation and moved him around the house, including the second bedroom where he would rape and abuse him further. Towards the end, Pearson summoned the energy to bite Berdella's penis during a session of forced fellatio. Berdella then beat him to death and later dismembered him in the basement. He stored Pearson's head in the freezer before burying it in the backyard.

Although Pearson was his last murder, another victim escaped his clutches in 1988. 22-year-old *Christopher Bryson* managed to escape from the house. He jumped from a second floor window and was wearing nothing except a dog collar around his neck. He broke his foot when he jumped but managed to call out for help. Someone heard him and called the police, and Berdella was subsequently arrested.

334 Polaroid images and 34 snapshot prints were found in the apartment when it was searched. There was a possible link with a total of 20 murders but only six could be verified using his notes and confession.

Berdella was sentenced to life in prison without parole. He died of a heart failure on October 8th 1992, while incarcerated at *Missouri State Penitentiary*.

Born **January 31st 1949.**

Active from **1984-1988.**

Arrested on **April 2nd 1988.**

Country: **USA. (Missouri).**

Victims: **6.**

AKA: **The Kansas City Butcher.**

Sentence: **Life in prison.**

Current whereabouts: **Died of a heart attack on October 8th 1992.**

(Research Article #1) The Lure of Celebrity Status

Becoming a celebrity can sometimes be an important motivation that gives impetus to a serial killer to carry on killing.

Not all killers seek fame, or infamy to put it in a better context. *Randy Kraft*, for example, hardly ever discussed his crimes, and definitely removed himself from them. Others like *Alexander Pichushkin* sought to better *Andrei Chikatilo's* body count, and in doing so, wanted to be known for his crimes.

It's not to say they don't all have their reasons for killing, they do, it's just that some killers seek fame and in some cases fortune. *Charles Bronson* would paint and then sell his art, *Charles Manson* wrote music and *Dennis Nilsen* penned an autobiography.

Nilsen is not the first killer to write an autobiography and have it released. The book was subsequently banned by the British Government as they felt that some of the details were glorified and not in the public interest.

At what point do you stop serial killers releasing detailed information and accounts of their crimes?

Confessions and interviews are mostly readily available after conviction so the information is already there. Although they do tend to be only the facts of the crimes and not the reasons or intricate details.

On the one hand, people have a macabre fascination with all things relating to serial killers. On the other hand, the public don't really want to see them get rich off the back of their crimes. It's a bizarre paradox where both sides are hungry for more but then morality comes into play.

By allowing the written accounts of their crimes to come out into the public and the public consuming them, we are in a sense fuelling the fire. We want to know the gory details so much that we strive to see live interviews with the killers. We want to know how they were moved to kill and the processes by which they were caught.

It has been suggested those who claim to be serial killer fanatics may have even considered an act of evil themselves at one point in their lives. To follow serial killers and to consume their lives is akin to the love of horror movies. They are far removed from our own ideals but because serial killers live in the real world, the fear and danger are awfully close to home. They are true-life horror stories without the special effects.

If we are to assume that most kill upon diminished responsibility, then the very act of reading their thoughts and memories is detrimental to the family members of the victims.

Fame then, surely is inevitable, as we strive to know more about those who commit the worse type of crimes. The *Son of Sam Law*, implemented after *David Berkowitz* came close to making money off his story, went some way to setting the standard for similar laws throughout the United States and some other countries.

But it's not always financial gain that serial killers are generally after, it's fame.

There would be no point in becoming financially rich whilst serving life or being remanded on death row.

David Berkowitz introduced the Son of Sam moniker to the world in 1977 when he communicated directly with the investigation for the first time. He left a handwritten letter addressed to the NYPD near the body of one of his victims. He had literally chosen the name by which he would become known.

The BTK Killer. *Dennis Rader*, sought to establish a brand name for himself and attract notoriety like the Son of Sam. He contacted the media in the Autumn of 1974 and left a letter for authorities at the local public library. It told them to call him; *Bind. Torture. Kill.*

Thus the BTK Killer was born and he himself had chosen the name for which he would be remembered and spoken about in years to come.

During the late 1960s and most of the 1970s, the rise of the celebrity took hold. It was something witnessed during World War Two and slowly moved into the public eye to take hold of the flower power era. Never had so many people sought fame or celebrity status.

Many children desired to be famous. The rise of popular culture was increasing at an astronomical rate. Gossip magazines, pulp fiction, celebrity in media and the increase in the output of movies would lead people to seek fame. Whilst some would seek it through legal and ethical avenues, others had already given up on all things moral.

It is evidenced that once a celebrity status or moniker has been given to an active serial killer, then the murder rates tend to increase. The killers then seek to prove the media and public right, to prove they deserve the bizarre celebrity status that has been given to them. Almost all will follow investigations and news reports about their crimes.

> "You know who I am, don't you? I'm the one they're writing about in the newspapers

and on the TV."

Richard Ramirez; *The Night Stalker.* To one of his victims who survived.

Then comes the danger of igniting the passions of those who might have held off acting on their dark thoughts. The celebrity status can motivate the killers to continue their crimes, but it can also inspire others. Many ignored and isolated potential serial killers become copycat killers, to achieve their own degree of celebrity status, or garner their own serial killer name.

The larger the body count, the greater the terror, the more chance they might make it to the front page of a newspaper or top-of-the-hour TV report.

Certain magazines devoted to popular culture have promoted infamy to the point of making serial killer's grim legends in their own way. The villains to the heroes of the movie, music and fashion world. Suddenly, true crime became entertainment for the masses.

People magazine once wrote huge swathes of information about the Unabomber, Ted Kaczynski, who began his campaign in 1978. Jeffrey Dahmer who began killing in 1978, shockingly made People's top 100 list of the most intriguing people of the Twentieth Century. Intriguing they may be but they are subsequently given a platform far greater than they deserve.

And it doesn't stop there. The media and books were the tip of the iceberg. Images of serial killers are sometimes slapped on t-shirts, comic books, calendars, trading cards, baseball caps, mugs, pendants and jackets. Their art is sold for thousands, they have their own fan followings, websites, member clubs, public funds and those who fall in love with them.

The lure of celebrity means so much more than a newspaper clipping. It could make them world famous and see their crimes become internationally recognised for decades to come.

(Research Article #2) The Lure of Social Media Fame

In the research article heading of *The Lure of Celebrity*, we discussed the relevance to serial killers and how they might seek fame without the fortune. Becoming known for their crimes could result in fame, or more correctly, infamy. The trappings of celebrity were often too much of a pull to refuse.

In a book I wrote on mental health I discussed the fallout with regards to social media and the damage it can spread knowingly or unknowingly.

"Ignore the eternal display of social media, it is not real life. If people thinking you are living a happy life is more important than actually being happy then something needs to change."

Mentacracy: Living Under the Rule of Mental Illness.

In the 1970s it was much harder to become famous. The entertainment industry was reserved only for the select few, if one had been lucky enough to get a foothold in the film, music, or art industry.

In 2021, we have social media.

One could become famous for simply '*doing a funny dance*' and posting it to *YouTube* with the right hashtags. You can film better quality movies on a $200 DSLR Camera than you could have done in the 1970s with camera equipment worth tens of thousands and sometimes more. You can write a song, record yourself singing it and then publish it to the public for reactions, feedback, or even a career platform.

The gateways to becoming famous have widened and more and more people are being lured into fame. *Facebook, Twitter, Instagram, YouTube* and many more, the platforms are eternal and perfectly suit either fame or infamy.

True stories have been written about murderers filming themselves killing someone and uploading it onto a social media platform. But they're not getting the infamy that was once afforded to those in 1978. Are people becoming desensitised to images of death, murder and killings? It's argued that as a society and as a civilisation, we have become emotionally dumbed down.

It's the same issue that links with the rise of pornography. You can find brutally violent images and videos online in just a matter of a few clicks. Mostly you can find those on social media platforms until they're taken down. There is moderation on some but only if its reported, meaning that some things that no human should ever see, are witnessed by millions.

Does this desensitisation pose an increasing problem as we move towards 2028 and the rise of the serial killer? As more people become desensitised to violent images and more people use social media to explore their individual tendencies then we could be walking into a hugely damaging second era of serial killing.

One has to wonder how much of an influence the supposed anonymity of social media will have as we move away from the carnage of 1978 and into a new age of murder.

Bergamo, Marco

Italian serial killer *Marco Bergamo,* AKA*: The Monster of Bolzano*, murdered five women between 1985 and 1992. During his childhood he suffered from a stutter and skin disease that saw him be bullied by family and school pupils. In his teenage years he collected knives and always had a knife on his person.

At the age of 26-years-old, in 1992, he had surgery to remove one of his testicles. This combined with his isolation and social awkwardness was one of the reasons why he went on to kill.

15-year-old *Marcella Casagrande* was his first victim in 1985. She had been butchered by Bergamo in her own home and he had stabbed her multiple times.

Six months later he murdered 41-year-old teacher, *Anna Maria Cipolletti*. She was known to have involved herself in prostitution to subsidise her teaching wage. She had been stabbed 19 times by Bergamo but no sexual abuse had taken place.

From then on until 1992, another three prostitutes were killed. For one victim, he even left a note on her grave that said he was sorry for what he did. He was caught when his car was stopped by police who found bloodstains on his passenger seat and documents of the last victim in the trunk.

He was convicted of five murders and sentenced to life in prison. He died of natural causes in October of 2017.

Born **August 6th 1966.**

Active from **1985-1992.**

Arrested in **1992.**

Country: **Italy.**

Victims: **5.**

AKA: **The Monster of Bolzano.**

Sentence: **Life imprisonment.**

Current whereabouts: **Died of natural causes in October 2017.**

Berkowitz, David: The Son of Sam (Extended Case File)

Berkowitz's campaign of terror brought 1977 to its knees and set the horrific standard for the year to follow. He killed six people between 1976 and 1977 but his trial in 1978 caught the public's interest.

Berkowitz's first victims are claimed by him to have begun on December 24th 1975. He stabbed two women using a hunting knife. One of the women was discovered to be *Michelle Forman*, the other was never identified.

In 1976, he walked up to a car window and fired three shots into the car then calmly walked away. He had killed 18-year-old *Donna Lauria* and injured 19-year-old *Jody Valenti*.

He would continue to kill in this impersonal manner until 1977 and just before his capture in August of that year.

"Well, you got me. How come it took you such a long time?"

David Berkowitz, to his arresting officers.

Berkowitz holds a unique place in the history of serial killers in that his crimes were not focused on sexual or personal predication. He used a gun and never stayed around to mutilate or damage the bodies further. Although not all serial killers mutilate victims or are driven by sexual perversity, it is a common trait.

Berkowitz didn't portray these traits and the way he would just walk away from his crimes showed a man who didn't seem to have a care in the world. In fact, Berkowitz would later claim that he was lashing out in anger against a world he felt had abandoned him. Though he did feel that he had been rejected too many times by women.

The level of rejection by women in serial killers can be considered quite high. For most serial killers who are known to have been rejected by women, their crimes are evidently sexualised. Berkowitz's were not. Though most of his victims were attractive young women.

When his apartment was searched, officers had found satanic symbols on the walls and doors. He would claim that he joined a satanic cult in 1975, which were not hard to find in the mid-1970s. He went on to say that other members of the cult would also kill people and would sometimes act as a lookout for his own murders.

PHOTO OF THE REAR OF FOX HOLLOW FARM

THE BUILDING AND GROUNDS ARE NOW CONSIDERED HAUNTED

IMAGE ATTRIBUTIONS
(ATTRIB A54) (ATTRIB A55)
(ATTRIB A56)

HERB BAUMEISTER

BERKOWITZ IN 2003

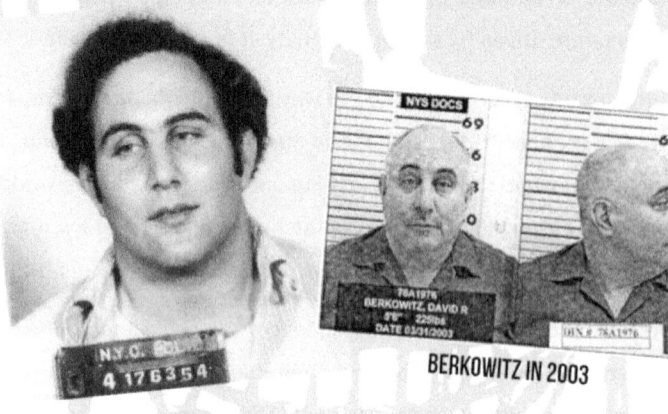

IMAGE ATTRIBUTIONS
(ATTRIB A58) (ATTRIB A59)

DAVID BERKOWITZ

Although the existence of the cult could never be proven, the investigation and indeed some of the survivors still maintained that Berkowitz was not acting alone. This tied into the reports of different people at the scene, different cars and different shapes in the shadows.

There was even a bizarre claim that Berkowitz's former neighbour, *Sam Carr*, had a dog possessed by a demon that told him to kill people. He would claim his nickname was based on this particular Sam.

Why is Berkowitz's case important for *1978: Year of the Serial Killer*? Because immediately after his conviction, the *Son of Sam Law* was passed as a pre-emptive legal statute by New York State Legislature.

The huge interest in Berkowitz's case and trial led publishers and producers stepping over each other to buy his story. The public curiosity and media presence in the case led many to believe that he would sell his story as quick as he could get it out. Many didn't want a serial killer to make money from his or her crimes.

It was the first legal restriction of its kind in the United States. The legislation would then be invoked eleven times from 1977 until 1990. It was even invoked in the case of *Mark David Chapman*, who had killed *John Lennon*.

The law was changed constantly in the years that followed 1991. It had been quashed and then reignited under a different type of legislature. All the way it had caused controversy. Similar laws are now in place in 44 States throughout the country.

As it was, the original *Son of Sam* moniker would come to change many laws within the United States.

Born **June 1st 1953.**

Active from **1976-1977.**

Arrested on **August 10th 1977.**

Country: **USA (New York).**

Victims: **6+**.

AKA: **Son of Sam / The .44 Calibre Killer / Richard David Falco.**

Sentence: **Six life sentences.**

Current whereabouts: **In prison.**

Bible Belt Strangler

Also known as '*The Redhead Murders*', the killings are a series of unidentified murders linked to an unidentified serial killer. The first victim was in October 1978 and the killings may have continued until 1992. Hardly any of the victims have been identified but most of them usually had red hair.

The killings that were linked to the Bible Belt killer took place in numerous states, including Tennessee, Arkansas, Kentucky, Mississippi, Pennsylvania, and West Virginia. The bodies were abandoned along major highway and interstate routes. It has long been suspected that the victims were either hitchhiking or involved in prostitution.

There is believed to be a total of six to 11 victims that have been attributed to one serial killer. The killer is so named due to the locations the murders had taken place.

Active from **1978-1992.**

Country: **USA**.

Victims: **6-11+**.

AKA: **The Redhead Murders.**

Current whereabouts: **Unidentified killer. Status unknown.**

Biegenwald, Richard

An American serial killer sometimes called 'ced *The Thrill Killer*' murdered at least six people over a 25-year period. He is suspected of two other murders in the same time frame. He would mostly shoot his victims but some were stabbed.

Biegenwald had a rough upbringing and was physically abused by his alcoholic father. When he was just five-years-old, Biegenwald set fire to the family home and was sent for psychiatric observation. He was drinking and gambling by the time he was eight-years-old, then set himself on fire when he was 11-years-old.

The first murder took place in 1958, when Biegenwald was only 18-years-old. He had stolen a car to rob a shop, where he gunned down the shop worker, *Steven Sladowski*. He was arrested two days later and convicted of murder. He served 16 years of a life sentence until his release for good behaviour in 1974.

In June 1978, he shot and killed police informant *John P. Petrone* at an abandoned airport. Then in 1981, he shot dead *Maria Ciallellam*, before dismembering her body and burying her remains at his own mother's house. He then stabbed to death *Deborah Osbourne* on April 8th 1982. He buried her body on top of Maria Ciallellam's remains.

In August 1982, he shot dead *Anna Olesiewicz* after luring her off the streets. He then disposed of her body behind a *Burger King* restaurant. His final victim was a drug dealer named *William Ward*, who he shot dead at his home.

Biegenwald was arrested in 1983 and died in 2008 of natural causes in prison.

Born **August 24th 1940**.

Active from **1958-1983**.

Arrested on **January 22nd 1983**.

Country: **USA**.

Victims: **6+**.

AKA: **The Thrill Killer.**

Sentence: **Death penalty later commuted to life.**

Current whereabouts: **Died of natural causes in 2008.**

Bishop, Arthur Gary

On October 14th 1979, in Utah, serial killer and sex offender **Arthur Gary Bishop** claimed his first victim. Four-year-old **Alonzo Daniels** was lured from the grounds of his family's apartment complex and was drowned in Bishop's bathtub. Bishop later buried the body in the desert.

In November 1980, Bishop lured 11-year-old Claude Peterson from an ice-rink under the pretence of purchasing some roller-skates. Peterson was then beaten to death and his body buried nearby that of Daniels. Despite being questioned, Bishop was not considered a suspect.

In October 1981, Bishop lured four-year-old Danny Davis from a supermarket and took him to his home. Again, despite numerous witnesses, Bishop was not a suspect in the disappearance. Davis was raped and beaten to death before buried near the locations of the first two. Investigators put numerous shoppers and shop workers through hypnosis in the hope they could find out any more information on the suspect but it proved unsuccessful.

It was almost another two years before Bishop killed again. He lured a young boy named Troy Ward to his home where he drowned him in the bathtub, assaulted him and beat him to death. His final victim was 13-year Graeme Cunningham, who vanished in July of 1983. He too was brutally murdered.

Police finally linked Bishop to the abductions and arrested him where he confessed to the five murders. He then led police to the burial sites of every victim. He was found guilty in March 1984 and sentenced to death. He was executed by lethal injection on June 10th 1988.

Born in **1951**.

Active from **1979-1983**.

Arrested in **January 1980**.

Country: **USA**.

Victims: **5**

AKA: **Roger Downs**.

Current whereabouts: **Executed by lethal injection on June 10th 1988.**

Black, Robert: Smelly Bob (Extended Case File)

In France, on May 30th 1987, 10-year-old *Hemma Greedharry* was raped and strangled to death. Her body was found beside a road in a Paris suburb. She is suspected to have been murdered by Scottish serial killer, *Robert Black*: AKA: *Smelly Bob*.

He was convicted in 1994 for the rapes and murders of four young girls in the United Kingdom. It is known he killed eight children across Europe and was suspected in 13 more.

Black was a paedophile and killer who operated from 1969 to 1987. He was a truck driver who made regular work trips to mainland Europe where it is suspected he murdered dozens more. He was also prime suspect in the infamous 1978 disappearance and murder of 13-year-old *Genette Tate*. She had vanished on her newspaper delivery round in Devon, on England's Southern Coast.

Black was born in Grangemouth, Scotland, in 1947. Because his mother didn't know who the father was, she had Black adopted and he was taken in by a couple who lived in Kinlochleven, in the Scottish Highlands. He went through life with the surname of Tulip, which he took from his adopted parents. He was called *'Smelly Bobby Tulip'* by school friends due to his poor hygiene – and the name stuck.

When he was growing up, he was prone to outbursts of anger and aggression and was a bully at the schools he attended. From an early age, Black believed he should have been born a girl, and at five-years-old was caught comparing his genitalia with a girl of the same age. From the age of eight-years-old, he would insert objects into his anus and carried on with the practice into his adulthood.

Black was knowing to wet the bed on regular occasions, one of the many pre-cursors to violence in later life. Every time he did so, he was beaten by his foster mother and couldn't fight back, resulting in numerous and regular bruising on his body.

When he was 11-years-old, both his foster parents died from apparent natural causes and he was adopted by another couple in the small village. There, he dragged a younger girl into a public toilet and attempted to rape her. His new foster parents had him removed from their care to a mixed-sex children's care home near Falkirk on the central belt of Scotland.

He abused girls there and was sent to a stricter care home for boys only. It was there that he was abused by a male carer for up to three years and would regularly be forced to perform oral sex on him.

In 1963, when he was 16-years-old, he left the care home and became a delivery boy for a local butchers. He stated that when he delivered to houses with young girls who were alone, he would sexually assault them. He claimed to have touched or attacked at least 30 young girls on his deliveries.

In 1963, he lured a seven-year-old girl to an abandoned air-raid shelter then throttled her until she passed out, before masturbating over her body. Black was only 16-years-old at the time. He was arrested but a psychiatrist's report claimed it was only a one-off and he was let go without punishment.

In 1968, he moved to London after being released from a borstal on another offence of child abuse. He moved to a bedsit near *King's Cross Station* where young children were in plentiful supply. He had multiple jobs, including a life-guard position that he was fired from for sexually touching a young girl – which comes as no surprise in hindsight.

He started collecting child pornography through a contact at an illegal book shop in King's Cross. He later managed to get hold of VHS tapes depicting child abuse. He also covertly took photos of children at swimming pools and in shops and kept the images in locked suitcases, due to the amount of material he had amassed.

He then moved into the attic of a Scottish couple in the area and got himself a long-distance driving job. In his truck he kept various disguises including different types of glasses. He also alternated between having a long beard and no beard at all.

His first confirmed murder victim was in August of 1981, when he abducted nine-year-old *Jennifer Cardy* in Northern Ireland, while on a long-haul journey. She had been riding her bike near to a main road when she vanished. Hundreds of volunteers joined the search for the girl and her body was found in a large lake, six days later by two fisherman. Black had raped and drowned the girl.

Even then, the police had suspected the killer might have been a truck driver due to the location of the lake to the trunk road. Even though it would have been someone who was familiar with the roads around it, no connection was made to Black.

His second confirmed murder victim was 11-year-old *Susan Claire Maxwell*, from Cornhill-on-Tweed, close to the Scottish border. Maxwell had been playing sports with friends before she walked home alone, before being kidnapped by Black. 300 officers and hundreds more volunteers were involved in the search and an investigation was made of every property in the area, along with a huge amount of open land.

A month later, in August of the same year, her decomposed body was found by a lorry driver in a shallow grave at the side of the road. She had been tied up and gagged, with her underwear carefully positioned under her head. Another three confirmed victims turned up from 1983 to 1987. There were also multiple disappearances and murders that were linked to Black.

In the United Kingdom alone, six disappearances and murders had been attributed to him.

8th April 1969 – 13-year-old *April Fabb* vanished while riding her bike in Norfolk. Her body was never found.

21st May 1973 – nine-year-old schoolgirl *Christine Markham* was last seen walking to school in Scunthorpe. Her body has never been found.

19th August 1978 – 13-year-old schoolgirl *Genette Tate* disappeared while delivering newspapers in the Devon town of Aylesbeare in England. Her body has never been found and the cause of her disappearance remains unsolved. It is one of Britain's most infamous and longest-running missing person inquiries. It has recently been reopened as a murder investigation by *Devon and Cornwall Police*.

28th July 1979 – 14-year-old *Suzanne Lawrence* vanished while walking from her house. Her body was never found but the location of her disappearance matched up with Blacks' route that day.

16th June 1980 – 14-year-old *Patricia Morris* vanished at the edge of her school. Her body was discovered two days later in Hounslow Heath near Heathrow. She had been strangled to death.

4th November 1981 - 16-year-old *Pamela Hastie* was found bludgeoned and strangled to death in Renfrewshire. An eyewitness put Black at the location at the time of the murder.

There were also disappearances and murders across Ireland, the Netherlands and Germany. All of the victims vanished or were killed at the same time as Black would have been in the areas on his long-haul European journeys.

In France, in 1987, a spate of child murders and disappearances have since been attributed to Black.

5th May 1987 – 10-year-old *Virginie Delmas* was abducted by Black. Her body was discovered months later in an orchard near Paris, in October of the same year. She had been strangled, and due to the decomposition of the body, it was unclear whether she had been sexually abused beforehand.

30th May 1987 – 10-year-old *Hemma Greedharry* was raped and strangled to death. Her body was found beside a road in a Paris suburb. Robert Black knew the road and area well, having made various deliveries there in the years prior to Greedharry's death.

3rd June 1987 – seven-year-old *Perrine Vigneron* vanished on her way to buy a Mother's Day card in the Bouleurs area of France. Her decomposing body was found over three weeks later. She had been raped and strangled to death in a similar fashion to the previous victim. A vehicle matching Black's truck was seen in the area around the time of the disappearance.

27th June 1987 – on the same day that the body of Perrine Vigneron was discovered, nine-year-old schoolgirl *Sabine Dumont* disappeared in Bièvres. On the following day, her body was discovered in the small area of Vauhallan. She had been raped and strangled. In 2001, Black was named as a prime suspect in her murder.

The nationwide manhunt for Robert Black was one of the most expensive and most resource-heavy UK murder investigations of the 20th century. But he was caught when a member of the public witnessed one of his abductions.

On July 14th 1990, 53-year-old retiree *David Herkes* was cutting his grass when he saw a blue van slow down on the other side of the road. Herkes started to clean the blades of his lawnmower and happened to look up to see the feet of a small girl lifting from the pavement and into the van. He watched as Black pushed the girl into the passenger seat before quickly getting in and driving away.

Already, Herkes believed he had witnessed an abduction and wrote down the registration number. He realised it might have been the six-year-old daughter of his neighbour and ran to her house where they called the police immediately. Within minutes the area was covered in police vehicles.

A short while passed and Herkes continued to describe what had happened to officers. Suddenly, Black had decided to drive back through the town on his way northwards and Herkes recognised the van instantly. He shouted to officers who jumped in front of the van and pulled Black from his seat.

The father of the missing girl charged into the van and found his daughter tied up in a sleeping bag. She had already been sexually abused but had survived and would go on to make a full recovery. It was the last child that Black would ever touch.

He was arrested and charged. In 1994 he was convicted of the rape and murder of three girls, along with kidnapping and sexual assault. He received a sentence of life imprisonment with a minimum of 35 years. The case caused outrage in the United Kingdom and saw protests calling for the death penalty to be reinstated in the country.

Up until his death, he was charged with another murder from 1981 and was about to be charged with more when he died of a heart attack in January 2016. He was already a prime suspect in most of his suspected victims.

Robert Black remains one of the worst serial killers to walk the streets of the United

Kingdom and Europe.

Born **April 21st 1947**.

Active from **1969-1990**.

Arrested on **July 14th 1990**.

Country: **United Kingdom / Europe-wide**.

Victims: **4-21+**.

AKA: **Smelly Bob**.

Sentence: **Life imprisonment with a minimum of 35 years.**

Current whereabouts: **Died of heart attack in January 2016.**

Bonin, William

In California, American serial killer, William George Bonin, AKA: The Freeway Killer, murdered at least 21 boys and young men between 1979 and 1980. He used frequent accomplices to help him kidnap and kill young men. Some of his crimes are listed below.

On August 5th 1979, in Newport Beach, California, 17-year-old German tourist Marcus Grabs was raped and brutally murdered. Grabs was backpacking the United States when he was approached by serial killer William George Bonin and accomplice Vernon Butts. Grabs was raped, beaten and stabbed 77 times. His restrained and nude body was discovered the next day beside a road in Malibu.

On September 12th 1979, in Los Angeles, the nude body of 17-year-old David Murillo was discovered near a highway. He had disappeared three days earlier while cycling to the movies. His head had been crushed with a tire iron and he had been raped and strangled. Bonin was later convicted of the murder.

On February 3rd 1980, in West Hollywood, 15-year-old Charles Miranda was picked up by Bonin and accomplice Gregory Matthew Miley. Charles was raped, beaten, and strangled to death with his own shirt because Miley was not able to get sexually aroused. His restrained and nude body was discovered the next morning beside an alley in Malibu.

On the same evening, after dumping Charles's body, the pair of murderers sought another victim. They picked up 12-year-old James McCabe who was on his way to Disneyland with family. Bonin raped McCabe in the back of the van and they both later beat and strangled him to death. McCabe's body was found in a dumpster three days later. Miley, who helped Bonin kill some of his victims, was sentenced to 25 years to life in prison.

On March 14th 1980, in Van Nuys, California, 19-year-old Ronald Gatlin was hitchhiking when he was picked up by Bonin. Gatlin's body was found the next day in Duarte, he had been raped, beaten, and strangled to death.

On March 20th 1980, in Hollywood, 14-year-old Harry Todd Turner was picked up by Bonin and accomplice William Ray Pugh. Turner's nude body was found the next day in an alley in downtown Los Angeles. He had been raped, beaten, and strangled to death by Bonin. Pugh, who was present during the murder of Turner, was sentenced to six years for voluntary manslaughter.

On April 10th 1980, in Los Angeles, 16-year-old Steven Wood was going about his business in the early afternoon when he was picked up by Bonin. Wood's nude body was discovered the next morning in an alley on an industrial estate. He had been raped, brutally beaten, and strangled to death with a ligature.

On April 29th 1980, in the parking lot of a supermarket in Stanton, California, 19-year-old Darin Lee Kendrick was abducted by Bonin and accomplice Vernon Butts. Kendrick had been collecting shopping carts and was lured into Bonin's van by the offer of free drugs. During the night, he was raped, tortured, and strangled to death.

He had been forced to ingest an acid which left him with internal burns and had an ice pick inserted into his ear that severed his upper spinal cord. His nude body was found the next day in an industrial park. Butts, who helped Bonin kill some of his victims, took his own life in 1981 while awaiting trial.

On June 13th 1980, in California, after extensive surveillance, Bonin was captured after having killed at least 21 people from 1979 to 1980. He was initially convicted of 10 murders in one trial and then another four in a separate trial.

Although convicted of 14 murders in total, he was known to have killed at least 21 with some investigators suspecting it may have been closer to 44. In 1986, after a lengthy trial, he was sentenced to death. He was executed by lethal injection in California on February 23rd 1996.

Born in **1947**.

Active from: **1972-1980**.

Arrested in **June 1980**.

Country: **USA**.

Victims: **21-44**.

AKA: **The Freeway Killer**.

Current whereabouts: **Executed by lethal injection on February 23rd 1996**.

Brandt, Charlie

Brandt killed himself in 2004 after stabbing his wife to death. Before that, he had decapitated and heavily mutilated his niece, even as far as removing her heart.

He had shot his parents dead in 1971, his mother was pregnant at the time and Brandt was only 13-years-old. After his parent's death, he spent only one year in a psychiatric hospital before being released.

On September 20th 1978, 12-year-old *Carol Sullivan* was abducted from a school bus stop in Volusia County. Her skull was found inside a bucket. Brandt was living in the area at the time but could not be tied to the murder. He then moved to Florida where things got worse.

On September 15th 2004, after not hearing from her friend for a while, *Debbie Knight* went to Brandt's niece's house. When she couldn't get in through the front door, she tried to get in through the garage, where she found the decomposing body of Brandt's niece hanging from the rafters.

When the police arrived, they got into the main part of the house and saw Brandt's wife laying on the couch, she had been stabbed seven times in the chest. *Michelle Jones*, the mother of Brandt's niece, had been decapitated and gutted, with her heart and organs removed. Her head had been left next to her body.

Brandt's suicide in 2004, after the murder of his wife, meant that no investigation was undertaken. He has been suspected of other murders in Florida since 1973.

Born in **1957**.

Active from **1971-1985**.

Country: **USA**.

Victims: **3-6+**.

Current whereabouts: **Committed suicide in 2004**.

Brashers, Robert Eugene

One of a few serial killers to have been identified after their death. *Robert Eugene Brashers* was identified in 2018 through the use of genetic genealogy, to the 1990 murder of *Genevieve Zitricki*, in South Carolina in 1990. he had previously been convicted of a 1985 assault and shooting in Florida.

The Zitricki murder had remained unsolved for 28 years. As part of a Greenville cold case investigation, in 2018 his body was exhumed in order to retrieve a full DNA sample. They linked Brashers to the murder. He had broken into her apartment, raped and beat her before strangling her to death. Her body was discovered in the bathtub.

He was then linked to the 1997 rape of a 14-year-old girl in Tennessee, and the 1998 double murder of a mother and daughter, *Sherri and Megan Scherer*, in

Missouri. It is claimed that each of his victims had a striking similarity to his wife at the time and may have been the motive for the rapes and murders.

In 1999, he shot himself dead, when police approached him about a different incident.

Born **March 13th 1958.**

Active from **1985-1999.**

Country: **USA.**

Victims: **3.**

AKA: **Mr. Maroon.**

Current whereabouts: **Suicide by shooting in 1999.**

Briley Brothers, The

The three brothers would kill 12 people between them during their reign of chaos. The brothers were raised in a happy home with caring parents. But while they were young they were collecting dangerous animals including tarantulas and piranhas.

Their father claimed his son's eyes would light up with glee when they fed small mice to their pets. It unnerved him so much that he padlocked his door at night in case they came into his room.

The first murder was committed by Linwood Briley in 1971 when he was 16-years-old. He pointed a rifle out of his bedroom window and shot his elderly neighbour dead. When a police investigation led back to the Briley brothers, Linwood stated that he thought the neighbour had heart problems so she was going to die soon anyway. It was his only motive for the murder. Linwood served one year in a rehabilitation home.

From 1979, Linwood and *James Briley*, along with another brother and an accomplice, committed a series of rapes, robberies and random murders over an eight-month period. The brutality and callousness of the murders had the city of Richmond in fear during their campaign.

They were all arrested in October 1979, after police heard gunfire in a residential house. Both James and Linwood were sentenced to death for their part in the murders.

Born **1954** (Linwood) and **1956** (James).

Active from **1971-1979**.

Arrested in **October 1979**.

Country: **USA (Virginia)**.

Victims: **12**.

Sentence: **Death penalty for both Linwood and James.**

Current whereabouts: **Linwood was executed by electrocution on October 12th 1984. James was executed by electrocution on April 18th 1985.**

Brown, Vernon

On August 25th 1980, in Indiana, the body of nine-year-old **Kimberly Campbell** was found in a vacant house. She had been raped and strangled to death by **Vernon Brown**. Despite the vacant house belonging to Brown's grandmother and the fact he was seen with Campbell the evening before, there was not enough physical evidence to charge him.

It was another year until warrants were issued for his arrest, but he had skipped town and moved to Missouri. In 1985, Brown killed two young women in Missouri, along with another in 1986. He was finally arrested on October 27th 1986 and sentenced to death for two of the murders.

Investigators have since linked him with at least five murders across Indiana and Missouri. Brown was executed by lethal injection on May 17th 2005.

Born in **1953.**

Active from **1980-1986.**

Arrested in **October 1986.**

Country: **USA.**

Victims: **3-5.**

Current whereabouts: **Executed by lethal injection on May 17th 2005.**

Browne, Robert Charles

He confessed to killing 48 people, mostly women, between 1970 and 1995. He was convicted of two murders and is serving two double-life sentences for them. He claims that he also killed women in South Korea and Vietnam when he was serving in the US Military. He was subsequently discharged for drug abuse. He was married six times before his conviction.

Investigators have discovered bodies and subsequently linked him to seven murders using Browne's confessions and story. Investigators said that there was information Browne knew that only the dead would know.

His seven victims were petite, not much higher than five feet. He claimed he would kill women because he was disgusted with them and they had low moral character traits. Browne was also an opportunistic killer which goes against most who choose their victims carefully. He would go for long drives, even road trips and stopped wherever he felt like it.

In his confession of 48 victims he claimed that bodies could be found in nine States. They included; Colorado, New Mexico, Washington, California, Louisiana,

Mississippi, Oklahoma, Texas and Arkansas.

He strangled his victims, stabbed, shot and used chemicals to kill them. He claimed he disposed of the bodies in lakes, rivers, ditches and over cliff faces. Browne also dismembered bodies and placed parts of them in garbage bins all over the country.

Although most of his murders have not been proven, some investigators claim there is a high percentage that do seem likely. He was arrested in 1995 and has been in and out of court since. On March 20th, 2000, he sent a cryptic letter to the district attorney's office.

"The score is, you one, the other team 48. Seven sacred virgins entombed side by side, those less worthy are scattered wide."

Part of Browne's letter to the DA.

Two years later a cold-case team decided to investigate the details of the letter and wrote letters back to him. Browne eventually provided enough information to substantiate the killings of seven people.

His crimes are still being investigated.

Born **October 31st 1952**.

Active from **1971-1985**.

Arrested on **March 28th 1995**.

Country: **USA / South Korea**.

Victims: **2-48+**.

Sentence: **Life imprisonment**.

Current whereabouts: **In prison**.

Bunday, Thomas Richard

On August 29th, in Fairbanks, Alaska, 19-year-old **Glinda Sodemann** went missing. Two months later, her decomposed body was found in a shallow grave near a highway in the city. She had been murdered by serial killer **Thomas Richard Bunday** who killed at least five girls and women from 1979 to 1981 by shooting them.

He was serving in the *Air Force* at the time at the **Eielson Air Force Base** near Fairbanks. On March 15th 1983, Bunday committed suicide by driving his motorcycle directly into an oncoming truck. An arrest warrant had been issued just days prior to his death. He remains one of Alaska's few known serial killers. His known victims were 19-year-old Glinda Sodemann, 11-year-old Doris Oehring, 20-year-old Marlene Peters, 16-year-old Wendy Wilson, and 19-year-old Lori King.

Born in **1948**.

Active from **1979-1981**.

Country: **USA**.

Victims: **5+**

Current whereabouts: **Took his own life before being arrested.**

Bundy, Ted (Extended Case File)

On January 15th 1978, serial killer Ted Bundy paid a visit to the Chi Omega sorority house of the *Florida State University* (FSU). He bludgeoned and strangled to death two female victims and bludgeoned another three victims who went on to survive the attack. He had intended to kill five people in one day and this had displayed the level of intensity that Ted Bundy had inflicted on the United States since 1974.

Unsolved murders that were thought to have been carried out by Bundy but not proven date back to 1966. He would go on to admit to 30 murders but he had been linked to many more and so the final death-toll could have been a little or a lot higher. Since he was executed in 1989, there is no way to know for sure how many he had killed.

Ted Bundy would come to hold a special place in the annals of serial killer history. He would become the face of the so-called epidemic and the infamous poster boy for the psychopathic few.

His story would culminate in 1979 with a trial that was televised to the world and threw the spotlight on serial killers like no other before him. Some would argue that *Jack The Ripper* had more stories in the media. While that might have been true in Victorian England, Bundy was different in that he had actually been caught.

There are many piles of information regarding Bundy out there, including a *Netflix* documentary series, a 2019 film starring *Zac Efron,* and at least 310 books and regurgitated pamphlets.

His capture by police officer, *David Lee*, is worthy of note. Lee had stopped Ted Bundy's car as it showed up as being stolen. After approaching Bundy, he was attacked, causing him to fire off two warning shots. He gave chase and fought Bundy to the ground, subduing him. David Lee then bundled him into the back of the car.

Lee was unaware he had just caught a man who was on the FBI's *Ten Most Wanted Fugitives* list.

"*I wish you had killed me,*" Bundy had said to Lee, in an extraordinary revelation.

It appears it could be one of the most interesting things that Bundy was ever recorded saying. It always appeared to many researchers that he thought himself beyond the law and would never be caught. If he *wanted* to be killed, then he did not wish to face any trial for his crimes. In psychology there is a difference between wanting to die and wanting to be killed.

Wanting to die is usually a consequence of having a mental illness and usually involves active or passive suicidal ideation. Wishing to be killed is a consequence of someone not willing to take their own life but wanting that responsibility to be placed on another. It is an attempt to hide away from one's sins and to not face the fear of judgement.

Why then did Bundy move to represent himself in the courts?

He oversaw the trials himself, regardless of the defence team he had amassed. The decision to represent himself in court was based on a rampant display of control and delusion. We know that delusion is strongly associated with mental health disorders, but in the 1970s it wasn't as intricately linked as it is now.

It's not untoward to say that Bundy saw himself as a higher class of human being, regardless of his own sins. Being able to speak about himself and his crimes in the third person narrative would have elevated his belief that he was more important than others.

He had a controlling, possessive personality that became even more evident while he was on death row.

"The ultimate possession was, in fact, the taking of life."

Ted Bundy to a fellow inmate.

He was also studied by and conversed with the *FBI Behavioural Analysis Unit* during his decade on death row. The reports and findings that arose from understanding Bundy would go on to assist investigators all over the world. They now had a new understanding of the serial killer phenomenon and it was mostly Bundy that had paved the way for this knowledge.

Every serial killer has their own individual intricacies that make them who they are and allows them to do what they do. Yet, profiling them became a little easier after the Bundy trial. Unknowingly, he had already kicked off a wave of killings in which some people would aim to *better* his death-toll.

Although he confessed to 30 murders, it has been suggested that he killed more than that. His sexual desires were sometimes sated on a return to his own crime scenes where he would perform sexual acts with the corpses. He also had removed the heads of 12 of his victims, keeping some of them as mementos.

Alongside Jack The Ripper, Ted Bundy is the most written about serial killer in history and is still firmly in the public spotlight as of 2021.

Born **November 24th 1946.**

Active from **1974-1978.**

Arrested on **February 15th 1978.**

Country: **USA.**

Victims: **30+.**

AKA: **Ted.**

Sentence: **Death penalty.**

Current whereabouts: **Executed by electrocution on January 24th 1989.**

PITKIN COUNTY COURTHOUSE IN ASPEN THAT BUNDY ESCAPED FROM

DR. RICHARD SOUVIRON PRESENTS DENTAL EVIDENCE AT THE TRIAL OF TED BUNDY FOR THE CHI OMEGA MURDERS

IMAGE ATTRIBUTIONS
(ATTRIB A7) (ATTRIB A8) (ATTRIB A12) (ATTRIB A13) (ATTRIB A14)

TED BUNDY

72

Bianchi, Kenneth & Buono, Angelo: The Hillside Stranglers (Extended Case File)

On February 16th 1978, *The Hillside Stranglers* had claimed their tenth and final victim. *Cindy Lee Hudspeth* was strangled, raped and murdered. Her body was put into the trunk of a car which was pushed off a cliff to cover up the crime. At the time, the crimes were suspected to be of one serial killer and so the moniker of *The Hillside Strangler* was used. It was only upon their capture that two serial killing cousins came to be known as the stranglers.

Kenneth Bianchi and his cousin, *Angelo Buono,* were convicted in early 1979 for the kidnapping, raping, torturing and murdering of ten females aged from 12 to 28-years-old.

They became known as The Hillside Stranglers as they dumped their victim's bodies in the hills surrounding the greater Los Angeles area. They began killing in October 1977 and would claim victims throughout the coming Winter.

It started with three sex workers, always deemed an easy target by violent individuals. Their bodies were discovered strangled and naked in the hills. It was only when they kidnapped girls from middle-class areas that the media and indeed the law picked up their investigation of the killers.

When we looked at post-war child abuse cases, we showed that if the children were from working class or impoverished backgrounds then their cases were not deemed as important. The war of the classes would be another feature within the rise of serial killers which we'll look at shortly.

Bianchi and Buono would sexually abuse and torture their victims before disposing of their bodies. They were known to have experimented with different methods of murder. Among them were lethal injections of chemicals, electric shocks and carbon monoxide poisoning.

Bianchi would become the downfall of the duo's reign. Their killings came to an end in February 1978 when they realised that the police were closing in on them.

In January of the following year, Bianchi's desire for death consumed him. He was working as a security guard when he lured two females into a house. *Karen Mandic* and *Diane Wilder* were pushed down the stairs and then strangled to death.

Because Bianchi had previously killed with Buono and not alone, he ended up leaving too many clues. A routine check linked him to the addresses of two of the Hillside Strangler's victims.

Their trial would go on to become one of the most expensive trials in the history of the California legal system at the time.

Kenneth Bianchi was born to an alcoholic prostitute in 1951, who disowned him shortly afterwards. His adoptive mother would come to call him a compulsive liar from the moment he could talk. He was diagnosed at the age of five-years-old, with *petit mal seizures*.

These seizures are caused by abnormal electrical activity in the brain. It causes a brief trance-like state where the person falls in and out of consciousness. Absence seizures, as they are otherwise known, usually have a genetic reason for someone suffering from them.

Due to his seizures, he was in and out of the doctors where it was discovered that he had involuntary urinating problems. This led to him feeling and suffering from a great deal of humiliation. From then he developed anger-led behavioural problems and was diagnosed at the age of ten-years-old with *passive aggressive personality disorder*.

When his adoptive father died in 1964, Bianchi showed no signs of emotional attachment nor responded with grief in any way. He had become devoid of emotion at the event and it was something that would break down the moral barrier further before taking his first victim.

It wasn't until 1977 when he began spending time with his cousin that he would begin to kill. Buono had been raised separate from Bianchi but they would both develop into the killers they became.

Buono was born in 1934 and was 17 years older than his younger cousin. He had developed a rising criminal career from grand theft auto, assault, and rape. Buono had also developed a controlling attitude towards women.

He used prostitutes regularly and even imprisoned two in his home at one point. It wasn't long before they both started working as pimps. Their passion for control and darkness came together and by late 1977 they had started killing. Bianchi would later testify against Buono.

The Hillside Stranglers would infect the national psyche as much as any other serial killer of the time. That their combined trial was one of the longest in history and was pounced upon by the media is a damning incitement of the way that serial killers had been portrayed.

Born **May 22nd 1951 (Bianchi), October 5th 1934 (Buono).**

Active from **1977-1978.**

Arrested on **January 13th 1979 (Bianchi), October 22nd 1979 (Buono).**

Country: **USA.**

Victims: **10.**

AKA: **The Hillside Stranglers.**

Sentence: **Life imprisonment for both Bianchi and Buono.**

Current whereabouts: **Bianchi remains in prison. Buono died of natural causes on September 21st 2002.**

Burkett, Nathan

In April of 1978, 22-year-old *Barbara Ann Cox's* body was discovered, she had been strangled to death. Burkett was responsible for at least three cold case murders in Las Vegas. The women were assaulted and strangled before their bodies were dumped near Burkett's apartment.

In 1994, Burkett brutally murdered 27-year-old *Tina Gayle Mitchell* and 32-year-old *Althea Williams Grier*. DNA found at the scene linked him conclusively to the murder of Cox and Mitchell. The way in which Grier had been killed and discovered, saw police link up that investigation to Burkett.

In the 1980s, Burkett had served time in prison for manslaughter when his mother had been found burned to death. The last known murder came in 2002 when he killed 41-year-old *Valetter Jean Bousley*. He was convicted of manslaughter and served six years in prison. While in prison, the other crimes were linked to him.

Burkett pleaded guilty to two murders but prosecutors say he may have been linked with at least five. He was sentenced to life in a rather quiet court case. His criminal record extends back to 1976. As of 2021, Burkett is 69-years-old and expected to spend the rest of his life in prison.

Born in **1950**.

Active from **1976-2002**.

Arrested in **October 2003**.

Country: **USA**.

Victims: **3-5+**.

Sentence: **Life imprisonment**.

Current whereabouts: **In prison**.

Burtsev, Roman

Russian serial killer and paedophile, *Roman Burtsev*, AKA; *The Kamensky Chikatilo*, raped and killed six children over a three year period. All of his victims were murdered in his hometown of Rostov Oblast.

He was born in 1971 and raised by alcoholic parents and older siblings. He committed his first murder when he was 22-years-old. On September 5th 1993, he murdered a brother and sister at the same time. He had spotted 12-year-old *Yevgeny Churilov* and his 7-year-old sister *Olesya Churilova* playing near a junk yard.

He decided that he wanted to take the girl's virginity as he took a fancy to her but didn't to leave any witnesses. He killed the boy by punching him and then hitting him over the head with a large piece of junk metal. He raped the girl and strangled her to death, before disposing of both their corpses in one of the garbage sites nearby.

He hid their corpses so well that they wouldn't be discovered until after his arrest. He then killed three more times, in 1994, 1995 and then two in 1996. On July 1st 1996, he abducted nine-year-old *Ira Ternovskaya*, from a riverbank where she was playing. He then raped her and killed her before burying her in a shallow grave.

On July 16th 1996, he raped and murdered 12-year-old *Natasha Kirbabina*. He then went to a nearby house and asked the elderly owner if he could borrow a spade. He then went back to where he left the body and buried it in a shallow grave, before throwing the spade away. The old lady contacted police and described him to police.

A day later, on July 17th, Burtsev was arrested, and confessed to six murders. His motive for the murder was the pleasure he received in taking virginity and the passion for hiding his victims, in which he took great care. It was only when he led police to the bodies that they were found.

He was convicted in the same year and sentenced to death, which was later commuted to life in prison, where he remains today.

Born in **1970**.

Active from **1993-1996**.

Arrested on **July 17th 1996**.

Country: **Russia**.

Victims: **6**.

AKA: **The Kamensky Chikatilo.**

Sentence: **Death penalty commuted to life.**

Current whereabouts: **In prison.**

Butcher of Mons, The. (Extended Case File)

In Belgium, at least five murders were committed by an unidentified serial killer named *The Butcher of Mons*. It is one of Belgium's most famous unsolved crimes. All the victims had been dismembered and their body parts placed in plastic bags on the side of public roads and other public areas for all to see.

The first murder took place in January of 1996 and the last in July of 1997. Because of the Marc Dutroux case, the Butcher of Mons case had become well known across Europe at the time. Because the body parts were discovered a while after their deaths, Marc Dutroux had instantly become the prime suspect.

Dutroux had been jailed in 1996, in the longest and most infamous trial in the country's history, and the case was still fresh on people's minds. As the investigators looked closer at the bodies in the bags, they realised that there was no evidence pointing to Dutroux as the killer. Not least because Dutroux was a murderer and rapist of children, and the Butcher of Mons killed adults.

It wasn't until March 1997 that the bags started to be discovered. A police officer named *Olivier Motte* found eight bags beneath the *Rue Emile Vandervelde* in Cuesmes. The various limbs and body parts came from three different victims. A further bag was found on the same street just one day later, and another later on in March along the *Path of Worry* in Mons.

On April 12th 1997, two more bags were found near the Hainre River, in Havré. The bags contained feet, a head and other body parts. All the remains were discovered in the Mons region and were dumped along streets and rivers with poetic names, including the aforementioned *Path of Worry*, the *River Haine (Hate)* and the *Chemin de Bethlehem*. All the victims were known to have passed through Mons Railway Station and were considered poor or having troubles in their lives.

As the investigation was finding the bags all over Mons, theories began to abound about who or what the killer was. In a striking resemblance to Jack the Ripper, aside from the remains of the bodies, the killer would have had medical training. The way in which the bodies had been dissected and mutilated had been carried out with a precision that only a medical professional would have had.

The local police reached out to the FBI for help, who came up with their own profile to assist the investigation. They claimed that the killer would have a stable job with a relatively normal life, as all the victims were killed on the weekends. As soon as the media got hold of it, they began mentioning religious sects and occult ritual as a possible reason for the bodies in the bags. The media at the same time, and for some inane reason, disagreed that the killer was a surgeon, instead leaning on the more newsworthy *cult* connection.

The first known victim was on January 4th 1996, when 42-year-old *Carmelina Russo* was reported missing. She had last been seen at her home in Mons and was known to have frequented the Mons Railway Station. On January 21st, in the Nord region of France, her pelvis was discovered.

On July 21st 1996, 43-year-old *Martine Bohn* was reported missing. Martine was a French transsexual who had previously worked as a prostitute and may or may not have been working as one at the time of her murder. She was known to have frequented various underground bars in Belgium and France.

She had left her family many years before and had no social life outside of drinking and prostitution. She was the only victim that appeared to have been killed out of a sexual motivation. A few days later her torso was pulled out of the River Haine by a fisherman. Both breasts had been sliced off, and no other body parts were found at the time.

On December 22nd 1996, 33-year-old *Jacqueline Leclercq* went missing. Some reports put her last-seen date in January of 1997, but newspaper reports at the time put her missing date as of December 22nd 1996, and a reported missing date as of January 1997.

Leclercq was a young mother of three who had split from her husband and had been denied custody of her children. She had become transient and began hanging around the Mons Railway Station for unknown reasons. She would officially be declared missing on January 23rd 1997. Her remains were discovered as part of the first eight bags beneath the Rue de Emile Vandervelde.

In March 1997, 21-year-old *Nathalie Godart* vanished. She had been a mother of one child who had been taken into care because of problems in Godart's own life. Godart lived in a rundown Mons bedsit and was a regular at various bars and gathering points in the city. People knew her as being extremely promiscuous with men but she had never charged for sex. Some of her body parts would be found in the River Haine.

The last confirmed victim of the Butcher was 37-year-old *Begonia Valencia*. She had vanished in July of 1997 from her home in the area of *Frameries*. Her bones and skull were found half a year later in *Hyon*, just outside of Mons. Valencia was known to have taken a local bus, like clockwork every evening, and it is claimed that the Butcher could have picked her up at a station in Mons.

Ten years after Valencia's disappearance, one of her neighbours gave an interview to reporters investigating the case. It was from this interview that the bus and station connection came about. The neighbour told a story of a mysterious person who came back to the town once a year.

This person would drop a wreath into the local river, on the anniversary of Valencia's disappearance, in order to keep her memory alive. No one has ever come forward to claim responsibility for the wreath, leading cold case investigators to believe there was a slim possibility it could have been the Butcher himself.

One of the prime suspects in the case was a Montenegro native named *Smail Tulja* (Smajo Džurlić). He changed his name to Tulja after fleeing New York were a murder took place that matched the victims in France.

In September of 1990, in New York City, Tulja's wife, *Mary Beal*, went missing. Her remains were discovered three weeks later in two garbage bags left on the side of the street. She had been beheaded and had been dismembered into smaller parts.

The similarities between the New York murder and the Belgium murders were overwhelming.

Tulja had fled to the Belgian city of Mons and then to Albania in the early 2000s. In 2006, two female victims were found in bags in Albania. They too had been dismembered and dissected. A year later, in 2007, Tulja was arrested in his home country of Montenegro. At the request of Albanian police, the FBI were brought in who made immediate connections between all the murders and subsequently the arrest in Montenegro.

Montenegro had become an independent nation in 2006 and did not have an extradition treaty with the United States. But the Montenegro court still managed to convict him in 2010 of the murder of Mary Beal, and he was sentenced to 12 years.

Unfortunately for the continuing investigation, Tulja died in prison in 2012, making his connection to the other murders more difficult. The FBI and NYPD suggested that Tulja had killed eight people, seven across Europe and one in New York. The Belgian and Albanian investigators failed to make any conclusive connections to Tulja and the murders in their countries.

This meant that since 2012, more suspects have been put forward as the Butcher of Mons. In 2010, 62-year-old French doctor, *Jacques Antoine*, was arrested for assaulting a woman. The investigators discovered two letters that had been sent to them a few months earlier by Antoine's son. In the letters he claimed that his father was the Butcher.

The letter claimed that his Strasbourg-based father had frequented the Mons region multiple times from the mid-1980s to 1997, with various garbage bags in his vehicle. There was also mention of a predilection towards firearms, and further stories of him carrying trash bags around. No evidence was found linking Antoine to the murders but he remains a tentative suspect to this day.

Another suspect is British murderer and suspected serial killer, *John Sweeney*, AKA: *The Canal Murderer*. He claimed his first victim in Amsterdam, in 1990. He had murdered 33-year-old American model *Melissa Halstead*, dismembered her body and put her remains in two holdalls, which were later fished out of the Amstel River.

In 2000, Sweeney murdered 31-year-old Paula Fields in London. Fields was a crack cocaine addict from Liverpool who worked as a prostitute in North London. Her remains were found in 2001, when six holdalls were fished out of the Regent's Canal at the King's Cross section. Ten of Field's body parts were discovered in them. Her head, hands, and feet were missing.

It was claimed that Sweeney may have lived in Belgium at the time of the Butcher murders but no solid link has been made. He was accused of attempted murder by one of his girlfriends. The murder and disposal of his victims demonstrated a great deal of planning and pre-meditation. He was also a carpenter who would have had access to specialist cutting tools. He was sentenced to life in prison in 2011.

The identity of the Butcher of Mons remains unknown to this day. As of 2021, various cold case investigations are ongoing, in the hope that one day, the Butcher will finally be identified.

Active from **1996-1997.**

Country: **Belgium.**

Victims: **5+.**

Current whereabouts: **Unidentified killer. Status unknown.**

Caputo, Richard

An Argentine-American serial killer, also known as *'The Lady Killer'*. He moved to the States in 1970 to New York City. He would later claim he was sexually abused as a child and that this kickstarted a wave of negative influence that manifested in acting out violence.

His known victims include the New York murders of 19-year-old *Nathalie Brown* on July 31st 1971, and 26-year-old psychologist *Judith Becker* in 1974. In San

Francisco in 1975 he murdered 28-year-old *Barbara Ann Taylor*. Then in 1977 he killed *Laura Gomez* in Mexico City. He has long been suspected of two more murders in 1981 and 1983.

For the murder of Nathalie Brown in 1971, Caputo was caught shortly after and charged with the crime. He was found incompetent to stand trial and was sent to the psychiatric unit of Matteawan State Hospital. While there he was treated by Judith Becker, his second known victim. Upon his discharge in 1973, he would turn up at Becker's door, in an attempt to befriend her. It was later suggested that they may have continued a platonic friendship before she was beaten and strangled to death.

At one point he was number one on the *FBI's Ten Most Wanted list*. At the trial, his lawyer claimed that Caputo had at least three distinct personalities, struggled to remember any details of the crimes.

Caputo killed four confirmed victims from 1971 to 1977 and remained a fugitive until 1994 when he turned himself in to law enforcement because he was afraid that his psychosis would manifest in more murders. He was suspected and heavily linked to two murders in 1981 and 1983 and could have killed more but none were officially confirmed.

He died of a heart attack in his prison cell in October 1997.

Born in **1949**.

Active from **1971-1983**.

Arrested on **January 18th 1994**.

Country: **USA / Mexico**.

Victims: **4-6+**.

AKA: **The Lady Killer**.

Sentence: **25 years in prison**.

Current whereabouts: **Died of a heart attack in October 1977**.

Catlin, Steven David

He was convicted of three murders in 1990 and sentenced to death. He was adopted as a toddler and was unruly growing up. He dropped out of high school and started with petty crime which led to him being arrested on forgery charges.

His first marriage was said to have been marred by domestic violence, abuse and his own drug addiction. He married again without divorcing his original wife after using a fake name on a marriage license. He then went on to marry another two times with most relationships ending because of his abuse.

He killed his mother and two of his wives by poisoning them with a toxic herbicide called '*paraquat*'. He killed for financial gain and for the control and power it gave him.

He was charged in 1985 for the 1976 murder of *Joyce Catlin*, and while serving time, he was charged on the other two counts.

As of 2021, he remains on death row at San Quentin State Prison.

Born in **1944**.

Active from **1976-1984**.

Arrested in **1986**.

Country: **USA**.

Victims: **3**.

Sentence: **Death penalty**.

Current whereabouts: **Death row**.

(Research Article #3) Child Abuse from the 1940s-1960s

One of the most difficult areas to research has the been the data surrounding child abuse from the 1940s to 1960s. Generally this is considered during and after World War Two but pre-1978.

Most serial killers who were either active, caught, or started in 1978, were around the age of 30-years-old and were generally white males. As of 2016, an astonishing 90.8% of serial killers were white males.

Statistics show that most children are abused from the age of five-years-old and upwards for reasons including social, physical and cultural.

In the disconnected world of the mid-Twentieth Century, most child abuse cases never reached the attention of the authorities. It is reported that when they did, the response from welfare workers was mostly inadequate.

In the recent *Northern Irish Historical Institutional Abuse Inquiry*, a lot of information and data was sent out into the public domain. There seemed to be a lack of joined up thinking and urgency up until the 1980s. This would have mostly been down to World War Two.

War is one of the other factors later on in this book. Pre-1950, children who were abused were often depicted as unintelligent and slow in mind, as well as being sexually active themselves.

Shockingly, before World War Two, and for some time after, welfare workers tended to place children into categories of sexual knowledge. By doing so, most children then became culpable for eliciting abuse from adults. To think this was only recent history is astonishing enough, but that was only the tip of the iceberg.

In over 2000 cases studied from 1927 to 1954, half the victims were under seven-years-old. Even then, they were not always portrayed as being the innocent party in the abuse. Less so if they were from a working class background.

In the British wartime evacuation of children from the cities, there had been a rise in young prostitution. This only served to move attention away from abuse. In another astonishing fact, during the evacuation of 827,000 children, only six psychiatric social workers were available during their removal.

It's obviously agreed that during wartime, there was a prevalence to have these kind of workers elsewhere. Yet, the chaos of World War Two on both sides of the Atlantic can never be underestimated.

The *Baby Boomer* generation from 1946 to 1964 are also seen as being partially to blame for the rise and nonchalance regarding the abuse of children.

Changes in social work and care saw a system that was open to neglect and abuse itself. Families were no longer being interviewed, especially foster parents and step-parents. Having young people in the workplace was still the way forward. Those from impoverished backgrounds were even more at risk. Record keeping was few and far between and siblings were often separated in the years that followed the war.

In the United States and across the Western world, there became a large focus on mother-child relationships. The main focus was the challenge of promoting marital bliss. There was a commitment from governments to keep family members at home and families together in a projected harmony of circumstance.

This meant that child abuse in all its forms was never seen as a good enough reason to remove that child from a family environment. In most cases there had deemed to be consent by the child. Some did not understand the abuse was wrong, and others were indifferent to it happening.

The downplay on post-war child abuse was obvious. They might as well have brushed any evidence of it under the carpet. As we have already learned, childhood abuse is one of the major factors when looking at why people become serial killers.

Childhood abuse throughout the 1950s and 1960s was generally being brushed aside. Disconnected authorities wrangled with families and the law, with most not knowing what needed to be done or even acknowledging it was taking place.

There was more concern placed on the promiscuity of sexually active young people than there was for actual abuse. There was little interest in framing anyone as a victim of sexual abuse. When child abuse was talked about in the 1950s and 1960s, it was generally regarded as delinquency or blamed on parents from foreign countries. The sexual abuse against young boys was even less talked about.

There is a link between childhood abuse and those who go onto commit violent crimes. A 2005 report of 50 serial killers showed that 68% of serial killers suffered from maltreatment of some kind.

It's important to understand what abuse is, as there are different ways of understanding it. The most common types are:

Physical abuse.

Violence and bullying towards another.

Sexual abuse.

Sexual violence and forced interaction with another.

Psychological abuse.

Emotional and controlling attitudes.

People make the obvious connection with sexual abuse in children as a precursor to later violence in adulthood and teen years. That's not always accurate but it has the evidence to back it up.

In the same report, it was shown that 26% suffered sexual abuse and 35% suffered physical abuse. Half of everyone in the study suffered some type of psychological abuse from adults or older children. Child abuse is generally common amongst serial killers but the results of the studies themselves are always brought into question.

Most of the data is retrieved from third parties, who sometimes only have a tenuous connection to the serial killer in question. There is also the knowledge that a suspected 90% of child abuse went unreported before the 1980s. It still mostly goes unreported today.

Any study involving childhood abuse and serial killers draws only from *substantiated* reports from social workers. Thus the scale of child abuse throughout the Twentieth Century could potentially be monstrously high.

Because child abuse from the post-war period was rarely recognised in the morally and lawful way we see it today, the information is not forthcoming. Statistics on child abuse from the 1940s and all the way through the early 1970s are flawed. Data wasn't kept properly, victims were made to feel like victims, and any statistics that do come out of the period are mostly assumed to be the tip of an exceptionally large iceberg.

More importantly, people kept getting away with it.

The next question becomes; why were so many people abusing children during or after World War Two and even in today's world? Most people ask why because they have a strong emotional connection to the question itself. The answer is not easy, the reasons are even harder.

It's especially important to note that these are common factors and should not be taken as overriding examples of those who might go on to abuse children. There are often more deeper factors involved.

Control.

A person who has control over a child might develop a sexual interest in them.

Betrayal.

They overcome the trust of the child and in doing so break down their own moral barriers in order to move to the next step.

Impulsion.

The abuser then acts on their sexual fantasies towards the child.

In understanding childhood sexual abuse, it is no way about forgiving the abusers. Every person that sexually, physically or psychologically abuses a child should rightfully be held accountable for their crimes.

We know that those abused in childhood have a higher risk of developing a tendency of violent acts in later life. This mostly happens when the person feels they have the required strength to overcome another human being.

Serial killers who were caught, active, or began killing in 1978, would have been in the correct suggested age bracket for having suffered abuse in their childhood years.

It's important in the modern world of connectivity that we continue to collect and store data efficiently. *NHS Digital* is a prime example of where data collection is flawed and mostly incorrect. Collation and inter-agency correlation is utterly imperfect. The various Trusts in the NHS don't always share with other Trusts making the collation of data difficult and somewhat political.

Without correct data, we will struggle for longer to understand the correlation between child abuse and violence in later life.

(Research Article #4) Child Abuse from the 1990s to 2000s

The decades that followed the 1980s had a lot to deal with. The satanic ritual claims of media and investigators led many to believe that evil cults were rampaging across the world. An astonishingly large number of people believed the cults were taking children and abusing them or even sacrificing them to the dark lord himself.

In an exceedingly small amount of cases, there had been elements of ritual abuse but generally they were considered rare. Unfortunately, this led to some police forces and departments scaling back on claims of child abuse that cited ritual elements. Yet, unbelievably, child abuse has been on the increase ever since.

Some people look back at the 1950s to 1980s as having the largest number of cases of child abuse. Sadly, that's not true. There has been one ruling factor from the late 1990s that has led to the current increase; the internet.

Because of the media-led satanic revelations and charges of false memories amongst children, the child protection movement developed serious setbacks. Threats were sky-high and it was about the time that people began locking their doors a little more often.

There was a constant and seeping doubt when accusations of parental abuse or abuse from strangers were reported. The threats were piling up but the authorities were struggling to play catch-up.

We can look back on this period with hindsight and discover paedophile rings that run to the highest levels of government (British), media (BBC), charity organisations (Oxfam), and religion (Catholic Church).

It was almost as if certain organisations were secretly blocking investigations into child abuse, and by all accounts they might well have been.

New laws were dropping in all over the world; Megan's Law in the USA, and Sarah's Law in the UK. They were both child sex-offender disclosure schemes brought about due to high-profile cases on both sides of the pond. Although it appeared that actually gaining information on offenders by concerned parents was not as easy as it seemed.

The internet created a perfect haven for paedophiles. Hundreds of thousands of cases across the United States and United Kingdom were reported. Mostly involving children who had been groomed using internet forums and chat services.

The subsequent public unveiling of the Tor network (the dark web) saw images and videos of child pornography proliferate computers and hard drives with millions of images.

It has been suggested if the media had never run stories on the dark web then it would have remained more underground than it currently is. As soon as media outlets started talking about it, the masses discovered it when it could have remained hidden away.

It led the curious to seek them out and the already disturbed to placate their own desires. Large sting operations went into place but only a small fraction were ever caught. To this day, the UK-based CEOP (Child Exploitation and Online Protection Command) have warned of huge increases in paedophilia due to the proliferation and distribution of images online.

From the 1950s to the 1980s, the criminals and perverts used to have to physically seek out hard copies of images, thereby putting themselves at obvious risk of being caught. Today, these offenders can access databases of images at the click of a button, on any device, anywhere in the world.

Even with all the laws and knowledge that was spreading through the new world, reports of abuse in developed countries was increasing exponentially from the 1990s onwards. In Japan, it was shown there was a 1000% increase in child abuse cases from 1990 to 2000.

From the late 1990s and right up until 2021, the Roman Catholic church has been embroiled in a scandal involving the sexual abuse of thousands of children and young teens by priests. Tens of thousands of cases have been brought against the church across the world and still it carries on.

The Pope astonishingly blamed it on '*Satan*' and '*the 1960s*'. One Australian priest claimed child abuse was acceptable as per the laws of the bible. This belief was held by a number of priests who came out in support of their brethren.

In the present day, there is the belief and knowledge that children are widely subject to physical and sexual abuse and it's not going away any time soon. As population increases and more people discover their dark desires online then the abuse will continue.

The interest in child abuse is claimed to have been one of the most significant developments of the 1990s, leading in to the 2000s.

What we do know is that child abuse can sometimes lead their victims to violent crime in their teens or early adulthood. And some, as we've already learned from the data provided in the 1970s, go on to become serial killers.

In 1978, we spoke about child abuse in the 1950s and 1960s being one of the driving factors of the increase in serial killers to 1978.

If we use the same principle then the huge increase in child abuse from 1990s to 2010s will also have an effect on violent crime from around 2020.

That the abuse is more rife and more common in the 1990s to the 2000s and beyond then it is an assumption there will be a rise of serial killing from around the 2028 mark.

Chagas, Francisco Das

Brazilian serial killer and former mechanic, *Francisco das Chagas Rodrigues de Brito*, raped and killed at least 30 children in the regions of Maranhão and Pará. He was suspected of killing at least 42.

Chagas claimed that he was exacting revenge because he was abused as a child and wanted others to feel his pain but didn't remember the details of his murders.

He claimed to have known that he was killing children but had no memory of the intricacies of the murders.

He was arrested in 2004 and initially charged with the murders of two young boys who were found buried beneath the floor of his shack, in a shanty town just off from Sao Jose do Ribamar. He would rape and then castrate his victims, before buying them in shallow graves.

"Something was guiding me, directing me. It was like a voice in my head. And it was that thing - the voice - that determined what happened. Sometimes I'm revolted by what I did, but you must understand that something was using me to do this. Good people will understand that."

Chagas, in a 2004 interview with the BBC.

The trial of Chagas was held in the auditorium of a local club in Sao Jose de Ribamar, because the courtroom wasn't big enough to hold the hundreds of victims' relatives.

Even though violence is common in Brazil, serial killing is rare and Chagas is now assumed to be the country's worst serial killer.

Born in **1965**.

Active from **1989-2003**.

Arrested in **December 2003**.

Country: **Brazil**.

Victims: **52+**.

AKA: **The Mechanic**.

Sentence: **237 years in prison**.

Current whereabouts: **In prison**.

Chanal, Pierre

French serial killing soldier Pierre Chanal murdered at least eight people between 1980 and 1988, although it is suspected he could have killed 17. The area if his killings became known as the *Triangle of Death*.

On August 8th 1987, the body of Irishman *Trevor O'Keeffe* was discovered in a shallow grave in France. He had been hitchhiking through the country when he was strangled to death by Chanal. At least eight young men had disappeared within the triangle since 1980.

In 1988, Chanal was stopped by police. When they opened his van doors, they discovered a Hungarian hitchhiker who had been tied and gagged. Chanal was convicted of kidnapping and rape but was suspected to have killed up to 17 people in the Mourmelon region of France.

His van was full of sex toys and a camera where he had been taking various images of men he had picked up. Astonishingly, Chanal was a Chief Warrant Officer in the *4th Dragoon Regiment* in France. He had previously earned a United Nations medal for his service as a UN peacekeeper in Lebanon.

Pierre Chanal committed suicide in 2003 whilst on trial for the murders.

Born **November 18th 1946.**

Active from **1980-1988.**

Arrested on **August 9th 1988.**

Country: **France.**

Victims: **8-17+.**

AKA: **The Triangle of Death Murders.**

Current whereabouts: **Committed suicide in 2003, while awaiting trial.**

Chase, Richard Trenton: The Vampire of Sacramento (Extended Case File)

Richard Trenton Chase killed six people over a one month period from December 29th 1977 to January 27th 1978. He became known as the *Vampire of Sacramento* because he drank the blood of his victims, engaged in necrophilia, and ate some of their remains.

Teresa Wallin's death five days earlier shocked the nation and would come to shock the world in time. After the aforementioned necrophilia, Chase then removed multiple organs. He cut off one of her nipples and drank her blood. He then stuffed dog faeces down her throat before leaving her to be found.

It's quite clear that Chase suffered from a mental disorder. For short periods of time, in 1973 and 1976, he was committed to a psychiatric ward and became known as *Dracula* after injecting rabbit's blood into his veins. He was subsequently diagnosed with paranoid schizophrenia and then released in late 1976 after being deemed no longer a risk to society.

He may also have been suffering from *Renfield Syndrome*, a form of clinical Vampirism which is added in detail as a research article in this book.

Chase was born in Sacramento in 1950 and was sexually abused by his mother over the first ten years of his life. During his teen years he became addicted to drink and drugs. Later on, he became a pyromaniac and also enjoyed torturing and killing small animals. After leaving his mother's house on the belief that she was trying to poison him, he rented an apartment with some friends.

During his time in the apartment, it was said that Chase enjoyed walking around in the nude and was constantly high on multiple types of drugs including LSD. Possibly even *Orange Sunshine LSD* which is discussed in a later chapter.

ROBERT ANDREW BERDELLA

IMAGE ATTRIB. A57

ROBERT BLACK

IMAGE ATTRIB. A60

STEVEN DAVID CATLIN

IMAGE ATTRIB. A15

RICHARD TRENTON CHASE

IMAGE ATTRIB. A61

This was only a few years before he would kill his victims and drink their blood in a misconstrued belief that he was keeping himself alive. It was because he believed Nazi's had carried out invasive experiments on him causing him to physically need the blood.

Chase was to become synonymous with the term of serial killer. His monstrous crimes are still talked about, discussed, and used as a basis for television shows to this very day.

When some people think of serial killers, they might think of schizophrenic individuals who as a child had a tendency for killing small animals and acting bizarrely. Chase fitted every profile available at the time.

He had a fascination with torturing small animals, like cats and small dogs. It was this feeling of ultimate power over another's life that would eventually drive him to kill a human.

By the age of 10-years-old, Chase killed a cat he found on the street. Some would say it was preparation for a larger kill. This could stem from the traumas of child abuse and the subsequent desire for control over another. As a child, the only power one might have over another is a small animal. As they grow up, they might be able to overpower larger animals or even humans.

During his teen years, he was able to hide his mental issues under a veil of alcohol and marijuana which was easily accessible at the time. He constantly got into trouble at school and at home because of it, but he saw it as an escape from the banalities of life and the troubles that plagued him.

It became known that Chase was unable to perform sexually as he couldn't maintain an erection. When he was 18-years-old, he voluntarily went to see a psychiatrist about his erection problem. It was under the counselling of his psychiatrist where he learned it was sometimes caused by the repression of anger.

During his time in the apartment he would go through many flatmates, all of which would complain to him and to the authorities about his bizarre behaviour and heavy drug use.

One time he nailed the closet door shut in his bedroom because he thought that people were coming out from the darkness and invading his private space. He began to develop severe paranoia and started to become a fully-fledged hypochondriac, believing that everything was going wrong with his body.

One time, he entered a hospital looking for the person who had stolen his pulmonary artery. He complained that his bones were coming out through the back of his head causing his skull to split and maintained a belief that his stomach was back to front.

He claimed his heart would stop beating and then start up again after a short amount of time. Chase would wallow in a pit of paranoid delusions and far-fetched hypochondria, brought on by child abuse and a massive consumption of drugs.

When he refused to leave the apartment, his flatmates moved out instead. His newfound isolation afforded him the possibility of acting on more darker desires. He started to trap then kill more small animals like rabbits and cats. He would disembowel them and eat the raw meat. He then moved onto purchasing small pets with the intention of killing them.

Chase was under the delusion that his heart was shrinking. The consumption of raw flesh and the drinking of animal blood would stop his heart disappearing from his body altogether. He believed this to such an extent that he once injected rabbit blood directly into his veins.

When he was 25-years-old, he was committed as a paranoid schizophrenic to *Beverly Manor Institute* for the mentally insane. It is reported that anti-psychotic medicines failed to work. This sometimes meant that his schizophrenia and psychosis may have been caused by the drugs that he had previously consumed.

One day nurses found him with blood around his mouth, they discovered two dead and mutilated birds outside his window that he had lured for capture. After a few months he was released as he was no longer considered a danger to the public.

He was able to move into another apartment in the city and restarted trapping cats and dogs to kill and consume. In his trial, his mother claimed that Chase appeared on her doorstep one day with a dead cat. He smiled, threw the cat to the ground and ripped it open with his bare hands. Then he smeared the animal's blood all over his neck and face. In an even more bizarre chain of events, his mother failed to contact anyone over the incident.

On December 29th 1977, he killed *Ambrose Griffin*, a 51-year-old engineer in the city. After a shopping trip, Griffin returned to his car to get the last of the items. When his wife stepped back outside, she saw her husband on the ground next to the grocery bags. Chase had shot him twice.

On January 23rd 1978, Chase tried to break into a house at *2909 Burnece Street*. When a neighbour approached him, he stopped, lit a cigarette, stared at her and casually walked away. That same afternoon, he broke into a house along the street but was interrupted by the owners and he ran off, but not before smearing his excrement on some of their belongings.

He moved along the street to *2360 Tioga Way* and casually walked into the home of the Wallin family. He bumped into *Teresa Wallin* as she was taking out the garbage. Chase shot her three times and dragged her corpse to the bedroom leaving a blood trail through the house. He raped her corpse whilst stabbing her multiple times with a kitchen knife.

Chase then proceeded to carve off her left nipple and cut her torso open below the sternum. He removed her spleen and intestines, cut out her kidneys and sliced her pancreas in half. He then placed the kidneys back inside the body as if they were one organ.

He used a yogurt pot to scoop up the blood from inside her body and drink it. He would then rub her blood over his face and neck. Before he left the house, Chase had gone into the garden, picked up some dog excrement and pushed it into her throat and mouth.

The extreme brutality of the Walling murder was to shock not just California, but the whole of the United States. The media got wind of the story and as the killer seemed to have a fascination with drinking blood, Chase earned the dubious title of '*Vampire of Sacramento*'.

Only one mile from the Wallin house, on January 27th 1978, the Miroth family would suffer a similar, if not worse fate. Chase entered the Miroth residence and firstly shot dead a family friend named *Danny Meredith*. He stole his wallet and car keys before rampaging through the house.

He shot 38-year-old *Evelyn Miroth* and her six-year-old son, *Jason Miroth*. He also shot and killed Evelyn's 22-month-old nephew. Evelyn was found half-naked on her bed with some of her organs removed.

Chase had drunk some of her blood and engaged in sexual intercourse with the corpse as he had done on the previous occasion. His desire for cannibalism and necrophilia had left nothing to the imagination.

The investigation moved forward very quickly. Chase hadn't tried to hide what he had done. Evidence was easy to come by and when they searched his apartment they found everything they needed but they didn't have to look too hard. Everything in the kitchen was blood stained, from the fridge to the drinking glasses. One container had pieces of brain fragments and others had small pieces of bone within them. The electric blender had never been cleaned.

Before his trial, it was claimed Chase virtually turned into an animal when they tried to extract blood for him for a sample. He was subsequently charged with six counts of murder in the first degree, it was a trial that was to last four months during the course of 1978.

On May 8th 1979, after only a few hours, the jury returned the obvious verdict of guilty of six counts of murder in the first degree. He was given the death penalty by gas chamber at *San Quentin Prison*.

Chase gave a series of interviews in which he spoke of his fear of Nazis and UFOs. He believed he had been killed by a combination of both and had been forced to kill others in order to keep himself alive. He asked the interviewer, *FBI Agent, Robert Ressler*, for a radar gun, so that he could capture the Nazi UFOs and bring them to justice for the murders.

It also emerged that Chase believed his blood was turning to powder and that he needed blood from other creatures to replenish it. He was to begin an appeal on the basis that he was only killing to preserve his own life. Chase was to become the poster boy for a paranoid schizophrenic serial killer.

On Boxing Day 1980, a guard found him dead in his cell. He had committed suicide with an overdose of antidepressants that he had collected and saved. When Chase's body was autopsied, it was found that his heart was in a perfectly healthy condition.

Born **May 23rd 1950.**

Active from **1977-1978.**

Arrested in **January 1978.**

Country: **USA (California).**

Victims: **6.**

AKA: **Vampire of Sacramento.**

Sentence: **Death penalty.**

Current whereabouts: **Suicide by hanging on December 26th 1980.**

Chikatilo, Andrei: The Red Ripper (Extended Case File)

On December 22nd 1978, Andrei Chikatilo lured nine-year-old *Yelena Zakotnova* into a secretly purchased house where he attempted to rape her. He failed to maintain an erection and because of her moaning and struggling, he strangled and stabbed her to death.

In an interview after his arrest, he stated that in the process of stabbing the child he found himself ejaculating. 1978 was the beginning of the reign of Russia's most evil serial killer.

Almost all of his victims suffered sexual assault and mutilation resulting in the murders of 52 children and women. He did however confess to 56 murders.

Andrei Chikatilo was one of the most revered killers to have ever tarnished the Russian motherland. You've read a little bit about his upbringing in the World War Two section. It is clear that he was hugely affected by the horrors of war as a child.

He would share a bed with his mother, in fear of the war. But because of his constant bed-wetting, she would berate and beat him for it. He saw the direct results of Nazi occupation and was recorded as saying that he literally saw bodies being blown up into the air to fall down in a crumpled bloody mess to the dangerous streets below.

He did say that the sight of this both scared him and excited him. From this obvious and saturated exposure to things that no human should have seen, he started to develop images of torture in his head. His brother also befell a horrific fate.

"They caught my brother, who was only ten, they ate him, and sold some of his flesh for food."

Andrei Chikatilo, speaking of a group of Ukrainian men.

His first sexual experience was when he was 17-years-old, with a ten-year-old friend of his sister's. It was the first time he was able to ejaculate, he said he was able to do it with images of torture in his mind. He was normally shy around girls but had wrestled his sister's friend to the ground and forced himself upon her.

Because he couldn't physically rape her, he violently sexually assaulted her instead, a pre-cursor of things to come. After a series of embarrassments when girls his age started to question his impotence, he tried to hang himself in his mother's home but his mother and some neighbours helped to lift the noose off. With the feeling of nothing left in his life and the embarrassment of his failures, he moved away to a small town near *Rostov-on-don*.

Chikatilo went directly into the army but it didn't last long. When he returned home he tried many times to find a girlfriend But he was still unable to perform sexually and rumours started spreading again about his sexual inadequacies. He felt humiliated and dreamed about torturing the girls who were cruel to him.

He then went on to become a schoolteacher and did finally get married in a somewhat arranged marriage by his sister. Yet, it was not too long before his wife criticised everything he did, including his actions in the bedroom. He felt at that time that his life was a disaster and thus his torture fantasies increased.

His wife and mother criticised him constantly and he even tried to have children with his wife. It is said that he could only attempt conception by ejaculating onto his hands and then pushing it inside his wife.

When his mother died in 1973, he began abusing some of the girls in his school. It started with gentle touching and stroking but then his lust got the better of him and he began to grope and forcefully touch the girls. He said this made him feel powerful and he enjoyed the feeling it gave him.

Most of the time, the school covered it up with denial and lies instead of prosecution. Some would say that with hindsight, this allowed a pervert to become a killer.

It was December 22nd 1978 and the killing of Yelena Zakotnova that would become the catalyst of further killings. Chikatilo later confirmed that he was only able to achieve orgasm through the stabbing of children and women and that the urge to relive the experience of Zakotnova was too overwhelming.

He claimed he didn't have to go looking for victims, he didn't have to seek them out. They were always right there and they were usually willing to follow him anywhere. It was however, another three years before he killed his second victim, 17-year-old *Larisa Tkachenko* who he lured to a forest to drink vodka.

Her body was found with mud in her mouth and she had been beaten and strangled to death. The body had been mutilated with a stick and Andrei's own teeth. He had also completely bitten off one of her nipples.

13-year-old *Lyubov Biryuk* was his third victim when he dragged her into the bushes from a secluded path. Her body was found with 22 knife wounds to the head, neck and pelvic region.

From then on, Chikatilo no longer attempted to resist the dark urges that were coming to him more often than he could control. He was free of any control and even the fear of being caught was lost on him. He had become a killer and nothing was going to stop him living out his fantasies.

He established a pattern, a plan of luring and killing children and young women in secluded areas. Most of the victims were runaways, prostitutes and homeless girls. They were easy to manipulate and gullible enough to do anything for a good drink.

For the next five victims and those that followed, each had evidence of mutilation to the eye sockets caused by a knife. In some cases, their eyes had been entirely gorged out and either allegedly eaten or disposed of somewhere else.

In 1982, he carried out a particularly horrific murder. Ten-year-old *Olga Stalmachenok* was lured to a cornfield on the outskirts of her town before she was brutally murdered. Her body was found a few days later. She had been stabbed 50 times in the head and body, her chest had been ripped open and he had cut out her lower bowel and uterus.

After having already brutally killed 15 children and young women, Chikatilo was arrested on suspicion of some of the murders, at least the ones that could be linked with the eye gorging signature. He had been spotted luring young girls away from bus stops and had a knife and rope in his bag when first arrested.

In 1984, Chikatilo was only one of 25,000 suspects, and details of the specifics of the crimes were sent to every police station in Russia. But the crimes were difficult to stomach, later victims appeared beheaded and so badly mutilated that one was even thought to have been caught in a harvesting machine.

The prime suspect became *Yuri Kalenik*, a 19-year-old who had lived in a home for mentally disabled children. He would return to the home to play games with the younger boys. The head nurse found him and another boy playing on the trolleys and accosted them. She then asked if they knew anything about the murders and the other boy said that *Yuri* was the killer.

Amazingly because of this soft accusation, the authorities believed they had broken the case and found the real killer. For the first few days after his arrest, he was beaten violently by investigators looking for a confession. Knowing that the only way to stop the beatings was to confess, Yuri gave a false confession.

Detective *Viktor Burakov* took over the investigation and changed direction with the case. Yuri's confession would one day be used as a basis for psychological false confession cases.

Yuri even managed to lead them to where the bodies were found, he did this by trying to understand what the police wanted of him. He even followed their direction when at one of the crime scenes. Burakov started to disbelieve Yuri's account but he was to remain in custody until it could be fully disproven.

Because Chikatilo had a strain of two blood types, he would constantly be discounted from the crimes. Many more brutal murders would take place. Before the Autumn of 1984, the investigation had attributed 24 victims to the unnamed murderer.

Semen found at each of the bodies matched up to blood type AB, yet every suspect who had that blood type was either found having an alibi or the incorrect personality match. The investigation was going out of control, the police and detectives knew nothing more than when they first started.

Chikatilo was then killing one victim every two weeks and the investigation could not work out how he was choosing his victims and why the evidence didn't seem to match up. The main issue was in the blood type against the original suspects list. It was the removal of that complete list that was causing the investigation to hit a dead end at every turn.

In August 1985, another body appeared near a small airport outside Moscow. Her body had been mutilated and exposed. Investigator Burakov went to Moscow to examine the victim and was in no doubt that it was the same killer.

Moscow detectives linked the killing of three young boys where one had been raped and one had been decapitated. At the same time, Burakov was called back to *Shakhty* where an 18-year-old girl was found dead with leaves stuffed into her mouth.

If any of this sounds slightly familiar, then you might have seen the film, *Child 44*, with *Gary Oldman* and *Tom Hardy*. The film is very loosely based on the Chikatilo murders.

On the girl's body they found the same blood type AB, red and blue thread under her fingernails and a single strand of grey hair. This was the most physical evidence found so far. Then the investigation brought in serial killer specialist, Chief Investigator *Issa Kostoyev*. Issa believed they had already come across the killer during their investigation but did not know it at the time. It was a low-blow to Burakov's investigation.

Issa began profiling the killer and used American profiling books that detailed cases of dismemberment and disfiguring of a killer's victims.

"Some killers were driven merely by arrogance and the idea that their victims were objects that belonged to them to do with as they pleased."

Serial killer specialist, Chief Investigator *Issa Kostoyev*

At this point in time, Issa discovered that Burakov's investigation had resulted in five false confessions, including that of Yuri Kalenik, who was still remanded in custody. Issa was furious and ordered all the information on all crime scenes to be compiled into one report and sent to everyone within the flawed investigation.

Then, having finally got hold of all the crime scene reports and known data, a *Dr. Bukhanovsky* spent months compiling a 65-page report on the suspect. He labelled the suspect; *Killer X*. He referred to Killer X as a *necro-sadist*, this would be someone who needed to watch people die in order to achieve sexual gratification.

He believed the multiple stabbing was a way to enter the victims sexually where the killer could not physically do so. The deepest cuts were representative of the height of his sexual pleasure. He even went as far as stating that Killer X mutilated or removed the eyes because he believed in the superstition that his image would be left on them.

Suddenly the investigation was picking up pace, with the report, the profiling and the evidence, they looked close to catching their killer. Then, just as suddenly as moral picked up again, the murders stopped and the investigation dried up. It would remain static for another *six* years.

Chikatilo had become wary and followed the investigation down to the most intimate detail. He held onto his urges somewhat and tried to change his methods of murder. He moved his killings away from Rostov-on-don to the Ukraine and further afield Ural towns in Russia, many of them were not ever linked to him at the time until after his confession.

It was six years later, in 1990, after the discovery of even more bodies linked to the same killer, a massive police operation got under way and a saturation of nearby bus stops, train stations and public gardens was evident by the amount of police acting as a deterrent. It was the biggest police investigation in Russia's history at the time. It seemed as though everyone had been involved at some point along the way.

On November 6th 1990, Chikatilo killed his last victim, ending a serial killer's reign that began in 1978.

He was arrested coming out of a cafe after being watched actively seeking out young females to talk to and attempt to lure. They arrested Chikatilo and placed him in a cell with a gifted informant but he was not willing to admit or say anything against himself.

The next day, Kostoyev chose to handle the interrogation himself. It was a meeting of a serial killer and detective that some would fill their books with, such was the information that eventually came out of it. Chikatilo confessed to being a sexual deviant but for days never actually confessed to having anything to do with the murders.

A medical examination showed that Andrei Chikatilo's blood type was A which was different to the blood type found in his other bodily fluids. Chikatilo's semen had a very weak type B antibody making him an exceedingly rare case. But it would not have been enough to stand up in court should the entire investigation fall on his rare blood type.

They needed a real confession and it would be down to Dr. Bukhanovsky to finally get the confession from him. Dr. Bukhanovsky agreed to question him but only out of a professional interest and not from a legal standpoint.

Chikatilo would later say that he gave up everything to Dr. Bukhanovsky because he seemed to be the only person who ever really understood him. Finally, he broke down and admitted that he had done everything and more.

It was immediately apparent that the initial number of 36 victims was going to be a long way off the final number. Chikatilo remembered the details of each of his murders and would go through them in turn, one by one. He would never stick to a pattern, sometimes he would learn someone's walking routes, yet other times would be opportunistic killings. He would squat beside the bodies and cut them so as not to get blood on his clothes.

Chikatilo would sometimes place his semen inside a uterus that he had just removed. Then as he walked along a path, he would chew on it. He never admitted to ingesting the remains but no missing body parts were ever found.

"The cries, the blood and the agony gave me relaxation and a certain pleasure."

Andrei Chikatilo, in his confession.

He claimed the reason for mutilating or cutting out his victim's eyes was because he had initially believed an old urban legend that the image of a murderer is left imprinted on the eyes of the victim. It confirmed the same fact that had been written in Dr. Bukhanovsky's report.

He had enjoyed playing with the blood of his victims and confessed to tearing at the victim's genitalia, nipples, tongues and lips with his teeth. He chewed upon the uterus of his female victims and the testicles of his few male victims. But he still maintained that he never ate them, he simply chewed and discarded. He was found guilty of 52 murders and sentenced to death for each and every one.

In 1992, another Russian serial killer, *Alexander Pichushkin,* came to the fore. Upon his arrest in 2006, he talks about Andrei Chikatilo in his own confessions. He claimed that he wanted to kill *more* than Chikatilo and some say he might have succeeded.

For it is a dark part of human nature that when one serial killer is captured, there will always be another in the shadows, awaiting his or her time in the spotlight.

Born **October 16th 1936.**

Active from **1978-1990.**

Arrested on **November 20th 1990.**

Country: **Soviet Union.**

Victims: **52-56.**

AKA: **The Red Ripper / The Butcher of Rostov.**

Sentence: **Death penalty.**

Current whereabouts: **Executed by shooting on February 16th 1994.**

Christiansen, Thor Nis

A Danish-American serial killer from California who killed four women with an intention of killing more. He had been obsessed with the idea of shooting women and having sex with their corpses since an early age.

After moving to California from Denmark with his family at a young age, Christiansen struggled to fit in. When he reached school-age he began drinking alcohol and smoking copious amounts of marijuana. He moved out of his parents' house, dropped out of high school, and began working as a gas station attendant.

On one day in 1976, he stole a 0.22 calibre pistol from a friend, as he was overcome with fantasies of shooting women and decided to act on his fantasies. He would find his victims while they were hitchhiking for a lift, then he would shoot them in the head. Afterwards, he would drag them away from the roadside to engage in necrophiliac acts with their bodies.

A fifth victim was shot in the head but miraculously survived. After her recovery she spotted Christiansen in another bar and immediately reported him to police whereupon he was captured.

He was killed in prison in 1981, after being stabbed in the exercise yard of Folsom State Prison. Surprisingly, psychiatrists had predicted that he might be killed in prison, as he was young with blonde hair, and his last victim was African-American. His own killer has never been found.

Born **December 28th 1957.**

Active from **1976-1979.**

Arrested on **July 7th 1979.**

Country: **USA.**

Victims: **4.**

AKA: **The Look-alike Murders.**

Sentence: **Life imprisonment.**

Current whereabouts: **Killed in prison in 1981.**

Ciudad Juarez Rebels, The

The *Ciudad Juárez Rebels* is the name of a group of Mexican serial killers who claimed their victims between 1995 and 1996, in Ciudad Juarez. The leaders of the group were *Sergio Armendáriz Diaz* and *Juan Contreras Jurado*. There were three other members who would also be sentenced in 2005.

A victim of one of their most notorious crimes was discovered on April 7th 1996.

The torso of 17-year-old *Rosario García Leal* was discovered in an abandoned parking lot on the outskirts of the city. She had vanished in December 1995.

Where she had been discovered, further bone fragments were also found belonging to other people. It was also suggested that Leal had been kept alive for at least a month before they had killed her. On April 8th 1996, a member of a different gang was arrested and confessed to taking part in Leal's kidnapping.

After the Ciudad Juárez Rebels were arrested, the five men confessed to the murders of eight women. They were subsequently convicted of all eight murders and sentenced to life in prison. It has long been suspected that they could have killed up to 14 people between them.

Active from **1995-1996.**

Arrested **during 1996 (all members).**

Country: **Mexico.**

Victims: **8-14+**

AKA: **Sergio Armendáriz Diaz and Juan Contreras Jurado (Group leaders).**

Sentence: **Life imprisonment.**

Current whereabouts: **In prison.**

Claremont Serial Killer, The

In Claremont, Australia, from 1996 to 1997, two women were murdered and one went missing after attending night clubs and bars in the area. Claremont is a wealthy suburb of Perth and not a place usually associated with violent crime. All three women vanished in similar circumstances, and the investigation concluded at the time that an unidentified serial killer was the culprit.

On January 27th 1996, 18-year-old *Sarah Spiers* left the *Bayview Club* in the early hours of the morning. She was last seen waiting for a taxi at gone two in the morning. Spiers was never seen again and no remains have ever been found, in spite of a long and expensive investigation.

On June 9th 1996, 23-year-old *Jane Rimmer* vanished. Her friends left her after seeing the length of the queue at the Bayview Club. Rimmer was last spotted on security footage outside the Continental Hotel nearby, and it would be the last time she was seen alive. Her nude body was discovered on August 3rd 1996, by a family who were picking wildflowers.

Then on March 14th 1997, 27-year-old *Ciara Glennon*, also vanished from the same area. She was last seen walking away from the Continental Hotel. Her nude body was discovered 19 days later near the side of a road in Eglinton, 40 kilometres north of the Continental Hotel.

The subsequent investigation was one of the largest in Australian criminal history with up to 100 investigators at its peak. One possible suspect was questioned in 1998 and remained on the suspect list for ten years before he was removed. After many more suspects and a possible fourth murder dating to before Spiers's disappearance, the investigation was struggling.

Then on December 22nd 2016, 48-year-old *Bradley Robert Edwards* was arrested as a suspect. In September 2020, Edwards was found guilty of the murders of Jane Rimmer and Ciara Glennon but acquitted of the murder of Sarah Spiers. It became too difficult for the prosecution to prove a connection between Edwards and Spiers due to the lack of a body. Though, he remains the only suspect in the Spiers disappearance.

Active from **1996-1997**.

Arrested on **December 22nd 2016**.

Country: **Australia**.

Victims: **3+**.

AKA: **Bayview Club Killer.**

Sentence: **Open case.**

Current whereabouts: **Awaiting trial.**

Clark, Hadden Irving: The Cross-dressing Cannibal (Extended Case File)

American murderer *Hadden Irving Clark*, AKA: *The Cross-dressing Cannibal* was suspected of being a serial killer. He is confirmed to have killed two people, one child and one adult, but it has been suggested he killed more when he confessed to killing dozens since 1974. His brother also killed a woman then dissected her, cooked her breasts and ate them.

During his childhood, he was raised by two alcoholic parents who were violent towards each other. When his mother was drunk, she referred to Clark as Kristen, and made him wear girl's clothing. His father committed suicide when he was a teenager and Clark turned to torturing and killing small animals. He also bullied other children and was generally anti-social.

He had two brothers, one of whom was *Bradfield Clark*, who was convicted of killing and cannibalising his girlfriend. His only sister ran away from home as a teenager and later proclaimed that she didn't have a family.

Hadden already had a reputation for being evil. If anyone crossed him or dared to belittle him then he would kill their pets, sometimes leaving the decapitated bodies on their doorsteps. A doctor's report later divulged that Clark believed birds and squirrels spoke to him.

Hadden Clark went on to join the U.S. Navy but was discharged with paranoid schizophrenia in the same way he was fired from most of his jobs. He claimed to police later that he had been killing since 1974, when he was 22-years-old. He said he would get away with it because he was a drifter and would roam the United States, living on the streets or getting small cash-in-hand jobs.

The first confirmed murder was on May 31st 1986. He killed a six-year-old girl named *Michelle Dorr*, who was a friend of his niece, *Eliza Clark*. She had grown bored of playing alone and wandered down the street looking for Eliza, but she wasn't in. Clark then lured Dorr to an upstairs room in his brother's house – the only brother to not be in prison.

He followed her upstairs, telling her that Eliza was in her bedroom. When she stepped into the room, he pushed her to the floor and slashed her with a knife on her back before stabbing her in the throat. He attempted to have sexual contact with her corpse but instead resorted to eating parts of her body. He then squashed the corpse into a bag, cleaned up the blood, and buried the girl in a remote park nearby.

"I think I have a split personality. I don't like to hurt people but I do things I am not aware of."

Hadden Clark – quoted in a doctor's report.

Shockingly, cannibalism ran in the family. In 1984, after a night of heavy drinking and drugs, Hadden Clark's brother, Bradfield Clark, killed his short-term girlfriend *Patricia Mak*. He beat and strangled to her death then dragged the body to the bathtub. There he dissected her body, cooked her breasts on a barbecue, and ate them. He confessed to his crime and was convicted of the murder.

Six years after his first confirmed kill, Hadden Clark claimed his second confirmed kill came when he murdered 23-year-old *Laura Houghteling* in Maryland. He entered the family home dressed as a woman, then stabbed her to death while she was in her bedroom.

He suffocated her with a pillow to ensure she was dead then dragged the body to another remote wooded area and buried her body. He then returned to the house, dressed in the same women's clothes and left the house pretending to be his victim, so that people thought she was still alive if spotted.

He was caught when a fingerprint on one of her pillows matched to him. He was arrested and confessed, leading police to the body less than a year later. At the same time he led them to where he buried Michelle Dorr. He then confessed to murdering tens of women since 1974 and claimed he was the killer of the infamous *Lady of the Dunes* murder, amongst others.

"We're dealing with a serial killer here. We don't know how many people he killed. The fact is, he was a transient and moved around. How much is truth and how much of it's not? He was a highly active guy for quite a long period of time. They have to see exactly what he's been up to."

Police Chief Richard Rosenthal – in a press interview for APB news. (2000).

Clark claimed there was a body buried in his grandparents' house. When police searched his grandparent's property, they didn't find a body but they found a plastic tub of over 200 pieces of jewellery, including one of Laura's rings. Clark maintained that all the jewellery came from his victims.

In 1993, Clark was convicted of the murder of Laura Houghteling and sentenced to 30 years in prison. In 1999, after another trial, he was convicted of the murder of six-year-old Michelle Dorr and was sentenced to an additional 30 years in prison.

He claims to have killed many more and if the jewellery in the plastic tub is anything to go by then there might be some truth in his confessions. As of 2021, he remains incarcerated.

Born in **April 1951**.

Active from **1986-1992**.

Arrested on **November 6**[th] **1992**.

Country: **USA.**

Victims: **2+.**

AKA: **The Cross-dressing Cannibal / Lady of the Dunes Murder (Claimed).**

Sentence: **Total of 60 years imprisonment.**

Current whereabouts: **In prison.**

Clepper, Gregory

In Chicago, on April 23rd 1996, *Gregory Clepper* murdered 30-year-old *Patricia Scott*. He had raped and strangled her before pushing her body into a trash bin behind a High School. Upon his arrest a few days later on May 2nd, Clepper was linked to another 12 murders.

Clepper is described as a sexual predator, one whose sole motivation is sexual. He was arrested after an acquaintance called the police because Clepper had been bragging about one of his murders. Once the murders were linked, the timeline of murder became clear.

They started in 1991 with bodies turning up in garbage bins all over Chicago, almost all of them had been raped or violently sexually abused. At the time, law enforcement wasn't making any connections with the victims and it wasn't until Clepper's arrest that the murders were linked. He had killed Patricia Scott in his own home, and his mother along with a friend helped him hide the body. They were later charged with helping to dispose of the body.

To secure a conviction, prosecutors dropped all the other 12 murder charges in exchange for a confession of the murder of Scott. He was subsequently sentenced to 80 years in prison for the murder. As time went on, Clepper was linked to another 15 murders but confessed to killing over 40, which would make him Chicago's most notorious serial killer by body count.

Born in **1968.**

Active during **1996**.

Arrested on **May 2nd 1996**.

Country: **USA (Chicago)**.

Victims: **1-13+**.

Sentence: **80 years in prison**.

Current whereabouts: **In prison**.

Cole, Carroll

Cole was mostly drunk when he killed his victims but still claimed to have killed 35 women across several states in America, although 15 women and one boy were evidentially linked. Most victims were strangled in parking lots and he would sometimes take their bodies home to sleep with their corpses because they reminded him of his mother.

He claimed he drowned a boy when he was only 10-years-old. The death of the boy had been listed as an accident until Cole's confession. During his childhood, while his father was fighting in World War Two, Cole was physically abused by his mother including being whipped, beaten, and forced to watch her adulterous relationships.

He acted out on his dark fantasies when he was 33-years-old. He began picking up women for sex and using prostitutes on regular occasions. He was known to have been rough with his women and decided to kill those who were married, simply because they reminded him of his mother, who he had come to hate.

There have been multiple reports that he ate some of his victims but this has never been proven. It is suggested that he falsely claimed he ate his victims to get an insanity charge. Cole was sentenced to death in **1981**.

Born **May 9th 1938**.

Active from **1971-1980.**

Arrested in **1980**.

Country: **USA.**

Victims: **16-35.**

Sentence: **Death penalty.**

Current whereabouts: **Executed by lethal injection on December 6th 1985.**

Colonial Parkway Murders, The. (Extended Case File)

Between 1986 and 1989, an unidentified serial killer was suspected of killing at least eight people along or nearby the Colonial Parkway of the United States Commonwealth of Virginia. Three couples were murdered and one couple went missing. It has also been suggested that another two people may have fallen victim to the same killer.

In most countries, the construction of highways or motorways was one of the reasons why serial killing increased through the 1970s and reached a peak in the 1980s. Life was also made extremely difficult for law enforcement because of various State boundaries that existed.

It also meant that a serial killer's potential victim might not be recognised as such due to the then disconnected reporting between authorities. The highways provided an opportunity where there wasn't one before. The killings in this three year period were referred to as *The Colonial Parkway Murders*.

The first recorded murders took place on October 9th 1986. 21-year-old student *Rebecca Ann Dowski* and 27-year-old *Cathleen Marian Thomas* disappeared while out together. It wasn't until October that a jogger spotted a white car alongside the

York River. Inside the car, both Thomas and Dowski were found, they had been strangled and mutilated.

A coroner's report confirmed they had been tied with rope, strangled and then had their throats slit. Gasoline had been poured on the bodies to hide evidence but the killer or killers had been unable to light it. Their belongings were found in the car meaning that it hadn't been a robbery. Since the murders took place on federal property, the case fell under FBI jurisdiction. Over 150 fingerprints were found but did not match any person on the FBI database.

On September 22nd 1987, in Isle of Wight County, Virginia, 20-year-old *David Knobling* and 14-year-old *Robin Edwards* were found shot to death. The dating couple were discovered in the *Ragged Island Wildlife Refuge*, on the south shore of the James River. The two bodies were found by Knobling's father and a search party who were scouring the edges of the river.

According to those who knew them, Robin Edwards was an older-looking 14-year-old and had been known for dating older men. However, if the relationship was a sexual one then it would have been illegal under the laws at the time. No shell casings were found and some believe a revolver could have been the murder weapon. Since the Ragged Island Wildlife Refuge was state property, then the case was taken over by the State Police and not the FBI.

On April 9th 1988, 18-year-old *Cassandra Lee Hailey* and 20-year-old *Richard Keith Call* went missing. Richard's abandoned vehicle was found on the Colonial Parkway, only three miles from where the bodies of the two previous victims were discovered. The keys were still in the ignition and the driver's side door was left open.

As of 2021, their disappearance has never been solved but it has been suggested they may have been murdered, as all the clothes they were wearing when they had gone missing were found inside the car. The case fell under FBI jurisdiction. The family said the car must have been positioned in its resting place as the couple had never used that section of road.

On September 5th 1989, 18-year-old *Annamaria Phelps* and 21-year-old *Daniel*

Lauer disappeared. At the time of the disappearance, Annamaria had been dating Daniel's brother and was assumed to be having an affair with Daniel. Their bodies were found by deer hunters in the area on October 19th 1989, at a secluded logging road.

The area they were found in was 30 miles away from the I-64 ramp onto Colonial Parkway. The two deer hunters had come across a blanket in the woods, when they lifted it up they found the skeletal remains. Although cause of death could not be determined, knife marks were found on the bones of Annamaria.

There were two more murders that may have been connected with the Colonial Parkway murders. In 1996, 24-year-old *Julie Williams* and 26-year-old *Lollie Winans*, who were a young couple, were backpacking through the *Shenandoah National Park* with their Golden Retriever. They set up camp just a few feet away from a horse trail. They were last seen by a Park Ranger who renewed the camping permit and dropped them off at the *Stony Man* car park.

When they were reported missing, park rangers found their car and the dog, who was roaming the area. They then found both bodies nearby. They had been bound and gagged with duct tape and were half-naked, their throats had been cut so deeply that they were virtually decapitated. It has never been clear whether these two murders were the work of the same killer who was operating in the mid to late 1980s, but it hasn't been ruled out.

In 2010, *Detective Steve Spingola* released a document regarding the murders and claimed they were possibly killed by different people. He claimed that the Thomas and Dowski murder could be connected to the Shenandoah murders of Lollie Winans and Julie Williams. He theorized that the two double murders could have been the work of a serial killer targeting lesbian couples.

Some other investigators believe that the killings might have been committed by someone who worked in law enforcement. The windows on the cars were all wound down, leading one investigator to suggest that the only reason to have done so was if they were being pulled over by an officer or ranger.

A deputy who was around at the time, named *Fred Atwell*, has constantly been mentioned as a person of interest. Most families of the victims stated that his obsession with the murders was unhealthy, and he worked his way into their lives, too intimately to just be friendly. He was arrested in 2011 for robbing a woman at gunpoint. As of 2021, The Colonial Parkway Murders have not been solved and remain a cold case investigation to this day.

Active from **1986-1989.**

Country: **USA.**

Victims: **8-10.**

Current whereabouts: **Unidentified killer. Status unknown.**

Cook, Anthony and Nathaniel

The serial killer brothers raped and murdered white people in Ohio from the 1970s to the 1980s. Both brothers were long-haul truck drivers and claimed a total of nine victims during their campaign of racially motivated violence.

They would generally kill their victims by either shooting them or beating them with a baseball bat, and in some instances; a concrete block. They would take advantage of young lovers parked in isolated locations.

In 1973 they raped and murdered a 12-year-old girl together. The pair were arrested in 1981, with Anthony initially being convicted of murdering a real estate agent. It wasn't until the early 1990s when DNA evidence improved, that the investigation was able to link both brothers to multiple cold case murders.

In 2000, Anthony pleaded guilty to nine counts of murder while Nathaniel pleaded guilty to three murders.

IMAGE ATTRIBUTIONS
(ATTRIB A62) TO (ATTRIB A69)

THE EIGHT KNOWN VICTIMS OF THE COLONIAL PARKWAY MURDERS
AS OF 2020, THE IDENTITY OF THE KILLER REMAINS A MYSTERY

COLONIAL PARKWAY MURDERS

Born **March 9th 1949 (Anthony), October 25th 1958 (Nathaniel)**.

Active from **1973-1981.**

Arrested during **1981**.

Country: **USA (Ohio)**.

Victims: **9**.

Sentence: **Nathaniel received 15-75 years. Anthony received 15 years to life in prison.**

Current whereabouts: **Nathaniel was released on August 8th 2018. Anthony remains in prison.**

Conahan Jr., Daniel Owen

Active in Florida over a two year period in the mid-1990s, *Conahan, AKA: The Hog Trail Killer*, would be convicted of one murder but positively linked to at least five more. Conahan had come out as gay during his school years, and his parents were not happy with the decision. Thinking it to be an illness, they sent him to a psychiatrist, which forced him to repress his feelings.

He joined the U.S. Navy shortly after school but was discharged in 1978 when he was the cause of a large fight because of his actions towards other men. In 1995, he became a nurse and worked at the Charlotte Regional Medical Center in Punta Gorda.

On January 1st 1996, a family living in North Port, Florida, were in for a shock. Their family dog had gone outside and wondered back in with a human skull hanging from its mouth. Police then discovered more bones and pieced together a skeleton, the victim bore resemblance to the body of a skeleton found in 1994. The skeleton found in North Port has never been identified.

On March 7th 1996, the body of *John William Melaragno* was discovered in North Port. Melaragno had been murdered just ten days prior to his discovery. His body had been mutilated and his genitals had been hacked at. He wouldn't be identified until June 1999.

On April 17th 1996, a police investigation had kicked into gear after Melaragno's body had been discovered. Investigators found a man's skull in the woods nearby, a few hours later they turned up the rest of the body, who was identified shortly after as *Kenneth Lee Smith*. A few more hours passed and another man's body was discovered nearby.

The second victim was identified as *Richard Allen Montgomery*, he had been raped and mutilated and his body dumped in the woods the day prior to the discovery. As soon as the media got wind of two bodies in the woods, talk of a serial killer operating in the area began to do the rounds.

On July 3rd 1996, Conahan was arrested after a number of different witness statements pointed him out as a possible suspect. Conahan was arrested on an attempted murder charge of a man in 1994, and his DNA was positively linked to the body of Montgomery. While in custody, further skeletal remains were discovered in the county including one who had been reported missing in 1993.

On August 17th 1999, Conahan was found guilty of first-degree murder and attempted murder and sentenced to death. But the story of the skeletons didn't end there. On March 23rd 2007, eight different skulls and skeletal remains were discovered in some woods in Fort Myers, Florida. Every single one of them was linked to Conahan and were found only a mile away from the attempted murder site.

As of 2021, Conahan remains on death row at a prison in Florida.

Born **May 11th 1954.**

Active from **1993-1996.**

Arrested on **July 3rd 1996.**

Country: **USA (Florida).**

Victims: **1-11+.**

AKA: **The Hog Trail Killer.**

Sentence: **Death penalty.**

Current whereabouts: **Death row.**

Connecticut River Valley Killer, The. (Extended Case File)

The *Connecticut River Valley Killer* is a suspected and as yet unidentified serial killer who is linked to at least seven murders on the New Hampshire and Vermont border. The murders were over a nine-year period from 1978 to 1987.

On January 10th 1987, In Stratton, Vermont, a 38-year-old nurse named *Barbara Agnew* was stabbed to death in her car during a snowstorm. She had been returning from a skiing trip but never made it home. A snowplough driver found the car at a rest stop and went to see if the driver needed assistance.

The window was cracked and blood covered the steering wheel, but there was no one inside. Agnew wouldn't be discovered until March 28th 1987. Her body was found beside an apple tree in Windsor County.

On October 24th 1978, 27-year-old *Cathy Millican* was seen photographing birds at the *Chandler Brook Wetland Preserve* in New London, New Hampshire. The next day, her body was found only a few feet away from where she had been seen. She had been stabbed 29 times.

On July 25th 1981, 37-year-old student *Mary Elizabeth Critchley*, disappeared while hitchhiking near *Interstate 91* at the Massachusetts and Vermont border. Two weeks later, her body was discovered in a wooded area in New Hampshire. Due to the viciousness of the attack and exposure to the elements, the coroner was unable to give an official cause of death.

On May 30th 1984, another hitchhiker on *Route 12* went missing. 17-year-old nurse *Bernice Courtemanche* vanished in New Hampshire. It wasn't until April 9th 1986, that her remains were found by a fisherman. In that instance, the cause of death was listed as knife wounds to the neck and head.

In New Hampshire on July 20th 1984, another nurse, 27-year-old *Ellen Fried*, vanished after calling her sister from a pay phone in Claremont. She spoke to her sister about a strange car that was coming and going along the road. Her own car was found abandoned the next day, just a few miles away from the pay phone. Her remains were found over a year later at a wooded area near the banks of the *Sugar River*. The coroner's report confirmed she had been stabbed to death.

A year later on July 10th 1985, 27-year-old *Eva Morse* vanished after hitchhiking home from work in Charlestown, New Hampshire. A logger found her remains a year later, reports showed she had been stabbed in the neck.

On April 25th 1986, 36-year-old *Lynda Moore* was working in her yard at her home in Vermont. She was then stabbed to death during a violent struggle and was found dead later that day by her husband. Witnesses claimed they saw a suspicious man in the area and a police sketch was subsequently drawn up.

Another possible link was the April 6th 1988 stabbing of seven-months pregnant *Jane Boroski*. She had stopped her car to use a vending machine in Winchester, New Hampshire. A man was waiting at her car when she returned and accused her of hurting his own girlfriend. Boroski ran off in fear but the man stabbed her 27 times.

Miraculously she survived, crawled back to her car and drove to a friend's house two miles away. She even managed to end up behind the attacker's car. Both Boroski and her child survived. Although her daughter grew up to live a relatively normal life, she was diagnosed with minor cerebral palsy due to having suffered brain damage in the attack.

As part of the investigation, Jane Boroski was put under hypnosis. She managed to describe the attack in detail. She remembered that the attacker seemed extremely calm and collected. When she stopped struggling with him, he seemed to lose interest and ceased his attack. She also described the car and partial number plate but the attacker has never been caught. After her attack, the killings stopped.

Many theories regarding the identity of the killer have been put forward in the years that followed. An Idaho police officer concluded that the police sketch was that of a convicted criminal who was in prison shortly after but nothing was confirmed.

Another suspect was *Michael Nicholaou*, a former Army helicopter pilot who served in the Vietnam War. He was accused of killing civilians in Vietnam and was discharged from the Army because of it. He claimed to have been bitter about the discharge but there are no details as to how he might have killed people in Vietnam. It is also claimed that he was responsible for the murder of his first wife but was never convicted. There is also no DNA evidence linking him to the murders.

Delbert Tallman was another suspect who confessed to killing a woman in 1984. Her murder was similar to most of the Connecticut River murders. He withdrew his confession and was found not-guilty of her murder. It is unclear why he withdrew his confession.

Gary Westover was also a suspect who confessed to being involved in the murder of Barbara Agnew; the final 1987 victim. He claimed to have abducted her with three other men and murdered her in the woods. He died shortly after the confession and no further evidence linked him to the crime.

As of 2021, the case of the Connecticut River Valley Killer remains unsolved.

Active from **1978-1987.**

Country: **USA (Connecticut).**

Victims: **7+.**

Current whereabouts: **Unidentified killer. Status unknown.**

Constanzo, Adolfo

American serial killer and cult leader *Adolfo de Jesús Constanzo* was responsible for the deaths of numerous people through ritualistic killings with members of his cult.

He was also a drug dealer and ran a cult named *The Narcosatanists*. He was nicknamed the Godfather by his disciples and took part in multiple murders within Mexico. By 1987, Constanzo had started to believe that his magic was responsible for the success of the Mexican drug cartels and wished to be a business partner to a crime syndicate known as *The Calzadas*.

When they rejected his wishes, seven members of the Calzadas family were brutally murdered. They were found later with body parts missing. Most of them had their brain removed and one had his entire spine ripped out. The spinal column was never discovered.

In 1988, he moved the cult to a ranch in the Mexican desert where together they carried out more ritual murders. They started killing drifters and other rival drug dealers. On March 13th, 1989, cult members abducted an American student from a Mexican bar. American *Mark Kilroy* was taken back to the ranch where Constanzo killed him in front of his cult.

The American authorities pressured the Mexican Police to get answers on Kilroy's disappearance. The investigation led to Constanzo and the infamous ranch, where fifteen mutilated corpses were unearthed. They also discovered a ritualistic cauldron which contained dead black cats and human brains.

Constanzo died in a firefight with Mexican Police when he had fled to Mexico City with some of the cult. A total of 14 other cult members were subsequently sentenced to 60 years each. Most are still incarcerated to this day.

Born **November 1st 1962**.

Active from **1986-1989**.

Country: **Mexico**.

Victims: **1-15+**.

AKA: **Adolfo de Jesús Constanzo / The Narcosatanist / The godfather.**

Sentence: **Died before trial.**

Current whereabouts: **Killed in a shoot-out by Mexican Police.**

Copeland, Faye and Ray

American serial killing couple *Faye Della Wilson Copeland* and *Ray Copeland* killed at least five people at their farm between 1986 and 1989. They ended up becoming the oldest couple to be sentenced to death. Faye was 69-years-old and Ray was 76-years-old.

Ray was born in Oklahoma in 1914 and began life taking part in petty crime such as stealing livestock for financial gain. He spent a year in prison for his petty crimes and was released in 1940 when he met Faye, whom he married shortly after. It would 46 years later that they would claim their first victim.

Before 1986, he had spent decades perfecting illegal money making methods which involved everything from scamming cattle auctions to not paying farm workers. He began employing drifters on his farm and used them to purchase cattle with bounced checks but when it didn't work the way he wanted it to, he moved up to murder.

In 1989, a previous drifter employee phoned the authorities through a crime stoppers phone number and claimed he had seen human bones and remains on the farm. He also stated that Ray Copeland had assaulted him with an attempt to murder him. The investigation firstly found three male bodies in a barn and then excavations unearthed further remains.

Faye was given four death sentences and life without parole. Ray was convicted of five counts of murder and sentenced to death but he died of natural causes in 1993 whilst on death row. In 1999, Faye's death sentence was commuted to life but following a stroke she was granted medical parole to a nursing home. She too died of natural causes, two days before Christmas Day in 2003.

It has been suggested that the couple may have killed up to 12 people on the farm.

Born **December 30th 1914 (Ray), August 4th 1921 (Faye).**

Active from **1986-1989.**

Arrested on **October 17th 1989.**

Country: **USA.**

Victims: **5-12.**

Sentence: **Both received death penalties. Faye's was later commuted to life imprisonment.**

Current whereabouts: **Ray died of natural causes in 1993. Faye died of natural causes in 2003.**

Corwin, Daniel Lee

On February 13th 1987, in California, 72-year-old *Alice Martin* was abducted by American serial killer *Daniel Lee Corwin* whilst out walking near her home. Her body was found the next day in a field. She had been raped before being strangled and stabbed to death.

On July 10th 1987, in Texas, 26-year-old *Debra Lynn Ewing* was abducted at gunpoint by Corwin whilst working at the *Vision Center* in the city. Her body was discovered two days later in an undeveloped plot of land. She had been raped before being strangled and stabbed.

On Halloween 1987, Corwin stabbed to death 36-year-old *Mary Carrell Risinger* at a car wash. He had attempted to abduct her but she fought back and screamed for help. Corwin then stabbed her in the neck as her three-year-old daughter looked on from inside the car. She bled to death at the scene.

He killed three people, all in 1987, but the seeds were laid 12 years earlier. In 1975 when he was just 17-years-old, Corwin abducted a classmate from his high school. He bound her in his car, drove her to a remote area and raped her. Then he dragged her from the car, beat her and stabbed her in the heart. Miraculously, she survived and pulled herself to a road to get help.

Corwin was sentenced to forty years in prison but astonishingly paroled after just nine years of the sentence served. He was released in November of 1985 and then went on to kill only 16 months later.

Corwin was subsequently convicted of three 1987 murders, sentenced to death and executed by lethal injection in December of 1988.

Born **September 13th 1958.**

Active during **1987.**

Arrested in **1989.**

Country: **USA.**

Victims: **3.**

Sentence: **Death penalty.**

Current whereabouts: **Executed by lethal injection on December 7th 1998.**

Cottingham, Richard

An American serial killer known to have killed six people. He would claim later that he was responsible for up to 100 murders. He is also known as *The New York Ripper, The Butcher of Times Square,* or *The Torso Killer.* He would generally kill prostitutes then dismember his victims and leave their torsos behind.

He first killed in 1968 by strangling a 29-year-old mother. Her nude body was found in a car park. In 1979, firemen uncovered two victims in a fire, both had their hands and heads removed and had been set alight. One of them was a Kuwaiti prostitute. The missing body parts were never found.

Cottingham was a respected member of the community, which made his arrest and confessions difficult for some to understand. He ran computer systems and networks for a major health insurance firm and was well-liked by colleagues. But when he was arrested, on his person he had a pair of handcuffs, a leather gag, two collars, a replica gun and a knife.

When police searched his home they found personal items that had been taken from many of the murdered prostitutes. Cottingham had become addicted to using prostitutes and sex workers and in some instances had become violent with them.

In May of 1980, police were called to a motel after people had complained of a screaming girl. When they arrived they caught Cottingham attempting to flee the scene. When police entered the motel room, they found a young sex worker handcuffed to the bed. She had been raped, beaten and stabbed. She also had her nipples partially bitten off. Initially receiving a sentence of up to 197 years in prison, he went on to receive further sentences in each successive trial.

In early 2020, the 73-year-old Cottingham confessed to three more murders. The deaths most recently connected to him include Jacalyn Harp of Midland Park, Irene Blase of Bogota and Denise Falasca of Closter. All three women were strangled in the late 1960s. As of 2021, he is currently serving multiple life sentences at New Jersey State Prison.

Born **November 25th 1946.**

Active from **1967-1980.**

Arrested in **May 1980.**

Country: **USA.**

Victims: **6-100+.**

AKA: **The New York Ripper / The Butcher of Times Square / The Torso Killer.**

Sentence: **Multiple life sentences.**

Current whereabouts: **In prison.**

Craine, Louis

On January 25th 1987, 24-year-old *Loretta Perry*, was found dead in a housing block. She had been raped and murdered by serial killer *Louis Craine*. Craine was sentenced to death for Perry's killing and the killing of three other women.

On March 18th 1987, the body of *Vivian Collins* was found in an abandoned house in the 1600 block of East Century Boulevard in the neighbourhood of Watts. She had been killed and dumped in the same manner as Craine's previous victims.

On May 29th 1987, in Los Angeles, 29-year-old *Carolyn Barney* was found dead in a vacant lot near a housing project. Her body was found in the same block where Craine's parents lived. At around the same time, a number of black serial killers were active in the Los Angeles region and two of Louis Craine's murders were previously attributed to *The Southside Slayer*.

Almost all of the victims were young black women who were either prostitutes or drug users. The bodies would be dumped in remote parks, in alleys or in vacant buildings.

In 1989, Craine was arrested and sentenced to death for the murders of four women. He was acquitted in the trial of the fifth victim but it has since been attributed to him. Within months of being convicted he died of unknown natural causes.

Born in **1957**.

Active from **1986-1987**.

Arrested on **May 29th 1987**.

Country: **USA**.

Victims: **5**.

Sentence: **Death penalty**.

Current whereabouts: **Died of natural causes in 1989**.

Crump, Thomas Wayne

On October 4th 1980, in Las Vegas, the body of 25-year-old call-girl **Jodie Jameson** was discovered in a motel room bathtub. She had been tied up and strangled with a ligature made of pillowcase fabric. She had been murdered in the early hours of the morning by serial killer **Thomas Wayne Crump** who killed at least four people during the 1970s to 1981.

Crump claimed he killed Jamieson because she had robbed him and deserved everything that happened to her. He later confessed to at least seven murders and was sentenced to death twice, once in a New Mexico trial, and again in a Nevada trial. He never once showed remorse for his crimes.

Born in **1940**.

Active from **1970s-1981**.

Arrested in **1981.**

Country: **USA.**

Victims: **4-7.**

Current whereabouts: **Died of natural causes in June 2018 while on death row.**

(Research Article #5) Attitudes towards Women in the 1970s

We'll get another few statistics out the way first, from a 2015 study of serial killers, cited in the appendices.

75% of male serial killers, kill because of sexual motives and gratification.

49% of male serial killers exclusively hunt women.

There is a branch of science known as *evolutionary psychology*. The argument is that humans have been evolving over such a huge amount of time that the human brain, genetics, and functions have become accustomed to a paternal ancestral society. It is said to be highly likely that these factors still genetically influence us in the modern era.

It is no surprise that male serial killers generally kill women. Females are generally weaker than men and make for an easier victim choice.

Men have the biological ability to reproduce in far greater quantities than women. Biologically, a female desires a mate for a lot longer time than a male desires a mate. It is in a male's nature to seek multiple mates to reproduce. This is scientific biology, caused by evolution.

Heading into the 1970s, it was all about to change, and rightfully so. This author agrees that the women's rights movement was a long overdue and needed societal evolutionary change. Yet it had varying effects on some men in the decade and the decades that followed.

The women's rights movements of the 1970s moved forward at a frenetic pace. Overcoming sexism, free access to legal abortion, challenging oppression and seeking equality. The 1970s marked the 50th anniversary of the women's right to vote in various Western countries including the United States and United Kingdom. So there was a large celebration of the movement and a push for greater rights for women.

The country of *Oman* only passed a law that women could vote in 2003, so there's clearly still a long way to go to reach equality.

Feminism, as it would come to be known, had landed at the small end of the 1970s in a big way. This, combined with the flower power movement, put women in the limelight, more than they ever had been before.

The movement led to many female-powered political organisations.

National Organization for Women (NOW) (1966)

National Women's Political Caucus (1971)

Equal Rights Amendment Ratification Council (1973)

Coalition of Labor Union Women (1973)

The above were just some of the more well-known ones in the United States alone.

Some men, because of their upbringing or abuse traumas from childhood, began to take offence to the notion that women should be equal. More sexual attacks had started to take place, more killings were occurring and a hidden divide between men and women began to open.

One researcher claims that it was women's fault that more violent crime was recorded against women from the 1970s. This author argues it was in the shallow-mindedness of some males that they were not able to accept that women should be equal to men.

Serial killers make up a ridiculously small percentage of murders in most countries. So to fear a serial killer is based on stories that have been spoken about them. Generally in the United Kingdom, you're more likely to die by suicide or drug-related deaths. In the United States, you're more likely to die by gang-violence or firearms. Those deaths remain separate from the ones caused by serial killers.

Serial killers have been a loud epidemic since the 1970s. The fascination began to slow down in the 1990s but it's coming back in a bigger way than before. This provides us with more insights into the minds of the broken.

A 2018 documentary entitled *Conversations with a Killer*, with Ted Bundy, offered up some telling quotes. He would say he loved women and indeed, loved his mother, which is an anomaly amongst serial murderers.

In one scene he appears to be helping profile his own murders. Bundy tended to refer to himself in the third person, either as way of disassociating from the crimes or allaying responsibility.

"A person of this type chooses his victims for a reason. His victims are young, attractive women. Women are possessions. Beings which are subservient, more often than not, to males. Women are merchandise."

In another section, he focused on the sexual aspect of his crimes which was something he rarely spoke of.

"Sex has significance, only in the context of a much broader scheme of things. That is possession, control, and violence."

Subservient females, women as possessions, and control; the very factors that the feminist movement had been trying to change. It appears serial killers in the 1970s and even in modern times, still see women as objects to be controlled, rather than being equal to men.

In interviews regarding the Bundy documentary, gender and sexuality psychiatrists were giving their own perspectives. In the 1970s, especially in the United States, it seemed that if you were white and male then you were naturally part of a so-called *privileged elite.*

Females suddenly had access to education and careers that were once exclusively for men. Suddenly these females had become rivals for someone like Bundy and others like him.

The one true threat to masculinity is a female of equal, or superior status. Ted Bundy's feelings of inferiority meant that he needed to have relationships with women *and* destroy others he was not in a relationship with.

His variable love and hate for women in equal measure, was reflected in a larger cultural misunderstanding that only certain females were worthy of a man's love. In Bundy's case, he held his mother in high esteem and those who he was in a relationship with.

A certain level of misogyny tends to be present in serial killers. It also holds the notion that a worthy woman could just as easily become unworthy. Bundy handled the threat of a move to unworthiness by killing *surrogate* females, standing in for those who he deemed worthy.

As of 2021, the situation has proved much better but women are still fighting for equality.

(Research Article #6) Attitudes towards Women in the Noughties

Due to the easy access of adult websites from 2000 and especially now in 2021, there has been a growing perverse view of women from some men due to this and other factors.

The feminist movements of the late 1960s and 1970s had their impact for many reasons already discussed. But it was nothing compared to the rise of girl-power and social media hashtag campaigns where men were constantly accused of saying the wrong thing.

Observing something like this from a psychological perspective is harder than one might imagine. It has to be reiterated that this is only an exceedingly small percentage of men but it is a growing percentage nonetheless and needs to be made known.

Women now make up more CEO positions than ever before and some state it's still not enough. The balance of power from men to women had been swaying ever since the mid Twentieth Century feminist movement kicked off.

Female-focused pop groups such as the Spice Girls, kicked off the new wave of feminism and media-centric girl power.

When combined with easy access to violent pornography and the proliferation of girl-power, some men focused their perverse attentions on their growing hate of women. Misogyny began to make a comeback. Stories of presidents making degrading remarks and white men feeling like a minority hit the headlines.

Serial killers are mostly men and their victims are usually female, in around three-quarters of cases. It's no coincidence as to why; males are generally stronger than women and have the means with which to overpower their victims. Females are the most vulnerable of serial killer victims.

Just as the rise of the feminist movement in the 1970s gave a reason for some men to kill, so might the recent rise of girl-power and hashtag campaigns do the same in the digital age

All of this is to do with anger at females who seem to be claiming power from men. In part, for serial killers, this might be due to some inadequacy they have received from a female in their life, either their mothers or a partner.

The rise of female prominence in both eras then suggests that some serial killers will use this as a catalyst to bring their dark fantasies to life if they are not already.

Cuellar, Cristopher Chavez

In Colombia, *Cristopher Chávez Cuellar*, AKA*: The Soulless*, killed at least 15 people over a period of 17 years. He first killed in 1998 when he was 25-year-old. He met a woman at a bar, then kidnapped, raped and stabbed her to death. A warrant went out for his arrest in connection with the crime but he managed to evade police until 2004.

Also in 1998, along with his brother, they murdered a man in cold blood for unknown reasons. They were both later arrested and charged with the murder, Cuellar was also charged with the death of the woman and sentenced to 44 years in prison for the crimes.

Amazingly, he was released only a few years later for good behaviour. In 2015, he killed a gas station manager during a robbery and then in February of the same year he committed a crime that shocked Colombia. In an argument over an area of land ownership, Cuellar sought out the children of the couple who would not give him the land.

He lined up their four young sons and executed them where they knelt. A fifth son managed to escape and went with a family member to a military base for protection. After escaping custody, authorities put a 50,000,000 Pesos reward on his head, and he was captured shortly after.

In November 2015, he was sentenced to 40 years imprisonment for the murders of the four brothers. It has long been suspected that he had killed many more before being caught.

Born in **1973**.

Active from **1998-2015**.

Arrested in **February 2015**.

Country: **Colombia**.

Victims: **15+**.

AKA: **The Soulless**.

Sentence: **40 years imprisonment**.

Current whereabouts: **In prison**.

Cullen, Charles: The Killer Nurse (Extended Case File)

In New Jersey, Pennsylvania, *Charles Cullen,* AKA*: The Killer Nurse*, claimed at least 35 confirmed victims. But it has been suspected he may have killed over 400, making him the world's worst serial killer. The claims have long been disputed but at least two investigation teams believe the count to be in the hundreds.

Unlike Harold Shipman, the British medical serial killer who was convicted on 215 counts of murder, Cullen has only ever been convicted of 29. Even if Cullen's disturbing count of 400 is ever reached, they would not have been confirmed or convicted and only suspected. However, Cullen's murders had an impact that was felt across the United States.

Born in New Jersey in 1960, he was the youngest of eight children, and his father died in the same year he was born. He would later claim that he was bullied from a young age by his older siblings, their partners and other children at school.

In what became the first of many suicide attempts, when he was nine-years-old, he mixed chemicals together from a science set and then drank them. He survived after having the chemicals flushed through his system. It would be one of at least 20 known suicide attempts, in what was a cry for help that in the 1960s and 1970s went largely ignored.

"You know, maybe if I was nine years old and would have had to die that day, all these lives, including my family, wouldn't be affected in this way."

In an interview with Cullen.

In 1977, when he was 16-years-old, his mother died in a car crash. He stated it affected him more than he let on at the time and he became aggrieved with the hospital for not releasing the body. Instead, they cremated the body without a funeral.

In 1978, he joined the U.S. Navy and served on a submarine. During his time in the Navy, he was bullied by his fellow comrades and didn't fit in with the team. On one occasion, his comrades found him sat at the missile controls, wearing a doctor's uniform, complete with medical gloves and mask. It was later suggested that it was about the power he had at his fingertips and how it would have made him feel like a god.

He was committed to a Navy psychiatric unit and then discharged in 1984, when it is suspected he claimed his first victim. A couple of years later, he took a medical job at the St. Barnabas Medical Center in Livingston. He married in the 1986 and had a daughter. In the same year, Cullen began abusing his dogs and exhibiting strange behaviour.

The first confirmed murder was on June 11th 1988, at St. Barnabas, where he gave a deadly overdose to a patient. He began killing more by contaminating their intravenous medicine bags. He left St. Barnabas in 1992 after an investigation into contaminated bags was opened. The hospital suspected Cullen in at least 20 murders but couldn't be confirmed.

He began working at another hospital in the area while going through a divorce with his wife. In 1993, he moved into a basement apartment by himself where he attempted suicide on multiple occasions. He then began stalking a fellow nurse, *Michelle Tomlinson*, under the delusion that she was his girlfriend.

He would follow her around the hospital and give her unwarranted gifts. On one night in March of 1993 he broke into Tomlinson's home, that she shared with her young son, pretending that they were a couple. He was arrested and received a year's suspended sentence for trespassing. He was then treated for depression in two psychiatric wards.

He then got a job at the Hunterdon Medical Center in Flemington, where he murdered five patients in 1996 alone. He moved around between hospitals, taking advantage of a nationwide shortage of nurses. The eagerness to take on new nurses at any hospital was something that played into Cullen's hands. He was also fired from at least three more hospitals for unknown reasons and spent more time in a psychiatric unit.

Every time he murdered a patient, Cullen was suspected of having tampered with the IV bags or having injected the patient direct. No conclusive evidence could be found and even with a history of mental health illnesses, he was still allowed to take nursing work at different hospitals. Even after being fired from most of them.

He could do this because at the time, the hospital managers were worried about the liability of the hospital, and so criminal investigations were not directed at him. In 2000, he attempted suicide again by lighting a charcoal grill in his bathroom, in an attempt to suffer from the smoke effects and carbon dioxide. He was rescued by neighbours and sent yet again to a psychiatric hospital.

Unbelievably, one hospital, *St. Luke's*, discovered that he had stolen medicinal drugs that could be used to kill. They offered him a choice; resign and be given a recommendation or be fired. Seven of his co-workers complained to authorities that Cullen might have been killing patients, a small investigation ensued but ended after a few months. They had not even investigated Cullen's past.

From September 2002, until his arrest in 2003, he worked at the *Somerset Medical Center* in Somerville, New Jersey. As his depression worsened, he killed at least 13 more people using a combination of easily accessible medicines. It was the managers of Somerset Hospital who saw things that others did not.

Cullen had been accessing patient's files who were not assigned to him. He had been requesting medication that had not been prescribed and cancelled orders of repeat prescriptions. But the hospital delayed in requesting assistance from authorities, allowing Cullen to kill at least five more people.

In October 2003, Cullen's final victim died of an insulin overdose. Records showed that Cullen had administered the overdose. Astonishingly, Somerset fired him, under suspicion only. It took a nurse named *Amy Loughren* to alert the police herself. Police then began a full investigation and kept Cullen under surveillance.

The investigation used Loughren to enter Cullen's house, with a recording device. From the talk she had with Cullen, the investigation was able to put together enough evidence to make an arrest.

After a lengthy trial in which he taunted judges and families of the victims, he was sentenced to 11 life sentences in 2006. He was later sentenced to additional life sentences for further murders. He avoided the death penalty by reaching a plea agreement with the prosecution team.

On March 10th 2006, when Cullen appeared in court again, he repeatedly taunted Judge William Platt by ordering him to stand down. He repeated his taunts for half an hour until the judge ordered Cullen to be gagged with a towel and duct tape. It still didn't stop him mumbling his discontent of the court, leading families of the victims to shout back.

"If my grandmother was alive right now, she'd say to you, 'I hope you rot in hell, you sick son of a bitch.'"

A family member of one of the victims.

In 2004, New Jersey passed the Patient Safety Act. It allowed hospitals and medical staff access to a confidential reporting system, to be used when someone is suspected or for adverse events. Cullen could move from job to job because each hospital was unwilling to share negative experiences of their own. The new reporting system allowed hospitals to be more open in their reporting of their own staff or colleagues, to an outside authority.

Since then, more than 30 States have passed laws to protect employees or managers who speak up against colleagues or employees. This also came off the back of numerous cases brought against each hospital from the families of the victims. Two investigations concluded that Cullen may have killed up to 400 patients over a 19-year period.

Cullen later claimed that he enjoyed watching his patient's deterioration over a period of days and that he killed on impulse. He claimed to have not remembered how many he had killed and how he chose his victims, stating that his entire life had been lived under a fog of mental health decline and delusion.

As of 2021, Cullen remains incarcerated at a prison in New Jersey.

Born **February 22nd 1960.**

Active from **1984-2003.**

Arrested on **December 14th 2003.**

Country: **USA.**

Victims: **35+.**

AKA: **The Killer Nurse.**

Sentence: **Multiple life sentences.**

Current whereabouts: **In prison in New Jersey.**

Dahmer, Jeffrey: The Milwaukee Cannibal (Extended Case File)

On June 18th 1978, *Jeffrey Dahmer, The Milwaukee Cannibal,* killed his first victim. He would go on to rape, mutilate, murder and dismember a total of 17 boys and men from 1978 until his arrest in 1991.

"I always had a sense that it was wrong. I don't think anybody can kill somebody and think that it's right."

Jeffrey Dahmer.

He would go on to become one of the most infamous serial killers in known history and he began in 1978. You only have to type his surname into a search engine to be met with tens of thousands of pages about him.

It was the way in which he killed his victims and kept their bodies that would go on to shock the world. He was only 18-years-old when he killed his first victim, a hitchhiker named *Steven Hicks*.

His parents were going through a messy divorce and Dahmer was left alone in the family house. He picked up Hicks and brought him back to have a night of drinking beer. Dahmer later claimed he saw an opportunity to act on dark thoughts that had been inside of him for quite some time.

He slammed a dumbbell weight into Hick's head. He then went on to mutilate, dissect and dissolve the body. Dahmer spread the misshapen remains throughout the family garden. He claimed he killed him simply because Hick's didn't want to stay.

Prior to the interstate systems, hitchhiking had never really been heard of or was limited to a certain mindset. The creation of the interstates, as shown in the

Highways to Hell section, gave rise to the hitchhiker. And thus gave rise to a greater pool of potential victims for those who would act on their dark fantasies. Just like Jeffrey Dahmer.

It would be another nine years before he killed again. All his victims were male and all his victims were mutilated, dissected and dissolved. That a killer would be able to hide the murder for nine years is horrific enough. But the longer that Dahmer wasn't punished for his crime, the more powerful he would have felt.

"I think in some way, I wanted it to end. Even it meant my own destruction."

From 1987, he would pick up men from gay bars and take them back to a hotel room and later his home. He discovered he was gay while in puberty and sought gay bars and gay bathhouses from an early age. He would drug his victims, rape them and mostly strangle them to death. It was his fascination with the corpses that would see him become infamous amongst serial killers.

Dahmer engaged multiple times in necrophilia, having sex with the corpses until *rigor mortis* had set in. He would take photographs of his victims to log each part of the dismemberment process. He would preserve the skulls and genitals for display in his home and sometimes cannibalise parts of their flesh.

By 1991, he had begun to kill on average one person each week.

"The only motive that there ever was, was to completely control a person; a person I found physically attractive. And keep them with me as long as possible, even if it meant just keeping a part of them."

He began to believe he could turn his victims into zombies who could be controlled as submissive sex toys. He started drilling holes into their skulls and injected boiling water or hydrochloric acid into their brains to lobotomise them.

Astonishingly, one victim managed to escape onto the street and call for help. Dahmer convinced police officers that it was his extremely drunk boyfriend. And he got away with it.

It was July 22nd 1991, when one of his victims, *Tracy Edwards*, escaped and flagged down a police car. When the officers entered Dahmer's home, the true extent of his crimes were displayed for them to see.

They found a severed head in the fridge and three more heads placed around his home. They found the pictures of the dead bodies and the stages of dismemberment and even found a human heart in the freezer. In Dahmer's closet, a bizarre altar was discovered made out of skulls and candles, all adjoined with wax. He confessed straight away to the true extent of his crimes.

When he was a child, he underwent a double hernia operation, not the most common of operations for a child. Before it, he was a happy energetic boy but after the operation, he was known to have changed and become withdrawn into himself.

It was also known that his mother was suffering from mental health disorders and was on large doses of anti-psychotic medication throughout her pregnancy with him. Might this have had an effect on Dahmer's own mental health in his formative years?

There are some other potential reasons why he would go on to kill in such a fashion. During school, he was drinking alcohol almost daily. Wine, spirits, beer, whatever he could lay his hands on and smuggle into his school. Alcohol at an early age is known to cause major issues in later life.

From the age of 10-years-old, Dahmer was obsessed with the bones of animals. His father, who was a chemist, believed that his son had found his calling and showed him how to clean bones using bleach. This bizarre education formulated his own unique view of the world and led to his passion for murder. He would use exactly the same methods in disposing of his victim's remains or cleaning their skulls using bleach.

"I don't care if I live or die, go ahead and kill me."

He was sentenced to 957 years in prison but was killed by another inmate in November of 1994. Dahmer's horrific legacy lives on to this day in books, films, music and pop culture.

Born **May 21st 1960**.

Active from **1978-1991**.

Arrested on **July 22nd 1991**.

Country: **USA (Milwaukee)**.

Victims: **17**.

AKA: **The Milwaukee Cannibal**.

Sentence: **957 years imprisonment**.

Current whereabouts: **Killed by another inmate in November 1994.**

Damergi, Naceur

Tunisian serial killer *Naceur Damergi* raped and killed 13 children in the Nabeul region of the country over a four year period from 1984 to 1988. Damergi had been born in prison to his prostitute mother and didn't meet his father until he was 30-years-old.

When he was 16-years-old, in 1960, he got engaged to his cousin then worked in France to raise money for the marriage. When he permanently returned in 1968, he found out that his cousin had married another man without telling him. It had enraged him so much so that in 1970 he raped a 12-year-old girl and then tried to kill the girl's sister.

IMAGE ATTRIB. A16

ANDREI CHIKATILO

IMAGE ATTRIB. A4   IMAGE ATTRIB. A70

JEFFREY DAHMER

He was sentenced in 1971 for the rape and attempted murder and wouldn't be released until 1984. During the time in prison he had built up an unhealthy image of children and over the following four years, raped and murdered 13 young girls.

In 1988 he was sentenced to death for the rapes and murders. He was hanged on November 17th 1990 and remains one of Tunisia's worst serial killers.

Born in **1944**.

Active from **1984-1988**.

Arrested in **1988**.

Country: **Tunisia**.

Victims: **13**.

Sentence: **Death penalty**.

Current whereabouts: **Executed by hanging on November 17th 1990**.

David, Horst

German serial killer *Horst David* killed at least seven people from 1975 to 1993. During his marriage from 1963 to 1984, he stayed away from the family as much as possible spending time in the cities of Munich and Hamburg. Due to his addiction with escorts and prostitutes, the family had financial difficulties.

The first murder in 1975 was a prostitute named *Waltraud Frank*. Just two days later, another prostitute, *Fatima Grossart* was found dead. David later claimed that he had argued with both victims because they had demanded more money than their standard rates.

He divorced in 1984 and moved to Regensburg where he lived on state handouts. It was suspected that towards the late 1980s, he may have murdered more women. But it wasn't until 1993 that he would be linked to another murder. His neighbour, *Mathilde Steindl*, was strangled in her home.

His fingerprints were found in Steindl's home but there was no other evidence linking him to the crime. In due course, his profile was sent to a new Automated Fingerprint Identification System (*AFIS*). It subsequently made a match with the fingerprints on Fatima Grossart's body from 1975.

Upon his arrest he confessed to a total of seven murders from 1975 to 1993. Three of the murders had never been investigated as murders because the crime scenes had been set up to look like household accidents. It is claimed that financial gain had been the sole motivation, along with a sexual perversity.

In 1995, David was sentenced to life imprisonment and remains incarcerated as of 2021.

Born **November 22nd 1938**.

Active from **1975-1993**.

Arrested in **August 1995**.

Country: **Germany**.

Victims: **7+**.

Sentence: **Life imprisonment**.

Current whereabouts: **In prison**.

DeAngelo, Joseph James: The Golden State Killer (Extended Case File)

Not since Ted Bundy has the case of a serial killer been so widely spoken about in media and especially in online forums. His capture brings to end one of the largest serial killing mysteries of the Twentieth Century.

It is a complicated case with so many threads of crime coming to a head. *The Golden State Killer* was a serial killer, rapist and burglar who killed at least 13 people, committed more than 50 rapes, and over 100 burglaries in California from 1974 to 1986.

Each of his known three crime sprees afforded him a new moniker in the media. This was before it became evident that the three monikers were one and the same person. So along with the Golden State Killer, which is what the press are currently running with, he was also the East Area Rapist (EAR) and the Original Night Stalker (ONS).

It has also been suggested that there are links to him being the Diamond Knot Killer, The Cordova Cat, The Rippon Court Shooter, and The Visalia Ransacker.

On February 2nd 1978, DeAngelo shot dead *Brian Maggiore* and *Katie Maggiore*. DNA has been matched against the two victims and the killer is confirmed to be DeAngelo. It is claimed by one witness that he had already killed 14 people before 1974 and it is an assumption that he killed again in 1978, probably more than once.

He was identified through a DNA match with his fourth cousin on an open data personal genomics website. Subsequently, the investigators built a family tree and zoned in on DeAngelo based on living locations, age at the time of the crimes, and serial killer profiling techniques. They secretly gained access to his DNA from a throw-away item as they were watching him and it came back to be a 100% match.

DeAngelo's father served in World War Two but not much is known about him beyond that. After his parents' divorce, his mother quickly remarried and they moved to California from New York. His childhood and developing years were formed by his father returning from war, divorce and displacement of his home life.

In 1964, he joined the U.S. Navy and was subsequently deployed to Vietnam. We've already spoken in this book about the toxic legacy of World War Two and the damaging effect of Vietnam on serving soldiers but divorce also plays a major factor.

In most of the rape cases, the crimes took place too long ago and cannot be tried in a court of law due to the statute of limitations. However, in their place, he is being charged with kidnapping.

In June 1972 he garnered a bachelor's degree in criminal justice at the *California State University* and subsequently joined the *Exeter Police Department* in 1973. He was promoted to sergeant and it is suggested that he was using the department as a stepping-stone to becoming an FBI Agent.

Whilst working on the force, he was already operating as the *Visalia Ransacker.* If witness statements are to be believed he had already killed many people by that point in time.

He then moved from the Exeter Department to the *Auburn Police Department* in 1976. June 1976 is the first confirmed attack of the East Area Rapist. In 1978, under the same moniker, he moved onto murder. The last known attack of his East Area Rapist name was on July 5th 1979, in Danville, California.

He was then fired from the Auburn Police Department for shoplifting in a *Pay & Save* store. If we base the assumption that DeAngelo had joined the police in order to use it as a stepping-stone to the FBI, then his dismissal from the Auburn PD would have put to bed any chance he ever had to work with the FBI.

October 1st 1979 is the date of the first attack attributed to the Original Night Stalker (ONS). The more famously known Night Stalker was Richard Ramirez who killed 14 people from 1984 to 1985.

On December 30th 1979, Dr. Robert Offerman and Alexandria Manning are killed in their home near Goleta, 100 miles northwest of Los Angeles.

Just three months later another double murder took place in Ventura. Lyman and Charlene Smith were bound and bludgeoned to death with a fireplace log. Charlene had been sexually assaulted and tied with a curtain cord. Their 12-year-old son found their bodies three days later. DNA collected from this scene was used to identify DeAngelo almost 40 years later.

On August 21st 1980, Keith and Patti Harrington of Laguna Niguel, California, were bludgeoned to death. Some sources bizarrely put this five years earlier but it was in fact 1980. Keith's father discovered their beaten bodies when he arrived for dinner on the Thursday night. There were more murders in the same area and it wasn't until September of 1981 that the killings stopped, for a while.

In September of that year, DeAngelo's first child was born in Sacramento. As we've discussed with Ted Bundy, some serial killers hold their own family in higher esteem than others. This might seem like a given notion but some serial killers are able to lift up their wives and children as being important to them, they respect and revere their own families. At the same they focus any hatred they might have garnered towards them on other females or children.

It's important because after DeAngelo's first child, there is an assumed five year gap where no crimes were committed. It wasn't until the May 4th, 1986, murder of Janelle Cruz in Irvine, that the investigation would start linking DeAngelo to the new spate of murders and rapes.

His second child was born in 1986 and the third in 1989. Beyond that, there are no crimes committed and some put this down to the fact he now had children of his own and was intent on raising his family.

He was arrested in July 2012 for driving under the influence. Little did the officers know they had one of the most notorious killers and rapists in their custody. It wasn't until March 2018 when he became a suspect due to a DNA match to his fourth cousin on a DNA database and then arrested in April 2018.

Which raises the important notion of *genetic informants*.

You didn't really think those ancestry DNA sites were just to find out more about your own family, did you? Mostly they are, of course, but they are being used to a massive extent in the investigation of cold cases and new cases.

You could unwittingly be a genetic informant and not ever know it. The rise of the genetic informant is something for debate in further discussions.

There is a theory that he was also the Zodiac Killer but there has been no evidence pointing towards it as of 2021, even though some of his killings were similar in style.

In June 2020, DeAngelo admitted to 13 murders in a deal with US prosecutors meant to spare him the death penalty. He also admitted to numerous rapes, burglaries and other crimes at the time. On August 20th 2020, DeAngelo was sentenced to multiple life sentences.

Prosecutors ultimately did not seek the death penalty, due partially to California's moratorium on executions. Judge Bowman said that the sentence he chose was the absolute maximum the court was able to impose under the law.

As such, DeAngelo is now serving a total of 11 consecutive life terms without the possibility of parole, alongside 15 concurrent life sentences and other time for weapons charges. Despite being convicted of 13 murders, most investigations and research suspect there could be at least 87 victims with many more unidentified and unaccounted for.

Born **November 8th 1945.**

Active from **1974-1986.**

Arrested on **April 24th 2018.**

Country: **USA.**

Victims: **13-87+**

AKA: **Golden State Killer / East Area Rapist / Original Night Stalker.**

Current whereabouts: **In prison serving 26 life sentences.**

Dudin, Nikolai Arkadievich

On December 3rd 1987, Russian serial killer *Nikolai Arkadievich Dudin*, AKA: *The Grim Maniac*, shot dead his father. He hid the body for a year before when an arrest for rape saw him confess to the murder.

He was only 13-years-old when he killed his father. Due to his age he escaped the death sentence and was imprisoned, where he incited riots along with an attempted murder. He was released in 2000 and two years later killed at least another 12 people in various incidents. He would use guns, knives and blunt objects to kill his victims.

During May of 2002 alone, he killed nine people in a month of terror. On the first two days of the month a young female disappeared without a trace, she was later found dead, having been killed by Dudin. On May 8th, he killed an entire family, first by shooting the father dead and then the mother. Then he chased their 11-year-old daughter before stabbing her repeatedly until she died.

Two days later on May 10th he killed three more people in a triple murder, in almost a replication of the murders on May 8th. And just a few days afterwards, he killed two more people in a double murder.

In July 2002, he was caught red-handed attempting to kill someone. He was arrested and sentenced to life imprisonment without parole. He was subsequently sent to a special regime colony; the *Supermax White Swan Prison*, where he remains to this day.

Born **December 22nd 1973**.

Active from **1987-2002**.

Arrested on **July 17th 2002**.

Country: **Russia**.

Victims: **13**.

AKA: **The Grim Maniac**.

Sentence: **Life imprisonment**.

Current whereabouts: **In prison at the Supermax White Swan Prison**.

Duncan III, Joseph Edward

Joseph Edward Duncan III is an American serial killer who killed at least five people from 1996 to 2005. He also confessed to the 1996 killing of two young sisters in Seattle. As of 2021, he hasn't been convicted of those murders.

At the age of 15-years-old, in 1980, Duncan was sentenced to 20 years in prison for sexually abusing a young boy. He was released in 1994 after 14 years in prison but returned to prison in 1997 for violating his parole.

During his first stint of freedom, he had already killed the two young girls and one young man. He was released from prison in 2000 and moved to North Dakota, with the authorities unaware they were releasing a serial killer.

On July 6th 1996, two sisters, 11-year-old *Sammiejo White* and nine-year-old *Carmen Cubias* vanished as they were out walking alone. They had left the Crest Motel in Seattle, only to never return. Their decomposed remains were discovered on February 10th 1998, in Washington. Duncan confessed to the murders after his next arrest in 2005.

On May 16th 2005, multiple bodies of the *Groene* family were discovered in their home outside the city of Coeur d'Alene, in North Idaho. 40-year-old *Brenda Groene* and her boyfriend, 37-year-old *Mark McKenzie*, were found dead along with Brenda's 13-year-old son, *Slade Groene*. They had all been tied up and bludgeoned to death.

Her two other children, nine-year-old *Dylan* and eight-year-old *Shasta* were missing from the property and a state-wide AMBER alert was put into action. Seven weeks later, Duncan was spotted in a restaurant holding the hand of Shasta. A waitress and some customers recognised her and subsequently stopped Duncan from leaving the premises. Police turned up to arrest him shortly after.

On July 4th 2005, investigators discovered the remains of Dylan Groene in a remote forest location. He had been shot in the head at close range by a sawn-off shotgun. It took DNA testing to confirm the rest of the remains. In the trial of Dylan Groene, a video was made by Duncan, detailing the torture of the boy, in it he is heard shouting at the top of his voice.

"The devil is here, boy, the devil himself. The devil likes to watch children suffer and cry."

Joseph E. Duncan – in a video with Dylan Groene.

By 2011, Duncan had been convicted by three courts. Two courts in Idaho for the murders of the Groene family members, and a Californian superior court, for the murder of a 10-year-old boy in 1997. In total he received six life sentences and three death sentences.

On March 22nd 2019, Duncan lost an appeal to commute the death sentences to life, which means he remains on death row awaiting execution.

Born **February 25th 1963.**

Active from **1996-2005.**

Arrested on **July 2nd 2005.**

Country: **USA.**

Victims: **7.**

Sentence: **Three death penalties and six life sentences.**

Current whereabouts: **Death row.**

Dutroux, Marc: The Monster of Belgium (Extended Case File)

One of Europe's most infamous serial killers and crime cases. Belgian-born, *Marc Paul Alain Dutroux*, killed at least four young girls and abused many more. His trial would cause such an uproar in Belgium that over 300,000 people would march in memory of the victims.

Dutroux was born in 1956 and was the eldest of five children. His parents moved to the Belgian section of the Congo before his first year, as they were teaching French in the region. As the Congo crisis deepened, the Dutroux's escaped back to Belgium, where they divorced in 1971.

Dutroux briefly married when he was 19-years-old, had two children and divorced eight years later in 1983. He met his future second wife, Michelle Martin, while he was still married to his first wife. Together, they would involve themselves in crime and go on to abduct five young girls before sexually abusing them.

At that time, Dutroux was unemployed and survived by carrying out robberies, muggings, and selling drugs. He even stole cars in Belgium and sold them over the border in Czechoslovakia and Hungary. He went on to own seven houses and used three of them for the sole purpose of torturing young girls. At one of his houses in Marcinelle, he built a torture dungeon in the basement and hid it by a concealed concrete door.

In February 1986, both Dutroux and Martin were arrested for the kidnapping and rape of five girls. After a lengthy trial in 1989, Dutroux was sentenced to just over 13 years in prison, and Martin received five years for her part in the crimes. Astonishingly, after only three years, Dutroux was released for good behaviour in 1992.

The dungeon had never been found and Dutroux decided to put it to full use. On June 24th 1995, eight-year-old *Julie Lejeune* and her friend, eight-year-old *Mélissa Russo* were kidnapped. They were held in Dutroux's dungeon and repeatedly raped, with their ordeals filmed and recorded on VHS. Around that time, Dutroux had garnered another accomplice, *Michel Lelièvre*, who would help him abduct girls.

Two months later and the two eight-year-old girls were still being abused and tortured in Dutroux's dungeon. On August 23rd 1995, Dutroux and Lelièvre kidnapped 17-year-old *An Marchal* and 19-year-old *Eefje Lambrecks*. Because the dungeon was still in use, they chained the two teenagers in one of the bedrooms of the house.

They suffered the same abuse as the girls in the dungeon but after a couple of weeks, Marchal and Lambrecks were drugged and moved to a different Belgian town. There, Dutroux and another accomplice, *Bernard Weinstein*, murdered the girls and buried them in a shallow grave.

There had always been questions asked about how Dutroux had so many accomplices. They were all suspected to be members of an underground gang of paedophiles and murderers who made sure that they looked out for and helped each other. This aspect of the Dutroux case gave rise to theories of cover-ups and secrets within the Belgian elite.

Weinstein and another man named *Philippe Divers* stole a van and thought they had hidden it well, but it was found by police. Dutroux then suspected that Divers and his friend, *Pierre Rochow*, had betrayed him, so he lured them to Weinstein's home in Jumet. They then went to search Rochow's home and found his girlfriend, *Bénédicte Jadot*. They interrogated her but she escaped and called the police.

Dutroux decided to cover his own tracks and kill Weinstein, so he kidnapped him and held him in the dungeon, where he tortured him and then buried him alive. During this time, the two eight-year-old girls were still in the house and were allowed to walk around freely while he was there.

On December 6th 1995, Dutroux was arrested on suspicion of stealing luxury cars. He remained in custody until March 20th 1996. Before he went into custody, he had told his partner, Michelle Martin, to feed the two girls in the house every day. Martin was scared of entering the dungeon and didn't feed the girls, they died of starvation sometime while Dutroux was in custody.

The day he was released on March 20th, he went back to the house, removed the bodies from the dungeon and buried them near to Weinstein's body in the grounds of another house. As much as Martin had disappointed him, Dutroux continued feeding his dark desires.

On May 28th 1996, Dutroux and his former accomplice, Lelièvre, kidnapped 12-year-old schoolgirl *Sabine Dardenne*. She was taken to the dungeon in the house and repeatedly raped, abused, tortured and starved, over a three month period.

On August 9th 1996, Dutroux and Lelièvre kidnapped 14-year-old schoolgirl *Laetitia Delhez*, as she was leaving her local swimming pool. There was an eyewitness to the kidnapping, who later described the van and partial license plate to police.

On August 13th, Dutroux, Martin, and Lelièvre, were arrested on suspicion of kidnapping. Police searched Dutroux's properties but didn't find anything, they failed to find the dungeon in the basement as it had been so well hidden. After intense interrogation, Dutroux and Lelièvre both confessed to the kidnappings.

On August 15th, Dutroux led police into the basement and showed them the secret concrete door to the dungeon. Inside they found 14-year-old Delhez alive and chained to the wall. Astonishingly, 12-year-old Dardenne had survived three months of torture and abuse and she too was rescued from the dungeon.

On August 17th, Dutroux led them to another of his properties and showed them where he had buried the bodies of the two eight-year-old girls and Weinstein. On September 3rd, he led police to the remains of Marchal and Lambrecks, in Jumet.

Once news of the murders and rapes got into the media, the public were outraged. Criticism of the police was made public as they could have stopped the situation from getting worse but they had failed on multiple levels. Dutroux had even offered money to a police informant to provide him with girls for his dungeon. Dutroux's own mother had written a letter to police, saying that her son scared her, and she was sure he was doing something evil.

Her letter was ignored.

On the night that he kidnapped the two teenage girls, he was already under police surveillance. However, the police had only set up the CCTV to operate during daylight hours. When police searched his house for the first time in December of 1995, they failed to discover the dungeon. If they had done, then the two eight-year-old girls might have been rescued before starving to death.

While the police were searching the property, the lead officer heard children's voices but assumed they were coming from outside the property. The police even collected VHS tapes from the house that showed Dutroux building the door to the dungeon. The police never played it because they claimed they didn't have a VCR player at the time.

As the mounting evidence against the incompetence of the police was made more public, the anger and frustrations grew within the country. Then came the accusations of cover-ups. Stories began to emerge of a paedophile sex-ring that included members of the police force and politicians within the government itself.

Some of the investigators and one judge then claimed that much of the evidence gathered was 'flimsy' and wouldn't stand up in a court of law. This led to one judge named *Jean-Marc Connerotte* to be dismissed, which led to a growing rage within the Belgian public.

On October 20th 1996, 300,000 people marched on Brussels in support of the families of the victims. The White March, as it became known, was also to protest against the ruling authorities and the police for the failures in their investigation into the missing girls. The demonstrators wanted higher levels of protection for children, along with an independent justice system that could investigate Dutroux without influence from parliament.

When the trial began, the fired judge, Connerotte, was called to the stand as a witness. He testified that he needed bullet-proof vehicles and an armed security team to protect him. When asked who they were protecting him from, he said there were shadowy figures in positions of power who were determined to stop the full truth coming out.

Connerotte testified that some suspects were being protected by people in government and it had hampered the investigation to the point of it being impossible. There were even rumours that the Mafia had some influence on the pre-trial hearings.

A 17-month pre-trial Parliamentary investigation into Dutroux was undertaken, leading to a report in February of 1998. It concluded that Dutroux did not have accomplices in high places. It enraged people further as it was pretty much the government investigating themselves and clearing their own name.

Dutroux hit the headlines again in April 1998, when he escaped from a courthouse while only one guard was watching him. There were meant to have been two guards but one of them decided to run an errand. Dutroux fought off the only guard, stole a car at gunpoint, and escaped into dense forest. 5000 officers and dozens of helicopters were called in to capture him. The borders of France, Luxembourg and Germany, were put on an '*all-borders-alert*' and effectively temporarily closed.

He was captured in the forest half a day later. The episode resulted in the resignations of a Police Chief, a Minister of Justice, and the Minister of the Interior.

Finally, in 2004, Dutroux's trial began, almost eight years since he had been arrested. Michelle Martin, and Lelièvre, along with one other were tried as accomplices to the crimes. Dutroux was put in a bullet proof glass cage during the trial, for his own protection.

Dutroux testified that he was part of a Europe-wide underground ring of paedophiles that included police officers, top businessmen, medical professionals and high-level government officials.

On June 17th 2004, the jury found Dutroux and Martin guilty of all the charges they had been put up on. Just a few months prior to Dutroux's arrest, the death penalty had been abolished in the country in early 1996. A petition to bring back the death penalty purely for Dutroux was created but fell on deaf ears.

He was sentenced to the maximum sentence of life imprisonment without parole. Michelle Martin received 30 years and Lelièvre was sentenced to 25 years. Then another failure by the justice system resulted in yet another uproar in the Belgian public.

After only 13 years of her sentence, Martin was paroled and released into the care of an isolated convent of nuns, known as the *Poor Clares of Malonne*. When news of her parole had come up, thousands of people protested against it, but again, their protests were ignored.

Astonishingly, the convent was sold shortly after which meant that Martin had to find new shelter or return to prison. Even more astonishingly, a former judge built an apartment in his farmhouse, purely so that Martin could live there, and she does – to this day. Lelièvre remains incarcerated as of 2021, despite numerous appeals and parole hearings.

Dutroux has also made numerous appeals, on the basis that he is no longer a danger to society, but they have been denied at every turn. As of 2021, he remains incarcerated in solitary confinement at a prison in the Nivelles area of Belgium.

The case affected Belgium so much that a third of people in the country with the surname of Dutroux, applied to have it changed. Conspiracy theories abound to this day, not least with the knowledge that over 20 witnesses in the original trial have died under mysterious circumstances.

In 1996, when she was 12-years-old, Sabine Dardenne was chained to a wall in Dutroux's dungeon for 79 days. She found the strength to testify against Dutroux during his trial. In 2006, 10 years after her abduction, she published a book about the experience called '*J'avais 12 ans, j'ai pris mon vélo et je suis partie à l'école*'.

It was published in the United Kingdom under the very apt title of '*I Choose to Live*'.

Born **November 6th 1956**.

Active from **1995-1996**.

Arrested on **August 13, 1996**.

Country: **Belgium**.

Victims: **5+**.

AKA: **The Monster of Belgium**.

Sentence: **Life imprisonment**.

Current whereabouts: **In prison, in solitary confinement**.

Eckert, Volker

A German serial killer who was convicted of killing six women in various European countries. He is known to have killed nine and accused of more murders in different countries throughout his life.

In most of the murders, he would strangle the women, mutilate them and photograph them. After, he would cut off the hair and dress the corpses. He would keep the hair as trophies of his crimes. The German lorry driver had confessed to killing three prostitutes in Spain and two others in France between 1999 and 2006.

He was caught in November of 2006 after a Europe-wide arrest warrant was issued by Spanish authorities. He had killed a 22-year-old Bulgarian woman in Spain called *Miglena Petrova*. He had strangled her to death and left her body near to a football pitch with no attempt to cover the crime. He also took photographs of his victims, some of which led to investigations being re-opened.

He was caught by a satellite tracking system which was installed in his truck. The investigation were able to retrace the truck's routes which put Eckert at the scene of the Petrova murder. In his truck they found photographs of Petrova's corpse along with another unidentified victim.

Eckert later confessed to killing a 14-year-old girl in East Germany in 1974. Investigations were closed after Eckert killed himself during proceedings in 2007.

Born in **1959**.

Active from **1974-2006**.

Arrested on **November 17th 2006**.

Country: **Germany / France / Spain / Italy / Czech Republic**.

Victims: **6-19+**.

AKA: **The Brummi Killer.**

Current whereabouts: **Suicide in 2007, while awaiting trial.**

Edwards, Edward

Born Charles Murray, *Edward Wayne Edwards* was suspected of murdering at least five people. He was on the *FBI's Ten Most Wanted Fugitives* list in 1961 for armed robberies at gas stations. He has been connected to many more crimes including the *Atlanta Murders* from 1979 to 1981.

Edwards grew up as an orphan after having witnessed the suicide of his own mother. While in an orphanage he was physically and emotionally abused by the carers. It is claimed that the level of abuse he received combined with watching his mother commit suicide led to his violent behaviour in later life.

Edwards foster son, *Dannie Law Gloeckner*, disappeared in May of 1996 and his body was discovered a year later in 1997, he had been murdered by Edwards with a shotgun. Five months before Gloeckner vanished, he legally changed his name to *Dannie Boy Edwards*.

Edwards was caught in 2009 but died of natural causes in 2011. He was linked many times as a suspect in the Zodiac Killer investigation.

Born **June 14th 1933.**

Active from **1977-1996.**

Arrested on **July 30th 2009.**

Country: **USA.**

Victims: **5+.**

Current whereabouts: **Died of natural causes in 2011 while awaiting trial.**

Eijk, Willem Van

The '*Beast of Harkstede*' was a Dutch serial killer who was convicted of five murders. His victims were all females and he would generally rape them before strangling them. In childhood, he was known for his cruelty to small animals including dogs, cats, and ducks.

He was also an outcast who was bullied both physically and emotionally. With no friends he began collecting dead frogs and insects. He claimed at the time he would dream about raping and killing women and turned to petty crime before committing murder.

The first murder came in 1971, when he was 30-years-old. He picked up a 15-year-old hitchhiker named *Cora Mantel*, who had allegedly missed her bus on the way to visit her boyfriend. Van Eijk then raped her and strangled her to death with her own clothing, before dumping her body in a ditch.

In 1974, he killed 43-year-old, *Aaltje van der Plaat*. Her body was found near a road in a field. She had been stabbed multiple times, her belly was ripped open and her left nipple had been cut off. Witnesses had seen Van Eijk flee the scene, he was arrested shortly after and sentenced to 18 years in prison.

He was released in 1990 and claimed his next victim in 1993. The body of 23-year-old prostitute *Antoanella Bertholda Fato* was discovered. She had been strangled to death during intercourse. Before Van Eijk was arrested for a second time, eight prostitutes had been murdered in the area where he lived.

Although not all could be conclusively linked to him, he was arrested in 2001 and charged with multiple murders. Many more bodies have since been attributed to Van Eijk.

Born **August 13th 1941.**

Active from **1971-2001.**

Arrested on **November 12th 2001.**

Country: **Netherlands.**

Victims: **5+.**

AKA: **The Beast of Harkstede / Crazy little William.**

Sentence: **Life imprisonment.**

Current whereabouts: **In prison.**

Ellis, Walter E.

American serial killer *Walter E. Ellis*, AKA: *The Milwaukee North Side Strangler* raped and strangled seven women in Milwaukee from 1986 to 2007. All seven of his victims were strangled by hand, with a rope, or with an item of clothing tied around their necks.

Upon his arrest in 2009, he refused to speak and remained silent until his death. Therefore the motivations of his killings remain unknown and he refused to cooperate with authorities and his own lawyers.

He was caught when his DNA matched semen samples found on six of victims and from a blood sample on a can of pepper spray at one of the crime scenes. He was sentenced to seven consecutive life sentences but died in 2013 from unknown natural causes.

Born in **1960.**

Active from **1986-2007.**

Arrested on **September 5th 2009.**

Country: **USA (Milwaukee).**

Victims: **7.**

AKA: **The Milwaukee North Side Strangler.**

Sentence: **Seven life sentences.**

Current whereabouts: **Died of natural causes in 2013.**

Escalero, Francisco Garcia

Spanish serial killer *Francisco García Escalero* was convicted for the murders of 11 people over a seven year period from 1987 to 1994. He was a diagnosed schizophrenic who had sex with his victim's corpses and engaged in cannibalism.

He claimed his first victim in August of 1987, a prostitute by the name of *Paula Martínez*. He claimed he killed people because the voices in his head told him to and his hallucinations caused by schizophrenia forced him to kill. He raped, killed and decapitated Martínez before burning her corpse.

In the years that followed he killed lots of homeless people and beggars. Sometimes he stabbed them to death and other times he crushed their skulls with rocks. The burned bodies of some victims were found decapitated. Alongside the murders he would go to local cemeteries and dig up bodies so he could have sex with them. He was also known to have eaten parts of the corpses.

He was arrested after escaping from a psychiatric hospital that he was in temporarily. Escalero attempted suicide but was stopped in the process. He confessed and was sent to trial in 1995. At the trial he was declared insane and sentenced to a life term at a high-security psychiatric hospital.

Born **May 24th 1948.**

Active from **1987-1994.**

Arrested in **April 1994.**

Country: **Spain.**

Victims: **11**.

Sentence: **Life term in psychiatric hospital.**

Current whereabouts: **High-security psychiatric hospital.**

Evans, Donald Leroy

American *Donald Leroy Evans* murdered at least three people from 1985 to 1991 but confessed to over 70 murders stretching back to 1977. He was born in 1957, the seventh of nine children. Their mother was a violent alcoholic who constantly beat her children.

By the time he dropped out of school, Evans was already involved in drug and gang culture. At the age of 16-years-old, he attempted to kill himself by mixing a combination of illegal drugs with cockroach poison. In 1986, he was convicted for the rape of a local woman and sentenced to fifteen years in prison. He only served five and was released in 1991.

On August 1st 1991, Evans kidnapped a 10-year-old girl who he raped and strangled her to death. He was arrested only four days later and confessed immediately. It had been suggested that the girl was alive during the rape and died shortly after of her wounds. For that particular crime he was sentenced to death.

He then confessed to more than 70 murders in 22 different States. At first, the investigation didn't believe him but some of the descriptions of his victims matched up to missing persons and he was convicted of another murder.

Evans was stabbed to death in 1999 by a fellow inmate, while in the showers of the Mississippi State Penitentiary. Whatever secrets he had, and the true number of his victims have now gone with him to the grave.

Born **July 5**th **1957.**

Active from **1977-1991.**

Arrested on **August 5th 1991.**

Country: **USA**.

Victims: **3-70+**.

Sentence: **Death penalty.**

Current whereabouts: **Killed by a fellow inmate in 1999.**

Evans, Gary Charles

American serial killer *Gary Charles Evans* was a lifetime criminal who terrorized New York until his death in 1998. In October 1991, he spent two weeks on top of a building while he was working out the routine of a coin shop below. He then walked into the shop, asked for a valuation and then shot the shop owner in the head.

By 1993, he claimed he had already killed four people. His robbery skills were reaching epidemic levels. He stole almost 1000 items of antiques from an antique departmental store in Vermont and then used an industrial crane to steal a bench from a cemetery.

In 1987, Evans managed to befriend *David Berkowitz*, AKA; *The Son of Sam*. Berkowitz from then on would refer to Evans as '*The Great Tricep King*', on account of his muscular appearance. It is claimed that on one occasion, Berkowitz had become angered by Evans as he had referred to him as '*David Berserk-o-witz*'.

Upon Evan's next arrest in 1998, he confessed to five murders and the led police to the resting places of his victims. Almost all of the victims had been dismembered. Shortly after, he escaped from a prison van and when police surrounded him, he committed suicide by jumping to his death from a bridge.

Born **October 7th 1954.**

Active from **1985-1997.**

Arrested on **June 18th 1998.**

Country: **USA.**

Victims: **5.**

Current whereabouts: **Committed suicide by jumping from bridge after escaping from a prison van en-route to his trial.**

Evonitz, Richard Marc

American rapist and serial killer, *Richard Marc Evonitz*, murdered three young girls in Spotsylvania County, Virginia. He was also convicted of the kidnapping and rape of a 15-year-old girl in South Carolina.

While serving in the U.S. Navy in 1987, when he was 23-years-old, he exposed himself in front of a 15-year-old girl and masturbated in front of her. When his ship returned to port, he was arrested for the act and given a three year suspended sentence. He was also suspected of raping two young girls in Virginia, in 1994 and 1995.

His first confirmed murder took place on September 9th 1996. He kidnapped 16-year-old schoolgirl *Sofia Silva* from her front garden in Spotsylvania County. He raped and strangled her to death, then bizarrely shaved her pubic hair off. Her body was discovered a month later in a wooded area just off from a main highway. She had been found wrapped in a white sheet and had started to decompose.

Half a year later on May 1st 1997, two sisters, 15-year-old *Kristin Lisk*, and 12-year-old Kati Lisk vanished after leaving their school buses. When their father arrived home and found their bags in the front yard, he raised the alarm, but it was too late. Five days later and 40 miles away, their two bodies were discovered in a river.

Like Silva, their pubic hair had been shaved off.

Although DNA from all victims was a match, the investigation struggled to find a suspect. Until June 24th 2002, when Evonitz kidnapped 15-year-old schoolgirl, Kara Robinson, from her friend's yard. He tied her to the bed in his apartment and raped her multiple times. Robinson was able to escape while Evonitz slept.

Robinson went straight to the police but Evonitz escaped to Florida. Police managed to track him down, and on June 27th, when police surrounded him, he put a gun to his head and shot himself dead. Before Evonitz committed suicide, he phoned his sister and confessed the murders, and more. Since his death, more rapes and murders have been attributed to him.

Born **July 29th 1963**.

Active from **1996-1997**.

Country: **USA**.

Victims: **3+**.

Current whereabouts: **Suicide by shooting before arrest.**

Ferrari, Werner

One of Switzerland's most infamous criminals. He killed five children in the 1970s. He would lure them away or kidnap them from popular music festivals before abusing and strangling them.

Ferrari was raised by various carers and was known to have been withdrawn from the people around him. It is unclear what might have happened in his childhood to have triggered the violence that he enacted on others.

He first killed a ten-year-old boy in 1971 before being arrested and serving just eight years. Between 1980 and 1989, another 11 children were abducted and eight were violently murdered. Three were never found and Ferrari denied any involvement in their disappearances.

Ferrari turned himself in just four days after his last murder. He called police stating that he had nothing to do with the girl's death, this enabled police to descend on his apartment. He was arrested and confessed to multiple murders.

As of 2021, he is still one of Switzerland's most notorious inmates.

Born **December 29th 1946.**

Active from **1971-1989.**

Arrested on **August 30th 1989.**

Country: **Switzerland.**

Victims: **5-13+.**

Sentence: **Life imprisonment.**

Current whereabouts: **In prison.**

Fischer, Joseph J.

On July 2nd 1979, in New York, serial killer **Joseph J. Fischer** walked into a police station and told officers that he had stabbed his wife to death and left her body in the bedroom of their trailer. After police found the body, Fischer confessed to killing more than 20 people across various States from 1978 to 1979.

He had previously served a life sentence for the murder of a 16-year-old boy in 1953 who had beaten to death with a rock. He was paroled in June 1978 and went on a murder rampage that investigators claimed may have included more than 40 victims. Fischer was convicted of the death of his wife and sentenced to life while investigators looked at the rest of the claims.

The investigation ended in December 1991 when Fischer died of natural causes in prison. It has long remained unclear if Fischer's claims had any basis in fact. Despite his claims, he was still convicted of two murders with at least two more positively linked to him.

Born in **1923**.

Active from **1953-1979**.

Arrested in **July 1979**.

Country: **USA**.

Victims: **2-20+**

Filho, Pedro Rodriguez

AKA: *The Pedrinho Matador*, is a Brazilian serial killer who actively sought to kill other criminals. He killed an astonishing 47 people while inside prison, including another serial killer who was named *Francisco de Assis Pereira*.

Filho has always been a unique serial killer in that he targeted other criminals, leading some to call him the *real life Dexter*. He was also known as the *Criminal Killer* or *Killer Petey*.

Filho said he first felt the need to kill when he was only 13-years-old but held off until he was 14-years-old, when he killed the Vice-Mayor of Alfenas in southern Brazil. He killed the Vice-Mayor because he had fired his father after accusing him of stealing.

He move to São Paulo where he killed a man who was said to have been the real thief that had framed his father. He then continued his route of violence and murdered a drug dealer before meeting a girl named *Maria Aparecida Olympia*.

She lived with him for a short while and they became close until she was brutally murdered by gang members in the city. It is unclear whether it was out of revenge for the murder of the drug dealer.

Filho then went on a rampage, torturing a large number of people and killing others in an attempt to find the person who killed his girlfriend. When he was 18-years-old, he had already killed 10 people. Then in a bizarre twist of fate, his father killed his mother with a machete. And so Filho went to the prison and killed his own father, where he cut out his father's heart and chewed on it.

In 1973, he was sent to prison where he killed 47 other inmates. Due to the Brazilian justice system and despite the fact his body count was huge, Filho was released in 2007. Unsurprisingly, he continued to kill other criminals outside of the prison walls.

He was arrested again in 2011, on previous charges of inciting riots and further murders. He was also imprisoned further for crimes within prison.

In 2018, he was released again and has converted to Christianity after he apologised for his sins upon the world. Filho is also in the process of writing an autobiography. Amazingly, he has a YouTube channel, where he gives advice to young people and others thinking of committing crime.

As of 2021, he dedicates his life to stop young people turning to crime.

Born **June 17th 1954.**

Active from **1967-2003.**

Arrested on **May 24th 1991.**

Country: **Brazil.**

Victims: **100+.**

AKA: **Pedrinho Matador / Killer Petey / The Brazilian Dexter.**

Current whereabouts: **Released in 2018.**

Fokin, Victor

Another Russian serial killer, *Viktor Viktorovich Fokin*, AKA: *The Grandfather Ripper*, killed at least 10 people over a four year period from 1996 to 2000. He was 60-years-old when he committed his first murder.

In April 1996, a year after his wife died, he lured a 35-year-old homeless woman to his apartment. He plied her with vodka and then hit her on the head with a hammer, killing her instantly. Fokin then dismembered her body and dumped the body pieces into the Yeltsovka River.

Approximately, every two months afterwards, the dismembered remains of females were found in different areas, leading to a task force being set up. He was arrested in 2000, much to the shock of the local community, due to his age and previous work within the area.

In 2001, Fokin was sentenced to only 19 years at a corrective prison colony. 10 murders were attributed to him with evidence found in his apartment but the investigators believed he may have murdered many more. He died of natural causes in 2003, aged 68-years-old.

Born **February 19th 1935.**

Active from **1996-2000.**

Arrested in **March 2000.**

Country: **Russia.**

Victims: **10+.**

AKA: **The Grandfather Ripper.**

Sentence: **19 years at a corrective prison colony.**

Current whereabouts: **Died of natural causes in 2003.**

Fourniret, Michel Paul: The Ogre of the Ardennes (Extended Case File)

On December 11th 1987, 17-year-old *Isabelle Laville* was the first victim to be murdered by the *Ogre of the Ardennes*. French serial killer *Michel Paul Fourniret* confessed to killing 11 people in France and Belgium between 1987 and 2001. His wife *Monique Pierrette Olivier* was complicit in some of the murders and would be sentenced alongside him.

It wouldn't be until July 11th 2006, when Isabelle Laville's remains would be recovered.

Born in 1942, in the middle of World War Two, he grew up in a poor household and the threat of violence hanging over the family's head. Michel stated that in his formative years he had sexual encounters with his mother. The continuing abuse caused him a great deal of trauma and he began to develop an unhealthy view of women as he went through puberty.

He became obsessed with the notion of virginity after he discovered his first wife was not a virgin. This had upset him after learning his wife had been with other men. It was this along with his mother's incestuous abuse that led to him trying to kill mostly virgins.

His accomplice and future wife, Monique, was already aware of Michel's personality and crimes before they married. While serving time in prison for 15 counts of sexual assault against minors in and around Paris, Michel sought pen pals and placed ads in a religious magazine. Monique answered the ads and many letters were sent between them until his release from jail in 1987.

Through their letters, they developed a pact that would lead to the murders of multiple people upon his release. Michel wrote to her about his fantasy and great desire to kill virgins and young women. Monique then pledged to help Michel abduct young women and girls if he would agree to kill her abusive husband who she had separated from.

Michel never ended up killing her husband but he kept promising he would. However, Monique kept up her side of the pact and helped Michel kidnap, rape and murder multiple victims over many years.

In March 1988, Michel was contacted by 30-year-old *Farida Hammiche*, who was the wife of a convicted bank robber that Michel had shared a cell with until his release. She claimed there was cash and gold coins buried in a cemetery and she needed help to unearth it. Michel agreed and received a share of half a million French Francs (approx. $87,000 USD at the time).

A month later Michel and Monique decided to steal the rest of the loot from Hammiche's apartment. They lured her out of her home and drove her to a secluded area where Michel strangled her to death. They then returned to her house to steal the rest of the haul. Hammiche's body was never found. It is unclear how much they managed to get but they purchased an expensive Château in Donchery.

In August 1988, the couple drove to a supermarket and lured 20-year-old *Fabienne Leroy* to their car. Monique was pregnant with Michel's child and pretended to be ill because of it in order to trap their next victim. They drove her to a forest near a military camp where Michel raped her and shot her in the chest. Her body was found a day later.

In January 1989, Michel took an evening train when he met 21-year-old *Jeanne-Marie Desramault*, only to learn she was staying at a convent. Once he knew her routine, he met her again at the train station two months later, this time with Monique by his side. They invited Desramault to their home and she accepted as Michel would drive her home after.

After finding out she wasn't a virgin, Michel beat her and attempted to rape her. She was gagged and strangled to death. They then buried the body in the garden of the Château. Her remains were found in 2004.

In July 1989, Michel and Monique finally married and drove to Belgian with the one-year-old son. They caught sight of 12-year-old *Elisabeth Brichet* and they waited for her to leave her friend's house. Michel asked for directions to a doctor's surgery, and she agreed to go with them in the car. The following day, Michel strangled her in their home and buried her in the garden of the Château close to where Desramault had been buried.

Her disappearance became prime time news and a number of sightings of her were recorded in the years that followed. Many suspects were put forward including *Marc Dutroux* who was an infamous child killer at the time. After Dutroux's arrest in 1996, the mother of Elisabeth Brichet organised a march in honour of the missing and murdered children of Belgium. Elisabeth's body was found the same day as Desramault on July 3rd 2004.

On November 21st 1990, the couple were convicted of burglary in a court in Nantes. They left the court shortly after and drove to a shopping centre where they lured 13-year-old *Natacha Danais*, into their vehicle. They drove her to a secluded area near the coast where Michel stabbed her twice in the chest with a screwdriver. He strangled her to death and dumped her body on a beach.

Eight days later, an innocent man named *Jean Groix*, who was a neighbour of the victim, was arrested after a witness said it was his van at the shopping centre. In a bizarre twist, he was putting up members of the ETA in his home. It was suspected that the 13-year-old neighbour had found out about it and Groix silenced her by killing her. A few months later, Groix killed himself in his cell, as he couldn't face being convicted of a child's murder.

Michel later confessed that he killed two more people in France in 2000 and 2001. This came after a 10 year break from killing when they had moved to Belgium to buy a small castle. In May of 2000, he abducted 18-year-old student *Céline Saison*. He drove her back to Belgium where he raped her before strangling her and dumping the body in a wooded area. Her remains were discovered two months later.

In May of 2001, he lured 13-year-old Thai girl *Mananya Thumpong*. He drove her to a secluded wooded area, raped her and strangled her to death. Some of her bones were found almost a year later, due to wild animals having eaten the flesh of the body. While in prison, in 2018, he confessed to killing two more women in 1988 and 1990.

In 2003, an unnamed 13-year-old girl escaped Michel's clutches and she ran from his van in Belgium. She had been tied by her ankles and wrists and managed to get help. She was able to identify Michel and he was arrested in June of 2003. A year later, Monique confessed that had her husband had killed numerous people since 1987. They were both extradited to France for their trials.

They assisted the investigation and led police to the bodies of three of the four missing victims over a two year period. The trial took place in 2008 where Michel was found guilty and sentenced to life for the murders of seven of the victims whose bodies had been discovered. Monique was sentenced to life for being an accomplice in the murders. They were ordered to pay 1.5million Euros in compensation to the families of the victims.

Although convicted of seven murders, he was linked to four more bringing the total to 11 victims. It remains one of France and Belgium's most notorious cases. As of 2021, both Michel and Monique are serving their sentences in separate prisons.

Born **April 4th 1942.**

Active from **1987-2001.**

Arrested on **June 26th 2003.**

Country: **France / Belgium.**

Victims: **8-11+.**

AKA: **the Ogre of the Ardennes.**

Sentence: **Both Michel and Monique were sentenced to life imprisonment.**

Current whereabouts: **In prison.**

(Research Article #7) Urban Strangers

In 1900, only 15% of the world's population lived in cities. According to the United Nations (UN), in 2007, 50% of the world's population lived in cities. As the cities grew in size it was suggested that crime was an unwanted side effect of urbanisation.

When more people live closer to each than before, meaning the cities instead of rural areas, there is a higher link with crime. In fact, urbanisation and crime go hand and hand and there are particularly good reasons for that. The higher the density of population, the higher the opportunity there is for crime.

Committing crime in cities is generally easier than it is in rural areas. Even covering a city with CCTV does not seem to make a difference because the population is much larger than before.

The modernisation of urban areas has led to a rise in crime because more of the areas have become associated with income gap division. The working class are more likely to find themselves in highly urbanised areas than those of a middle or upper class. Within these highly urbanised areas, you find that crime is more evident than in the richer areas. This is a consequence of urbanisation

The Monstrous Book of Serial Killers (2nd edition)

CHATEAU DU SAUTOU, FORMER HOME OF MICHEL FOURNIRET

POLICE SEARCH AT CHATEAU DU SAUTOU

MONIQUE PIERRETTE OLIVIER

IMAGE ATTRIBUTIONS
(ATTRIB A19) (ATTRIB A20)
(ATTRIB A21A) (ATTRIB A21B)

MICHEL PAUL FOURNIRET

185

And serial killers became quite aware of that fact, taking advantage of urbanisation to their violent benefit.

Urban centres have been around since the dawn of human civilisation. It's evidenced that people will always strive to be part of communities as our species are known as social animals. Except the communities of 10,000 BC and the urban communities of the 1970s are so vastly different in their structure and design. It's difficult to see any similarity beyond the point that both have humans in their societies.

Some of the reasons for more crime in urban areas are income inequality, population density per square mile, police fatigue, police funding and unemployment rates. The very presence of crime only serves to influence more crime in an area. The talk of communities and neighbourhood groups within urban areas is honourable but are rarely cohesive or connected enough to prevent the rise of crime.

This type of urbanisation is part of the modern area. There were cities thousands of years ago but population increases saw a wide-ranging change to the fundamental structure of their existence. The council estates and projects from the middle of the Twentieth Century were far more conducive to crime than those at the beginning of human history.

Projects, council estates and any area with a high population density allows for an unprecedented level of anonymity. Potential anonymity leads to more crime and might result in murders. A serial killer can take advantage of populous urban environments and exploit them to bring their own dark thoughts into reality.

Urbanisation causes yet another but inextricably linked reason; *the stranger.*

Before modern times, people tended to know one another by name. Communities were tighter and you would have known the family name of everyone in your settlement. People knew each other's routines, family history and personal details. Strangers, as rare as they were, were hardly ever encountered and when they were, they were met with fear and wariness.

A thousand years ago, one might have only seen a hundred or so strangers in their entire lives. In modern times, you could come across hundreds, if not thousands, on the streets of a city or on the journey to work.

We live now amongst the urban stranger. We have no idea who is sitting opposite us on the train, we do not know who is in front or behind us in the queue of a supermarket.

Some people feign niceties so that they move on quicker with their own isolated existence. We do not always wish to know someone's name or routines; it puts us in the firing line for modern-day repercussions.

We have to worry about saying the wrong thing to someone we don't know for fear of reprisal, unwarranted or not. Urbanisation hasn't brought communities together, it has allowed strangers to live in their own worlds, sometimes right next door or in the flat above. We don't know anything about them and for the most part we don't wish too.

As population increases and people live longer, urban areas are becoming more packed than ever before and it will continue on an upward curve for as long as humans exist on the planet. There's no halting the bandwagon of evolution, we will continue to expand our numbers at the detriment of our own future and safety.

Serial killers usually prey on strangers, urban areas have provided them with a constant flow of what they need. It provides them with an ideal setting to act on their violent or perverse desires. As the world changes and moves towards more privacy than ever before, people are deliberately cutting themselves off from the world, not wishing to participate in social media or internet use.

This in turn provides more victims for the potential serial killer. Just as in the 1970s when urbanisation was forcing the world into a new era.

(Research Article #8) Disconnected Living

The internet brought the world together – and then allowed people to live in isolation without ever leaving their homes.

Loneliness or isolation is one of the biggest factors that lead to mental health disorder or suicidal ideation. It also allows some people to harvest their dark thoughts and subsequently see them in action. Some serial killers have spoken of isolation as one of their largest mitigating factors, and of course most serial killers murder in isolation.

In the 1978, video games were few and far between, sometimes only reserved for the better-off in society. Jump forward to 2020 and gaming is one of the biggest industries on Earth. By 2028, many will be using virtual reality as often as they use the internet, in fact both might be intertwined.

The internet will have more control over our daily lives and mobile devices will soon be able to access the internet wherever we go in the world. We can order food from a phone and have it delivered, there is no need to go out shopping anymore.

We can stream the latest films and music to any device in the home. There's no need to even order DVDs, no reason to go out and leave the house. We talk through microphones to people all over the world we meet in virtual worlds but we don't really know who they are.

In 2028, social media will have become more prevalent, taking over face to face interactions for the first time. We're interviewed online, befriended, loved or hated. We shop, download, stream and interact. Disconnected living becomes the norm and we focus more on the inverted unreal world of *The Net* than we do with reality.

Apply that thesis to one of an already disconnected mindset then the results can and will be devastating. Porn, violence, extremism, occult activity, terrorism, brutal imagery, hate, all are within easy reach with no real censorship. The governments of the world might attempt to put a stop to it but it's not going to slow down people seeking it out.

The British Government have already implemented a *soft* ban on hardcore BDSM with the *Audio-visual Media Services Regulations act of 2014*. But it hasn't worked, the images detailed in the list of banned activities are said to be more prevalent than ever before.

People are floating through their lives and not really connecting with the people around them. This level of disconnection and inward distraction is a boiling pot of mental health issues, violence and disassociation.

Leading up to 2028, the line between the real world and the virtual world are already blurred for some. There is a desperation at the heart of social media that holds validation over truth.

The danger in disconnected living is that it is too easy to float by in life and not contact anyone outside of online *friends*. Those with instincts to act on their dark thoughts have never found a bigger outlet and resource than there is in today's world.

That line blurs fantasy with reality. The mind of a serial killer might already find it hard to associate with either. Disconnected living might give those thinking of acting on dark thoughts a more realistic opportunity of doing so.

Fowler, Bobby Jack

American rapist and serial killer *Bobby Jack Fowler* is suspected of killing over 20 people. Advancements in cold case investigation and DNA technology has linked him to a number of murders over a 23 year period from 1973 to 1995.

As part of the *Royal Canadian Mounted Police E-Pana* Investigations, there is DNA evidence that matches Bobby Jack Fowler to the murder of 16-year-old *Colleen MacMillen* in August 1974. Her body was discovered in September 1974. She was last seen leaving her home to hitchhike to a nearby friend's house.

In November 1973, 19-year-old *Pamela Darlington* vanished from Kamloops while hitchhiking to a local bar. Her body was found the next day. She has been strongly suggested to have been a victim of Fowler's. In October 1973, 19-year-old *Gale*

Weys vanished while hitchhiking from Clearwater to Kamloops. Her body was found in a ditch on Highway 5 just south of Clearwater. Her death was also linked to Fowler.

In 2012, they used the advancement in DNA technology to positively identify him in the murder of MacMillen. The Royal Canadian Mounted Police strongly believe that he was responsible for at least 10 of the other victims on the list. However, many more murders took place after his arrest in 1995 when he was picked up on a rape charge.

As Fowler died in prison in 2006, the investigation of his suspected murders has been made more difficult. As of 2021, many of the cold cases remain an open investigation.

Born **June 12th 1939**.

Active from **1973-1995**.

Arrested on **June 28th 1995**.

Country: **USA**.

Victims: **1-20+**.

Sentence: **16 years in prison**.

Current whereabouts: **Died of natural causes in 2006**.

Francois, Kendall: The Poughkeepsie Killer (Extended Case File)

In Poughkeepsie, New York, serial killer *Kendall Francois*, AKA: *The Poughkeepsie Killer*, took the lives of at least eight women over a two year period from 1996 to 1998. He took the bodies home and stored them in his house that he shared with his parents.

As a child and into his teen years, Francois had poor hygiene and was bullied because of it. Other children in school called him 'Stinky' and the name stuck to become his nickname for years afterwards. He was also mocked for his weight and size, and because of it he became withdrawn from society, not talking much and keeping himself to himself.

The first murders began at the tail end of 1996 when Francois was 25-years-old. 30-year-old *Wendy Meyers* was murdered on October 24th 1996, she had last been seen at a Valley Rest Motel on the banks of the Hudson River. She had been spotted talking with Francois in his car over prices for her services. He then took her home and when she wanted to leave quickly, according to his confession, Francois strangled her to death.

He then took her body into one of the bathrooms and washed her corpse clean. Then he put her into a black bin bag and took it to his attic, where the body stayed for almost two years before being discovered. After Meyers death, Francois discovered his blood lust and went on to murder many more in quick succession.

On November 29th 1996, 28-year-old prostitute *Gina Barone* got into Francois's car and they drove to his garage where they had sex. Francois claimed that after sex, Barone wanted more money and so he strangled her to death in his car, leaving her body in the trunk until the next day. Then he cleaned her body and put in his attic next to the body of Meyers.

On November 31st 1996, just two days after his second murder, Francois kills 31-year-old prostitute Cathy Marsh. He had strangled her so hard that he had broken her hyoid bone, which is a bone in the upper spine just beneath the jawbone. He took the body home, cleaned it and put her in the attic next to the other bodies. Her mother wouldn't report her missing until four months later in March 1997.

In January of 1997, a 47-year-old prostitute named *Kathleen Hurley* vanished from the street she was working on. She had been brutally murdered by Francois who kept the body in his attic. Shortly after her disappearance, the media starting to latch on to the story of prostitutes being listed as missing and the police investigation finally began.

After a local newspaper report asked the question of a serial killer in the county, many prostitutes in the area pointed the finger at Francois, among others. They claimed that Francois preferred rough sex and enjoyed choking them at the same time. At the time, the police couldn't confirm either way if Francois was the killer so they had him and his home under surveillance.

In the Spring of 1997, the Poughkeepsie Police reached out to the FBI for help. On first look, the FBI didn't take the case because there were no bodies and no crime scene. Most times when people were reported missing, there was a simpler reason other than murder.

Due to individual circumstances, this could have included people who wished to live off-the-grid, committed a crime themselves, became homeless, family problems, drug issues, and multiple other reasons. A serial killer was the least likely reason.

Francois, aware of the investigation, held his bloodlust at bay, but not for long. On October 9th 1997, 27-year-old prostitute *Michelle Eason* vanished from the downtown area she was working. She was the first black woman to be killed by Francois, all of the previous and later victims were white and of a smaller build.

One month later, on November 13th 1997, 29-year-old *Mary Healy Giaccone* was reported missing by her father. Giaccone's mother had just died, and her father went to the police to ask for help in finding her to give her the bad news. When they investigated, it appeared that Giaccone was last seen working the streets back in February of 1997.

Suddenly, the media and area began to fear that a serial killer really was stalking the streets. The Poughkeepsie Journal ran multiple stories on the missing women, and the police kept up the investigation. On January 18th 1998, a police officer followed Francois to his mother's workplace where Francois was giving her a lift. After he dropped her off, police arrested him and asked him to come in for questioning. They gave him a lie-detector test which he passed with flying colours.

Just five days later, he picked up prostitute *Lora Gallagher*, and took her back to his house. He throttled her during sex, and she passed out, only to awaken later underneath Francois's full body weight. She fought herself free and demanded to be taken back to the streets.

Surprisingly, Francois agreed and took her back downtown, where Gallagher told others about her experience. Prostitutes who heard the story then took their concerns to the vice squad. It took an entire month to convince Gallagher to sign an official statement against Francois. But as soon as she did, Francois was arrested, on February 26th 1998.

On May 18th 1998, Francois was convicted of the assault on Gallagher. Astonishingly he was only sentenced to 15 days in prison for the assault. Even more astonishingly, he would serve only seven days in prison. It would only be four weeks after his release that he would kill again.

June 12th 1998, he killed 51-year-old *Sandra French*, during sex. He hid her body in the attic after cleaning her body. Due to the smell and the overcrowding of corpses in the attic, he decided to move her body to the crawlspace of his house.

August 12th 1998, 34-year-old *Audrey Pugliese* was killed by Francois. She suffered the most brutal murder of all the prostitutes he killed. Francois claimed that he 'flipped-out' during sex and started punching her in the face, but Pugliese got away and ran into the basement, in an attempt to run out the basement door.

Francois grabbed her and pulled her back to the concrete floor where he continued a barrage of punches to her face. Angry with her, and not content with the punching, Francois started stamping on her. He crushed her ribs, and her stomach, then stamped on her face. Then he strangled her to ensure she was dead, before dumping her body in the crawlspace.

Just two weeks later on August 26th, he killed his final victim; 25-year-old prostitute *Catina Newmaster*. A day later, he moved her cleaned body to the crawlspace to join the others.

The prostitute community was outraged and claimed the police didn't care about them.

"We're low life's, that's what it comes down to. People don't care that we're missing

because they think we don't belong on the streets in the first place. It's not just the police, it's the community."

Interview with a prostitute – Poughkeepsie Journal, July 26th 1998.

Unknown to the community and Francois at the time, there had been an ongoing investigation that involved the local police, State police, and the FBI, who had finally pooled their resources. Yet even though Francois had already been convicted of assault, he still hadn't been caught.

On September 2nd, Francois picked up *Diane Franco* and took her back to his house where he attacked her during sex. She fought him off and convinced him to take her back to the street. Surprisingly, he agreed, and took her back to where he had picked her up. She reported the attack immediately and police arrested Francois shortly after.

That same evening, a warrant was served on Francois's house, and an army of police and investigators descended on the property. Amazingly, his parents and sister were in the house and were asked to leave so a search could begin.

Detectives later stated that the inside of the house had the most overpowering stench of death they had ever encountered. The house was a complete mess, with clothes and rubbish on the floor, dirty washing, mouldy food strewn about the place, and maggots in the sink. One forensic expert stated the house to be '*completely toxic*'. A couple of days later, a total of eight bodies were brought out of the house, as media vans lined the streets. A month later, Francois was charged with eight murders. He pleaded guilty and a trial by jury was not required, thus avoiding the death penalty. He was sentenced to life in prison without the possibility of parole.

Once he was sentenced, more disturbing details of the case were released. One investigator claimed that after spending a few hours in the house that his boots were eroded because of the amount of human '*sludge*'. When the bodies decomposed to skeletons, Francois removed their skulls and placed them in a children's paddling pool in the attic.

Back in 1995, he had contracted HIV from a prostitute, and may have been one of the reasons why he decided to kill. His only claimed motive was that he became angry during sex and couldn't control what he was doing.

His parents and sister claimed to have no idea what he was doing, despite living in disgusting conditions. They said that Francois claimed a Raccoon had died somewhere in the house and that's what was causing the smell. His neighbours were aware of the smell and the rundown look of the house but didn't complain to authorities or call the police.

On September 11th 2014, aged only 43-years-old, Francois died in prison of natural causes. The cause of death has never been listed but is assumed to be a condition related to him being HIV positive.

Born **July 26th 1971.**

Active from **1996-1998.**

Arrested on **September 1st 1998.**

Country: **USA.**

Victims: **8+.**

AKA: **The Poughkeepsie Killer.**

Current whereabouts: **Died of natural causes on September 11th 2014.**

KENDALL FRANCOIS

IMAGE ATTRIBUTIONS
(ATTRIB A22) (ATTRIB A23)

KENDALL FRANCOIS' FORMER HOME TAKEN THREE MONTHS AFTER POLICE SEARCHED THE HOUSE AND REMOVED THE BODIES

LONNIE DAVID FRANKLIN JR.

IMAGE ATTRIB. A24

PEDRO RODRIGUEZ FILHO

IMAGE ATTRIB. A79

Frankford Slasher, The. (Extended Case File)

The Frankford Slasher is a moniker for a serial killer who was active in and around the Frankford region of Philadelphia, in Pennsylvania, from 1985 to 1990. A black man named *Leonard Christopher* was convicted for one of the nine linked victims. He was convicted on minimal evidence and most witnesses saw the victims with a middle-aged white man before their deaths. All of the victims were sexually assaulted and stabbed to death.

On August 26th 1985, the body of 52-year-old *Helen Patent* was found by transit workers at a train yard in Philadelphia. She had been left half-naked and laid out in a provocative manner. She had been stabbed 47 times and her organs had been exposed by the vicious attack.

On January 3rd 1986, only a few miles from the first victim, the brutalised body of *Anna Carroll* was found on the floor of her bedroom. She too had been left nude and in a provocative position. She had been stabbed six times and had been gutted, exposing her insides. The kitchen knife used in the attack was left inside of her.

After a third victim was discovered on Christmas Day, 1986, investigators began to make connections. All three victims had been regulars at the *Goldie's Bar* on Frankford Avenue. The area had been well known for drug users and had a reputation as a big nightlife centre.

On January 8th 1987, the body of *Jeanne Durkin* was discovered beneath a storage truck just off of Frankford Avenue. She had been stabbed 74 times and was found in a pool of her own blood. She was naked from the waist down and had also been positioned in a provocative position. Durkin was a homeless woman who was commonly seen sleeping in an entranceway just a few doors down from Goldie's Bar. It was then that investigators realised a serial killer was at large.

They informed the media that the crimes were not related and the killings stopped for an entire year. Until January 1988 when 66-year-old *Margaret Vaughan* was found murdered in a similar fashion to the previous four victims. They created a sketch of the murderer who had been seen drinking with her in Goldie's Bar, and asked the public for help.

Another year passed and another victim was found in January of 1989. 30-year-old *Theresa Sciortino* was found in her apartment just outside of the Frankford region of the city. She had been stabbed 25 times and was found on the kitchen floor in a pool of her own blood.

Her wounds had been caused by a kitchen knife which was left at the scene. Next to her body was a three-foot section of wood that had been used to sexually violate her with. Investigators discovered that she was also a regular at the Goldie's Bar.

Another year passed and yet another body turned up on April 19th 1990. The body of *Carol Dowd* was discovered in an alley near a fish market. She had been raped and stabbed 36 times. Due to the brutality of the attack, her intestines had spilled out of her body. Then a connection was made between Dowd and two of the previous victims; Sciortino and Durkin. They had all been in and out of psychiatric wards in the years prior to their murders.

Upon interviewing some of the fish market employees they met with Leonard Christopher who worked there and lived in the area. He said that he knew one of the victims; Margaret Vaughan. Because he did not have an alibi, he was arrested on May 5th 1990 and charged with Dowd's murder.

Witness stories were all over the place, some placed him at the scene of the crime, while others said he was of good character and was nowhere near the murder scenes. On June 20th 1990, Christopher stood trial for the murder of Carol Dowd as the evidence was deemed sufficient enough.

His description didn't fit the one given by witnesses for the other murders but on December 12th 1990, Christopher was sentenced to life for the murder of Dowd. The evidence was circumstantial at best but it didn't matter. Not even when another body was found.

Two months earlier on September 6th, while Christopher was in prison awaiting trial, the body of 30-year-old *Michelle Denher* was found in her apartment just one block away from Frankford. She had been raped and stabbed 23 times. Her body had been found in a provocative position and she had a large slash to her stomach which exposed her intestines.

Astonishingly, Denher was also a psychiatric patient, who lived just three blocks away from the previous murder, and also drank in Goldie's Bar. A day before her murder, she had been seen with a middle-aged white man who fitted the original description of The Frankford Slasher.

The public were not convinced that Christopher had killed Dowd, and so the story had caught the attention of local media and community groups. One theory even pointed to witchcraft, due to a cult presence in the area that held rituals in a local park.

Investigators have since claimed there is no evidence that pointed to Christopher being The Frankford Slasher. As of 2021, the eight other murders are now part of an active cold case.

Leonard Christopher has since died of cancer.

Active from **1985-1990.**

Country: **USA.**

Victims: **9.**

Current whereabouts: **Unidentified killer. Status unknown.**

Franklin, Joseph Paul: The Racist Killer (Extended Case File)

In March of 1978, American porn king, *Larry Flynt*, was shot and paralysed by *Joseph Paul Franklin*, AKA: *The Racist Killer*. He ambushed Larry Flynt and his lawyer, in retaliation for an edition of *Hustler* displaying interracial sex. He would go on to kill between seven and 22 victims.

Born in 1950, he became a white supremacist and killed most of his victims from the late 1970s to the early 1980s. It is still unknown to this day how many he actually killed. He was executed by lethal injection in November of 2013.

He was born *James Clayton Vaughn Jr.* to a turbulent family. His father was a World War Two veteran who would physically abuse his children. His mother was considered to be an extremely strict disciplinarian who also physically abused him and his siblings. Franklin would go on to have stunted development in childhood and didn't mature as fast as his peers.

In his school years, he developed an interest in *Nazi's*, the *Ku Klux Klan*, and the *National Socialist White People's Party*. He changed his name to Joseph Paul Franklin to honour Nazi propagandist *Paul Joseph Goebbels* and former president *Benjamin Franklin*. He was inspired to kill 'blacks' after consuming *Hitler's Mein Kampf*.

The July 29th killing of *Bryant Tatum* outside a *Pizza Hut* in Tennessee was slap-bang in the middle of his horrific campaign of killings. That same moment, he also shot Tatum's white girlfriend, *Nancy Hilton*, who would go on to survive the shooting.

His first notable crime was exactly one year before on July 29th, 1977. He firebombed a Synagogue in Tennessee, completely razing it to the ground. Luckily, there were no deaths as not many worshippers had turned up on the evening he chose.

Would he deliberately seek to kill exactly one year later? It has never been made known. But the fact it was the same date suggests more than just coincidence. It's possible Franklin felt the failure of a lack of deaths the year before and sought revenge on the same date in 1978.

"I was looking to cleanse the world of the inferior races."

Joseph Paul Franklin.

Franklin fitted the *Drifter Killer* personality and used the newly constructed highways and interstates to roam up and down the East Coast of the United States. He would look to cleanse the world of mostly black and Jewish people. He paid his way by committing armed robberies at banks and also with blood-bank donations.

Over the years he had covered himself in racist tattoos and it wasn't long until the FBI discovered he had been visiting blood-banks. They put out a nationwide alert and a Florida-based blood-bank worker recognised the tattoos and phoned it in. It led to him being caught by the FBI in 1980.

"A government that forbids killing among its citizens should not be in the business of killing people itself."

Franklin's defence of his crimes.

He had attempted to incite a race war and had failed. He was sentenced to death and executed by lethal injection on November 20th 2013. He did not make a final written statement or say any last words before his death.

Born **April 13th 1950**.

Active from **1977-1980**.

Arrested on **September 25th 1980.**

Country: **USA.**

Victims: **7-22.**

AKA: **The Racist Killer / James Clayton Vaughn, Jr.**

Sentence: **Death penalty.**

Current whereabouts: **Executed by lethal injection on November 20th 2013.**

Franklin Jr., Lonnie David: The Grim Sleeper (Extended Case File)

On April 15th 1987, the body of 26-year-old *Bernita Sparks* was discovered in Gramercy Park, Los Angeles. She had died at the hands of LA-based serial killer *Lonnie David Franklin Jr.* When he was arrested in 2010 he had claimed at least 10 victims but is suspected and linked to a possible 25.

Franklin killed seven people from 1985 to 1988 but then came a 14 year gap when there were no killings. He then killed again three more times from 2002 to 2007. The gap between the killings earned him the notorious moniker of *The Grim Sleeper*.

Franklin killed over many decades and is one of the serial killers with the longest time-span of murders. He murdered destitute black women in South Central Los Angeles over a three year period from 1985 to 1988 but resurfaced in 2002 to begin killing again.

Franklin, Jr. was a respected member of the local community and would help people to take their bins out or do some handiwork. So no one would have ever expected him to be a serial killer. In his other life as a killer of women, he would murder prostitutes, drug addicts, or homeless runaways. He generally raped them before shooting them in the chest at close range. He then left their bodies in alleyways, in trash cans, or beside industrial bins. He knew the alleys well as he was a sanitation worker at the time.

He kept his victim's underwear and jewellery as a keepsake of his crimes. When he was arrested, the investigators found a large collection of pornographic Polaroids. They depicted unconscious women, either dead or alive. There were more photographs than the killings he was convicted of, leading to speculation that he may have killed many more.

Not too much is known about his childhood but he grew up in South Central, an area of Los Angeles known for its violence and high crime rate. Police relations at the time were non-existent, and gang violence became an epidemic in the area.

However, in 1974 while in his early twenties, serving in the U.S Army as a cook, he took part in a gang-rape of a German girl whilst based in Stuttgart. He was discharged a year later due to the incident. In a 1974 trial, the victim; *Ingrid W*, explained with the help of an interpreter that Franklin and two others jumped out a car and held a knife to her throat. She was gang-raped by the three of them over the course of an entire night.

Franklin testified the encounter was consensual but was convicted in a German court where he served less than a year in prison. During the rape, Franklin was known to have taken photos of the incident, in a dark foreshadowing of the murders to come.

In 1987, he became injured while working as a sanitation worker and spent the following two decades on disability handouts. In 1988, one of his victims was *Enietra Washington*, who was 30-years-old when she accepted a ride from Franklin. He drove her to an alley, raped, beat and shot her. Washington was left for dead near some trash cans but survived. She got away alive and her testimony was instrumental in the recent court case against him.

In 2007, the *LAPD* created a task force to find *The Grim Sleeper* and this was partly due to the reporting of an *LA Weekly* journalist named *Christine Pelisek*. She had noticed a pattern of murdered black women but with no reports of any arrests, so she wrote a story about it which led to the creation of the task force. It was Pelisk herself who had come up with Grim Sleeper moniker.

In 2010, Franklin was arrested after the investigation had used familial DNA searching. Franklin's son had previously been arrested for gun and drug offences, and his DNA was on the systems they searched. When they made the match, Franklin was found soon after and charged.

In June of 2016, Franklin was sentenced to death for 10 murders and one attempted murder. It has been suggested that he killed many more. He is currently on death row awaiting execution.

Born **August 30th 1952**.

Active from **1985-2007**.

Arrested on **July 7th 2010**.

Country: **USA**.

Victims: **10-25+**.

AKA: **The Grim Sleeper**.

Sentence: **Death penalty**.

Current whereabouts: **Death row**.

Fyfe, William Patrick

William Patrick Fyfe, AKA: *The Killer Handyman* is a Canadian serial killer convicted of the murders of five women in the Montreal. He confessed to killing four more and killed his victim when he was 24-years-old, in 1979.

He was arrested in December of 1999 when DNA evidence on a door frame of a victim's house led police to him. He killed his victims by bludgeoning or stabbing them to death and was motivated by sexual perversity. He was convicted in 2000 and is now serving a life sentence at a psychiatric hospital in Saskatchewan.

Montreal Police also believe he was the serial rapist who had been referred to as *The Plumber.* The rapist carried out a large number of violent rapes throughout the 1980s in the Montreal area.

Born **February 27th 1955.**

Active from **1979-1999.**

Arrested in **December 1999.**

Country: **Canada**.

Victims: **5-9+**.

AKA: **The Killer Handyman / The Plumber.**

Sentence: **Life sentence in a psychiatric hospital.**

Current whereabouts: **High-security psychiatric hospital.**

Furlan, Marco and Abel, Wolfgang

German-Italian serial killing duo, *Wolfgang Abel and Marco Furlan* were sentenced to 30 years each on February 10th 1987. They took part in the murders of at least 10 people from 1977 to 1984 in Germany, Italy and the Netherlands.

On December 17th 1978, a gay waiter in Italy was stabbed 30 times with two blades left sticking out of his back. It was suggested that between them they may have claimed up to 28 victims.

At each crime scene they left a leaflet, written in Italian, it showed a Nazi Eagle and swastika and each of them had a different slogan. *"We are the last of the Nazis"* and *"Death comes to those who betray the true god"* being two of them.

They were caught in 1984 and were both sentenced to 30 years each on February 10th 1987. Furlan was subsequently released in 2010. Abel was released to house arrest and then finally released to live amongst us in 2016.

Born **March 25th 1959 (Abel), January 16th 1960 (Furlan).**

Active from **1977-1984.**

Arrested on **March 4th 1984.**

Country: **Italy / Germany / Netherlands.**

Victims: **10-28.**

AKA: **Ludwig.**

Sentence: **Life sentences.**

Current whereabouts: **Furlan was released in 2010. Abel was released in 2016. Their current whereabouts are unknown.**

Gacy, John Wayne: The Killer Clown (Extended Case File)

On December 22nd 1978, the very same day as Andrei Chikatilo's first victim, *John Wayne Gacy, The Killer Clown,* is arrested.

In February of 1978, Gacy killed a 19-year-old man named *William Kindred.* William told his girlfriend he was going to a bar for the evening but ended up becoming another of Gacy's 33 victims. The figure of 33 is speculative as it is suggested there could be many more victims attributed to him. William Kindred was the last victim to be buried in Gacy's crawl space.

The Killer Clown would rape and kill 33 young men over a small time period of just a few years. 29 of his victim's remains were discovered in the crawlspace and other areas beneath his home. He would kill his victims mostly in the middle of sexual acts of bondage or raping them with various sex toys. He would find an orgasmic-like feel in taking their lives in such a manner.

Gacy, born in Chicago, was one of three children. He was born in 1942, in the middle of World War Two. His father was a World War One veteran and would physically abuse his wife and his children. He had also become an alcoholic after his return from the war.

In one of this book's research articles, we talk about the legacy of World War Two and not so much about The Great War, 30 years before. It goes without saying that a survivor or veteran of any war is susceptible to various mental disorders or depression. That Gacy's father abused him could have been a direct result of his own traumas experienced in World War One.

Gacy's father would beat him with leather belts and broomsticks and put his sisters in higher esteem than him. It was this sexual belittlement that led to Gacy growing up believing he was a '*sissy*' and would grow up '*queer*'. Something that would be one of the main elements of his murders in that he only killed boys and men.

When he was seven-years-old, Gacy was caught sexually playing with a young girl. His father then whipped him with a strip of hardened leather. That same year, Gacy was sexually abused by a family friend, in a van. He kept the abuse secret through fear of his father's punishments.

John Wayne Gacy became an extremely complicated person growing up. His sexual confusion was coming to the forefront of his mind and his inability to fit in simply wasn't working for him. He moved to Las Vegas in 1962 and became a mortuary attendant. He would sleep on a bed behind the embalming room and watch the morticians embalm the bodies. Once, when he was alone, he laid in a coffin with a deceased teenage boy, where he embraced and caressed the body.

He moved back to Illinois, married for the first time and became a candidate for the *Democrat Party*. He then became a *KFC* franchise manager and was generally respected in the community. His wife gave birth to two children but then started divorce proceedings when he was convicted of male rape. During his killing campaign and because of his services at fund-raisers, children's parties and parades, he would regularly dress up as *Pogo the Clown*. Sometimes he would be *Patches the Clown*. These monikers led to Gacy being nicknamed The Killer Clown.

Rumours had begun to spread that he was having sexual relationships with other men who worked for him in the KFC restaurants. He was a member of the United States Junior Chamber Organisation known as *Jaycees*, which is a training organisation for people aged between 18 and 40-years-old. The *Waterloo Jaycees Club* had a dark side where Gacy relished in prostitution, drug addiction and ample amounts of pornography.

In 1968 he lured a man to his home, on the same day his wife was giving birth to his son. He tied him up and raped him. The man went straight to the police and Gacy was arrested. He was sentenced to ten years but astonishingly served less than two years for good behaviour. He was so angered at his wife for the divorce proceedings that he disowned her and his two children, never seeing any of them again.

He then married a second time to an old school friend, never had children and subsequently divorced a few years later. During their marriage he was heavily involved in gay pornography and his wife would find wallets and personal items of other men but never questioned it.

A few months before he married again, Gacy had claimed his first known victim. In January 1972 he had picked up a 16-year-old boy name *Timothy McCoy*. Gacy would claim that McCoy approached him with a knife and he defended himself only to then stab McCoy in the chest multiple times. Gacy would bury him in the crawlspace of his house and cover the body with a layer of concrete.

He would go on to rape many more men before his step up to murder had taken over him. One of Gacy's employees named *David Cram*, lived with Gacy for a while after his second divorce. Together they dug the trenches under the crawlspace in his house. It is claimed later than Cram could have been helping Gacy with the killings and movement of the bodies.

His second victim in 1974 was a teenage boy of unknown origin. He put the body in his closet but fluid leaked from the boy's mouth and nose and so for subsequent victims, Gacy would push rags or the victim's own underwear into their mouths.

He killed most of his victims in a two year period from 1976 to 1978. He would generally rape them as part of sex games and then stab or strangle them to death. He would sometimes torture them, and one surviving victim was testament to his perversity.

In 1977 he abducted 19-year-old student *Robert Donnelly* from a bus stop at gunpoint. Gacy abused, tortured and raped him with various sex toys and tools. He tortured him with water torture by dunking his head in a bath, raped him constantly, violently assaulted him and beat him. But then Gacy threw him in his car and drove him back to Donnelly's own home.

Donnelly stated in an interview that the pain from the torture had been so bad, he wished Gacy had killed him. Police turned up at Gacy's house but he claimed they had consensual BDSM sex and he was released with no charge. As the net closed in, Gacy would later state he knew he was going to be caught. When he started dumping bodies in the river instead of burying them in the crawlspace of his house then the investigation led back to him.

Gacy quickly flooded the crawlspace under the house to hide the evidence. When an evidence technician named *Daniel Genty* went down there as part of the investigation, he waited for the water to drain away.

He found skeletal remains, decaying flesh and obvious signs of multiple murders. He told the investigation; "I think this place is full of kids."

Upon his arrest Gacy confessed to the murders and claimed that he had lost count of the amount of bodies in the crawlspace. He had thought about covering the crawlspace in concrete to hide the evidence but he never got around to it.

He killed five people in 1978 and they were all dumped in the river. During the investigation, 26 bodies were recovered from the crawlspace and one beneath the concrete floor of his garage. A week later, another body was recovered under the dining room floor.

Gacy was convicted of 33 murders and was sentenced to death by lethal injection for 12 of them. He was executed in 1994 but the execution was marred by a botched IV tube. There was a problem with the tube when the drugs solidified and had to be replaced, the execution subsequently took 18 minutes.

Following his death, Gacy's brain was removed for medical study.

Born **March 17th 1942.**

Active from **1972-1978.**

Arrested on **December 21st 1978.**

Country: **USA.**

Victims: **33+.**

AKA: **The Killer Clown.**

Sentence: **Death penalty.**

Current whereabouts: **Executed by lethal injection in 1994.**

WHITE HOUSE PHOTOGRAPH OF FIRST LADY ROSALYNN CARTER WITH DEMOCRATIC PARTY ACTIVIST AND SERIAL KILLER JOHN WAYNE GACY

JOHN WAYNE GACY IN CLOWN SUIT

PAINTING BY GACY

IMAGE ATTRIBUTIONS
(ATTRIB A3) (ATTRIB A25)
(ATTRIB A26) (ATTRIB A71)

JOHN WAYNE GACY

Gallego, Gerald and Charlene: The Love Slave Killers (Extended Case File)

On September 11th 1978, two teenagers were abducted by *Gerald Armond Gallego* and *Charlene Adell Gallego* who became known as *The Love Slave Killers*.

Between 1978 and 1980, the Gallego's hunted young girls and turned them into sex slaves before brutally murdering them. They would go on to kill ten people before their arrest in 1980.

Gerald came from a disruptive childhood, his mother was a prostitute and his father was a violent criminal who killed two policeman. He was the first person to be executed in a gas chamber in Mississippi, in 1955.

His mother and her various boyfriends abused Gerald in his formative years. During her time as a prostitute, she allowed some of her clients to sexually abuse him. It is said that this level of abuse and neglect led him to sexually abuse a six-year-old girl when he was only 13-years-old. During his teens and shortly after, he was arrested 23 times on various criminal charges.

When Charlene was young, her mother was badly hurt in a car crash. She would then join her father on his business trips when her mother was home bound. She was said to have been a smart and intelligent young girl. For unexplained reasons, she turned to heavy alcohol and drug use in her early teens and told everyone she was having sex with a black man.

She would be married twice before meeting Gerald. Her first husband was a wealthy heroin addict, and his drug addiction increased her dependency on drugs. Her first husband would later claim that Charlene was a sex addict whose fetishes included lesbian sex and threesomes with prostitutes. It is unclear why sex would become overtly important to someone of such a young age. It was never known if she was abused in childhood or not.

Gerald worked as a barman and truck driver. Amazingly, he was married a total of seven times, including two marriages to the same woman. He would leave them mostly because they were running out of money. He would also begin to abuse his daughter on a regular basis. When he married Charlene, he was already married to his previous wife.

Gerald enjoyed rough sex and Charlene was happy to oblige his violent perversity. It is claimed they were more sexually compatible than others had been in their own lives. Charlene said in court that Gerald preferred to sodomise her during most sessions and that it was a painful experience, though she would feign enjoyment to make him happy.

On September 11th, 1978, two teens, *Rhonsa Scheffler* and *Kippi Vaught* went missing from a mall in Sacramento. It was Charlene who lured them into a van that was parked close by. Gerald used a handgun to threaten the girls before tying them up.

They drove all the way to Baxter where he abused and raped the girls before shooting them in the back of the head. In June of 1979, two more girls were abducted in Nevada. Gerald beat them to a bloody death with a hammer and a shovel. Their bodies remained undiscovered for over two decades.

They would abduct and kill six more people before their final two victims. In November of 1980, they kidnapped two students at a fraternity party. The man was shot and found later near a lake. The girl, *Mary Sowers*, was taken to the Gallego's apartment. She remained captive as Gerald abused and raped her. Afterwards, he took her to the middle of a field and shot her in the back of the head.

The kidnapping of the two students was witnessed and the police tracked the Gallego's number plate. It seems the Gallego's had been sloppy in their final abduction and were subsequently arrested.

Charlene testified against her husband in a plea deal that only saw her receive a 16-year sentence. Charlene claims that it was Gerald who killed every single one of them.

"There were victims who died, and there were victims who lived. It's taken me a

hell of a long time to realize that I'm one of the ones who lived."

Charlene Gallego, in one of her interviews.

Doubt has sometimes been thrown on her responsibility of the crimes but she was released in 1997 under a new identity. She was discovered a few years later living a life in the same neighbourhood where the murders took place and has shown no remorse for her crimes.

She was revealed by a local reporter in a bizarre interview regarding a different matter, which has never been made public. However, the community discovered and have revered her presence ever since.

One resident claimed that Charlene had been a thanksgiving guest of hers the year before. She had been sitting across from the parents of one of her victims and they never knew. Due to potential lawsuits, her new identity will not be revealed here but the community in question is enraged.

"Gallego's audacity at moving back to the area where most of the killings took place pales to her ongoing audacity of hosting fundraising events, and leading a veterans' event, including posing for photographs. She doesn't care."

Local reporter.

Gerald was sentenced in 1983 to death by gas chamber at the notorious *San Quentin State Prison*. He died of cancer in a Nevada prison medical centre, in 2002.

Born **July 17th 1946 (Gerald), October 10th 1956 (Charlene).**

Active from **1978-1980.**

Arrested on **November 17th 1980.**

Country: **USA.**

Victims: **10.**

AKA: **The Love Slave Killers.**

Sentence: **Gerald - death penalty. Charlene - 16 years in prison.**

Current whereabouts: **Gerald died of cancer in 2002. Charlene was released in 1997 to live among us.**

Garavito, Luis: The Beast (Extended Case File)

Luis Garavito, AKA*: The Beast*, killed children and teenagers in Colombia, from 1992 until 1999. In just a seven year period, his confirmed number of victims totals 138 but is suspected to be around 300. He has since been described as the world's worst serial killer.

In terms of number of *convicted* victims, *Harold 'Dr. Death' Shipman*, from the United Kingdom, is the world's worst serial killer after being convicted of 215 murders and linked to a total of 250. Another Colombian, *Pedro Lopez*, was convicted of 110 murders and is sometimes listed as the world's worst serial killer, but The Beast is even worse.

On June 8th 1996, a young boy went missing in the town of Boyaca. He had been lured to his death by The Beast. Five days later, the decapitated body was discovered in a remote area, the boy's penis had been sliced off and stuck inside his mouth.

The mother discovered that Garavito had bought her son sweets before the disappearance and he was arrested on suspicion of the murder. He told police he bought the boy sweets but nothing more, he was believed and the police didn't follow up on it. Just four days later, he killed a 13-year-old boy in the nearby town of Pereira.

Born in Genova, Colombia, in 1957, he was the eldest of seven children. Garavito and his brothers were beaten regularly by their father. Garavito was also emotionally, physically, and sexually abused by his neighbour. And for the crimes inflicted on him, he would take revenge by hurting hundreds of children.

Before he turned to murder, he drifted from job to job, becoming an alcoholic in the process. From his alcoholism, he turned to a more aggressive personality and would have a temper that he found difficult to control. It is claimed that he attempted suicide at least once and had been in and out of psychiatric care for five years before the killings began.

"We are not facing some sort of criminal genius, we are confronting an individual who had no inhibiting restraints to killing."

Pablo Gonzalez – state prosecutor's investigative team. (1999).

His victims were mainly young boys between the ages of six-years-old to 16-years-old. He would lure them from the streets of Colombia and just over the border in Ecuador. He would rape, beat, torture and slaughter his victims, burying them in shallow graves.

In Colombia, in the early 1990s, the country was suffering from the effects of a long-running civil war and many children were either abandoned or living below the poverty line. Many children were not listed as missing and Garavito's crimes went unnoticed for many years.

As with Pedro Lopez, Garavito would bury his victims in mass graves and once one site was discovered, the authorities finally took notice. Even in 2021, some bodies are still being discovered on the outskirts of rural villages where the victims match Garavito's other victims.

He kept souvenirs of his victims, which sometimes included their passport photos.

He also kept a detailed list of when and where most of them died. Most of the remains were found with broken bones, most likely inflicted whilst the boys were alive.

Garavito admitted to raping or sexually abusing every one of his victims. He kept some of the victims tied up for two or three days, usually to a tree by a leash. He would play with them and abuse them softly before raping them in a rising crescendo that would end with their deaths. Some victims were found with bite marks on their genitals.

He would kill them by cutting their throats and bleeding them dry. He would usually go on to dismember the corpses with a dull knife before burying parts of them in different places. He remembered where he buried every single one of his victims, so much so that he would draw the investigators a map to most of them. He led police to one mass grave at a ravine that consisted of 25 skeletal remains.

In a similar fashion to Pedro Lopez, he would lure boys with the promise of cakes or candy. Sometimes, he would be pretend to be a priest in order to gain their trust. Shockingly, a lot of children were addicted to drugs in Colombia at the time, and the promise of drugs was another method that Garavito used to lure them to isolated areas.

He did this in over 54 cities across the two countries, making the links and investigation even more difficult. He would also spend time watching his victims to ensure that a boy was *worthy* of being his victim. His preference was for lighter-skinned boys with soft skin.

Upon his arrest, Garavito confessed and asked forgiveness from the investigators. He claimed that a demon would possess him and take control of his body during the murders. This combined with the alcohol consumption meant that he was not in control of his body when raping and killing. He even said that upon his release from prison, he wished to begin a political career, with a focus on helping abused children.

In 1998, the bodies of three children were found on the outskirts of Genua, Colombia, and an investigation into a possible serial killer opened. A mother of one of the boys told police about an older man who was seen with him before he disappeared.

On April 22nd 1999, Garavito was arrested on an attempted rape charge, after being stopped by a member of the public. The investigators looking into the rape began to believe they had *The Beast* in custody. An interrogation led to Garavito confessing to the murders, it is claimed the descriptions of his murders brought him to tears.

At one of the mass graves, a pair of glasses had been found. The glasses were designed for a rare eye condition that Garavito happened to suffer from. At other graves, empty bottles of alcohol, his shoes or his own underwear were found buried with the victims. The police took DNA from the pillow and bedsheets in his police cell and it matched the DNA found at the mass graves.

He was charged with 172 murders and convicted of 138. The exact location of the prison where he is serving his sentence is unavailable to the public due to the fear that he would be killed immediately.

Garavito was sentenced to 1,853 years in prison. Astonishingly because of good behaviour and the way the Colombian sentencing system works, his sentenced was reduced. Even more astonishingly, he is now eligible for release at some point during 2021.

Born **January 25th 1957.**

Active from **1992-1999.**

Arrested on **April 22nd 1999.**

Country: **Colombia.**

Victims: **138-300.**

AKA: **The Beast / El Loco.**

Sentence: **1,853 years in prison.**

Current whereabouts: **In prison with a release date of 2021.**

Gargiulo, Michael Thomas

American serial killer, *Michael Thomas Gargiulo*, AKA: *The Hollywood Ripper*, killed at least two women but has been linked with at least two more murders. In 2019, he was convicted of two murders. He has been heavily linked to a murder in 1993.

In Illinois, where Gargiulo grew up, he murdered his 18-year-old neighbour, Tricia Pacaccio, by stabbing her to death on her porch. A few years later, Gargiulo moved to Los Angeles in a suspected effort to escape the investigation. While living in Hollywood, he began killing again.

On February 21st 2001, Gargiulo stabbed up-and-coming actress *Ashley Ellerin* 47 times, in a frenzied attack at the victim's home. The stabbing was so brutal that her head had nearly been severed. The depth of the blade had passed through her body on numerous occasions. One of the stab wounds to the head entered the skull and removed a section of bone, as if it was a piece of a puzzle.

On the night she was killed, she had a planned dinner with Hollywood actor *Ashton Kutcher.* In May 2019, Kutcher would testify at Gargiulo's trial about his planned evening with Ellerin. Kutcher had knocked on Ellerin's door later that night but there was no answer. He then assumed Ellerin had left early because he was a little late and left the property. Ellerin was discovered by her housemate the following day.

In December of 2005, Gargiulo stabbed to death his neighbour. 32-year-old *Mario Bruno* was stabbed 17 times at her home in El Monte. She had been asleep in her bed when the attack began.

In April 2008, Gargiulo went to the home of his neighbour, *Michelle Murphy*, and attempted to kill her. Murphy fought back and overpowered him, kicking him away from the bed. Gargiulo had apparently expressed his apologies before he left her home.

Gargiulo was arrested shortly after and charged with the two Hollywood murders, the murder of his 18-year-old neighbour in 1993, and one of attempted murder. Due to multiple delays, the trial wouldn't begin until 2019. In August of 2019, he was convicted of the two Hollywood murders.

In March 2020, a jury handed down the death sentence. But sentencing has been delayed indefinitely while Judge Larry P. Fidler considers a defence motion regarding a sheriff who may have been smuggling contraband into the county jail at the time of the trial. As of October 2020, the defence motion is still being heard.

Born **February 15th 1976.**

Active from **1993-2005.**

Arrested on **June 6th 2008.**

Country: **USA.**

Victims: **3.**

AKA: **The Hollywood Ripper.**

Sentence: **Awaiting sentencing.**

Gary, Carlton: The Stocking Strangler (Extended Case File)

February 12th 1978 saw Georgia's most famous serial killer step up his campaign of violence against elderly women.

African-American, *Carlton Michael Gary* was finally executed on March 15th, 2018. He was convicted of armed robbery and the murders of three elderly women in Columbus, Georgia. He is suspected of killing four more but was never convicted. His suspected number of victims are seven.

Carlton's father abandoned him until a brief meeting when he was 12-years-old. He constantly moved around with his mother and was found to be malnourished most of the time. In the modern era, malnourishment in children is generally the responsibility of the parents and classified as child abuse.

His aunt was a maid for elderly, wealthy women. It was in his time spent with his aunt that his hatred and fascination with elderly women seeped into his thought processes.

His childhood saw him turn to crime pretty quickly. He began to use drugs heavily and was arrested multiple times before he was 18-years-old. Mostly for robbery, arson, or assault. When he was 20-years-old, two elderly women were killed in the Albany region, and a third was assaulted.

Upon his capture by way of fingerprints, he claimed that it was an accomplice that had murdered the women and that he only robbed them. His testimony against *John Lee Mitchell*, the 'accomplice', had no material evidence except Carlton's own words. Even so, Mitchell was convicted of the murders while Carlton served time on a robbery charge.

On parole in 1975, he moved to New York, where two elderly women were attacked. One was killed and the other survived. The survivor claimed it was a black man who had attacked her. Carlton wasn't charged but due to parole violation for robbery was sent back to prison. In 1977, he escaped from prison and moved back to Columbus, Georgia.

On September 16th 1977, a 60-year-old woman named *Feme Jackson* was brutally raped, beaten and subsequently strangled to death with a nylon stocking. In the following weeks, another five elderly women were beaten and killed in a similar fashion.

On February 12th 1978, an elderly lady named *Ruth Schwob* was attacked. Ruth managed to trigger her bedside alarm causing Carlton Gary to flee the scene. Not being able to end the night without killing, he broke into another house only two blocks away and raped and strangled 78-year-old, *Mildred Borom*.

His final victim was in April of 1978. He would be arrested in December and subsequently sentenced to death in 1986. Carlton Gary would spend 22 years on death row before being executed in 2018.

Born **December 15th 1952**.

Active from **1977-1978**.

Arrested on **May 3rd 1984.**

Country: **USA.**

Victims: **3-7.**

AKA: **The Stocking Strangler.**

Sentence: **Death penalty.**

Current whereabouts: **Executed in 2018.**

Gaskins, Donald Henry

Nicknamed '*Pee Wee*', Gaskins would be convicted of nine murders. He could claim that he killed 110 but it has never been proven. There was a suspicion that he just wished to be known as the serial killer with the highest body count.

When he was a child, Gaskins was bullied and mocked for having a smaller stature, which is where his nickname came from. He was neglected as a child, so much so that he only learned his given name of Donald when it was read out in court. At one-year-old, Gaskin drank a bottle of kerosene which caused convulsions that lasted through his early years.

As he grew up, he became involved in robberies, assaults and gang rape with some acquaintances. He was subsequently charged with the crimes and sent to a reform school, where it is claimed he was raped by other inmates. He escaped only to be re-sentenced when he attacked a teenage girl with a hammer. During his time in prison, he was raped again and *owned* by another prisoner. Then he killed the most feared man in the prison and no longer became a victim.

He escaped again only to recaptured and re-released in 1961. He killed a female hitchhiker in 1969, tortured her and sunk her body in a swamp.

"All I could think about is how I could do anything I wanted to her."

Gaskin, in his memoir.

He claimed to have picked up his victims on the new American highway systems. He killed for pleasure potentially once every six weeks at his peak. He tortured and mutilated his victims while keeping them alive as long as he could.

Born **March 31st 1933**.

Active from **1953-1982**.

Arrested in **December 1975**.

Country: **USA**.

Victims: **9-110**.

AKA: **Pee Wee**.

Sentence: **Death penalty**.

Current whereabouts: **Executed in the electric chair on September 6th 1991**.

Georgiev, Hristo Bogdanov

On August 28th 1980, in Sofia City, Bulgaria, serial killer **Hristo Bogdanov Georgiev**, AKA: **The Sadist**, was executed for the murders of five women between 1974 and 1980. His final victim was in March of 1980 when he attacked **Angelo Pantova** on a train line. He stabbed her in the back but she managed to crawl over 30 metres, before Georgiev walked up behind her, raped her, and then strangled her to death.

The murders were only connected in 1979, when similarities began to arise. Investigators discovered a world of major criminals, sex parties, mentally ill suspects, and murder which led to arrests of multiple criminals over the course of just one year.

Georgiev was arrested in April of 1980 and fast-tracked through the courts. He was executed by firing squad on August 28th 1980.

Born in **1956**.

Active from **1974-1980**.

Arrested in **1980**.

Country: **Bulgaria**.

Victims: **5**.

AKA: **The Sadist**.

Current whereabouts: **Executed by firing squad on August 28th 1980.**

Gilbert, Kristen Heather

In Massachusetts, a former nurse, soccer-mom, and serial killer, *Kristen Heather Gilbert*, killed at least four patients who were under her care at the *Veterans Affairs Medical Centre*, in the State. She killed them by injecting their IV bags with epinephrine, which resulted in cardiac arrest.

To show herself as a heroine, she would respond to the emergency herself and aim to resuscitate the patient, on some occasions she would succeed. When she was growing up, Gilbert was known as a life-long manipulator and liar, who faked suicide attempts in order to gain sympathy and subsequently manipulate people around her.

She gained a nursing diploma when she was 21-years-old, in 1988, and married in the same year. She joined the VAMC site in 1989 and almost immediately she was suspected of being the cause of an increasing number of deaths.

In 1996, three nurses at the centre, reported their suspicions to authorities and an investigation began. Gilbert even tried to derail the investigation by phoning in a bomb threat, and then checked herself into various psychiatric hospitals to throw people off the scent. Gilbert was arrested on July 11th 1996.

In January of 1998, she was convicted firstly of making a bomb-threat and then went to trial for some of the murders that could be attribute to her. Staff at the hospital suggested that Gilbert was responsible for at least 80 deaths and at least 300 medical emergencies, in which she tried to show herself as the hero.

In March 2001, Gilbert was convicted of four counts of murder and two counts of attempted murder. She received four consecutive life sentences and an additional 20 years, to be served without the possibility of parole. She was transferred to a special federal prison in Texas, where she has been ever since.

Born **November 13th 1967.**

Active from **1995-1996.**

Arrested on **July 11th 1996.**

Country: **USA**.

Victims: **4+**.

Sentence: **Four life sentences plus 20 years.**

Current whereabouts: **In prison.**

Gillis, Sean Vincent: The Other Baton Rouge Killer (Extended Case File)

In Louisiana, American serial killer *Sean Vincent Gillis*, stalked, kidnapped, raped, murdered, and mutilated eight women over a 10 year period. Born in 1962, it was claimed by his mother that his upbringing had been healthy and sociable and that he was a well-behaved child who got good grades in school. It was a far cry from the murders he committed later in his life.

Yet, his father had left the family the year he was born and it was something that infected his formative years, resulting in mental illness and alcoholism. From his later teens, he began drinking and taking drugs, and was arrested in 1980 for driving under the influence.

He was also prone to outbursts of anger and violence, with one witness saying he would go outside at three in the morning and start punching garbage cans to release his tension. He would commit his first murder in 1994, when he was 30-years-old. He would later testify that he killed because he was stressed.

Just before the first murder, his mother moved away to take a job in Atlanta, and for the first time, Gillis would be living alone. The loneliness he found himself in, saw him turn to pornography in a big way and he became obsessive with it. He became angry at his mother for leaving and would sometimes be heard screaming in the middle of the night.

His neighbours would often hear banging and cries of anguish in the early hours of the morning. On one occasion, he was caught spying on one of his female neighbours through their window. His obsession with porn led him to discover the dark side of the internet. He consumed images of rape, dead bodies and torture of women. But despite all of this, he still managed to find a girlfriend.

In March 1994, he attempted to rape 81-year-old *Ann Bryan* in her own home. When she screamed, Gillis claimed he had become scared and killed her to stop her screaming. He cut her throat and stabbed her over 50 times. He refrained from killing again for five years but during this time he began stalking joggers and other women across the county, watching their every move.

On May 30th 1999, he drove his car into 52-year-old jogger, *Hardee Schmidt*, who he had spotted three weeks earlier. The force of the collision threw her into a ditch. He then dragged her body into his car, drove to a remote area and raped her multiple times. After stabbing her to death, he dumped her body in a shallow grave.

As the murders continued, the police couldn't make any connections, as the victims were random and no evidence of a suspect was forthcoming. It meant that Gillis carried on killing for another five years. Some of his victims would have their hands or feet chopped off and other body parts would be removed.

On one occasion, the local sheriff claimed that one of his victims had been so brutally hacked to pieces that it was difficult to believe they were looking at a human being. One of the victims was left in a ballet pose next to a sign that read; '*Dead End*'.

His final victim was in February 2004, 43-year-old *Donna Bennett Johnston* was raped and strangled to death with a nylon tie. As she lay dead in front of him, Gillis sliced off her nipples and mutilated her breasts with a knife. He then sliced off one of her tattoos and cut off her left arm. Her body was found a few days later in a drainage canal near Louisiana State University.

In April of 2004, tire tracks near the body of Johnston linked to Gillis's vehicle. Due to the specific type of tire, only 90 purchases had been made in the area over a three year period which made it easier to track him down. Later in the same month, Gillis was arrested and charged with multiple smaller crimes, so the investigators had time to find further evidence against him.

Gillis confessed to eight murders but police were struggling to prove them all. When they searched his vehicle, they found 45 digital images on his computer of Johnsons's body. There were also photos of her corpse in the trunk of his car. Then the investigation hit a goldmine of evidence, they found photos of other victims, at various stages of their death. Some of the photos were then used in the subsequent trial.

Through all of his years killing women, his girlfriend had no idea that she was living with a serial killer. When they searched his home, they discovered various body parts, which he used in conjunction with the photographs to fantasise about the killings.

"What he is, is a narcissistic, self-centred, ego-maniac serial killer."

Prosecutor Prem Burns – at the trial of Gillis.

In 2008, Gillis was convicted and sentenced to life without parole. While under arrest and awaiting his sentencing, he exchanged letters with a friend of his final victim, in which he was apologetic but also referred to himself as evil. He particularly regretted mutilating the bodies. His confession was somewhat different.

"I'm sorry I hurt people, but I would do it again. You let me out on the street, I'll find somebody before sundown."

"If anything in my useless life comes out, help the little girls today not to be the premature corpses of tomorrow."

Sean Vincent Gillis – in his confession.

The reason Gillis was known as 'The Other Baton Rouge Killer', was because another serial killer was already operating in and would be caught during Gillis's campaign.

The *Baton Rouge Serial Killer,* AKA*: Derrick Todd Lee* was arrested in 2003, and at the time, the area breathed a sigh of relief, believing Lee to be responsible for all the murders. Lee killed at least seven women from 1992 to 2003 and was sentenced to death in 2004. He died of a heart failure in 2016 while awaiting his execution.

As of 2021, Gillis remains incarcerated at a prison in The Louisiana State Penitentiary, AKA: *The Alcatraz of the South*.

Born in **1963**.

Active from **1994-2004**.

Arrested on **April 29th 2004**.

Country: **USA**.

Victims: **8**.

AKA: **The Other Baton Rouge Killer**.

Sentence: **Life imprisonment**.

Current whereabouts: **In prison**.

(Research Article #9) Highways to Hell

In the United Kingdom, the *Preston Bypass* opened in 1958, it would become part of the M6 motorway. In 1959, the first full-length motorway; the M1, opened for traffic. The United Kingdom could almost be seen a microcosm for the United States.

You can drive from the South of England to the North of Scotland in approximately 14 hours if the roads are clear. By comparison, the United States is huge.

Construction on the United States highway systems began in 1956. In an act of congress known as the *Federal Aid Highway Act of 1956*. As of 2016, over 25% of all miles used by vehicles, use the interstates. Construction carried on through the 1950s, 1960s, 1970s and beyond.

American society reorganised its culture around the highway and led to the new wave of the commuting lifestyle. Before the introduction of the highways, the road to work would have been long and winding roads that slowed economic evolution.

Psychologically, the Interstates opened up huge areas of land connecting places that were only tentatively connected before. As construction passed through urban areas, they would isolate communities and create physical ghettos. Sound barriers protected them from the noise of the roads but hid them as well, becoming isolated communities to the millions of drivers passing them by.

There is an even more unfortunate dark side that came out of the interstates; it opened up the country to *the drifter*. It allowed potential serial killers to widen their geographical catchment area. They didn't have to stay in their hometowns or States anymore and could just as easily drive to the next State over. Or even across the entire country if they wished.

By the 1970s, the free-love generation had landed. Hippies were the in-thing and peace was the pledge of the decade. There was more trust amongst people than there was for governments. War and Watergate had seen people move from politics to pop culture.

Although hitchhiking was banned in almost all of the United States, many people were still using it as a form of travel. The more people that thumbed for rides on the country's interstates, the more potential victims there were for drifter killers.

Randy Kraft, The Scorecard Killer, would mostly dump his victims on the side of highways. He killed between 16 and 67 people from 1971 to 1983.

William Bonin, The Freeway Killer, would also dump his victim's bodies on the side of freeways. He killed at least 21 people from 1979 to 1980.

Jeffrey Dahmer, The Milwaukee Cannibal, would count hitchhikers among his victims. He killed 17 young men and boys between 1978 and 1991.

Gerald Stano, The Boardwalk Serial Killer, would prey on prostitutes and hitchhikers. He killed at least 22 women from 1969 to 1980.

The Highways of Tears list is made public in 2007 by the *Royal Canadian Mounted Police's E-Pana investigation*. It is a task force set up to investigate the disappearances and murders of at least 18 girls and women along Vancouver Highways in a 40 year period from 1977.

The **FBI** officially launched their **Highway Serial Killing database** in 2009. Their investigation showed over 500 cases where bodies had been dumped on highways in the decades before. As of 2012, the FBI suggested there were approximately 300 '*highway serial killers*' active in the United States.

In most countries, the construction of these types of roads was one of the reasons why serial killing increased through the 1970s. Life was also made extremely difficult for law enforcement because of various State boundaries that existed.

It also meant that a serial killer's potential victim might not be recognised as such due to the then disconnected reporting between authorities. The highways to hell provided an opportunity where there wasn't one before.

(Research Article #10) Project E-Pana: Highway of Tears

Project E-PANA was created in 2005 to review and investigate numerous unsolved murders on *Highway 16*, which became known as the *Highway of Tears*. The investigators chose the name of PANA as it is an Inuit word describing the spirit goddess who looks after souls before they go to heaven.

The task force was set up by the *Royal Canadian Mounted Police* (RCMP) with the exclusive purpose of solving cases of missing and murdered people along the Highway. Highway 16 runs between Prince Rupert and Prince George, two cities in British Columbia that are 446 miles (718 km) apart. After just one year from the formation of the project, the investigation expanded to include Highways 5, 24 and 97.

In 2006, the task force had nine active investigations on the books. A year later in 2007 they had doubled to eighteen. The cases being investigated were cold cases from 1969 to 2006 and because more murders were diluting the investigation, they created a specific set of rules. These rules allowed them to focus on specific cases in the region and meant they could be added to the project E-PANA list.

Victims had to be female.

Involved in hitchhiking or prostitution, or other high-risk behaviours.

Last known location to be within a mile of the three major British Columbia highways; 5, 16 and 97. This could have been the last time she was seen alive or where her body had been found.

Cases where evidence pointed to a stranger having committed the crime rather

than a domestic attack or accident.

The murder victim list.

October **1969** – 26-year-old *Gloria Moody* – Last seen leaving a bar in Williams Lake. Her body was found in the woods at a cattle ranch six miles away.

July **1973** – 18-year-old *Micheline Pare* – Last seen beside the gates of Tompkins Ranch near Hudson's Hope. Two women had previously dropped her off there. Her body was found in the area in August 1973.

October **1973** – 19-year-old *Gale Weys* – She vanished while hitchhiking from Clearwater to Kamloops. Body was found in a ditch on *Highway 5* just south of Clearwater. Suggested to have been a victim of serial killer *Bobby Jack Fowler*.

November **1973** – 19-year-old *Pamela Darlington* – Vanished from Kamloops while hitchhiking to a local bar. Her body was found the next day. Suggested to have been a victim of serial killer *Bobby Jack Fowler*.

December **1974** – 14-year-old *Monica Ignas* – last seen walking home alone from school. Her remains were found in April 1975, hidden in a dense forest. She had been strangled to death.

August **1974** – 16-year-old *Colleen MacMillen* – her body was discovered in September 1974. She was last seen leaving her home to hitchhike to a nearby friend's house. DNA evidence matched *Bobby Jack Fowler* to the murder who was also working in the area at the time.

May **1978** – 12-year-old *Monica Jack* – In one of the more well-known crimes in the area, Monica was last seen riding her bike near her home. Her disappearance remained a mystery until her skeletal remains were found by forestry workers in 1995. Serial murderer *Garry Taylor Handlen* was charged with her death along with another 11-year-old girl. On January 18th 2019, Handlen was finally convicted.

May **1981** – 33-year-old *Maureen Mosie* – She had been hitchhiking from Salmon Arm to Kamloops when she disappeared. Her body was found the next day by a woman walking her dog. She had been beaten to death.

August **1989** – 24-year-old *Alberta Williams* – Her body was discovered a month later, just over 20 miles east of Prince Rupert. She had been raped and strangled to death.

June **1994** – 16-year-old *Ramona Wilson* – She was hitchhiking from Smithers to stay with friends in Hazelton but she vanished. Her remains were discovered in April 1995 near the Smithers Airport. Several items were in a small, organized pile a few feet away from her, these included a section of rope, three interlocking ties and a small pink water pistol.

July **1994** – 15-year-old *Roxanne Thiara* – A prostitute who went missing in Prince George. She told her friend she was going off with a customer and she was never heard of again. Her body was found a month later in a bush along Highway 16. She was friends with the next victim on the list.

December **1994** – 15-year-old *Alishia Germaine* – Her body was found behind an elementary school outside of Prince George, just off Highway 16. She had been stabbed to death and was friends with Roxanne Thiara who had been killed a few months earlier. They had been seen working together multiple times before their deaths.

February 2006 – 14-year-old *Aielah Saric Auger* – Her body was discovered in a ditch on Highway 16, just a few days after she went missing.

The missing persons list.

1983 – 17-year-old *Shelley-Anne Bascu* – Vanished in 1983 and her body has never been discovered. However, personal items such as clothing and blood matching her blood type were found beside the Athabasca River. She is still officially a missing person's case.

June 1990 – 16-year-old *Delphine Nikal* – She had been hitchhiking from Smithers in an Easterly direction when she vanished. The teenager's body has never been discovered and she is a missing person's case to this day.

October 1995 – 19-year-old *Lana Derrick* – She was last spotted getting into a car with two unidentified men, at a service station in Thornhill. She has been missing ever since and no sign of a body has ever been found.

June 2002 – 24-year-old *Nicole Hoar* – in a similar fashion to the others, she was last seen hitchhiking to Smithers. She had been spotted at a service station just west of Prince George. An investigation suspected convicted murderer *Leland Vincent Switzer*. A search was carried out on his property but they found no sign of any human remains. Hoar has been missing ever since.

September 2005 – 22-year-old *Tamara Chipman* – She was last seen in Prince Rupert and had been hitchhiking east on Highway 16. As of 2021, no sign of her has ever been found and she remains a missing person.

As of 2021, only one murder has been solved and that was the infamous death of

12-year-old *Monica Jack*. Serial murderer, *Garry Taylor Handlen* was charged with her murder and the death of another 11-year-old girl.

American serial killer *Bobby Jack Fowler* was linked with DNA evidence to the murder of 16-year-old Colleen MacMillen. Fowler had also been working in the area at the time. He has also been linked with a number of other E-Pana investigations and is the prime suspect in the murders of Gale Weys and Pamela Darlington.

In 2012, they used the advancement in DNA technology to positively identify him in the murder of MacMillen. The Royal Canadian Mounted Police strongly believe that he was responsible for at least 10 of the other victims on the list. However, many more murders took place after his arrest in 1995, when he was picked up on a rape charge.

As Fowler died in prison in 2006, the investigation of his suspected murders has been made more difficult. Since 2010, the E-Pana investigation has lost 58 officers, dropping from 70 at its peak, to just 12. This has been due to budget cuts for the E-Pana caseloads.

As of 2021, all cases are still active.

(Research Article #11) Cheap Travel and Open Borders

Back in the 1950s, the construction of the interstates and highways in the United States and motorways in the United Kingdom connected cities easily for the first time.

By the 1970s, the highways allowed the drifter killer to navigate easily between populous areas, finding possible victims along the way. In essence it created a surge in hitchhiking and a massive rise in cross-state serial killing.

Jump forward to the late 2010s and it's not just the cities in each country that are well connected, the entire world has opened up. As a foot passenger, you can travel from Portsmouth in the United Kingdom to Cherbourg-Octeville in France for around $40 (£30). From France you can catch buses or trains to every region of Europe and beyond.

If you book at the right time, you can pick up a flight from London to New York for $300 (£225). Travel has never been easier. Even in the 1990s, countries like Cambodia, Vietnam and Laos were virtually off-limits, now you can get a package holiday from a high street shop.

You can go to Everest Base Camp for the price you used to pay for two weeks on the coast of Spain. Holidays used to be week-long torments in a caravan to Great Yarmouth or Blackpool. Now they are cheap flights and comparison sites.

If serial killers saw opportunity in the creation of the highway systems, then they are more than likely seeing larger opportunities with the connection of the entire world. It would not be difficult for someone to take a domestic or international flight, spend a few days indulging their fantasies, and then head back home as if nothing had happened.

Sex tourism has become a thing and since doing so it has increased exponentially. The Thai sex trade mostly makes its money from white westerners. Sex-tourism forums are some of the most popular adult forums out there.

Some of them include questions such as; *why would a white man fight for a woman back home when he could have petite tanned girls on tap for the price of a DVD*? There are even sites where men rate and review worldwide prostitutes and escorts in the same way one might review a show.

The world in 2020 has afforded more opportunity than ever before for someone to act on their dark thoughts and fantasies. Maybe there is a link between the supposed decline of the serial killer because of this easily accessible fantasy fulfilment.

Some have suggested that serial killers have not declined. The data shows this because they might have evolved with different methods and new ways of disposing of bodies.

The more connected the world is, the easier it might be for a potential serial killer to plan their next victim.

Gilyard, Lorenzo Jerome

Gilyard was a former trash company supervisor who raped and killed 13 women and girls but was convicted of six counts of murder in 2007. He had sex with the victims, usually by force, and left their bodies in secluded or isolated locations. His campaign of terror lasted from 1977 to 1993.

Most of the victims were sex workers in and around Kansas City. All of them were strangled and had put up a struggle against him. Bizarrely, every victim was missing their shoes, and the bodies had been dumped in secluded locations around the city. But no effort apart from that was made to conceal the remains.

Almost all the victims had cloth or paper stuffed into the mouths, in a suspected attempt to silence them while he raped them. Back in 1969 for a five year period, he was linked to five rapes but was never convicted for them. He also served an unlisted amount of time in prison for sexually abusing children.

Gilyard was arrested in 2004, and it is suggested many more victims could have been attributed to him. He was sentenced to life in prison without parole, where he remains to this day.

Born **May 24**[th] **1950**.

Active from **1977-1993**.

Arrested on **April 19**[th] **2004**.

Country: **USA**.

Victims: **13**.

AKA: **The Kansas City Strangler**.

Sentence: **Life imprisonment**.

Current whereabouts: **In prison**.

Glaze, Billy Richard

On August 31st 1987, American serial killer *Billy Richard Glaze* AKA*: Jesse Sitting Crow*, was arrested. Glaze was a suspect in the murders of three Native American women in the Minneapolis area at the time and was arrested while driving under the influence of alcohol. The officers found a bloody shirt and a crowbar in the car.

Evidence in hair samples taken from the crowbar were used to convict him of the three murders. Glaze was suspected of involvement in a possible 50 murders but with the evolution of DNA technology, Glaze's guilt has been brought into question.

It is suspected that he was not involved in the crimes as DNA evidence points to an unknown male in the murders but a new investigation is ongoing.

Glaze died of lung cancer in prison in 2015 after spending 25 years inside.

Born **July 13th 1944**.

Active from **1986-1987**.

Arrested on **August 31st 1987**.

Country: **USA**.

Victims: **3-50+**.

AKA: **Jesse Sitting Crow / Butcher Knife Billy.**

Sentence: **Life imprisonment.**

Current whereabouts: **Died of lung cancer in 2015.**

Graham, Harrison

American serial killer *Harrison Graham* was convicted of seven murders committed in 1986 but wasn't arrested until August 1987 when he was evicted because of the terrible smell coming from his apartment.

On August 17th 1987, in Pennsylvania, Graham was arrested and charged with the murders. He said he killed all of them while he was under the influence of drugs and mostly at the same time as having sex with the victims.

He kept the bodies of his victims in his apartment, in the slum district of Pennsylvania, wrapping them in bedding and piling them up in his bedroom. The bodies were found after an eviction notice was served due to bad smells coming from the apartment. He turned himself in after a week on the run after his mother convinced him to.

Graham was arrested only months after another Philadelphia serial killer *Gary M. Heidnik* was arrested for similar crimes. A criminal justice professor named *Anthony Walsh* suggested that the lack of media attention to Graham's crimes was a media neglect of black serial killers in America. Because people at the time didn't really believe black people were capable of serial killing, except the 1980s saw a large number of black serial killers.

Graham was convicted of seven murders and sentenced to death which was later commuted to life after an appeal regarding his mental health. As of 2021, he resides at the State Correctional Institution Coal Township (*SCI Coal Township*) in Pennsylvania.

Born **October 9th 1958**.

Active from **1986-1987**.

Arrested on **August 17th 1987**.

Country: **USA**.

Victims: **7**.

AKA: **Marty**.

Sentence: **Death penalty, later commuted to life imprisonment.**

Current whereabouts: **In prison.**

Greba, Alexander

A Russian serial killer known as '*The Goblin*'. He first killed when he was just 16-years-old and would go on to murder five people. He was raised by a single mother with alcohol problems, who physically abused her children whenever she got angry.

By the age of 10-years-old, Greba's criminal career had already begun and he began to shoplift and steal from people. In his early teens, he left home to live on his own in the forests surrounding the region of Oblast. In 1996, when he was 16-years-old, he broke into a house to get refuge from the cold of the winter months. He claimed that the woman who owned the house looked a lot like his own mother and so he murdered her in cold blood for that simple reason.

He was arrested in the same year and sentenced to eight years for the murder. He served the full sentence before being released in 2004. Just two weeks after he came out of prison, he broke into another house and killed the male owner. He went on to kill another three people in a similar fashion.

He was arrested shortly after and convicted of the four murders. In March 2005, Greba was sentenced to life without the possibility of parole.

Born **September 23rd 1980.**

Active from **1996-2004.**

Arrested on **July 6th 2004.**

Country: **Russia.**

Victims: **5.**

AKA: **The Goblin.**

Sentence: **Life imprisonment.**

Current whereabouts: **In prison.**

Greenwood, Vaughn Orrin

In Los Angeles, California, **Vaughn Orrin Greenwood**, AKA: **The Skid Row Slasher**, killed at least eleven people and attacked at least one more victim, who went on to survive. In 1964, he killed two homeless men by slashing their necks from ear to ear. The victims were posed by Greenwood in a ritualistic fashion. As with all of his victims, there was salt found sprinkled around their bodies.

In 1966, in Chicago, Greenwood attacked a man with a knife but the man survived and Greenwood was arrested. He was sentenced for assault and served almost six years in prison. At the time, there had been no connection with the two homeless men in 1964. Greenwood then went on a rampage from 1974 to 1975.

From December 1974 to February 1975, Greenwood brutally killed at least nine more men, most of whom were homeless or staying in homeless hostels. As in the 1964 killings, Greenwood would kill them in a ritualistic fashion by posing their bodies and surrounding them with occult markings. In some cases, cups full of the victim's blood was found nearby leading to the suspicion that Greenwood was in fact drinking their blood.

Investigators on the case believed the man to be white but Greenwood was black, this was despite bringing in experts and psychics to assist them. Their mistakes in the profiling allowed Greenwood to get away with more killings than he should have done.

He was arrested in 1975 and subsequently convicted of nine counts of murder. In 1977, he was sentenced to life in prison and remains incarcerated in a Californian prison to this day.

Born in **1944**.

Active from **1964-1975**

Arrested in **February 1975.**

Country: **USA**.

Victims: **11.**

AKA: **The Skid Row Slasher**

Current whereabouts: **Incarcerated at the California Men's Colony.**

Groves, Vincent Darrell

On July 4th 1987, 18-year-old *Karolyn Walker*, was brutally murdered in Aurora by American serial killer *Vincent Darrell Groves*. Her body was found a day later. Upon his second capture in 1988, Groves was suspected of killing 17 prostitutes over a ten year period from 1978 to 1988.

This was despite being in prison on a five year term for second degree murder from

1982 to 1987. Almost immediately upon his release, he began to kill again with three bodies discovered in 1987 alone. He would eventually be convicted on two more counts of murder.

He was sentenced to life for murder In 1996, while investigations were still continuing, Groves died in prison, leaving behind a dark legacy that affected many lives.

Born in **1953**.

Active from **1978-1988**.

Arrested on **September 1st 1988**.

Country: **USA**.

Victims: **14-17+**.

Sentence: **Life imprisonment**.

Current whereabouts: **Died of natural causes in prison on October 31st 1996.**

Grzesik, Tadeusz

In Poland, strawberry grower and serial killer, *Tadeusz Grzesik*, killed at least eight people as part of a gang known as the *'Moneychangers Gang'*. The first confirmed murders took place in September of 1991, when he was involved in the shooting of two Ukrainian men and one Ukrainian women in a car park. Before he killed the woman, he raped her, and his DNA would later prove his involvement, 18 years later.

The killings continued until 2007, and Grzesik was suspected of having killed over 20 people, with some of the bodies remaining undiscovered to this day. In 1998, he is suspected of having shot dead three men who were sitting at a table in front of a bar. Again in 1998, he was linked to the violent beating and stabbing of a 17-

year-old clubber who was returning from a night out. The teenager's body was discovered the following morning.

In 2005, he created a gang to attack owners of exchange offices in the country. Up until 2007, the gang were linked to numerous robberies and at least five murders, and multiple attempted murders.

In 2007, Grzesik was arrested and DNA linked him to multiple murders and unsolved cases from 1991. A lengthy trial led to the 2013 conviction for three murders and one rape, and he was sentenced to 25 years in prison. Some of the cases are still being investigated to this day and he has been positively linked to eight murders and a suspected 20.

Born in **1960**.

Active from **1991-2007**.

Arrested in **2007**.

Country: **Poland**.

Victims: **8-20+**

AKA: **Moneychangers Gang (member)**.

Sentence: **25 years in prison**.

Current whereabouts: **In prison**.

Haigh, Paul Steven

An Australian serial killer who shot and killed seven people in the late 1970s and then again in the early 1990s. In 1978, Haigh shot dead a 58-year-old Lotto Agency worker and a 45-year-old pizza shop operator. This was just two weeks after being paroled for multiple armed robberies.

A year later in 1979, he began killing people who he thought knew about his crimes. He killed an acquaintance named *Wayne Keith Smith* as he suspected he was about to contact the police. He also shot dead Smith's 31-year-old girlfriend, *Sheryle Gardner*. He then proceeded to shoot dead Gardner's 10-year-old son, as he would have been a witness to her murder.

One of Haigh's most brutal attacks was committed against his girlfriend, 19-year-old *Lisa Brearley*, in 1979. Haigh stabbed her 157 times after allowing another man to rape her at knifepoint.

He believed she was sleeping with other men and needed to die for her sins. It was one of the worst murders ever committed on Australian soil. He was caught in 1979 and killed another inmate in 1991 by hanging him.

Born **September 5th 1957.**

Active from **1978-1979** then in **1991.**

Arrested in **1979.**

Country: **Australia.**

Victims: **7.**

Sentence: **Life imprisonment.**

Current whereabouts: **In prison.**

Hall, Archibald

Archibald Thomson Hall was known as *The Monster Butler,* who committed his crimes whilst working for the British upper class. He killed five people during his campaign.

After being sentenced to prison for a number of crimes including robbery, he was released in 1975 and went on to kill his first victim shortly after. He returned to his home country of Scotland and began working as a butler for *Margaret Hudson* who lived in Kirtleton House.

In 1977, a man named *David Wright* began work at the house as a gamekeeper. It turned out that Wright and Hall had been in prison together and Wright threatened to tell the lady of the house about Hall's previous convictions. Hall then shot Wright dead while using a rabbit hunt as cover for the murder. He then moved to London and began working for *Walter Scott-Elliot* and his wife.

Hall's plan was to rob them of all their money and retire in a foreign country but when Mrs. Scott-Elliot walked in on Hall and an accomplice discussing their plan, the accomplice *Michael Kitto* suffocated her to death. They then drugged Walter and took him and his wife's body back to Scotland. They beat him to death, before enlisting the help of a local prostitute to assist with burying both bodies.

The prostitute was known only as *Coggles*. She had been seen wearing Mrs. Scott-Elliot's fur coat around town which Hall saw as drawing too much attention to herself. So Hall and Kitto killed her and buried her body in a barn. The final victim was his half-brother named Donald, who was a convicted paedophile just released from prison. Hall drowned him in the bath after having drugged him with chloroform.

Hall was subsequently captured in January of 1978 and attempted suicide while in custody. When it failed, he led police to the locations of the bodies. Kitto received 15 years to life in prison for his part in the crimes. Hall was sentenced to life imprisonment.

Born **July 17th 1924**.

Active from **1977-1978**.

Arrested on **January 16th 1978**

Country: **United Kingdom.**

Victims: **5.**

AKA: **Roy Fontaine / The Monster Butler.**

Sentence: **Life imprisonment.**

Current whereabouts: **Died of natural causes on September 16th 2002.**

Hance, William Henry

An American serial killer who is suspected to have killed four women in and around military bases before his arrest in 1978. *Hance* was killing at the same time as *Carlton Gary, The Stocking Strangler*, and so Georgia was playing host to a wave of serial killers.

In September of 1977, the nude body of 24-year-old *Karen Hickman* was discovered near Fort Benning in Georgia. She had been beaten to death and then run over with a car by Hance. Due to media attention being focused on Carlton Gary, Hance decided to take advantage of Gary's press by drawing attention away from his own murders.

He wrote a letter to the investigation claiming that he was part of a group of white supremacists called the *Forces of Evil*, and if they didn't catch Carlton Gary then a black woman would die at regular intervals. He had just killed a black prostitute named *Gail Jackson*. In his letter he claimed that the Forces of Evil were holding her hostage and would kill her if Gary wasn't captured. This was all in an attempt to deflect attention away from him.

After two more murders, police closed in on Hance, after realising early on that the culprit was from the nearby military base. He was arrested shortly after, found guilty and sentenced to life with hard labour. However, a review board did not agree and a re-trial was ordered.

Hance was subsequently convicted of killing three of the victims, sentenced to death, and executed in the electric chair in 1994.

Born in **1951**.

Active from **1972-1989**.

Arrested on April 4th **1978**.

Country: **USA**.

Victims: **4+**.

AKA: **Chairman of the Forces of Evil**.

Sentence: **Death penalty**.

Current whereabouts: **Executed by electrocution in 1994**.

Hansen, Robert

He was an Alaskan serial killer who raped and murdered at least 17 women in Alaska between 1971 and 1983. He is known to have killed over 30. Most of his crimes took place in Anchorage and he preferred to hunt them in the wilderness with a gun and a knife. He would generally abduct them before killing them.

Born in Iowa, he became withdrawn from society at a young age and was known to have had a bad relationship with his aggressive father. He was bullied in school and grew up with a stutter that saw him struggle in social environments. He was jailed multiple times for various crimes, including burning down a local bus garage.

In 1967 he moved to Anchorage, Alaska with his second wife. He became well-liked in the area and was known to have involved himself with community events. He was jailed in 1977 for stealing a chainsaw but was released after a year when he was diagnosed with bipolar disorder.

From 1980, he began killing prostitutes by paying for their services then flying them to his private cabin. He used his small private airplane that he had acquired at some point while in Alaska. When he got them to his cabin, he raped and beat them before releasing them into the open. Then he would stalk and hunt them with a rifle or hunting knife.

In 1983, the FBI were called in to assist with the investigation, as Alaska State Troopers were unsure what they were dealing with. It led to Hansen's arrest in 1983 and he was subsequently sentenced to life in prison where he died in 2014. His killings were the subject of the film *'The Frozen Ground*' with *Nicholas Cage* and *John Cusack*.

Born **February 15th 1939.**

Active from **1971-1983.**

Arrested in **June 1983.**

Country: **USA (Alaska).**

Victims: **17-30+.**

AKA: **The Alaska's Serial Killer.**

Sentence: **Life imprisonment.**

Current whereabouts: **Died of natural causes in 2014.**

Hansson, Anders

Also referred to as the *'Malmo Ostra Hospital Murders'*. In a four month period in the late 1970s, 18-year-old Hansson poisoned at least 15 victims whilst working as an orderly in the hospital, by killing them with detergents. It was discovered that 27 patients had been poisoned to death.

He was convicted of 15 murders and another 15 attempted murders. He was sent to a psychiatric hospital in 1979 and stayed there until 1994. It is unclear what happened to him after 1994.

There are some suggestions he was discharged with a new identity or had died and no statement was made available.

Born in **1960**.

Active from **1979-1979**.

Arrested in **1979**.

Country: **Sweden**.

Victims: **15-27+**.

AKA: **Malmo Ostra Hospital Murders**.

Sentence: **Admittance to high security psychiatric hospital.**

Current whereabouts: **Discharged from hospital in 1994. His status since leaving the hospital is unknown.**

Harding, Donald Eugene

On September 17th 1979, in Arkansas, criminal and future serial killer **Donald Eugene Harding** escaped jail by sawing his way out. After his escape, he went on to kill at least six people and took part in numerous robberies and other crimes before his eventual recapture in 1980.

On December 10th 1979, in Dallas, Texas, Harding shot dead **Stanton Winston Blanton** during a robbery. One day later he kidnapped the entire **Baker** family before robbing their home and leaving with an unknown amount of cash and goods. He left the family tied up before moving across the State to Waco to continue his campaign of crime and murder across America's Southern and middle States.

After his recapture in 1980, he was charged, convicted and sentenced to death for his crimes including the murders of at least six people. Harding was executed in the gas chamber in Arizona on April 6th 1992.

Born in **1954**.

Active from **1979-1980**.

Arrested in **January 1980**.

Country: **USA**.

Victims: **6+**

Current whereabouts: **Executed by gas chamber on April 6th 1992.**

Harvey, Donald

On October 26th 1987, American medical serial killer *Donald Harvey*, AKA: *the Angel of Death*, was admitted to the Toledo Correctional Institution in Ohio. This was after being convicted in August 1987 of killing 37 people. Harvey was a hospital orderly who claimed to have murdered 87 people between 1970 to April 1987 when he was arrested.

Harvey had worked in the medical profession from the age of 18-years-old. When he worked at the Marymount Hospital in London, Kentucky, he claimed to have killed at least a dozen patients there alone. Harvey claimed that he initially killed his victims because they enraged him but then he insisted it was because he didn't want to see terminally ill patients suffering.

He killed by administering many different types of drugs, mostly whatever was available at the time. He used arsenic, cyanide, insulin or morphine. He even suffocated some of them or drip fed them liquid tainted with HIV. Because he had worked in so many hospitals and his crimes didn't come to light for over 17 years, investigators suspected he could have killed hundreds of people.

Harvey claimed to have killed to ease the pain of his patients but stated that as time progressed his enjoyment rose. He was given 28 life sentences after pleading guilty in order to avoid the death penalty.

In 2017 he was savagely beaten in his cell and died of his injuries on March 30th of that year.

Born **April 15th 1952**.

Active from **1970-1987**.

Arrested in **April 1987**.

Country: **USA**.

Victims: **37-87+**.

AKA: **Angel of Death**.

Sentence: **28 life sentences**.

Current whereabouts: **Killed in prison in 2017**.

Hatcher, Charles Ray: One Man Crime Wave (Extended Case File)

May 27th 1978 is seen as a notorious date in St. Joseph's history. It was the day that four-year-old *Eric Christgen* was raped and killed by one of the worst killers to ever live in the United States; *Charles Ray Hatcher*.

Charles Ray Hatcher was a one-man crime wave who was born in 1929, he started killing when he was 40-years-old. Over a 13 year period, he would kill 16 people. He was born into a family with an abusive alcoholic father and was bullied at school.

His oldest brother died when he was 16-years-old. After that moment, his parents split and his father left the family home. When Hatcher was 26-years-old, he moved to St. Joseph, Missouri, with his mother and her third husband. It was there that his life of darkness began.

Hatcher lived a life of crime before he first killed and he was able to fool the authorities by feigning mental illness. He is one of the world's worst criminals and his murders of many children were seen as some of the most horrific of all time.

When Hatcher was six-years-old he witnessed an incident that some psychologists say would have affected him more deeply than people knew at the time. In 1935, he was flying copper-wire kites with his older brothers. Just as his oldest brother was about to hand him the kite, it hit a high-voltage overhead line and electrocuted him. *Arthur Allen Hatcher* was killed instantly.

Their father, Jesse, never got over the pain of losing his eldest son and turned to drink for solace. This downward spiral of grief and anguish finally led to his father leaving home and divorcing his mother. Hatcher's father was an ex-convict who had a violent streak within him. Whenever he drank, he became abusive towards his wife and children. Hatcher became a prolific petty criminal after leaving school and was twice sent to the infamous *The Walls* prison in Missouri. After six convictions and served sentences, he was finally released back into the world on March 18th, 1959.

Only a few months after being out of Jail, Hatcher turned from a life of petty crime to those of a more serious nature. For most criminals, an escalation in what they do or perceive to love can sometimes be inevitable. The same can be said for most serial killers. Each kill is normally within a smaller time scale than the previous and usually more brutal or apparent.

In the Summer of 1959, again only a few months after being released, he attempted to abduct a 16-year-old newspaper boy, *Steven Pellham*. He tried to abduct him whilst waving a butcher's knife maniacally. It was unclear how Pellham managed to get away but he called the police and Hatcher was subsequently arrested yet again after being caught in a stolen vehicle.

Hatcher was sentenced to five years for the attempted abduction, along with the car theft. He was moved to maximum security after having spent most of his life behind bars. For the next two years, he would thrive on his criminal status within the prison until his release.

One month after mankind landed on the Moon, hailing in a new era of technological and human marvels, Charles Ray Hatcher was strangling a young boy to death in a creek.

On August 27th 1969, he asked a 12-year-old boy to take a ride with him in his car. He drove to a local creek and strangled him until he died. He would later confess this at his trial.

Only two days had passed when a six-year-old boy was reported missing. Hatcher had offered the little boy an ice cream to lure him away from his friends, who later spoke of the incident.

A passer-by walking his dog came across the horrific scene. Hatcher was caught red-handed sexually abusing and violently beating the young boy. He was arrested within a few minutes and fortunately, the boy survived the attack.

It marked the beginning of Hatcher's game of multiple identities that he had most likely planned for a long time. He seemed to know, having spent most of his time in jail, how to *game* the system and the authorities. He refused to answer any questions and gave multiple names when asked who he was.

Before a judge in a Californian court, he would give the name of *Albert Ralph Price*. Because of this steadfast belief in another personality, the judge ordered Hatcher to be taken away for psychiatric evaluation. In 1970, Hatcher was diagnosed as unfit to stand trial with tendencies of insanity and notions of paedophilia.

Although not one psychiatrist could actually agree on Hatcher's condition. Hospital staff felt that Hatcher was fabricating a lot of his mental suffering in order to stay out of prison and to make himself a more special case.

In the Winter of 1972 he was finally convicted of the murder and rape of Gilbert Martinez and was committed to the *Californian State Hospital* for the mentally insane. He was classed as a mentally disordered sex offender.

In May of 1977, Hatcher was shockingly released to a halfway-house in San Francisco. This was because of the findings at a parole board hearing that stated Hatcher had improved dramatically during his time in prison. It stated that he was no longer a danger to the public. How wrong they were.

Almost immediately after release, he tried to stab a seven-year-old boy but the charges were dropped. His record of arrests, evaluations and sentences read like a horror book that surpassed even the worst criminals at the time. Hatcher was then considered a parolee at large and was not seen for an entire year.

Until he returned to Saint Joseph, Missouri.

On May 27th 1978, four-year-old Eric Christgen was raped and killed by Hatcher. A search party found Eric's body in an area of weeds and marsh on the banks of the Missouri River. He had been molested and smothered to death. Eric's funeral was the largest ever held in the city and the public wanted an arrest.

The police were all too happy to oblige and only one suspect came to the forefront of their investigations. It was *not* Charles Ray Hatcher but a man named *Melvin Lee Reynolds*, who was subsequently charged with the boy's murder.

The police had forced the arrest of Reynolds and he was sentenced to life in prison after nine months of intense interrogation where he signed a false confession. It was going to be another four years until the truth would come out.

In September of 1978, Hatcher was arrested for sexually attacking another 16-year-old boy. Hatcher was placed into the *Douglas County Mental Institution*, in Omaha, Nebraska but again was released only a few months later.

Bizarrely, due to police procedures at the time, no one actually knew it was Hatcher. He had given a fake name to his arresting officers. Hatcher was subsequently released to continue his pattern of sexually abusing and killing young boys.

On June 20th 1981, *James Churchill* was stabbed to death on the banks of the

Missouri River, in Illinois. Hatcher would later confess to the murder stating that his desire to kill had gotten ahead of him. He said that he and Churchill had been drinking together and he snapped and then stabbed him ten times. He had left the knife sticking out of his chest near the heart.

On July 29th 1982, when Hatcher was 51-years-old, he killed an 11-year-old girl. *Michelle Steele* disappeared after a dentist appointment. A day later, under the name of *Richard Clark*, he checked himself into the *Saint Joseph State Hospital*. This was in an attempt to deflect attention from him or to rid himself of another prison sentence. At the same moment, a group of hikers stumbled across Michelle Steele's abused and broken body.

A few days later on August 3rd 1982, after matching his description to a man seen on the river bank the day of Michelle's disappearance, Hatcher was charged with murder in the first degree. But he was charged under the name of Richard Clark.

It would not be until April of 1983 when Hatcher was declared fit to stand at trial in the case of Michelle Steele. He was sent back to the Buchanan County Jail to await trial, whilst there, he gave a note to a young deputy.

"Please call the FBI and tell them I would like to see them today. Very important case."

Hatcher's hand-written note.

When the FBI agents arrived, Hatcher told them everything and confessed to the murders of 16 people including many children. Apart from Michelle Steele, all of them were male. He drew a map to the body of Churchill and described burial grounds and positions of each corpse. In return for the information he was handing out, Hatcher pleaded for the death penalty.

On October 13th 1983, Hatcher was finally sentenced to life in prison for the murder of Eric Christgen. This was on the same day that Melvin Lee Reynolds was released from prison after being wrongfully convicted of the crime.

A year later Hatcher was sentenced to another 50 years for the murder of Michelle Steele. Before the rest of his crimes could be brought to trial in separate cases,

Hatcher hung himself in his cell.

It has been suggested that *Chucky* from the *Child's Play* films was based on Charles Ray Hatcher and his murders. The name of the killer doll in the film is *Charles Lee 'Chucky' Ray* and the doll would attempt to kill children.

Hatcher would sometimes wear a horizontally striped top, just like the character from the films.

Born **July 16th 1929.**

Active from **1969-1982.**

Arrested on **August 3rd 1982.**

Country: **USA**.

Victims: **16+.**

AKA: **One Man Crime Wave / Chucky.**

Sentence: **Life imprisonment plus 50 years.**

Current whereabouts: **Committed suicide by hanging in 1984, to avoid further charges.**

Heaulme, Francis

Francis Heaulme, AKA*: The Criminal Backpacker*, was a French serial killer. He had the rare condition of *Klinefelter's syndrome*, which meant he had a supplemental X chromosome, was infertile and had small testicles. In his formative years he was abused by his father and turned to drink before becoming suicidal.

At the age of 28-years-old, he left home to backpack around France, either by hitchhiking or cycling. Whatever money he earned was spent on drink and drugs. He would kill his victims with different methods and on random dates making his capture all the more difficult. He brazenly killed 44-year-old *Aline Peres* on a busy public beach in broad daylight, surrounded by people who witnessed nothing. Yet, it was this murder he was finally arrested for.

Among others, he murdered two children in 1986 and dumped their bodies alongside a railroad track in Montigny-lès-Metz. A man named *Patrick Dils* was convicted of the crime and served 15 years in prison before being exonerated in 2002.

Heaulme was arrested in 1992 and went on to describe each murder scene in detail. He was sentenced to 22 years in May of 1997. Then he was subsequently sentenced to another 30 years in 2004 for three murders, and life imprisonment in 2017 for the murder of two boys. As of 2021, he remains incarcerated.

Born **February 25th 1959.**

Active from **1984-1992.**

Arrested on **January 7th 1992.**

Country: **France.**

Victims: **9+.**

AKA: **The Criminal Backpacker.**

Sentence: **Life imprisonment plus a total of 52 years.**

Current whereabouts: **In prison.**

ARCHIBALD HALL

IMAGE ATTRIB. A81

CHARLES RAY HATCHER

IMAGE ATTRIB. A80

PHILLIP CARL JABLONSKI

IMAGE ATTRIB. A82

GILBERT PAUL JORDAN

IMAGE ATTRIB. A83

Heidnik, Gary Michael

On January 2nd 1987, in Philadelphia, 23-year-old *Deborah Dudley* was kidnapped by rapist and murderer *Gary Michael Heidnik*. AKA: *Brother Bishop*. She was held captive and murdered on March 19th, 1987. In less than six months from November 1986 to March 1987, Heidnik had kidnapped, tortured, and raped six African-American women.

During his childhood, Heidnik was emotionally abused by his father. He had long suffered with bed-wetting as he grew up and his father would punish him for it. He would humiliate his son by forcing him to hang his stained bedsheets from his bedroom window in full view of the passing public.

He would keep his victim's prisoner in a pit in the basement of his home and would go on to kill two of them. Another victim, 24-year-old *Sandra Lindsay*, was kidnapped on December 3, 1986 and killed in February 1987. She died of starvation and the effects of torture. He went on to dismember her body, cook her ribs in an oven, and boil her head.

It was suggested he may have minced the flesh, mixed it with dog food and fed it to his other victims but those reports remain uncorroborated. Heidnik was arrested on March 24th 1987, after a new captive managed to call for help. He was sentenced to death and executed by lethal injection in July 1999.

Born **November 22nd 1943**.

Active from **1986-1987**.

Arrested on **March 24th 1987**.

Country: **USA**.

Victims: **3**.

AKA: **Brother Bishop**.

Sentence: **Death penalty**.

Current whereabouts: **Executed by lethal injection in July 1999**.

Hertogs, Jacobus Dirk

On April 5th 1979, in the Netherlands, the body of 18-year-old **Emy den Boer** was discovered by a hiker in a forest near *Nistelrode*. She had gone missing two days earlier and had been shot dead. She had been murdered by Dutch serial killer **Jacobus Dirk 'Koos' Hertogs**.

On May 11th 1979, Hertogs abducted and murdered 12-year-old **Tialda Visser**. She was reported missing after failing to return home from ballet class at the *Royal Conservatory of The Hague*. Four days later her body was found not too far from where she had gone missing.

On September 29th, 1980, Hertogs abducted and murdered 11-year-old **Edith Post** who disappeared while she was at school. She had left her classroom to get some study materials from a closet in the hallway but never returned to her class. Her body was found a few days later on October 2nd in the dunes of *Wassenaar*.

On October 3rd 1980, Hertogs was arrested and charged with the three murders. He was caught when an anonymous tip led to his arrest. In a press conference, the police claimed that his last victim, 11-year-old **Edith Post**, had bitten her attacker. A visitor to a nightclub noticed the bouncer had bite marks on his fingers. That bouncer turned out to be Hertogs. He is one of the Netherland's most notorious criminals and was sentenced to life in prison for the murders.

Born in **1949**.

Active from **1979-1980**.

Arrested in **October 1980**.

Country: **Netherlands**.

Victims: **3**

AKA: **Koos**

Current whereabouts: **Died of natural causes while in prison in 2015.**

Hicks, James R.

In Maine, American serial killer *James Hicks* goes on to kill three people. In 1977, he killed his 23-year-old wife, *Jennie Lynn Hicks*. He dismembered her body and dumped the body parts in a nearby river, and in buckets in concrete near roadsides.

On October 16th 1982, he murdered 34-year-old *Jerilyn Towers*. She was last seen leaving a bar with Hicks. He raped and murdered her, before dismembering her and dumping her in the same river as his ex-wife.

The investigation into Jerilyn Towers' disappearance, meant that the Jennie Hicks's case was also re-opened, due to the similarities and location they lived in. Hicks was arrested in 1983 and was convicted of Jennie Hicks's murder. He couldn't be charged with the Towers murder due to a lack of evidence against him. He was sentenced to 10 years in prison but released after only six years, in 1990.

Shortly after, he starting seeing 40-year-old *Lynn Willette*, who he met at the motel they both worked in. They moved in together pretty quickly but on May 26th 1996, Hicks brutally murdered her and dumped her remains in the river. Due to lack of evidence in her disappearance, he was not charged at the time.

In 2000, he moved to Levelland in Texas and robbed a 67-year-old woman. He held a gun to her head and forced her to write a cheque and a suicide note. Fortunately, she had managed to escape and it led to his arrest. He was convicted and sentenced to 55 years in prison. He then made a deal with authorities that he would lead them to the remains of the murder victims in Maine, only if he could serve his time in Maine.

Some of the remains of his former wife and Towers were found buried at the side of the road near his former home in Maine. The remains of Willette were mostly found in concrete buckets, buried near to the river. The parts discarded into the river were never found.

Born in **1951**.

Active from **1977-1996**.

Arrested in **April 2000**.

Country: **USA**.

Victims: **3**.

Sentence: **55 years in prison**.

Current whereabouts: **In prison**.

Hojer, Ladislav

A Czechoslovakian serial killer and cannibal who killed five women over a three-year period. On December 1st 1978, he attacked and killed his first victim, known as *Eva R*. He dragged her into some bushes and strangled her. He then abused the corpse and masturbated onto her body. He would kill again twice more in 1980 and twice in 1981 before his capture in the same year.

In January of 1981, he committed a particularly brutal murder. He dragged a victim known as *Ivana M*, into a local park. He attempted to rape her but failed, then he stabbed her and strangled her to death.

He cut off her breasts and genitalia with scissors and took them home in a plastic bag. Once home, he used the pieces of flesh in a sexual manner. A week later he cooked them in salted water and ate as much as he could before feeling ill.

Hojer was executed by hanging in 1986.

Born **March 15th 1958**.

Active from **1978-1981**.

Arrested in **1982**.

Country: **Czechoslovakia**.

Victims: **5-7**.

Sentence: **Death penalty**.

Current whereabouts: **Executed by hanging in 1986.**

Holst, Thomas

In Germany, on November 25th 1987, 21-year-old student *Andrea Grube-Nagel* goes missing. She was the first victim to be abducted and murdered by German serial killer *Thomas Holst, AKA: Heidemörder.*

As Andrea was leaving the Rissen Train Station in Hamburg, Holst had forced her into his car by putting a knife to her throat and threatening to stab her. He raped, tortured and dismembered her as he would his next two victims. Two days later, Andrea's remains were found by construction workers in the town of Kaltenkirchen, which is just north of Hamburg.

Over a two year period from November 1987 to November 1989, Thomas Holst abducted, raped and killed three women from Hamburg. Upon his arrest a psychiatric stated that he was '*untreatable and with extreme relapse probability*.' He was sent to trial for the violent murders of three victims and subsequently to a high-security wing of a psychiatric hospital.

Astonishingly, his therapist, *Tamar Segal*, helped him escape in 1995 as she had fallen in love with him. Holst gave himself up three months later and was detained at the Hamburg Detention Center where he has been ever since. In another bizarre twist, Thomas Holst married Segal while he was in prison in 1997 and by all accounts they are still married to this day.

Born **February 18th 1964.**

Active from **1987-1989.**

Country: **Germany.**

Victims: **3.**

AKA: **Heidemörder.**

Sentence: **Life imprisonment.**

Current whereabouts: **In prison.**

Hubal, Abdullah

A rare serial killer from the Yemen, *Abdullah al-Hubal* killed 12 people in the country from 1990 to 1998. In 1990, Hubal killed seven people after Northern and Southern Yemen were reunited to make a singular country. He was arrested shortly after and sent to prison.

After a short prison sentence, he disappeared for a while until 1998 when he killed a couple in the area of Beit al Fakieh. He went on to murder three more people in the same area and was a wanted man in the Yemen. On August 16th 1998, when police tracked him down, he killed an officer by shooting him.

He remains the country's most notorious killer.

Born in **1955**.

Active from **1990-1998**.

Country: **Yemen**.

Victims: **13**.

Current whereabouts: **Died during a police shoot out on August 16th 1998.**

Hughes, Michael

On December 1st 1987, in California, 30-year-old *Deborah Jackson* was murdered by serial killer *Michael Hughes*, AKA: *the Southside Slayer*. He killed seven females between the ages of 15-years-old to 38-years-old over a six year period from 1986 to his arrest in 1993.

He was first convicted in 1993 and given a life sentence without parole for the murders of four women who he had strangled to death. Then, due to advancements in DNA technology, Hughes was charged with further murders in 2008. He had raped and killed two more women and two more teenage girls during his active years.

One of the charges was later dropped as evidence wasn't as certain as the other murders, but it has still been attributed to him. Some of the confusion with the victims was due to the fact that another serial killer was operating in the same area. *Lonnie David Franklin Jr.* AKA: *The Grim Sleeper*, had left bodies in a similar fashion within the area.

Hughes was convicted in 2011 and sentenced to death. As of 2021, he is on death row at San Quentin State Prison.

Born in **1957**.

Active from **1986-1993**.

Arrested in **December 1993**.

Country: **USA**.

Victims: **7+**.

AKA: **The Southside Slayer.**

Sentence: **Death penalty.**

Current whereabouts: **Death row.**

Hwaseong Serial Murders

On January 10th 1987, in South Korea, 19-year-old *Hong Jin-young* is found murdered. She is a victim of the unsolved *Hwaseong Serial Murders*. At least ten females between the age of 14-years-old to 71-years-old were found tied, raped and strangled with their own clothing. The murders took place between 1986 and 1991 and remain unsolved to this day.

On May 2nd, 1987, the body of 29-year-old *Park Eun-joo* is discovered. She too had been tied, raped and strangled with her own clothing. She is one of ten victims of the unsolved *Hwaseong Serial Murders*. The killings are one of South Korea's most notorious unsolved crimes.

Serial killing is rare in South Korea or at the least, not brought into the public eye. This is one of the only cases where a killer using the same modus operandi had been identified in the country. Because of the ridiculous notion of statute of limitations, the killings could not be investigated after 2006. Police still keep records due to the infamy of the case.

Statute of limitations that there is a maximum time limit placed on crimes for when legal proceedings can be brought to an individual. Many Western countries have a statute of limitations in place. The United Kingdom is the exception in that there is no current time limit in place.

A list of over 21,000 suspects has been put together over the years but as of 2021, the murders remain a mystery.

Active from **1986-1991**.

Country: **South Korea**.

Victims: **10+**.

Current whereabouts: **Unidentified killer. Status unknown.**

(Research Article #12) Victim Selection in the 1970s

The argument given for the decrease in serial killers from the 1990s onwards is that law enforcement simply got better. This might have meant that some potential serial killers were caught after just one kill or even with only the threat of murder on personal social media accounts.

The counter-argument is that there was simply a larger pool of victims in the 1970s than there is nowadays. And that counter-argument is somewhat true. As we've already seen, the rise of the interstates and highways from the 1950s gave rise to the drifter killer. This meant that one could drive great distances, across States or Counties and open themselves up to larger opportunity.

The rise of urbanisation also played a major factor in the number of potential victims available. From 2000, urbanisation has increased even more but so has surveillance, both online and offline. Law enforcement has become more effective in the modern age than it was in the pre-DNA technology era of the 1970s.

We know that most serial killers are not opportunistic and have general plans in their heads or written down as to how they are going to kill. Mostly, they already have a victim in mind. The 1970s and 1980s offered more possibility than ever before and so serial killers were jumping at the opportunity.

The world was changing too quickly, less care was given to people's own personal safety. Hitchhiking became common as the highways expanded, and children played outdoors all the time. The rise of porn, true crime magazines, and an increase in prostitution, all led to people taking bigger risks than before.

Flower power was embedded into the minds of a generation, free love was theirs to share, and to lose. Population was increasing and the fallout of recent wars gave rise to a higher percentage of mental health problems.

When all is said and done, there was a larger pool of victims to choose from. This also goes hand in hand with the disconnected law enforcement of the period.

Mostly due to a lack of internet and proper networking, it was more difficult to share information with other department's quick enough to catch the criminals. This is where the highways played such a huge part in the rise of the serial killer.

For gay men and women, the rise of the gay activist movements in the late 1960s and early 1970s gave rise to greater freedom than before. Although the 1970s were not as free as they are in the 21st Century, *coming out* was slowly becoming more acceptable.

There was an increase in gay magazines, celebrities and rallies. The rise of gay bars, bathhouses and gay saunas across the Western world, allowed men to live out their gay fantasies in somewhat anonymity. It also opened the door to a greater selection of victims.

The same could be said for the rise of prostitution. Sex workers were and still are at greater risk of becoming a victim of a serial killer than most other people. Ever since the stories of *Jack The Ripper* in Victorian England, the lure of killing a prostitute has never been too far from the minds of serial killers.

According to FBI data it shows that female sex workers are 18 times more likely to be killed by a serial killer than someone who is not involved in the industry. Female victims are generally much higher in serial killer cases than in general murder cases.

FBI research shows us how serial killers have opened up about their crimes, revealing their various dark sexual fantasies that evolve into murder. This was more prevalent with the rise of true crime magazines depicting scantily-clad women tied up and about to murdered by a man. This along with the rise of porn, influenced some people to enact on their fantasies.

Most serial killers only choose a victim whereby the chances of success are extremely high. Of course, not all killers do this. Richard Trenton Chase, simply ripped through people without a thought on evidence and being tracked afterwards, but he still would have chosen his victims.

This is why the first murder victim might be a street prostitute or homeless person. Beyond that, once they've got that out the way, then the victim choice might be someone of a higher standing; a student, office worker, or nurse.

Combine this with the construction of new highways and a rise in unemployment leading to homelessness or prostitution then victims became easier. The Green River Killer, *Gary Ridgeway*, was a truck driver. He later claimed that picking up prostitutes or hitchhikers was easy without anyone noticing or knowing any different.

He said he knew that no one would be looking for them straight away and a window of freedom would open up after the killing. At least for a short while after and in some cases much longer.

The murder of a prostitute is especially difficult for police and other law enforcement. The very nature of the victim having had sex with multiple men and the interactions with hundreds, if not thousands of strangers, makes it even harder to investigate. They are also less likely than most rape or assault victims to report the crimes to police for exactly the same reason.

There was also the belief that law enforcement themselves wouldn't even worry too much about prostitutes being murdered. It was the disconnection of various agencies and departments that slowed down the flow of information between them. There is also the possibility that some officers in the 1970s had used prostitutes themselves and didn't want anything linking back to them.

Record-keeping and crime detection in the 1970s was far more difficult and disorganised than it is in today's digital world. Improvements in data collection and statistics is at a far greater level now. The sharing of information was indifferent and sometimes frowned upon between different departments. The FBI was one of the solutions to this but then the discrepancies between their own investigations and the police ones were not always shared.

Simply put, in the 1970s and 1980s, it was easier to get away with serial killing than in later decades, partly because victims were easier to find.

(Research Article #13) Victim Selection in the 2010s

Some say the decrease in the amount of serial killers in today's world is down to the fact that people are not getting away with it anymore. Victims are harder to find and investigations have become state of the art.

Others aren't so sure.

In the *Urban Strangers* article we discussed the rise of urbanisation in the towns and cities. Jump forward to today's world and urbanisation has increased dramatically.

In 1978, the population of the earth was estimated at 4.287 billion. In 2020, it is estimated at 7.700 billion. That's almost double in just over 40 years. By 2050, Earth's human population is expected to be in the region of 10 billion.

There are more potential victims than ever before and more people are going missing than ever before. This could be to do with population increase or it could be that more reports are being made for missing people. It could also be that the authorities are recording the data better than in the 1970s which is generally considered to be true.

But people are still going missing. In places like India and Africa, people are going missing on an astronomical scale. We long thought the slave trade to be a thing of the past. Yet, human trafficking has only increased, forced child prostitution is on the rise, and real life human beings are being traded for monetary value as a product or possession.

Serial killers choose their prey generally because they can overpower them. This is one of the reasons why male serial killer victims tend to be female. They also tend to be slim, young, and easy to overcome.

With social media on the increase, women are still being told to look a certain way. This leads to more people crafting themselves into the perfect victim of a serial killer. We tend to compare the worst parts of ourselves with the best parts of others.

Online forums, chatrooms, social media sites, private messaging and hidden chat services have led to an increase in private information sharing, hacking and stalking. One can find a lot about a person with just a few clicks.

Potential serial killers can stalk a victim online and find out everything about them. A lot of social media users share their home address, what they eat, where they shop, when they're out of their homes, relationships, thoughts, just damn near everything. The pool of victims is immeasurably immense.

The difficulty in the modern era is getting away with it. Some cite the belief that serial killers are stopped before they get to their second murder. And whilst in some instances this is true, it's certainly not for all cases.

In the United States in 2018, 239,847 females under 21-years-old were reported missing. Over half of these are found within a week, some runaway and return home, mistakes in reporting, or arguments with family. A lot more are found later but still thousands of young females simply never return home or are never found.

It is estimated that over 90,000 people are missing in the United States at any one time. In the United Kingdom, 180,000 are reported missing every year with London reporting a 72% increase in missing persons from 2008 to 2018.

The BBC called the rise of missing persons; *unsustainable*. The fact is that police are required to follow up each missing person. When crimes take precedent, sometimes they are never followed up and they wait for someone to book a flight or use their credit card.

With stories of people simply vanishing, there is a precedent for the rise of the serial killer. With access to a universe of information online, maybe serial killers have simply got better at not being caught.

Ivanov, Yuri

A Soviet Union rapist and serial killer who raped and killed 16 girls and women over a 13-year period. From a young age he had developed a hate for women and if they belittled men then he would seek to kill them. He would mostly rape and then strangle his victims to death before taking some of their personal belongings as trophies.

He mostly killed in the mid to late 1970s. But in 1987 he killed a 16-year-old girl that led to his arrest because he returned to the crime scene. He confessed to the rape and murder of 16 girls and women and another 14 rapes without murder.

He then identified all of his victims by photographs proving he had killed them all. In 1989, he was executed by firing squad.

Born in **1956**.

Active from **1974-1987**.

Arrested in **1987**.

Country: **Soviet Union**.

Victims: **16**.

AKA: **Ust-Kamenogorsk Maniac**.

Sentence: **Death penalty**.

Current whereabouts: **Executed by firing squad in 1989**.

Ivanyutina, Tamara

Ukrainian female serial killer murdered nine people over an 11-year period. As most female serial killers tend to do, she used poisoning as her modus operandi. From 1976, she used thallium and poisoned those she simply didn't like, there was no other reason. She would source thallium by saying it was to kill rats in and around hers and her parent's property.

In 1987, at a school where she was working at, several pupils and staff were hospitalised for extreme food poisoning. Two adults died and nine others went to intensive care. An investigation ensued leading to her arrest and subsequent confessions going back to 1976.

She claimed she targeted the school canteen because the sixth-graders refused to set up tables and chairs and so she decided to punish them.

Executed by firing squad in 1987.

Born in **1941**.

Active from **1976-1987**.

Country: **Ukraine**.

Victims: **9**.

AKA: **The Kiev Poisoner.**

Sentence: **Death penalty.**

Current whereabouts: **Executed by firing squad in 1987.**

Jablonski, Phillip Carl

An American serial killer convicted of killing five women in California and Utah. On July 16th 1978, he killed *Linda Kimball*, his former partner. She was stabbed, strangled and beaten to death. Prior to this he had met her in February of 1977 and lived with her before she gave birth to their daughter.

On July 6th 1978, he went to her mother's house with the intention of raping her. He didn't go through with it but the rest of the family found out. Kimball left him a few days later and he killed her on July 16th. He was arrested, convicted and released in 1990 to sate his bloodlust even more.

In 1991 he would kill his new wife and her mother along with two others. He would sexually assault all of his victims and either shoot or strangle them. In the case of *Fathyma Vann*, he had carved the words; '*I Love Jesus*', into her back. When her body was found, her eyes and ears were missing.

Some label Jablonski as a spree killer but his crimes and the sexual satisfaction he gained from them cannot be overlooked.

As of 2021, he remains on death row and accepts and replies to pen-pal letters.

Born **January 3rd 1946.**

Active from **1978-1991.**

Arrested on **April 28th 1991.**

Country: **USA.**

Victims: **5.**

Sentence: **Death penalty.**

Current whereabouts: **Death row.**

Jackson, Elton Manning

In Virginia, serial killer *Elton Manning Jackson,* AKA*: The Hampton Roads Killer*, was convicted of one murder but confirmed to have killed 12 gay men. A suspected serial killer was stalking victims in the Norfolk gay community, and he remained unidentified for many years until Jackson's arrest.

On July 22nd 1996, 38-year-old gay man, *Andrew D. Smith*, was strangled to death and his nude body was dumped on the side of a road in Chesapeake. Smith was considered to be the 12th victim of the unidentified serial killer who had first killed in July 1987.

When he was arrested in 1997, Jackson wasn't immediately confirmed to have been the serial killer. Instead, the authorities stated that the murder of smith was similar in fashion to the previous victims. The method of killing and the disposal of the body on the side of the road, matched all previous **11** murders.

The bodies were found at the entrance of major highway systems around the area, the men were gay or were those who had frequented gay establishments and were usually unemployed or of no-fixed-abode. Some of the men were known to have been male prostitutes. Seven men were white and five were black, which profilers called a rarity, as a serial killer usually only killed a specific type of victim.

After Jackson's arrest, no further killings took place and evidence against Jackson began to mount up. In August of 1998, Jackson was found guilty of Smith's murder and sentenced to life in prison, where he has been ever since. With regards to the other 11 murders, Jackson remains the sole suspect and most investigators consider the cases closed.

Born in **1956**.

Active from **1987-1996**.

Arrested on **May 6**th **1997**.

Country: **USA**.

Victims: **12**.

AKA: **The Hampton Roads Killer**.

Sentence: **Life imprisonment**.

Current whereabouts: **In prison**.

Johnson, Martha Ann

An American female serial killer convicted of smothering to death three of her children over a five-year period. Even by 22-years-old, she was already married for the third time. She had children from each of her three marriages.

In 1977 she killed her 23-month-old son by smothering him. She would do the same in 1980, 1981 and 1982 to her other daughters and eldest son. Her eldest daughter was known to have died of asphyxia. She was linked to all four murders but convicted of only three.

She horrifically killed them by rolling her 250LB (113kg) body on them as they slept. She was arrested in 1989 and sentenced to death in 1990, later commuted to life.

She is currently detained at Pulaski State Women's Prison in Georgia.

Born in **1955**.

Active from **1977-1982**.

Arrested on **July 3rd 1989**.

Country: **USA**.

Victims: **4**.

Sentence: **Death penalty, later commuted to life imprisonment**.

Current whereabouts: **In prison.**

Jones, Genene

A female serial killer from the United States who killed up to 60 toddlers and children in her care when she was a nurse in the late 1970s and 1980s. She killed by injecting her victims with *digoxin, heparin* or *succinylcholine*, to cause the deaths.

Unfortunately, the true number of victims remains unknown. The hospital deliberately misplaced her records to avoid further pressure on them. The drugs would cause paralysis of skeletal muscles which also means the patient wouldn't be able to breathe under their own control. In children, they would suffer heart attacks or stop breathing.

Jones's motivation for the murders was to see herself become the hero. She enjoyed putting small children in real danger and then jumping in to save the same child. She was sentenced to a total of 159 years in prison.

As of 2021, Jones remains in prison with no known parole date.

Born **July 13th 1950**.

Active from **1977-1982**.

Arrested on **November 21st 1982**.

Country: **USA**.

Victims: **60+**.

Sentence: **Total of 159 years in prison.**

Current whereabouts: **In prison.**

Jordan, Gilbert Paul

Known as *The Boozing Barber*, he was linked to the murders of up to ten women over a 22 year period. He used alcohol as a murder weapon. His other convictions are for rape, assault, kidnapping, hit and run and car theft.

On October 12th 1987, in Vancouver, *Vanessa Lee Buckner's* body was found naked on the floor of the *Niagara Hotel*. Buckner's death was caused by Jordan supplying her with a fatal level of alcohol. He would seek women in bars and ply them with drink, sometimes paying them for sex.

He was arrested multiple times but no murder charges could be brought against him because of the nature of the deaths. However it didn't stop police putting out a warning in relation to Jordan. The police warning was released by the Saanich Police Department on February 5th 2005. Release listed in partial form below.

JORDAN is currently in the Victoria area but has no fixed address. JORDAN has a significant criminal record including manslaughter and indecent assault of a female. He uses alcohol to lure his victims. JORDAN's target victim group is adult females. JORDAN is subject to court ordered conditions including:

1) Abstain absolutely from the consumption of alcohol.

2) Not to be in the company of any female person or persons in any place where alcohol is being either consumed or possessed by that person or persons.

Because some of his victims were alcoholics, the police paid little attention. He was known to have drunk almost two bottles of vodka every day.

Born December 12th 1931.

Active from **1965-2004.**

Country: **Canada.**

Victims: **8-10.**

AKA: **The Boozing Barber.**

Sentence: **15 years for manslaughter.**

Current whereabouts: **Died of natural causes in 2006.**

Junco, Francisco del

In Miami, Cuban-American serial killer *Francisco del Junco* killed four female prostitutes in less than one year between 1995 and 1996. Born in Cuba to a troubled family, he was taking medication for epilepsy at the age of three-years-old. He grew to suffer from delusions where he would hear people's voices and their negative influences.

When he was 16-years-old, he consulted black magic practitioners, including a high priestess. He began to withdraw from society and hide away from people who he believed were out to kill him, or who the voices said were going to kill him. In 1980, when he was 23-years-old, he moved to Miami with relatives and suffered even further with delusions.

He was sectioned to a Miami mental health facility on three separate occasions from 1987 to 1992. Then from August 1995 to March 1996, he killed four black prostitutes by bludgeoning them to death with iron bars. After he killed them, he set their corpses alight with gasoline.

On June 3rd 1996, del junco was arrested, after a speedy investigation. He was found by police with a container of gasoline in his hand, almost red-handed. A homeless women had contacted the authorities after he had become violent with her.

He later confessed to the murders and was convicted in 2002 of four murders and sentenced to four life sentences. He escaped the death penalty due to his mental illness.

Born in **1958**.

Active from **1995-1996**.

Arrested on **June 3rd 1996**.

Country: **USA**.

Victims: **4**.

AKA: **June 3rd 1996**.

Sentence: **Four life sentences.**

Current whereabouts: **In prison.**

Junni, Ismo Kullervo

Born in 1943, Finnish serial killer *Ismo Kullervo Junni* would go on to murder 5 people from 1980 to 1988. Most of his crimes were committed at the Kivinokka summer camp area in Helsinki. He became known for removing his victim's teeth.

Growing up he had witnessed his father killing his mother by stamping on her head and dragging her body to their bathtub. It was a traumatic experience that never left Junni. Throughout his formative years and in his adult life, he grew a bizarre interest in cadavers and would often visit mortuaries.

In August of 1980, Junni killed his wife and then pulled out her teeth. He was investigated but due to insufficient evidence the case was recorded as an accident. It wasn't until 1986 when he killed again, he killed two of his colleagues at the summer camp and then set fire to the crime scene in order to hide the evidence.

In July 1986, Junni killed his friend, *Matti Haapanen*, by smashing a glass bowl over his head then he proceeded to set fire to his friend's summer home. Again in 1988, he killed another person by burning them alive in their summer home. When Matti's wife reported Junni's strange behaviour of telling stories about the fire, he was arrested and charged.

He was convicted of four murders and confessed to the murder of his wife.

Born in **June 1943**.

Active from **1980-1988**.

Country: **Finland**.

Victims: **5**.

Sentence: **Life imprisonment**.

Current whereabouts: **Died of natural causes on November 3rd 1995.**

Kibbe, Roger: The I-5 Strangler (Extended Case File)

On September 17th 1987, American serial killer *Roger Reece Kibbe* killed 17-year-old runaway and prostitute *Darcie Frackenpohl*. He strangled her to death after raping and beating her. He went on to remove her hair and then dumped her body near Echo Summit in California.

Darcie was Kibbe's final known victim as most of his murders took place in 1986. Most of the bodies were dumped on the side of the *Interstate 5 (I-5)*, one of the longest road systems in the United States. Police discovered abandoned cars on the highway that belonged to some of the victims. At the time it was suspected that Kibbe patrolled the area searching out females with broken-down cars.

They were very much murders of the time which harks back to the notion that the highways opened up *killing channels* for serial killers to move back forth between states.

Roger Kibbe was born in 1949 to a violent mother who regularly beat him. He spoke with a stutter and was bullied by other children in school because of it. He developed an unhealthy view of women in his teenage years, most likely caused by the abuse he had received.

In his teenage years he was arrested for stealing women's underwear from clotheslines. Unknown to the police at the time, Kibbe took pleasure in tying himself up with the underwear and taking sexual satisfaction in doing so. He would always cut up the items he stole with a pair of his mother's scissors, something that would be his modus operandi in years to come.

He married in his adult years to a dominant woman that reminded him of his mother, but not too much is known about that particular relationship.

Roger Kibbe's brother was a homicide detective and so it was suspected that he used his brother's knowledge about crime scenes to hide his true identity from any investigation that ensued. He learned how investigators would approach cases similar to his own murders. Because of this, no fingerprints or semen was found on his victims.

His first victim was in September of 1977, when he put a fake job advertisement in a business school. The job was for a secretary at a fake cosmetics studio. He did it with the sole purpose of finding a young female to rape and murder. 21-year-old student *Lou Ellen Burleigh* responded to the advertisement. Kibbe told her that his office was under construction and to meet in his van where he drove her to Lake Berryessa in Napa County.

He raped and strangled her before dumping her body near a riverbed. It would take 34 years for Burleigh's remains to be found. In 2011, a small bone was found in the area and DNA results confirmed it had belonged to her. Kibbe wouldn't kill again until April 1986, when he would kill five people in the same year.

He killed *Karen Finch* on June 21st 1987, before the September 1987 slaying of Darcie Frackenpohl. And it was Frackenpohl's murder that would lead to his arrest and conviction. Her body was discovered by a jogger two weeks after she was killed.

After abducting, raping and strangling his victims he would proceed to cut open their clothes in irregular shapes with his mother's scissors. It was never clear why he did this but it stemmed back to his childhood fascination of cutting up the underwear he had stolen.

It has been proposed he did this to mentally cleanse himself of the crime. Another suggestion is that he touched the person in those areas and cut the clothing away to hide the evidence. Although this seems unlikely as it would have been easier to remove the clothing entirely, thus a deeper psychological reason must have been prevalent. He also removed the hair of some of his victims to remove the duct tape he had bound them with.

In April 1988, Kibbe was arrested and went to trial later in the year for Darcie's murder. At the time there was insufficient evidence to link him to the other murders, even though police were sure he was the I-5 Strangler. In March of 1991 he was finally convicted of Darcie's murder and sentenced to 25 years.

When DNA technology advanced enough, further charges were brought to Kibbe and he made a plea bargain in 2009 to avoid the death penalty. He received six additional life sentences for the murders and remains incarcerated at *Mule Creek State Prison* in California. He is known to have killed eight people but has been linked to numerous more.

Born in **1941**.

Active from **1977-1987**.

Arrested in **April 1988**.

Country: **USA**.

Victims: **8+**.

AKA: **The I-5 Strangler**.

Sentence: **Six life sentences plus 25 years**.

Current whereabouts: **In prison**.

Kirkland, Anthony

On May 20th 1987, Ohio serial killer, *Anthony Kirkland*, murdered his 27-year-old girlfriend, *Leola Douglas*. After killing her, he then set her body on fire. For her murder, he served 16 years in prison and was released in 2004.

In the five years after his release, he would go on to kill another four females. Including the aggravated murders and rapes of 14-year-old *Casonya Crawford* in 2006, and 13-year-old *Esme Kenney* in 2009, both of Cincinnati. He would burn the bodies in an attempt to hide any forensic evidence.

He was caught near the scene of the Esme Kenney murder, and was found to be in possession of her watch and *iPod*. He had dragged her into a secluded area as she was jogging around a lake then raped and brutally murdered her, before burning her body.

After various appeals and court proceedings, he was finally sentenced to death in 2018 and currently awaits his execution.

Born **September 13th 1968.**

Active from **1987-2009.**

Arrested on **March 8th 2009.**

Country: **USA.**

Victims: **5.**

Sentence: **Death penalty.**

Current whereabouts: **Death row.**

Knychala, Jaochim

A Polish serial killer sometimes known as '*The Vampire of Bytom*' or '*Frankenstein*'. He killed five women over a five year period. As a child, his mother would neglect him and have sex with her many boyfriends in front of him. His grandmother would also violently and physically abuse him.

Knychala would kill all of his victims with an axe, butchering and dismembering their bodies after he killed them. It is claimed that he was killing using the same methods as serial killers who had already been caught. It is unclear who he was supposed to have copied. However, Knychala's crimes are listed as some of the worst among Polish serial killers.

He was sentenced to death in 1985 and was hung three days before Halloween.

Born **September 8th 1952**.

Active from **1975-1982**.

Arrested in **May 1982**.

Country: **Poland**.

Victims: **5**.

AKA: **The Vampire of Bytom / Frankenstein**.

Sentence: **Death penalty**.

Current whereabouts: **Executed by hanging on October 28th 1985**.

Koltun, Joseph

On August 31st 1980 in Podlaski, Poland, serial killer **Julian Koltun**, AKA: **The Podlaski Vampire**, claimed his first victim. She was an unnamed Russian female who was raped at knife point and bitten multiple times. She went on to survive the attack which occurred at the Polish-Soviet border.

Koltun was a railroad worker who was later arrested for raping seven women, killing two of them and drinking their blood. On September 17th 1980, he brutally murdered a teenage girl named **Dorota**. She had been so badly mutilated and beaten that the killer was labelled a vampire by the Polish press.

Koltun was active from 1980 to 1981 and has since been linked to at least six other disappearances in the region. He was arrested in January 1981 and sentenced to death in August of 1982.

Active from **1980-1981**.

Arrested in **1981**.

Country: **Poland**.

Victims: **2-8**.

AKA: **The Podlaski Vampire**.

Current whereabouts: **Executed in 1982**.

Komin, Alexander: The Vyatka Maniac (Extended Case File)

In Russia, *Alexander Komin* killed at least four people over a two year period in the mid-1990s and kidnapped and tortured many more. He became known as *The Slaveholder*, due to the way he kept his victims in a nine-metre bunker under his garage on his property. At one point over the two year period, he had six slaves chained up in the dungeon.

At the age of 18-years-old, Komin was sentenced to three years in prison for vandalism and hooliganism. While in prison, he met a fellow prisoner who had kept homeless people in his basement. The prisoner spoke of how he felt like God and had unlimited power and control over the people in his basement. It was an experience that Komin grew to want for himself.

A few years after being released from prison, he yearned for his own dungeon but knew he couldn't get away with it. So he came up with the idea of creating his own sewing production company. He roped in some friends to help him build a bunker under the garage that could hold the necessary space to begin the company as a start-up.

By 1995, the *'factory'* had multiple rooms, electric connection, ventilation and a makeshift elevator designed to move goods up and down. Komin was creating an underground prison and one of his friends, *Alexander Mikheyev*, became his accomplice toward the end of the build. However, he still kept up the facade of it being a sewing facility and lured people there with the promise of work.

One room had three bunk beds and an old television set. Another room had three sewing machines. Three trapdoors separated the bunker from the garage, with one of the doors having been stolen from a military base. Komin ensured that the steel ladder to the bunker was electrified so that his slaves couldn't escape. Images of naked women adorned the walls, to add to the bizarreness of the set up.

In January 1995, he met a woman named *Vera Talpayeva* outside a school and took her back to the garage. He then drugged her with clonidine laced vodka and she became his first victim and prisoner. She helped him lure a tailor named *Tatyana Melnikova* to the bunker.

When Komin went to find the tailor, he bumped into Talpayeva's boyfriend, *Nikolai Malykh*. Together they brought Melnikova to the bunker to meet with his girlfriend, but Komin drugged them both. He decided he didn't want any men as a slave and so he poisoned Malykh, stripped him, and dumped his body in a remote field where he died of exposure. His body was discovered a week later.

Now with two slaves in his bunker, he abused and raped both of them as and when he wanted. But his passion for keeping slaves grew and he wanted more workers for his business. Melnikova was the better tailor and put together various types of clothing that Komin would sell to other businesses, and at markets.

At the same time, he wanted to extend the bunker, and when his first victim, Talpayeva, proved unable to carry out the works, he went looking for another victim. Komin and Mikheyev lured 37-year-old alcoholic *Yevgeny Shishov* to the bunker. A few days later upon realising that Shishov was an electrician, they decided to kill him in case he worked out how to turn off the electrics and escape through the doors.

Komin created an electric chair purely to execute Shishov. He tied Shishov to the chair naked and secured him with exposed electric wires. He then ordered the two female slaves to push the two switches. Shishov was barbarically electrocuted in front of them and his body was later removed and buried in the forest.

He decided that because Talpayeva was now an accomplice to murder, that he knew she could be trusted. Komin released her out into the open for the sole purpose of finding him a new prisoner. Talpayeva had her back against a wall and followed Komin's orders. She brought another female back to the bunker named *Tatiana Kozikova*.

Komin ordered the three of them to work 16 hours a day, creating dressing gowns and shorts for the business. The two latter prisoners decided to escape and managed to force Komin into one of the rooms where they jammed the door shut. Komin got out and dragged them back before they had a chance to escape.

He gave them a choice of punishment; have their mouths cut to their ears or have RAB (раб) tattooed on their foreheads. The word translates as 'slave'. They both chose the tattoo over the slashing. From then on, Komin would regularly beat and rape his slaves to keep them under control. He had them wear collars and shackles and chained them to the wall.

Talpayeva was then sent out to get another slave but she disappeared, deciding to runaway instead. Komin then lured 27-year-old homeless person *Tatyana Nazimova*. She jumped at the chance of being fed with a roof over her head. When he and Mikheyev released that Nazimova was mentally and physically disabled, they decided to only use her for sexual purposes.

Over the following year, the conditions in the bunker were becoming atrocious and disgusting. The prisoners begged Komin to give them more food as he starved them on regular occasions. He responded by saying that if they wanted more food then he would cut up the body of a dead slave and feed it to them.

A year passed and Komin had become bored with Nazimova and starved her for almost a week before injecting her with brake fluid. He put her corpse on a sled, drove to a nearby field and dumped her body in the open.

In January 1997, his first victim bumped into him while Komin was out looking for a new prisoner. Astonishingly, Talpayeva agreed to rewards for finding him new markets to sell at and any more slaves. He got her on board by telling her that she had pressed the switch that killed Shishov in the electric chair.

Two days later, Talpayeva lured 22-year-old *Irina Ganyushkina* to the bunker. Amazingly, Komin tried to fertilise her with injections in order to grow an army of slaves he could control. Then he decided to punish Talpayeva for leaving him. He tortured and beat her for half a day before giving her a choice of drinking antifreeze or having it injected into her. She chose to drink it and made the other slaves watch her ordeal before she died of her injuries.

Shortly after, Komin claimed he fell in love with his latest prisoner and wanted to marry her. Kozikova and Melnikova suddenly knew that it was an opening to escaping and begged Ganyushkina to agree to the marriage. On July 21st 1997, Komin brought Ganyushkina to his apartment to prepare for the wedding but she escaped and ran to the police.

Komin was arrested shortly after and the two remaining prisoners Melnikova and Kozikova, were removed from the bunker. They had been underground for two years and had to wear a special bandage around their eyes, so their eyesight wouldn't be damaged by the light. Mikheyev was arrested shortly after and testified against Komin.

In 1999, Komin was sentenced to life imprisonment for four murders and various slave trade charges. Mikheyev was given 20 years in prison. Four days later, Komin killed himself by cutting the iliac artery at the base of his abdomen. He bled out before he could be saved.

When the two remaining victims had a fundraiser set up for them to remove the tattoos on their heads, not one person donated to them. In fact, the Russian public blamed the victims for their ordeal claiming that real women would have either died or killed their captor. Many saw the victims as having brought it upon themselves, which later caused uproar when their story was published in the New York Times.

Komin's story remains one of Russia's most disturbing crimes.

Born in **1953**.

Active from **1995-1997**.

Arrested on **January 21st 1997**.

Country: **Russia**.

Victims: **4+**.

AKA: **The Vyatka Maniac / The Slaveholder**.

Sentence: **Life imprisonment**.

Current whereabouts: **Committed suicide by cutting artery in 1999**.

Kraft, Randy: The Scorecard Killer (Extended Case File)

On April 16th 1978, *Randy Kraft* abducted an 18-year-old Marine named *Scott Michael Hughes*. Hughes was plied with Valium before Kraft slit open his scrotum and removed one of his testicles. All before strangling him to death with a ligature and discarding his fully clothed body beside a freeway.

Randy Steven Kraft is sometimes known as the *Southern California Strangler* or *The Freeway Killer*. The Freeway Killer is generally considered to be a mistaken moniker. The name was coined by the media to describe a serial killer from early 1979. His name was *William Bonin* and he would go on to murder at least 21 young men until his arrest in the Summer of 1980.

The Southern California Strangler was the name that the investigation attributed to Kraft's murders. The Scorecard Killer attribute is given to Kraft because he kept coded references to his victims. He was convicted of 16 murders but it is suggested he may have been responsible for 67 killings during his campaign of terror.

He was born in 1945 at the tail end of World War Two. His childhood was better than one might have expected compared to others who went on to become a serial killer. There has never been any notion of abuse or trauma in his childhood save for the fallout of the war.

Randy Kraft would also stand out as an anomaly amongst serial killers. Most serial killers are happy to discuss their crimes or prove their involvement in certain murders or disappearances. Kraft has never given any obvious reasons or motive for killing so many people. He also denies any involvement with his crimes and disregards the attention put on him as a serial killer.

Although he has never given reasons himself, there are things we know about him that might have led one to kill. His killings were about control and sating perversity, his crimes show this many times over.

In 1964 he campaigned for presidential candidate, *Barry Goldwater*. He also joined demonstrations in support of the Vietnam War. During this time he became a bartender at a gay bar and started to use Valium heavily. A few years later he earned a degree in economics. So far, there was nothing to think that he would go on to kill a possible 67 men.

His job at the gay bar would see him wrestle with his own sexuality. It was known that Kraft struggled with the possibility of being gay. In 1968 he joined the *U.S. Air Force* and was provided with high-level clearance. A year later, he openly came out as gay to his family and friends. He was discharged for medical reasons in 1969 and went back to bartending at the gay bar.

Although Kraft coming out as gay might not have had any link with the discharge, he was said to have felt *'forced out'*. The lack of belonging and somewhat isolation could have seen his mental state deteriorate.

Wayne Joseph Dukette was said to have been his first victim. Dukette's decomposing body was found near Ortega Highway in 1971. The naked body had been there for months and his clothes were never found. Kraft is said to have killed from the early 1970s until his arrest in 1983. His victims were mostly homosexual men and he would torture and mutilate most of them, sometimes while they were alive.

The April 16th 1978 killing of Scott Michael Hughes would see Kraft go on to murder many more in the same year. Kraft had killed Scott with a ligature before throwing the body to the side of a freeway. It is suggested that he strangled Scott with his own shoelaces.

Later in June of 1978, he would kill 23-year-old Roland Young. The victim's testicles and penis had been removed before being stabbed to death. In the same month, another Marine named Richard Keith was killed. He had been tied up by his wrists and strangled.

On July 6th 1978, Kraft killed a hitchhiker named *Keith Klingbeil*. It was evidenced that the victim ingested a huge amount of paracetamol and alcohol before being strangled with his own shoelace. His left nipple had also been burned with a car's cigarette lighter. Unbelievably, Klingbeil was found alive but died shortly after his arrival at hospital.

Again, on September 29th 1978, *Richard Crosby* would become Kraft's next victim. Another hitchhiker picked up by Kraft who had subsequently died of suffocation. As with other victims, his left nipple had been mutilated with a car's cigarette lighter.

On November 18th 1978, the body of *Michael Inderbieten* was found beside the San Diego freeway. He had been castrated, sexually abused, burned and suffocated to death.

Kraft would be convicted of 16 murders. However, his coded '*scorecard*' would take his suspected murder count to an astonishing 67.

It was clear that Randy Kraft could kill because of unlimited access to the highways and interstates. Maybe he thought the highways offered him anonymity with his killings which is why a lot of his victims would be hitchhikers. The interstates had offered the means with which to kill.

He has never shown any interest or given any assistance in clearing his name in unsolved murders and remains as tight-lipped about them to this day. As of 2021, he remains on death row in *San Quentin State Prison* in California.

Born **March 19th 1945.**

Active from **1971-1983.**

Arrested on **May 14th 1983.**

Country: **USA**.

Victims: **16-67+.**

AKA: **The Southern California Strangler. / The Scorecard Killer.**

Sentence: **Death penalty.**

Current whereabouts: **Death row.**

(Research Article #14) DNA Evidence Exploded in the 1980s

In England, on November 13th 1987, *Robert Melias* becomes the first person to be convicted of a crime using DNA evidence. He had been found guilty of rape and convicted by a British court. Scientists calculated that the chance of the sample from the crime scene *not* coming from Melias was 1 in 4 million of the male population.

Following Melias's conviction and in the same month, *Tommy Lee Andrews* became the first American to be convicted on DNA evidence. Andrews was also charged with rape, in Florida.

DNA profiling was originally developed as a method of determining paternity that could link a child with a parent. But it was the Robert Melias case in England that changed it all. The investigation had sought the help of a molecular biologist named *Alec Jeffreys,* as he had begun to use DNA for forensic testing. The perpetrator was caught based on the DNA evidence and subsequently convicted because of it.

In Florida, Tommy Lee Andrews was convicted because DNA tests found a match from his blood and semen in a rape victim. In the years that followed, no one disputed or argued against DNA evidence in criminal trials. As soon as prosecutors began using DNA to convict then defence lawyers began questioning the admissibility of DNA.

During the late 1980s and early 1990s, there were a number of legal challenges against DNA evidence. The challenges against DNA evidence mostly arose because the validity of the techniques used were coming under scrutiny. Out of these cases came a national standard for collecting DNA evidence.

In many cases, a DNA testing laboratory protocols would be brought into question. Their validation processes were deemed insufficient, meaning evidence was denied. Once lawful protocols came into place then DNA testing would become common in criminal cases that required DNA as evidence.

The federal *DNA Identification Act of 1994* meant that DNA profiles could be held on record for a set amount of time. It meant that laboratories had to adhere to a strict set of protocols for testing and uploading profiles to the database. In the same year, these protocols became uniform standards when the *Violent Crime Control and Law Enforcement Act* was implemented.

In the late 1990s and through the 2000s, the DNA databases helped solved a number of cold cases from the 1970s onwards. In 2002, Virginia became the first state to execute a criminal based on DNA evidence assisting in a cold case investigation. *James Earl Patterson* was already serving time for rape when he was linked to the murder.

The ability to use DNA testing to convict and to exonerate suspects changed the way that criminals were convicted, especially in rape and murder cases. It is now one of the most powerful tools that it used within the criminal justice system.

Krajcir, Timothy

An American serial killer who confessed to killing nine women; five in Missouri and four more in Illinois and Pennsylvania. He spent most of his life in prison for various sex crimes he had committed. During the gaps when he was released, he would act on his desire to murder.

He would travel to different towns where he had no connection. Then he would stalk his victims before breaking into their houses and wait for them to arrive home.

Some victims were found tied to their beds, others had been kidnapped and transported across state lines on the highway systems. Most would be raped and forced to perform demeaning sexual acts. His victims were either shot, stabbed or strangled. He has been in prison since 1982 and has been charged with various murders along the way, adding to his sentence.

As of 2021, he is currently serving time in the Pontiac Correctional Center in Illinois.

Born **November 28th 1944.**

Active from **1977-1982.**

Arrested on **August 29th 2007.**

Country: **USA.**

Victims: **9.**

Sentence: **Life imprisonment.**

Current whereabouts: **In prison.**

Kuklinski, Richard

Known as '*The Iceman*', Kuklinski holds a special place on this list as he is sometimes listed as a hitman, which is true, but he was also one of the worst serial killers in America's history. The classification of serial killer from the FBI is the unlawful killing of two or more people. The Iceman falls deep into the serial killer category.

He was convicted of murdering six people but it is suggested he may have killed between 100 and 150 people. He confessed to many more than he was convicted for. He was mostly a hitman for the American Mafia and was given the moniker of 'The Iceman' for freezing his victims to hide the time and date of death.

Mobsters came to call him '*the devil himself*' due to his fearsome reputation. At the time of his arrest, his family claimed to know nothing about his double life as a hitman and serial killer. He would become sloppy in the disposal of his victims and it led to his arrest in 1986 and conviction to life in 1988.

Some theories suggest he killed up to 250 people and by his own confessions was the man behind the murder of *Jimmy Hoffa*. He died in prison of natural causes in 2005.

Born **April 11th 1935.**

Active from **1948-1986.**

Arrested in **1986.**

Country: **USA.**

Victims: **6-150+.**

AKA: **The Iceman / The Devil Himself.**

Sentence: **Life imprisonment.**

Current whereabouts: **Died of natural causes in 2005.**

Kukula, Henryk

Polish serial killer *Henryk Kukula,* AKA: *the Monster from Chorzow*, raped and murdered at least four children over a ten year period from 1980 to 1990. He was only 14-years-old when he claimed his first victim.

During his childhood, Kukula showed signs of aggression towards people around him and was treated in a psychiatric hospital for suspected mental health issues. His mother allowed him to stop the medication and a year after he was discharged, he murdered a five-year-old girl then engaged in necrophilia with the body.

In 1984, he was sent to an educational facility where he beat a nine-year-old boy to death before having sex with the corpse afterwards. He was arrested and sentenced to 15 years in prison but was released only five years later. He claimed to have been raped multiple times by other inmates during his incarceration.

After his release in 1990, he raped and murdered two brothers aged five-years-old and seven-years-old. He was arrested again and sentenced to a further 25 years.

Kukula was due to be released in 2020 but in January 2020, it was decided that he would be transferred to the *Regional Center of Forensic Psychiatry* in Gostnin. He will remain there for an undefined length of time.

Born in **1966**.

Active from **1980-1990.**

Country: **Poland.**

Victims: **4.**

AKA: **The Monster from Chorzow.**

Sentence: **Current sentence of 25 years.**

Current whereabouts: **High-security psychiatric unit.**

Lainz Angels of Death

In Austria, a group of four women killed their patients over a six year period from 1983 to 1989. *Maria Gruber, Irene Leidolf, Stephanija Meyer,* and *Waltraud Wagner* were the four who made up the serial killing group.

They were nurse's aides at the *Geriatriezentrum am Wienerwald* in Lainz, Vienna. They killed their victims by administering overdoses of morphine or by forcing water into the lungs. Because elderly patients were prone to having liquid in their lungs, the murders were virtually unprovable.

The investigation claimed the hospital refused to help them when they looked at one of the deaths in 1988 and that they could have stopped more murders from taking place. The group were caught when a doctor heard them talking about their latest murder while they were out drinking in a local bar.

When they were arrested they all confessed to a total of 49 murders. They were sentenced to between 15 years and life in prison.

By 2008, all four women had been released from prison and are supposed to be living in Austria under new identities.

Active from **1980-1990**.

Country: **Austria**.

Victims: **49**.

AKA: **Maria Gruber / Irene Leidolf / Stephanija Meyer / Waltraud Wagner**.

Sentence: **15 years to life in prison**.

Current whereabouts: **All four have been released since 2008. Current whereabouts unknown**.

Lee, Bruce George Peter

Lee was convicted of 26 murders and is one of Britain's most prolific serial killers. He would kill mostly by setting fire to people's houses with the owners inside. Hardly any media spoke about Lee at the time.

Lee grew up with his grandmother and then mother until her husband left them. He was born with epilepsy and partial paralysis. He became gay in his teen years and changed his name to *Bruce Lee* in honour of his favourite movie star. He associated the tingling in his fingers with starting fires. It was as if there was a subconscious trigger that meant it was time to start a fire.

He first killed in 1973 and then again in 1977 when 11 people died in a nursing home fire. It was suggested that he set fire to the nursing home because one of the residents had slapped him for kicking pigeons. That same man burned to death in his chair.

Lee killed a total of 26 people but mostly went unnoticed by media at the time. Because his convictions were manslaughter rather than murder, he was mostly forgotten about. It was also around the time that the trial of Peter Sutcliffe had taken precedent within the country.

Born **July 31st 1960**.

Active from **1973-1979**.

The Monstrous Book of Serial Killers (2nd edition)

ROGER KIBBE

IMAGE ATTRIB. A85

RANDY KRAFT

TIMOTHY KRAJCIR

IMAGE ATTRIB. A86

PEDRO LOPEZ

IMAGE ATTRIB. A6

Arrested on **December 4th 1979.**

Country: **United Kingdom.**

Victims: **26**.

AKA: **Peter George Dinsdale.**

Sentence: **Committed to a psychiatric institution.**

Current whereabouts: **High-security psychiatric hospital.**

Lee, Derrick Todd

In Louisiana, *Derrick Todd Lee, AKA: The Baton Rouge Serial Killer*, murdered at least seven women over a ten year period. Another serial killer was operating in the region at the same time. *Sean Vincent Gillis,* AKA: *The Other Baton Rouge Serial Killer*, killed at least eight women around the same time period.

Gillis was known as the '*other*' serial killer, as Lee was captured first and suspected of all the murders. But when Gillis continued his campaign, investigators realised they had two serial killers in their county. An urban legend surrounding Lee still perpetuates to this day. It claims that he would play the taped sounds of crying babies to lure his victims outside their homes.

Lee would stalk his victims before killing them, to get to know their routines. He was also caught looking into the homes of women but was ignored as a suspect because the police believed the killer to be white. He first killed in 1992, and his last victim was in 2003.

He was arrested on May 27th 2003, on suspicion of rape. When DNA was put through the system, it linked to one of the murder victims. Shortly after, DNA technology conclusively linked Lee to seven victims in Louisiana. In 2004, he was convicted of all the murders in separate trials.

In most trials, it took the jury just over one hour to come back with a guilty charge. At the time he was suspected of the eight unsolved murders and would come off the suspect list when Gillis was arrested and convicted of them.

On January 21st 2016, Lee died of natural causes involving heart disease in a Louisiana hospital. He had been on death row awaiting execution.

Born **November 5th 1968.**

Active from **1992-2003.**

Arrested on **May 27th 2003.**

Country: **USA (Louisiana).**

Victims: **7+.**

AKA: **The Baton Rouge Serial Killer.**

Sentence: **Death penalty.**

Current whereabouts: **Died of natural causes on January 21st 2016.**

Lindholm, Jukka Torsten

Born in 1965 as *Jukka Torsten Lindholm*, the Finnish serial killer changed his name multiple times to be known as *Michael Maria Pentholm* and then *Michael Penttila*. His crimes had started in his early life and showed no signs of letting up. When he was 16-years-old, in 1981, he abducted a 16-year-old girl and dragged her into a basement where he beat and choked her.

The girl escaped and identified Lindholm as the attacker. He was sent to a youth prison in 1984 for one year for various other attacks and thefts. In 1985, upon his release, he killed his 48-year-old mother in the apartment they shared. Despite being a suspect, he was not charged with the murder.

In July of 1986, he lured two 12-year-old girls to his apartment for alcohol. He locked one of the girls in the bathroom as he choked the other one to death. When he released the girl in the bathroom, he raped and beat her but she escaped and ran from the apartment. Lindholm was caught shortly after whilst hiding out in a forest.

On March 17th 1987, he was found guilty of two charges of manslaughter along with other crimes. He was sentenced to nine years in prison but was released on parole in 1992. He attacked more people in the year that followed, killed a 42-year-old woman, then escaped a police station in June of 1993. When he was recaptured, he was sentenced to another nine years in prison then sent to a psychiatric unit.

Astonishingly he was released twice more in the years that followed only to attack more women and kill again. His final victim was on April 13th 2018 when he killed a prostitute in a Helsinki apartment. Lindholm as Michael Penttila was then sentenced to life in prison. Presumably until he is released on parole again.

Born in **July 1965.**

Active from **1985-2018.**

Arrested on **May 6th 2018.**

Country: **Finland.**

Victims: **4+.**

AKA: **Michael Maria Pentholm / Michael Penttila.**

Sentence: **Life imprisonment.**

Current whereabouts: **In prison.**

Lindsey, William Darrell

Active in St. Augustine, Florida, *William Darrell Lindsey* AKA: *Crazy Bill*, was responsible for at least seven murders in the area over a 13 year period. Lindsey became an orphan when he was just five-months-old, after his parents died in a car crash. He was quickly adopted into a household where suspicions of abuse were pointed towards the foster mother.

During his childhood years, he formulated an alter ego he would come to call '*Bad Bill*'. The alter ego was a sadistic sexual deviant who would torture animals, be prone to violent outbursts, and go on to brutally murder at least seven women. It was known that he only became aroused when he was angry, leading to the violence against women.

"You've got to understand that there's a good Bill and a bad Bill. Good Bill is a decent person...Bad Bill is a person society needs to be afraid of."

Lindsey, in a police interview.

He was known to have used prostitutes regularly and found solace in the cocaine drug culture of Northeast Florida. He was said to have killed for so long because his murders had no common link aside from the sex and drug culture. Lindsey was able to continue killing by floating through society unnoticed.

His first murder took place on October 9th 1983, after a drinking session at a bar known as the Tradewinds Lounge. He drove *Lisa Foley* to a local beach where an argument ended in murder. The murder wouldn't be solved until 14 years later when Lindsey confessed to the killing.

"We had intercourse and she wanted three hundred dollars. I said fifty dollars is all you're going to get. This started us fighting. I strangled her and took her body down to Pacetti Road and dumped her in a borrow pit down there."

Lindsey's confession.

Lindsey would confess to another six murders in the area and go on to describe them all in detail. Though he often stated that he didn't remember why he had become so enraged with each of his victims. He was arrested on suspicion of murder on December 29th 1996 and was linked to a possible 20 murders.

He was sentenced to 30 years in prison, after bargaining his way out of a death penalty. He is due to be released in 2025, at the age of 90-years-old.

Born **March 18th 1935.**

Active from **1983-1996.**

Arrested on **December 29th 1996.**

Country: **USA.**

Victims: **7+.**

AKA: **Crazy Bill / Red Bird.**

Sentence: **30 years in prison.**

Current whereabouts: **In prison, due for release in 2025.**

Little, Samuel

On January 22nd 1978, the body of 36-year-old **Julia Critchfield** was discovered near a dirt track in Saucier, Mississippi, by friends riding dirt bikes. She was found nude with a black dress draped over her. She had been raped and died from strangulation.

Critchfield's case had been a cold case up until 2016, when it became linked with American Serial Killer; **Samuel Little**. As of 2021, investigations into Samuel Little are still active, but he has confessed to 93 murders (as of November 2020).

Little was tried for the murders of three women, in September 2014. The prosecution presented the DNA evidence as well as testimony of witnesses who were attacked by the accused at different times throughout his criminal career. He was sentenced to life imprisonment without the possibility of parole.

Samuel Little was in a homeless shelter in Kentucky when he was arrested in 2012 following DNA testing on various cold cases. Despite multiple investigations being carried out, he could be America's most prolific serial killer. The cases are still ongoing as more and more victims are attributed to Little. He remains in prison, serving the original 2014 life sentences, while at the same time assisting law enforcement in their investigations.

Born **June 7th 1940.**

Active from **1970-2005.**

Arrested on **September 5th 2012**

Country: **USA.**

Victims: **93+**

Current whereabouts: **In prison.**

Lockhart, Michael Lee

American serial killer *Michael Lee Lockhart* was a multi-state serial killer who became infamous for receiving three different death sentences in three different states. He had killed in Florida, Indiana, and Texas.

In Indiana on October 13th 1987, Lockhart killed 16-year-old *Wendy Gallagher*. He raped her and mutilated her before killing her. Her body was discovered in the bedroom of her family home by her sister. She was partially clothed with her hands tied behind her back. She had been stabbed four times in the neck and 17 times in the upper body.

A large pool of blood surrounded her body. As she had been so brutally murdered, her intestines were exposed and hanging out. Forensics turned up fingerprints that matched Lockhart's DNA.

In Florida, in January 1988, he killed 14-year-old schoolgirl *Jennifer Colhouer* in the same manner. He sexually assaulted her, mutilated her and left her body to be found by family. He was arrested shortly after and sentenced to death for each of three murders he committed.

"*A lot of people view what is happening here as evil, but I want you to know that I found love and compassion here. The people who work here, I thank them for the kindness they have shown me and I deeply appreciate all that has been done for me by the people who work here. That's all, Warden, I'm ready.*"

Lockhart's final words – December 9th 1997.

Lockhart claimed to have killed dozens of people during his reign, across many states. He also shot dead a police officer who was trying to arrest him. Although convicted of three murders, it is unclear how many he might have murdered.

Born **September 30th 1960**.

Active from **1987-1988**.

Arrested on **March 22nd 1988**.

Country: **USA**.

Victims: **3+**.

Sentence: **Death penalty**.

Current whereabouts: **Executed in 1997**.

Long Island Serial Killer: The Craigslist Killer (Extended Case File)

One of the most infamous unidentified serial killer cases in New York's history. *The Long Island serial killer,* AKA*: The Craigslist Killer,* is an unidentified serial killer who is suspected to be linked to at least 16 murders over a 17 year period from 1996 to 2013. Almost all the victims were prostitutes or escorts, and their bodies would be found on the South Shore of Long Island.

Many of the victims were discovered along the Ocean parkway which is near remote beach towns in the area, *Gilgo, Oak Beach, and Jones Beach*. At one point, the killer was being referred to as the *Gilgo Beach Serial Killer*. Ten of the victims were not discovered until 2010 and 2011, when an investigation started picking up pace.

Investigators concluded that all ten had been the victims of a single serial killer, and so more connections were being made in relation to the killings.

In November of 2000, hunters discovered the body of a decapitated female in a wooded area. She had been placed in garbage bags and left out in the open. Four days later, in the same area, a nude male corpse was discovered, he had been strangled to death. Both bodies had been discovered near the Long Island Expressway and would go on to become involved in the entire Long Island Serial Killer investigation.

Ever since the discovery of those two bodies, the Suffolk County Police Department had constantly come under a barrage of criticism for not doing enough to catch the killer. It had led conspiracy theorists to talk of a cover up within the SCPD. And as we continue down the rabbit hole of the investigation, it is clear that over the years the case has become more and more difficult.

It was left to the media to draw up a profile of the killer, who suggested that the killer was white in his mid-20s to mid-40s and was familiar with the South Shore of Long Island. The killer would also have access to burlap sacks, which was what he stuffed the bodies into before disposing of them. The media also claimed that the killer might have been a member of law enforcement, possibly involved with the Suffolk County Police Department.

In 2016, the former Suffolk County Police Chief *James Burke* was suspected of having rough sex with escorts on the same beach where the bodies were found. It was also claimed by an escort who was with him that Burke stated he had been involved in the killings.

In November of 2016, he was sentenced to four years in prison for violently beating a man who stole a bag from his car. The bag included various sex toys, BDSM toys, and various pornography. It was also later proven that Burke stopped the FBI from getting involved in the Long Island Serial Killer Case. He had personally blocked all attempts from the FBI when they had decided to take the case and get involved.

Although many others were and have been suspected, Burke has long been the stand-out suspect for many. However, nothing has been proven and the case is still ongoing to this day. But then comes the twist of the Craigslist advertisements.

In December of 2010, four bodies and remains were discovered along the Gilgo Beach area of the region. Every victim had been strangled, and placed in a burlap sack, then dumped or buried in a shallow grave in the area. All of them were later identified as sex workers who had also advertised their services on the Craigslist personal advertisement site.

The body of 25-year-old *Maureen Brainard-Barnes* from Connecticut, was amongst the victims. She was an escort who used Craigslist to advertise herself and was last seen on July 9th 2007.

Shortly after she vanished, a friend of hers received a phone call where the caller claimed that Maureen was alive and '*working at a whorehouse in Queens*'. Because Maureen was a mother who only rarely escorted, it was assumed the phone call had been from the killer to throw any investigation off track.

Another body found in the same month was that of 24-year-old escort *Melissa Barthélemy*, who lived in New York and had vanished a year earlier. She too had been advertising her sexual services on Craigslist across New York State.

For an entire month after her disappearance, her teenage sister would get sexually vulgar calls from a man who was using Melissa's phone. The man then claimed he had killed her sister and would relish seeing her rot. The calls were traced to Madison Square Garden in New York but no identification could be made.

The other two bodies were 22-year-old *Megan Waterman*, from Maine, and 27-year-old *Amber Lynn Costello*, from New York. Both had used Craigslist advertisements to seek clients. Costello's sister, who was also an escort, claimed that she was using Craigslist to catch her sister's killer, but nothing has turned up as of 2021.

In 2011, more bodies were discovered in the area. The community around the South Shore of Long Island were outraged that the killer could seemingly not be caught. Back in 2003, the naked and dismembered body of 20-year-old prostitute *Jessica Taylor* from Manhattan, was discovered close to Gilgo Beach. She would be identified by DNA a few months later. In 2011, her skull and hands were discovered close to where the body had been found.

Over the course of 2011, multiple body parts and dismembered remains were discovered in the area. To this day, most have not been identified. The remains of four more young women and one young man then became part of the same investigation. It is suspected that all five of them were working as prostitutes. The male body was dressed in women's clothing and was killed in the same manner as the others.

Up to 2013, another six victims have been added to the investigation as showing similarities to the other remains that had been found. One of the victims was linked by DNA to a set of dismembered legs that had been found in a garbage bag on April 20th 1996. It appeared the killer or killers had been active for at least 17 years.

Another connection was made from 1997, when the torso of a woman was found just off from Gilgo Beach. She had a tattoo of fruit on her body and was known henceforth as *Peaches*. During the 2011 investigation of the shorelines, a dismembered skeleton was found, and DNA linked the bones to that of Peaches.

Later in 2011, the body of a two-year-old girl was discovered, DNA confirmed that the toddler was the daughter of Peaches. All of the body parts had been dispersed across County lines which some saw as a deliberate attempt to confuse any resulting investigation.

Like the Texas Killing Fields, it has been suggested that there might be multiple serial killers who use the Long Island shoreline as a dumping ground for their victims. It could be that a lone serial killer knew of the police routines on the beach areas and worked around the gaps in their workforce.

What is clear, is that he would contact them mostly through Craigslist and arrange a meeting with the escort of his choice. He would then meet them on his own terms and then brutally murder them. After their deaths he would dismember them and then drive out to Ocean Parkway and dispose of them on the beaches.

It has since been claimed that the Suffolk County Police Department were responsible for the killer being active for so long and remaining unidentified. The fact that the victims were prostitutes led recent investigators to ascertain that it was because of their profession that investigations didn't move forward.

Fear and paranoia among locals was infesting the Summer tourist season and the SCPD still hadn't caught the killer. Frustrated by the lack of progress, many locals decided to take matters into their own hands and started their own vigilante groups to hunt the killer. One bought a disused bulletproof DEA van to spy on the beaches, and many more have started up their own websites dedicated to catching the killer.

As of 2021, the identity of the Long Island Serial Killer remains a mystery.

Active from **1996-2013.**

Country: **USA.**

Victims: **16+.**

AKA: **The Craigslist Killer / Gilgo Beach Serial Killer.**

Current whereabouts: **Unidentified killer. Status unknown.**

Lopez, Pedro: Monster of the Andes (Extended Case File)

On January 1st 1978, Colombian-born *Pedro Alonso Lopez* was released from a Colombian state prison and went to Peru to continue his killings. Lopez is known as the *Monster of the Andes*. There is a very slim chance that he still roams South America today, taking victims as he pleases.

His mother; *Benilda Lopez de Casteneda,* was a prostitute who was having an affair with the man who would be Lopez's father. He was shot and killed before Lopez was born. He was the seventh of 11 children and his mother abused him from an early age, allowing him to watch her have sex with her punters. Lopez would claim that she let her clients hit her if they wished to.

When he was eight-years-old, he was caught abusing his younger sister and was thrown out of the house. It is said that he was found by a sex offender who took him into an abandoned house and raped him over and over. After the attack on him, he joined a street gang for protection and learned how to fight with knives and sticks.

In his late teens and early twenties, he would steal cars and sell them for money. He was arrested in 1969 and sent to prison for seven years. This is where the next level of Lopez's violence was formed. When he was 21-years-old and serving time inside, he was violently gang-raped by three other inmates. It was said to be an event that traumatised him more than his childhood rape had done.

A few weeks later, he killed his rapists using a handmade weapon. As it was considered self-defence, he only received an additional two years on his sentence, to be released on January 1st 1978. It was then that the Monster of Andes would be born and he would take his revenge out on the world.

"I lost my innocence at age of eight-years-old. So I decided to do the same to as many girls as I could."

Pedro Lopez.

Upon his release and until his subsequent arrest in 1980, he would kill on average three children every week. He preferred to kill girls between eight and 12-years-old and had no racial preference. He attempted to abduct and kill white foreign girls but he said they were too closely watched by their families.

The Monster of the Andes would roam the streets of Peru, Ecuador and Colombia, looking for 'good' girls to lure to their deaths, with the promise of gifts. He would prepare graves for the girls and generally take them from one area to one mass grave. Mostly, they were filled with the bodies of other small girls he had killed.

He claimed that he would make the child calm through the night, then at sunrise he would rape and strangle them. He chose strangling as he wished to see the child's eyes fade into nothing as they died in his hands. He always killed when the sun was out as he '*needed*' to see the eyes of his countless victims.

Only then would he feel that the killing had been worthwhile. There was only ever a gap of a few days before he would hunt the next child to feed his pervasive and perverse desires.

If the killings were bad enough, it was what he did after that proved him more the monster. In Lopez's confession, upon his second capture in 1980, he told authorities details that would shock them to their core.

As he buried some of the children in one location, he would go back to the sites and sit the corpses of the girls in their graves. He claimed he would hold tea parties and play other child-like games with them, talking to the dead as he did so.

He convinced himself that the corpses enjoyed his company and liked his games. But when the children didn't answer back or confirm their enjoyment then he would have to go and search for a new victim. He would sometimes ask the girls for directions and lead them off to his pre-meditated killing zone where the murders would take place.

He claims that he killed over 310 young girls in Colombia, Peru and Ecuador. The police deduced that the girls were either runaways or used as child prostitutes. This was also due to the views on child abuse and child prostitutes at the time. It wasn't only a United States or United Kingdom issue, most countries in the 1970s had a very lax view on those type of crimes.

After his confession, the police didn't believe he could have killed so many. So he offered to take them to some of the grave sites. They subsequently found the bodies of 53 young girls in just one mass grave alone.

For raping, killing, and mutilating over 100 confirmed murders of children, Pedro Lopez received life in prison. But *life in prison* in Ecuador, meant just 14 years.

He was released in 1994 but immediately arrested again and sent back to Colombia where he stood trial for the murder of a girl in 1979. In 1995, he was declared insane and was sectioned to a psychiatric hospital instead of prison.

Unbelievably, in 1998 he was deemed fit for a return to normal society and was released. His conditions of release deemed he would continue his psychiatric treatment and report to the police once a month.

He was never seen again.

No one truly knows what happened to Pedro Lopez beyond 1998. But in an interview from inside prison, he said he would happily return to killing young children upon his release. Indeed, he *'looked forward'* to when he could get his hands around the throat of another child.

There are many theories including the horrific one that he may still be alive and killing today. There's also the belief that he was caught by a vigilante gang and murdered. Another one suggests the authorities executed him in secret as they couldn't have him running amok but couldn't change their own laws.

One thing's for sure, he was more active in 1978 than in any other year. It seemed that South America had also fallen foul to the year of the serial killer.

Born **October 8th 1948**.

Active from **1969-2002**.

Arrested on **March 9th 1980**.

Country: **Colombia / Peru / Ecuador**.

Victims: **300+.**

AKA: **Monster of the Andes.**

Sentence: **Life sentence of 14 years.**

Current whereabouts: **Status unknown.**

Louis, Emile

A French serial killer who killed seven victims during the 1970s. Over 30 women were said to have gone missing in the same area but Louis retracted his initial confession and has remained silent ever since. There are verified suspicions that he did not act alone.

The seven young girls all had mild mental deficiencies and lived in homes for the handicapped and orphaned. It was assumed by law enforcement that the girls had simply runaway and no further investigations were needed. During his investigation, Louis led police to the remains of two of the seven girls.

Efforts by a military investigator named *Christian Jambert* were blocked and the investigator subsequently took his own life. When his case was reopened it was confirmed that Jambert had been shot twice in the head.

He had been murdered to cover up something potentially far more brutal; a secret criminal network that would pay to torture and rape young girls.

Louis was arrested in 2000 and is currently serving a life sentence.

Born **January 26th 1934.**

Active from **1975-1979.**

Arrested **in December 2000.**

Country: **France.**

Victims: **7-30+.**

AKA: **The Disappeared of the Yonne.**

Sentence: **Life imprisonment.**

Current whereabouts: **In prison.**

Lucas, David Allen

In San Diego, California, on May 4th 1979, serial killer **David Allen Lucas** brutally murdered 31-year-old **Suzanne Jacobs** and her three-year-old son in their home. He raped Suzanne and then slashed both their throats before leaving their bodies to be discovered by family and friends.

On November 20th 1984, Lucas raped and murdered University of San Diego student, **Anne Catherine Swanke**. Her body was discovered four days later in a remote area of the Spring Valley. Her vehicle had run out of gas at the time of her disappearance.

From 1979 to 1984, he murdered between three to six people in addition to kidnappings and attempted murders. He was arrested shortly after the Swanke murder in 1984 and sentenced to death in 1989 after a five-year long case and trial. In 2016, after a lengthy appeal, the death penalty was upheld and he remains on death row.

Born in **1956.**

Active from **1979-1984**

Arrested in **1984.**

Country: **USA**.

Victims: **3-6**

Current whereabouts: **Death row.**

Lucas, Henry Lee

A controversial name to put on the list but a serial killer nonetheless who was active through 1978. Hundreds of unsolved murders were attributed to him in what was described as a '*clearing up*' of old cases. He was convicted of 11 murders but sentenced to death for just one of them.

Lucas had lost an eye at ten-years-old, after an infection caused by fighting. His mother was a prostitute who would force him to watch her have sex with clients and would also force him to dress as a girl in public. His father, who had his legs amputated in a train accident, died in a blizzard when he was drunk.

In 1951, Lucas claimed his first victim, he strangled a 17-year-old girl named *Laura Burnsley*. She had apparently refused his sexual advances, although he later retracted his claim.

There have been many books and documentaries on Henry Lee Lucas, mostly because of the absurdity of the investigation and the clearing up of cases that surrounded him. He claimed he killed over 100 people and then suddenly a figure of 3,000 came to light when cases from various states were being attributed to him.

It is suggested that his real victim count comes to around 40. He died in 2001 of a heart attack, leaving his true dark legacy a mystery and a talking point that is still being discussed today.

Born **August 23rd 1936.**

Active from **1951-1983**.

Arrested on **June 11th 1983**.

Country: **USA**.

Victims: **11-40+**.

AKA: **The Confession Killer / The Highway Stalker**.

Sentence: **Death penalty later commuted to life.**

Current whereabouts: **Died of a heart attack in 2001.**

Luptak, Juraj

He raped and murdered three women from the late 1970s to the early 1980s. *The Strangler from Banska Bystrica* was raised in an orphanage and fell into alcoholism in his teens.

On May 6th 1978, Juraj Luptak was working in a meadow when he saw 20-year-old *Elena Adamova* walking nearby. He hit her on the head with a stone, raped her and strangled her to death. The shrivelled corpse of Elena was found in April 1979, hidden in thick bushes. He was arrested for tax evasion and spent two years in prison.

In 1982, he was released from prison and saw 15-year-old *Lýdia Rydlová* going home from school. He dragged her into a secluded area, raped, and strangled her. He buried her alive in a shallow grave, her decomposed corpse was discovered a month later.

Shortly after, her body was discovered he abducted 15-year-old *Ivana Turová*. He knocked her unconscious and was about to rape her when he saw she was on her period. When she awoke, he beat her to death in anger. Due to media and police pressure, Luptak ran off into the mountains and lived in the wild for a week. Shortly after he broke into a house for supplies but was arrested after being recognised from a description photo.

He was sentenced to death and hung for his crimes in 1987.

Born **January 2nd 1942**.

Active from **1971-1982**.

Arrested in **1982**.

Country: **Czechoslovakia**.

Victims: **3**.

AKA: **The Strangler from Banska Bystrica**.

Sentence: **Death penalty**.

Current whereabouts: **Executed by hanging in 1987**.

Maake, Maoupa Cedric

South African serial killer and criminal, *Maoupa Cedric Maake,* AKA*: The Wemmer Pan Killer*, took the lives of at least 27 people from 1996 to 1997. The moniker came about because of the area of Johannesburg where he was claiming most of his victims.

It took a number of months for the Johannesburg Police Force to link some of the murders together and it was then they realised that they had a serial killer at large in the city. Maake would kill men and women using two distinct methods of tracking and killing.

In the first, he would follow men or women who were walking alone then attack them from behind with a small rock to the back of the head. In the case of the men he would bludgeon them to death. In the case of the women, he would rape and abuse them first before killing them also.

The second targets were young couples in cars, in and around his local area. He would surprise the couple and then shoot the man in the head before dragging the female from the car and raping her, before shooting her dead.

Maake was arrested in December of 1997 and immediately confessed to some of the crimes, showing police the areas where he carried out the murders. He was charged with 36 counts of murder, 28 attempted murders, 15 rapes and various other charges relating to robbery and assault.

He pleaded not guilty but in September of 2000, he was convicted of 27 of the murders, 26 attempted murders, 14 rapes, and a raft of other charges. He was sentenced to 27 life sentences which along with the other charges amounted to 1,340 years in prison.

As of 2021, Maake remains incarcerated in a South African prison.

Born in **1965**.

Active from **1996-1997**.

Arrested on **December 23rd 1997**.

Country: **South Africa**.

Victims: **27+**.

AKA: **The Wemmer Pan Killer / Hammer Killer**.

Sentence: **27 life sentences plus extra convictions. Total 1,340 years**.

Current whereabouts: **In prison**.

Martynov, Sergei

A Russian serial killer, *Sergei Martynov*, killed nine people in the Chelyabinsk Oblast of the country. His first murder came in 1992, when he raped and murdered a teenage girl. He was arrested shortly after and convicted of the murder. His sentence of 14 years was served out and he was released in 2005, when he began killing more.

A few months after his release, he raped a teenage girl at knifepoint. He became a suspect straight away but had gone off-the-grid, so he remained on a wanted list for the years that followed. He wouldn't kill again until June 2007, when he raped and killed a woman, before dismembering her body and burying her in a shallow grave.

In July of 2007, he raped an eight-year-old girl and was suspected of further crimes in the same year but could not be proven. He went on to kill a man during a robbery in 2008 and committed the rape and murder of a 70-year-old woman.

His crimes were being committed all over the country, which made the hunt for him extremely difficult. He even left notes near some of his victims that taunted the police for not being able to capture him. Some of his victims had been mutilated and their breasts or sexual organs had been cut off.

After his final murder in 2010, Martynov was arrested in November of the same year, when he had used a mobile phone belonging to one of the victims. After his arrest, he confessed to crimes across ten different regions of Russia, including multiple rapes and eight murders.

He claimed that his motivation for the crimes was simply to rid the country of undesirables in what he called the '*cleaning of society*'. When he was awaiting sentencing, he requested to have another inmate in his cell purely so he could kill him out of boredom.

In 2012, Martynov was sentenced to life in prison.

Born **June 2nd 1962.**

Active from **1992-2010.**

Arrested in **October 2010.**

Country: **Russia.**

Victims: **9.**

Sentence: **Life imprisonment.**

Current whereabouts: **In prison.**

(Research Article #15) Toxic Legacy of World War Two

Most readers might have heard of PTSD (Post-Traumatic Stress Disorder) but up until the time of World War Two, the term was not in use.

Other terms including *shell shock* and *battle fatigue* were the sound-bites of the era. It wasn't until World War Two that *Combat Stress Reaction* (CSR) replaced the more poetic of the terms.

World War Two and indeed The Great War, left a toxic legacy of mental health issues and depression. It created a societal divide that remained difficult to return from. To put it simply, both wars led to a silent epidemic of mental disorders and isolation.

A study showed that adults who were around during World War Two, were 6% more likely to suffer from depression than those before the war.

An astonishing 3% of the entire world's population was wiped out during World War Two alone. Even more humbling when it is noted that the United States currently makes up only 5% of the world's population. In Europe alone, 39 million people died and over half were civilians.

After the war, health problems and poverty increased and class divides were temporarily stalled as the affected countries struggled to pull through. The middle classes witnessed a higher loss of wealth as people rushed to rebuild their lives.

The true cost of such a war was far greater than the financial cost. Lives and families were destroyed, homes were bombed, poverty and hunger became the norm and education was few and far between. The world became a far different place than it was before. It was to be a long climb out of a deep dark hole.

A couple of decades later, one of the most prominent factors towards the rise of the serial killer was the destruction of family values. This also included the physical destruction and loss of family members. Many children lost their fathers and would witness the emotional fallout of war.

Some fathers who survived and returned home displayed poor mental and physical health and struggled to survive in the world they came home to. For the children, in all cases, a deterioration of family values would set in.

Gender ratios changed shortly after the war caused by the higher death of men during wartime. High stress and lower marriage rates caused more depression and the onset of mental disorders. These were then mostly put on the backburner of medical professionals. There was simply no time to focus on it when attention was needed and diverted to physical wounds and ailments.

The current data of the fallout of World War Two is astonishingly hard to come by. Not enough has been done to measure the effects of war on families and children. However, if we link what we know about mental illness after the war with child abuse data as previously spoken about in January 1978, then we do see a connection.

It is no surprise that the abuse of children following World War Two increased more in that time period than any other. We see that more children were raised in broken families or without their biological fathers.

The government push with the *Baby Boomer* generation virtually punished families if they didn't seek a nuclear-family model. Those without husbands would mostly find new loves and expand their broken family.

The disregard of child abuse after the war in favour of the Baby Boomer's was something that would historically not go unnoticed. The link between broken families and abuse in childhood to violent criminals is well documented.

There were also many children growing up without a family. Though some might have had a family of sorts, they were raised in a vastly different world than the one before the war.

I've recently run a study about the *Y2K Generation*. It is a generation of people who were born in a pre-digital world and then have to live through the extreme technological advances of the present day. It has been a struggle for many to find their place in this new world. The same could be said for those living after the war.

Just 40 years earlier, the world was only just coming out of the Victorian era and then suddenly the industrial revolution had provided mass weapons of war. That transition for some would have been harder than the transition from the pre-digital to the digital age of the present era.

During the war, many children would have seen dead bodies and some would have been adversely affected by the war. Point in case is *Andrei Chikatilo*, a Russian serial killer who was convicted of 52 murders. His first victim was in December of 1978, and there is a heading on Chikatilo in that section of this book. Yet, the seeds for his crimes, were developed during *Joseph Stalin's* rule of Russia.

Chikatilo suffered hunger in his childhood and also in the years leading up to World War Two. His family was forced to eat grass and leaves to fight hunger in the Ukrainian SSR.

During the Nazi occupation of Ukraine, he witnessed the true horrors of war. Bombings, fires, shootings, raping, dead bodies, and a complete disruption to an already damaged childhood. His mother was raped by a German soldier, possibly in front of Chikatilo, who then gave birth to his sister.

Does war potentially create violent criminals?

No, not to everyone. Most people, even in the face of utmost adversary, will maintain their moral stance. Yet, some people who lived through World War Two as a child or were born to a broken family during the war, might have gone on to commit violent crimes.

For some of those people, the act of murder would become an outlet for their own suffering. Some might even go on to become serial killers, just like The Red Ripper.

(Research Article #16) Toxic Legacy of the Iraq War

The 2003 Iraq War was the first fully televised war. It was when 24-hour news was at its peak and they might as well have been live-streaming it, it was that detailed.

Audiences remember watching the news as the first of the tanks rumbled over the border into Iraq. There has never been any war since that has been documented so vigorously by the media.

In the UK alone, the Ministry of Defence (MOD) and the NHS failed to meet the mental health needs of soldiers returning from the second Iraq War. This lack of support is evident in every conflict before and after.

Mentalhealth.org began a campaign to raise awareness of mental health and social problems in former military men and women, especially those involved in conflict. MOD figures from the 1991 Gulf War showed that 20% of returning servicemen and women were diagnosed with psychological problems.

These included depression, PTSD, suicidal ideation, anxiety and alcohol or substance abuse. With approx. 13% of those suffering from PTSD. Another study found that servicemen and women were being diagnosed with related mental health problems an entire decade after being in conflict.

If the very governmental body who send soldiers to war cannot deal with the mental health fallout then it is no wonder many will suffer as a result of serving in a conflict.

The same argument that has been used regarding mental health services across the Western world 30 years ago is still being used today. They say that mental health services are over-stretched and under-funded and do not offer sufficient services to meet soldier's needs. Then the question remains; why not?

We've already discussed in the section on World War Two, how damaging it can be on the returning military and the effect on the families of those coming home. If children are being raised by father's who are mentally ill, through no fault of their own, then that child might have to grow up witnessing the fallout of war and how it affects their parents. And indeed, their perception of the world around them.

If soldiers are returning home, suffering from PTSD, then they too will struggle to live in the world they are coming back to. Some might not re-integrate back into society as well as others and those that don't, might go back into the world with toxicity on their minds.

According to Shelter (UK homeless charity) and the Government's Social Exclusion Unit, 25% of homeless people in the United Kingdom are former members of the armed services. 41% of homeless people who attended homeless shelters had previously been in prison. It remains a melting pot of mental health disorders that are simply not being treated. They are virtually going unnoticed and somewhat ignored.

During the Falkland's War, 237 British deaths were recorded. Since then and up to 2013, an astonishing 95 ex-servicemen and women who returned from the Falkland's have taken their own lives. For the Gulf War, 107 suicides have been registered of returning servicemen or women.

We know the Iraq war was bigger and more lives were lost. More soldiers were there than most other modern conflicts worldwide. The resulting fallout from it is deeply worrying.

Mashiane, Johannes

South African serial killer *Johannes Mashiane,* AKA: *The Beast of Atteridgeville,* killed 13 people over a 12 year period from 1977 to 1989. His first victim in 1977 was his girlfriend who he strangled to death. He was sentenced to only five years and released in **1982**.

From his release until his death in 1989, he raped and killed at least **12** small boys. He would either strangle them or stone them to death and would sodomise them before and after their deaths.

Mashiane was caught red-handed while molesting his fourteenth victim but police were informed and gave chase through a large Pretoria suburb. Before he could be caught he threw himself in front of a bus and was killed instantly. His suicide robbed the victims' families of motive and justice.

Active from **1977-1989**.

Country: **South Africa**.

Victims: **13+**.

AKA: **The Beast of Atteridgeville**.

Current whereabouts: **Committed suicide before capture.**

Mason, David Edwin

On August 18th 1980, in California, a 75-year-old male was beaten and strangled to death during a home invasion robbery. He had been murdered by serial killer **David Edwin Mason**, who killed four elderly people during 1980. Mason was also wanted in Butte County for shooting and killing his male lover while he was sleeping.

Mason knew most of his victims and found it easy to access their properties before killing them to not leave any witnesses. Mason was arrested in 1982 and convicted of four murders. While awaiting trial, along with an accomplice, they killed another inmate and hung him from the showers to make it look like a suicide.

Mason was later sentenced to death and executed on August 24th 1993

Born in **1956**.

Active from **1980-1982**.

Arrested in **1982**.

Country: **USA**.

Victims: **6**.

Current whereabouts: **Executed by gas chamber on August 24th 1993.**

Matteucci, Andrea

Italian serial killer *Andrea Matteucci,* AKA*: The Monster of Aosta*, killed four people from 1980 to 1995. His childhood was marred with a criminal father who abandoned Andrea the year he was born. His mother was a prostitute who allowed him to watch her liaisons with clients. Andrea then grew a hatred of women who were paid to be with men.

He killed his first victim on April 30th 1980. He met a man at an abandoned Roman Theatre but the man made sexual advances towards him and he killed him by stabbing him to death. From then on Matteucci grew a second hatred for people who have affairs or sexual contact with others while having a family of their own.

It remains unclear whether he killed anyone else before 1992 when his second confirmed victim was noted. Going against his own ideals, he met a prostitute named *Daniela Zago*. They argued about the money and Matteucci shot her in the head.

Two years later a Nigerian prostitute died at his hands, apparently over an argument relating to her '*unsatisfactory performance*'. He beat her before shooting her dead. He then proceeded to engage in necrophiliac acts with her corpse before taking the body home and dissecting it with a kitchen knife.

All of his victims remains were burned which made the investigation difficult and it is also suggested that he may have killed more. On June 26th 1995, he was arrested in connection with the disappearance of his final victim. He confessed to all the murders and was sentenced to 28 years.

In March 2017 he was released from prison and sent to a psychiatric hospital. As of 2021, it is unclear whether Matteucci still remains there or has been released into the public domain.

Born **April 24th 1962.**

Active from **1980-1995.**

Arrested on **June 26th 1995.**

Country: **Italy.**

Victims: **4+.**

AKA: **The Monster of Aosta.**

Sentence: **28 years in prison.**

Current whereabouts: **Released in 2017. Status unknown.**

Maudsley, Robert: Hannibal the Cannibal (Extended Case File)

On July 28th 1978, in the United Kingdom, *Robert Maudsley* killed a fellow inmate in prison. His case is a unique one in that he would kill more people in prison than he did on the outside. He was considered such a dangerous killer that a special isolation cage was built purely to house him.

His story would be associated with the *Hannibal Lecter* books and is worthy of mention due to the infamy he holds in the United Kingdom.

His childhood was as typical a childhood as some other known violent criminals. He had 11 siblings growing up, some in orphanages, some back at home. When he was eight-years-old, Maudsley was physically and sexually abused by his parents. He had been raped as a child and didn't escape the rotating door of abuse until social services stepped in and removed him from his parents' care.

There are some mixed beliefs as to whether he should have been given the label of serial killer, multiple murderer or even a vigilante. Either way, he was deemed to be Britain's most dangerous prisoner.

His broken childhood led him to a deep drug addiction in his teenage years. To subsidise his addiction to drugs he turned to prostitution, working as a rent boy in London. He attempted suicide on many occasions, seeing him fall into temporary psychiatric care. He told doctors that he was hearing voices telling him to go back and kill his parents.

"If I had killed my parents in 1970, none of these people need have died."

Robert Maudsley.

In 1974, a punter named *John Farrell*, picked him up for sex. The man would go on to show Maudsley photographs of the children he had sexually abused. Enraged, he killed Farrell by strangling him with a garotte, stabbing him and hitting him over the head with a hammer. He was arrested and sentenced to life in prison.

In 1977, he was transferred to the infamous *Broadmoor Hospital*. While there, he and another patient, locked themselves in a room with a known convicted paedophile. They both tortured the child abuser to death over a period of almost ten hours. Maudsley was subsequently convicted of manslaughter, deemed sane, and sent to *Wakefield Prison*.

On that fateful day in July 1978, Maudsley lured *Salney Darwood*, a man who murdered his own wife, into his cell. He tied a garotte around his neck and smashed Darwood's head repeatedly into the wall. He hid the body under his bed and tried to lure other prisoners into his cell.

When no one came in, he prowled the prison and walked into the cell of *Bill Roberts* before stabbing him to death with a *shiv*. After having killed the two men, he calmly walked into a prison guard's office and placed the bloody handmade weapon on the table.

"There'll be two short when it comes to the next roll call."

Maudsley's comment to the prison guard.

He was convicted and sentenced to life at Wakefield Prison. In 1983, a specially-constructed cell was designed at HMP Wakefield, where he has resided ever since. The glass cage, 5.5 metres by 4.5 metres, has bulletproof windows and an entire team of prison officers assigned to watch him. *The Cage* is in the basement of Wakefield Prison.

In order to access *The Cage* you would have to go through an astonishing 17 locked steel doors. The only furniture is a cardboard table and chair with a toilet and sink bolted to the floor. His bed is a thin mattress on a concrete slab.

Unsurprisingly there are some people who see Maudsley as a hero vigilante, who killed paedophiles and wife beaters. There is still an active campaign to move Maudsley out of *The Cage* where he has resided 23 hours a day for the past 45 years.

He has also never eaten any part of a human being. The cannibal legend came about because of the way one of the bodies had been found with the skull split open. This gave rise to a myth that a spoon was found in the man's head.

Still, the legend perpetuates to this day.

Born in **June 1953**.

Active from **1974-1978**.

Arrested in **1974**.

Country: **United Kingdom**.

Victims: **4**.

AKA: **Hannibal the Cannibal / Spoons**.

Sentence: **Life imprisonment**.

Current whereabouts: **In prison, in solitary confinement**.

Maust, David Edward

An American serial killer who killed in West Germany and the United States. He killed boys and men aged between 13 to 19-years-old. He was sent to a mental institution at nine-years-old at the request of his mother. His mother was claimed to be mentally suffering herself and was clinically psychotic. It was said that his mother had dumped him into mental health care, neglecting him.

A few years later Maust would choke two of his friends but not kill them. The event was not lost on his brother, who said Maust would beat to death squirrels with a baseball bat. He was also abused by other boys in a children's home when he was 13-years-old.

In 1974, while based in Germany, he killed a 13-year-old boy. He was sentenced to four years of military prison. He then requested not to be freed but was released in 1977 anyway.

Two years later he stabbed a friend while he was sleeping. He would go on to murder more young teens as the years progressed. Astonishingly, after being imprisoned in 1982, he was finally tried in 1994. Maust was sentenced to 35 years but was released in 1999.

Upon his release, he killed three more people before being arrested again. This time he killed himself in prison in 2006.

Born **April 5th 1954**.

Active from **1974-2003**.

Arrested on **December 9th 2003**.

Country: **Germany / USA**.

Victims: **5+**.

Sentence: **Life imprisonment**.

Current whereabouts: **Committed suicide by hanging on January 20th 2006**.

Maxwell, Bobby Joe

In Los Angeles, on January 21st 1979, **Bobby Joe Maxwell**, AKA: **The Skid Row Stabber**, killed 26-year-old **Luis Alvarez**. In mid-1978, Maxwell had been sentenced to just two months in jail for mild offences. Shortly after his release, from October 1978 to December 1978, Maxwell was alleged to have brutally killed 10 people.

On December 14th 1978, police arrested him again for concealing a weapon on his person and he was only sentenced to one month in prison. After his second release, he killed Alvarez who would become his final victim. On April 4th 1979, Maxwell was arrested for the final time after having been under surveillance for two months.

There had been a two-month gap in the Skid Row killings and that gap just happened to coincide with the two-month prison sentence that Maxwell had received in late 1978. Armed with this and fingerprints from one of the murders, Maxwell was captured. He was charged with 10 of 11 murders but convicted of two and later sentenced to two life terms. In prison, he confessed to another inmate that he killed '*to obtain the souls for Satan.*'

Thirty years later in 2010, Maxwell's lawyers proved that most of the witnesses to Maxwell's killings had given false statements to the police as they had been pressured by investigators. The courts overturned Maxwell's conviction in the same year which led to a new trial. In late 2017, while the new trial was ongoing, Maxwell suffered a massive heart attack which resulted in a coma.

In 2018, due to the condition of Maxwell, the prosecutors dropped all charges against him and the trial was thrown out of court. His convictions and sentence were labelled as a miscarriage of justice. Maxwell died in April 2019 while still in a coma. He never recovered to hear that he had been found innocent after nearly forty years. Despite Maxwell claiming his innocence, some investigators believe he was the true culprit. Officially, the true identity of the Skid Row Stabber still remains unsolved.

The Skid Row Stabber is sometimes confused with Vaughn Orrin Greenwood, AKA: The Skid Row Slasher. Greenwood was active from 1964 to 1975 and killed eleven people along with one victim who survived. He was arrested in 1975 and subsequently convicted of nine counts of murder. In 1977, he was sentenced to life in prison and remains incarcerated in a Californian prison.

Born in **1945**.

Active from **1978-1979**.

Arrested in **April 1979**.

Country: **USA**.

Victims: **11**.

AKA: **The Skid Row Stabber / The Skid Row Killer**

Current whereabouts: **Died of natural causes in April 2019.**

McDuff, Kenneth

An American serial killer who murdered at least nine people. By 1966, he had already made claims of raping and killing two women. He was then convicted in 1966 of the murders of three teenagers. He raped one of them so violently that he broke her neck with a broom handle.

He received three death sentences and was due to be executed in the electric chair. His accomplice, *Roy Green*, was released after 11 years. In 1977, McDuff's sentence was reduced to life. But then he hired a lawyer who amassed a huge amount of evidence to prove that Green was the real killer.

Unbelievably, the parole board deemed McDuff fit for society and he was released in 1989. He would then go on to a kill an unknown number of victims. The ones he would be convicted of were raped, tortured and strangled.

In 1992 he was arrested and yet again sentenced to death. He was finally executed in 1998.

Born **March 21st 1946.**

Active from **1966-1992.**

Arrested on **May 4th 1992.**

Country: **USA.**

Victims: **9-14+.**

AKA: **Broomstick Murderer.**

Sentence: **Death penalty.**

Current whereabouts: **Executed in 1998.**

McGown, Richard Gladwell

Richard Gladwell McGown was a Scottish-Zimbabwean murderer and suspected medical serial killer. He was convicted of the murders of two children from 1986 to 1992 but had been linked to at least three more. He had injected an overdose of morphine into their bloodstream which killed them within minutes.

Back in 1981, McGown had started to hold his own medical experiments to test new drugs and anaesthetics. He did this in Zimbabwe where he had been settled since the 1960s. Without the knowledge of his patients he is said to have experimented on at least 500 Zimbabwean children. Some of those children would later die from his experiments.

He was arrested in 1993 and an investigation into his conduct took place. A group of Zimbabwean students turned up outside the court and threatened to kill white people if the doctor wasn't sentenced. The case caused uproar in the country and a lead prosecutor stated that McGown was a 'messenger of death stalking our hospitals.'

He was charged with five murders but convicted of only two. It was unclear why the other charges were dropped. McGown was referred to as a Nazi and a racist but Zimbabwean media and the general public.

Despite being convicted for two murders, he was only sentenced to one year in prison which was reduced to six months because of a suspended sentence. He was told to pay $1,250 USD to the families of the victims. The families called the case and sentence a mockery of justice.

After his release, he returned to the United Kingdom and even went as far as appealing his medical license in a British Court. The British General Medical Court banned him from entering a medical profession or practising medicine anywhere in the world.

Since 1995, Richard McGown has been free to live among us.

As of 2021, his whereabouts remain unknown.

Born in **1937**.

Active from **1986-1992**.

Arrested in **1993**.

Country: **Zimbabwe**.

Victims: **5+**.

Sentence: **One year in prison and banned from any medical profession.**

Current whereabouts: **Released in 1995. Status unknown.**

McGray, Michael Wayne

Canadian serial killer *Michael Wayne McGray* was convicted of killing seven people but claimed to have killed 11 more. He killed over a 14 year period between 1984 and 1998.

The first murder was in May of 1985 when McGray was only 19-years-old. He picked up a 17-year-old hitchhiker named *Elizabeth Gale Tucker* then drove her to a remote wooded area in Nova Scotia, where he brutally killed her and dumped the body in a shallow grave.

On November 14th 1987, McGray robbed a taxi driver with two newfound accomplices. It is claimed that McGray killed the driver but evidence was thin. A trial for one of his accomplices, *Norm Warren*, ended with a not-guilty verdict. McGray was however sentenced to five years for the robbery and couldn't be charged in the taxi driver's death.

On March 30th 1991, he was given a three-day parole pass to a halfway house in Montreal. During the three days, McGray killed three more people and then returned to prison over a month late. The day he was paroled he was invited back to a gay man's house where McGray stabbed him multiple times in the throat and chest.

A day later on March 31st, he went back to a gay meeting area and was invited back to another man's house. He stayed the night before waking up and stabbing the man to death. A day later he killed another gay man, which meant he had killed three victims in three days.

Upon his release he went on to kill many more. More confirmed victims came in 1998 when he killed a mother and daughter in their apartment. *Joan Hicks* and her 11-year-old daughter *Nina* were living in New Brunswick when McGray broke into their home. Joan was beaten to death and her throat had been cut. Nina was discovered in her bedroom closet hanging from her neck.

The next day he was arrested and confessed to all the murders and more. He claimed 11 victims across the entirety of Canada and one in Seattle. He said if he was ever released that he would kill again. While in prison he killed another inmate and was transferred to a high security prison to live out the rest of his life sentence without parole.

In Nova Scotia on July 12th 2019, cold case investigators confirmed another female victim from 1995. Shockingly, her boyfriend had been convicted and spent 17 years in jail for a crime he didn't commit. That case is now active and ongoing.

Born in **1965**.

Active from **1984-1998**.

Arrested in **October 1999**.

Country: **Canada**.

Victims: **7-18+**.

Sentence: **Life imprisonment**.

Current whereabouts: **In prison**.

McRae, John Rodney

On September 15th 1987, in Michigan, 15-year-old *Randy Laufer* vanished. He was murdered by serial killer and paedophile *John Rodney McRae*, who killed up to five young boys between 1950 and 1997.

Back in 1950, when McRae was only 16-years-old, he killed his eight-year-old neighbour and was subsequently sentenced to life in prison to be paroled in 1972. Up until his second arrest in 1998, many children had gone missing that would soon be linked to him.

Laufer's bones were discovered on McRae's former Michigan property in 1997 and McRae was arrested shortly after. In 1998, he was sentenced to life for the Laufer murder but is suspected to have been involved in the disappearance of at least five boys in total.

In 2005, McRae died in prison of natural causes.

Born in **1935**.

Active from **1950-1997**.

Arrested in **October 1987**.

Country: **USA**.

Victims: **5+**.

Sentence: **Life imprisonment.**

Current whereabouts: **Died of natural causes in 2005.**

Metheny, Joseph Roy

An American serial killer who is said to have killed ten people but was charged on three counts of murder. He was an alcoholic and drug addict, as were most of his victims. He joined the *U.S. Army* in 1973 and claimed to have served in Vietnam although this was never substantiated.

He also claimed to have first killed in 1976 and was linked to more murders in the late 1970s. He would deliberately hunt women with drug or alcohol problems and in 1994 he killed a prostitute named *Cathy Ann Magaziner*.

He buried her body in a shallow grave and then returned six months later to dig up her corpse and remove the head. He unceremoniously threw the head in the trash. Her body would remain undiscovered for another year and a half.

In 1996, the decomposed body of *Kimberly Spicer* was discovered under a trailer just ten feet from Metheny's own trailer. He would usually stab and strangle his victims to death. It is also said that he dismembered some of the bodies and stored the '*meat*' in his freezer.

Then he would mix the flesh with a mixture of beef and pork to make burger patties. Over the following weekends he would sell the burgers on a small barbecue at the side of the road.

During his trial, he said he committed the murders because he enjoyed it and got a rush out of it, making him a prime example of a thrill killer. He also claimed he had no real excuse other than he liked killing.

He was found dead in his cell in 2017.

Born in **1955**.

Active from **1976-1995**.

Arrested on **December 15th 1996**.

Country: **USA**.

Victims: **3-10+**.

Sentence: **Death penalty later commuted to life.**

Current whereabouts: **Died of natural causes in 2017.**

Mfeka, Samuel Bongani

Another South African serial killer to make the list, *Samuel Bongani Mfeka*, AKA: *The Kranskop Killer*, raped and killed six women in the KwaZulu Natal area of the country. He was also accused at one point of being the *Nasrec Strangler*, who had left 15 bodies in his wake around the same time.

On September 8th 1996, the body of his final victim was discovered. On the same day Mfeka was arrested on a rape charge. While in custody, Mfeka confessed to six murders and told police he would show them where the bodies were. Four of the victims were unearthed nearby to where Mfeka lived, and most bodies were in a severe stage of decomposition.

One of the victims was dated to 1993 and was said to have been Mfeka's first murder. There were similarities between the victims of Mfeka and the Nasrec Strangler, and the investigation went on longer than expected.

Mfeka was convicted of the six murders and sentenced to life. He was one of a number of black serial killers in South Africa during the 1990s, who raped and killed an extremely high number of women between them. These included *David Selepe, Sipho Thwala*, and *Moses Sithole*, among others. Sithole alone murdered at least 38 women from 1994 to 1995.

Mfeka's current status remains unknown.

Active from **1993-1996.**

Arrested on **September 8th 1996.**

Country: **South Africa.**

Victims: **6.**

AKA: **The Kranskop Killer.**

Sentence: **Life imprisonment.**

Current whereabouts: **Status unknown.**

Mikhasevich, Gennady

He murdered 36 women but confessed to over 43. He strangled and smothered his victims, mostly in secluded locations. He would rape them or sexually assault them before and sometimes after the murders. He then robbed them of all belongings.

He had joined the army at a young age and served in various locations around the country. He returned home one day to find that his girlfriend had left him and was married to another man, all without his knowledge. He would later claim that this was the trigger that sent him into a violent rage.

On May 14th 1971, he had planned to commit suicide by hanging but had met a young girl waiting on the side of the road as he walked home. He decided in that moment to take out all his anger on her, by killing her in a brutal frenzy. From that moment, killing became easier, he decided not to kill himself but to kill women as an outlet for his rage.

He was arrested in 1985 after a large investigation. His case became known as *The Vitebsk Case*, and would unveil corruption of law enforcement agencies in the process. Mikhasevich was confirmed to have killed 36 women.

Born in **1947.**

Active from **1971-1985**.

Arrested on **December 9th 1985**.

Country: **Soviet Union.**

AKA: **The Vitebsk Case.**

Victims: **36-43+.**

Sentence: **Death penalty.**

Current whereabouts: **Executed by firing squad on February 3rd 1988.**

Minghella, Maurizio: The Valpocevera Strangler (Extended Case File)

On April 18th 1978, Italian serial killer *Maurizio Minghella* killed a prostitute named *Anna Pagano*. The corpse was found by shepherds, her head had been bashed in and a ballpoint pen was embedded in her anal cavity. He would kill again on July 8th, July 18th, August 22nd and November 1978. In separate killing spans, he would kill a total of 15 women before his arrest in 2001 with five of them in 1978.

The Italian press gave him the nickname *Killer of Prostitutes*. In the heading of *Victim Selection*, we learn that sex workers and prostitutes are more likely to be targeted by serial killers than any other female. Yet, in Italy, serial killers were not as common as they were in the United States, Russia or even the United Kingdom.

Minghella was born in Genoa in 1958 and was raised from the age of six-years-old by his single mother. She then married a new man who would subsequently beat her and Minghella's four siblings. It was later confirmed that Minghella's stepfather was an abusive alcoholic who would brutally beat every member of the family.

"I hated him a lot, I often dreamed of killing him, pulling a rope around his neck

from behind his back."

Minghella, about his stepfather, recorded in his interrogation in 2001.

He was failing in school as a result of the abuse and started to bully other pupils. He would get them in headlocks or push them by their necks. Sometimes he would drag them by their noses or mouths. Beyond his school life he had taken on many small jobs and had been seen with plenty of girls on his arm.

He had then been nicknamed the *Travoltino of Val Polcevera* due to his affection for women and disco music. Travoltino translates to Travolta.

Beyond his bit-part jobs he would steal motorbikes and small cars to charge around the streets of Val Polcervera. Shortly after, his brother was killed in a car crash and it is suggested that this event had a huge psychological impact on him. Afterwards, he developed a morbid fascination with dead bodies but somehow held off from killing.

He married a 15-year-old girl named *Rosa Manfredi*. Although that might shock a lot of people in other countries, the age of consent in Italy was 14-years-old in 1977 and remains the same today. The law even stretches to 13-years-old if their partner is under the age of 18-years-old.

Rosa died shortly after their marriage of a drug overdose, related to suffering depression after a miscarriage. She was already dependent on psychotropic drugs when they had met. Her death just a few months after their marriage had an even deeper psychological impact on Minghella's own mental health.

He began to visit prostitutes more so after Rosa's death, but even while they were married. At the beginning of 1978, he was briefly under the care of a psychiatric clinic in Genoa but they failed to see the path he was going to take.

On April 18th, he killed 20-year-old prostitute, Anna Pagano. He attempted to divert any following investigation by writing messages related to the *Red Brigades* on her body. It is said that the police didn't take notice of it and saw it as misdirection immediately.

On July 8th 1978, he killed another prostitute and hid her body in an abandoned car. Just ten days later, he would kill 14-year-old *Maria Catena Alba* who had gone missing the previous day. Her nude body was found tied to a tree by her neck. She had been raped and abused before and after her death.

Two more victims were raped and murdered before his arrest in December of 1978. He confessed to two immediately but pleaded not guilty on the others. The writing on the body of his first victim and the pen in the victim's anus was enough to link him directly with that crime.

On April 3rd 1981, he was sentenced to life in a maximum security prison for the five murders. He then proclaimed his innocence and in a twist of fate he was released to community care in 1995, which acted as a gateway between prison life and full freedom. But Minghella was a killer, he had killed before out of sexual perversity and would kill again. There was no doubt of this in the minds of some psychologists who were against his soft-release.

In March of 1997 he killed a 53-year-old prostitute in Turin. It was his new first victim of his second era of freedom. He would kill again in 1997, 1998, and in 1999.

His last victim was in February 2001, when he killed 27-year-old *Florentina Motoc*. Her face and head had been bashed in and she had been sexually abused. He attempted to burn her clothing but failed to get rid of all of his DNA. He was subsequently arrested, just six years after his release.

Beyond the DNA, the investigation had used mobile phone tracking technology to place Minghella in the area where Motoc had been discovered. In that six year period, he had killed a suspected ten more women.

After a brief escape in 2003, he was only convicted of four murders but linked with the ten. He was sentenced to life in prison in *Pavia*, where he is currently incarcerated. It is suspected he had killed at least 15 prostitutes over the course of his life.

Born in **1954**.

Active from **1978-2001**.

Arrested in **March 2001**.

Country: **Italy**.

Victims: **15+.**

AKA: **The Valpocevera Strangler / Killer of Prostitutes.**

Sentence: **Life imprisonment.**

Current whereabouts: **In prison.**

(Research Article #17) The Macdonald Triad

This is a set of three factors first proposed by psychiatrist; *J.M. Macdonald.* It was written as a thesis in 1963 and published in the American Journal of Psychiatry.

Cruelty to animals.

Obsession with starting fires.

Bed-wetting past the age of five-years-old.

It is said if all three factors are present in a child's behaviour then there is a higher chance they will go on to commit violent crime as time progresses. Generally this is linked to murderous behaviour and sexual predation. Although subsequent research has not validated the thesis, it still remains one of the starting points in diagnosis and awareness of serial killers.

What it did do was open up the research and debate amongst other psychiatrists and investigators. It is interesting to note that Richard Trenton Chase exhibited all the factors of the Macdonald Triad.

Since 1963, more reports have stated that this Triad is linked more to childhood experiences of neglect and abuse.

Setting fire to objects or property was seen as a way to release anger without resorting to dehumanising others or animal life. It has since been argued that the fire factor of the Triad can easily be replaced with other anti-social activities or behaviour. None of which are proof that a child will go on to become a serial killer.

Bed-wetting is seen as a humiliating factor for a child, especially when ridiculed by a parent or older sibling. There is evidence that abused children are more likely to feel or suffer humiliation than those raised in better households.

This humiliation is transferred in cruelty to animals. When a child is abused, they cannot retaliate to their abusers or captors. There is an obvious size differential should that child wish to fight back in any way.

Cruelty against animals, generally small animals, is a route one might take because those animals are viewed as weak and vulnerable. In the same way that they themselves are seen as weak and vulnerable when an adult inflicts cruelty upon them.

In one study of serial killers, it was noted that the same infliction of cruelty to an animal in their childhood years, was the same type of cruelty then inflicted on their human victims.

The Vampire of Sacramento fits into this thesis perfectly. Firstly, his fascination with torturing small animals and removing their organs was evident in what he would do to his victims. He would then drink the blood of small animals, just as he would with humans.

In a study of violent inmates, over half admitted to having committed acts of violence against animals either in childhood, adolescence or their teenage years. The link was then made between animal abusers and childhood abuse, particular parental abuse. It showed that those children who abused animals would have mostly suffered some kind of parental abuse in their formative years.

In a 2004 study regarding patterns of violence, the authors found a link between repetitive animal cruelty and subsequent cruelty towards humans. They noted that although the links were more obvious than first thought, they offered a warning. By focusing on just one aspect of possible rises to violent crime, it was detracting from other possible causes and reasons.

It is clear now that most psychiatrists and investigators focus on more than three factors in relation to research and evidence of serial killer foundations. But it was the Macdonald Triad that paved the way.

Since the Macdonald Triad, there have been more attempts to create factors as to why someone might go on to commit serial murder. *The Dark Triad*, being one of them cited in numerous research papers.

The Dark Triad is more of a psychological attempt at understanding why some might go on to kill. It includes the following factors:

Narcissism.

Traits include; grand-standing, pride, egotism, lack of empathy.

Machiavellianism.

Traits include; manipulation, exploitation, cynicism, deception.

Psychopathy.

Traits include; antisocial behaviour, impulsiveness, selfishness, callousness, remorselessness.

The problem with the Dark Triad is that the three psychological aspects are virtually interchangeable to the point of cancelling each other out.

Psychopathy and narcissism both can be mostly inherited by genetic components and then by how a child is raised. Machiavellianism is generally less found to be inherited than the others. This has led many to argue that the Dark Triad is virtually baseless in its theory but it certainly does add more to the database of psychological understanding.

Far beyond the psychological Triads, there are a greater number of factors present in what led to the rise of the serial killer.

Mmbengwa, David

Another South African serial killer, *David Mmbengwa,* AKA: *The Lover's Lane Killer,* would be convicted of seven counts of murder in 2001. Mmbengwa first killed in 1991 during a robbery. He was arrested and sentenced to six years in prison for culpable murder.

After four years, Mmbengwa was released from prison, to go and kill seven more people. Most of his killings came about from robberies and were couples who were making love in their cars, hence the moniker the press attributed to him. Among his victims, he claimed a Police Inspector, a Police Sergeant, and a Government Agriculture Official.

On November 14th 1996, he was arrested but managed to escape the Silverton Police Station. He was recaptured a few hours later and 23 counts of murder were laid at his feet. He was convicted of seven murders and given a life sentence for each of them. He also received another 46 years for various other crimes including robbery. As of 2021, he remains incarcerated at a prison in South Africa.

Born **October 10th 1966.**

Active from **1991-1996.**

Arrested on **November 14th 1996.**

Country: **South Africa.**

Victims: **7+.**

AKA: **The Lover's Lane Killer.**

Sentence: **Seven life sentences plus 46 years.**

Current whereabouts: **In prison.**

Monster of Florence

The mysterious murders in Florence over a 17-year period still baffles investigators to this day. They deduced that the murders were not committed by just one person but a group of people. The victims were generally young couples parked in isolated areas and were either shot or stabbed. The female victims would have their sex organs removed.

Another young couple were killed in September of 1974. They had been shot and stabbed to death in a country lane near Borgo San Lorenzo, while having sex in their car. The female had been raped with a grapevine stalk and disfigured with 97 stab wounds.

The Monster or Monsters of Florence would claim at least 14 victims. The murders have never been solved. Due to the dates and the methods of killing, it has been suggested that the Monster of Florence and the Zodiac Killer could have been the same person.

Active from **1968-1985.**

Country: **Italy.**

Victims: **14+.**

Current whereabouts: **Unidentified killer. Status unknown.**

Moore, Blanche Taylor

An American female serial killer also known as *'The Black Widow Killer'*, was convicted of three murders but linked with at least two more. She poisoned all her victims with arsenic.

Her victims were mostly in or previously in some kind of relationship with her, or their family members. After her arrest, people that knew her said she was vindictive and two-faced but others said she was the perfect member of their community.

As of 2021, she is currently the oldest woman on death row in Northern Carolina, at 86-years-old.

Born **February 17th 1933.**

Active from **1968-1989.**

Arrested on **July 18th 1989.**

Country: **USA.**

Victims: **3-5+.**

AKA: **The Black Widow Killer.**

Sentence: **Death penalty.**

Current whereabouts: **Death row.**

The Monstrous Book of Serial Killers (2nd edition)

PHOTO OF STEFANO BALDI AND SUSANNA CAMBI, VICTIMS OF THE MONSTER OF FLORENCE, KILLED OCTOBER 23, 1981

FLORENCE, ITALY

PHOTO OF HORST WILHELM MEYER AND JENS-UWE RüSCH, VICTIMS O THE MONSTER OF FLORENCE, KILLED ON SEPTEMBER 9TH 1983

PHOTO OF JEAN-MICHEL KRAVEICHVILI AND NADINE MAURIOT, VICTIMS OF THE MONSTER OF FLORENCE, KILLED BETWEEN 7TH AND 8TH SEPTEMBER 1985

IMAGE ATTRIBUTIONS
(ATTRIB A32) (ATTRIB A33)
(ATTRIB A34) (ATTRIB A84)

MONSTER OF FLORENCE

Morus, Henryk

In Poland, serial killer *Henryk Morus* killed seven people in a six year period from 1986 to 1992. His first murder in 1986 was 60-year-old shop owner *Teresa Grabowska*, who was killed in her own shop.

He went on to kill another six people including a young couple in their home where the woman was pregnant, two more business owners and a pensioner. According to those who knew Morus, he was a caring husband and a good man.

For four of the murders, he was sentenced to death. For the other three, he was sentenced to life along with other crimes.

He died in 2013 in a prison hospital when he was 70-years-old. Up until his death he had been a model inmate and had repeatedly apologised for his crimes. He died of a suspected heart attack and was buried by the prison as his family refused to have the corpse collected.

Born in **1943**.

Active from **1986-1992**.

Country: **Poland**.

Victims: **7**.

Sentence: **Death penalty and a life sentence.**

Current whereabouts: **Died of natural causes in 2013.**

Mulaudzi, Mukosi Freddy

In South Africa, serial killer *Mukosi Freddy Mulaudzi*, AKA: *The Limpopo Serial Killer*, murdered at least 13 people. Mulaudzi was originally convicted for two murders and an armed robbery in 1990 but managed to escape in 1996.

He carried on a life of crime and murder until his re-arrest in July of 2006. A year before, he raped and killed four young girls at the same time. 19-year-old *Ndivhuwo Winnity Tshilimandila* was raped and then hacked to death. Her cousins aged seven-years-old, 10-years-old, and 14-years-old, were also raped and brutally murdered. It was a crime that shocked South Africa.

A few months later, in Tshsdza Village, he killed a mother and her two young children in their home. He stabbed 30-year-old *Phophi Tracy Radzilani* to death then tied her two children to their bed. He then set fire to the house. Five-year-old *Moses Mushiana* and seven-year-old *Rotondwa* were burned alive in their bedroom.

His last victim was in 2006, when he killed *Shonisani Thinandavha* in Mulodi. She had been found partially cannibalised. Her breasts, right hand, left ear, and lips had been sliced off. Mulaudzi was captured shortly after.

After his trial in 2006, he was sentenced to 11 life sentences for 13 murders. As of 2021, he remains incarcerated in a prison in Limpopo, South Africa.

Born in **1962**.

Active from **1990-2006**.

Arrested in **July 2006**.

Country: **South Africa**.

Victims: **13**.

AKA: **The Limpopo Serial Killer**.

Sentence: **11 life sentences**.

Current whereabouts: **In prison**.

Murphy, Donald

On December 15th 1980, American serial killer and sex offender **Donald Murphy** was arrested and charged with six murders of prostitutes in Detroit. On the evidence available to the jury in his trial, he was convicted of two murders and sentenced to 30 years for each of them. But the bodies had been piling up.

On April 19th 1980, the body of 24-year-old prostitute **Jeanette Woods** was discovered on a sidewalk on Melrose, near the *I-375*. She had been raped, beaten, and strangled before having her throat cut. She had left her mother's house the evening before to meet with an unidentified boyfriend but never returned. She had previously been admitted twice to the *Detroit Osteopathic Hospital* for injuries suffered from beatings.

On June 15th 1980, the nude body of 22-year-old **Diane Burks** was discovered by a dog walker at a known lover's lane area. Burks hands had been tied behind her back and she had been strangled to death by Murphy. She had last been seen leaving her sister's boyfriend's house and heading towards her home.

On August 19th 1980, the nude and battered body of 17-year-old **Cassandra Ann Johnson** was discovered in a field by a 14-year-old neighbour. She had gone missing the day before and was last seen entering a store after leaving her boyfriend's house. Johnson had been beaten to death by Murphy and had died of head injuries as a result.

On October 8th 1980, the body of 26-year-old former cheerleader **Betty Jean Rembert** was discovered under some hedges on a vacant lot. She had died from a stab wound to the neck and head injuries that had caused a fractured skull.

On October 23rd 1980, the body of 23-year-old prostitute **Cynthia Angela Warren** was discovered a few blocks away from the red-light district of *Eight Mile Road*, where she worked. A man flagged down a police car to inform them he had found a body. Warren had been stabbed and beaten Murphy and he was convicted on her murder.

Murphy was never convicted of the Rembert murder and her death remains listed as unsolved. Despite being linked to the Woods murder, he was never convicted and her death also remains listed as unsolved. In the late 1970s and 1980, 18 prostitutes were killed in Detroit. It led investigators to believe that two serial killers had been active in the area at the same time as Murphy. The other, if there was another killer, remains unidentified.

Murphy was sentenced to a total of 60 years in prison, where he remains to this day.

Born in **1944**.

Active during **1980**.

Arrested in **December 1980**.

Country: **USA**.

Victims: **2-6**

Current whereabouts: **In prison**.

Nance, Wayne

Wayne Nance was one of the rare serial killers to have been killed by his final intended victim. It is claimed he killed more than five people over a minimum 12-year period. He was a truck driver from Montana who had been known as the local 'weirdo' ever since his teens.

He would boast of worshipping Satan and had once used a hot coat hanger to burn himself with satanic symbols and occult signs. He would kill his victims by hitting them over the head or stabbing them.

Due to the botched murder of his final victim in 1986, he was then positively linked to unsolved murder cases from 1974, 1980 and 1985.

Born in **1955**.

Active from **1974-1986**.

Country: **USA**.

Victims: **5+**.

Current whereabouts: **Killed by intended victim in 1986.**

Naso, Joseph

Convicted of the death of six women but claimed up to ten victims. On August 13th 1978, a decomposing nude body had been found on the Carquinez Scenic Highway. Later identified as *Carmen Colon*, one of Naso's victims. In an uncanny twist, a victim attributed to *'The Alphabet Killer'* a few years earlier, was also named Carmen Colon.

Naso ended up claiming victims with the same letter on their first and second name. It has long remained unclear if that was his selection choice for victims. On January 10th 1977, 18-year-old *Roxenne Roggasch* was found dead. In 1993, the body of waitress Pamela Parsons was found near to where Naso had lived at the time.

Naso killed many more women over the years and was able to escape detection for almost three decades. He wasn't arrested until 2011 and was sentenced to death in 2013.

Born in **1934**.

Active from **1977-1994**.

Arrested on **April 11th 2011**.

Country: **USA**.

Victims: **6-10.**

AKA: **Double Initial Killer.**

Sentence: **Death penalty.**

Current whereabouts: **Death row.**

Night-time Killers, The

In Kiev, Ukraine, between 1991 and 1997, two men murdered 16 people, together they became known as the Night-time Killers. *Vladyslav Volkovich* and *Volodymyr Kondratenko* were charged and convicted of 16 murders and claimed they had started killing as practice to becoming contract killers.

Their victims were killed in a number of different ways. Most were killed with a rifle but others were stabbed or bludgeoned to death. They killed mostly homeless people as 'practice' before they could kill for profit. It remains unclear how they thought they would become contract killers.

On June 18th 1996, 44-year-old *Yevheniy Osechkin* was shot dead near a railway station in Kiev. Robbery was ruled out as motive as Osechkin still had cash in his pockets. Investigators then began looking at other murders in the area and noticed a pattern of homeless people being shot or stabbed to death. Including one who was found dead just 100 metres from Osechkin.

On July 2nd 1996, a well-liked doctor named *Oleksandr Yehorov* was shot dead in his car. One hour later, another male victim was found just a few streets away. He too had been shot with the same weapon and also stabbed. As more victims piled up, the investigation increased its manpower. But although they had DNA, there was no match on the database.

In October 1996, the pair were arrested after the investigation collated all the information they had gathered. The day they were arrested, they had planned to kill a security guard. Two more men were also arrested as co-conspirators in some of the crimes. Not long after the trial began, Kondratenko committed suicide by taking an overdose of painkillers.

"They were nothing to me, not people, just items in a list. Killing them made me feel like a superman."

Volkovich in his confession – regarding his victims.

In 2000, Volkovich was convicted of 16 murders. The pair had originally claimed 20, but four of them were homeless victims who couldn't be proven. After Kondratenko died, Volkovich attempted to blame him for everything. Even so, Volkovich received a sentence of life in prison, as did the two co-conspirators.

Active from **1991-1996.**

Arrested in **October 1996.**

Country: **Ukraine.**

Victims: **16.**

AKA: **Vladyslav Volkovich / Volodymyr Kondratenko.**

Sentence: **Volkovich got life imprisonment.**

Current whereabouts: **Kondratenko committed suicide during the trial. Volkovich remains in prison.**

Nilsen, Dennis: The Muswell Hill Murderer (Extended Case File)

On December 30th 1978, in England, *Dennis Nilsen, The Muswell Hill Murderer*, killed his first victim, 14-year-old *Stephen Holmes*.

Dennis Nilsen is one of Britain's most infamous serial killers. Some see him as the British version of *Jeffrey Dahmer* and in a lot of ways, the similarities are striking. They both killed gay men and they made their first kill within five months of each other in 1978. Nilsen killed 15, Dahmer killed 17, and they both carried out necrophilia acts upon the bodies of their victims.

Yet, the very nature of their crimes are inherently different. Because of the United Kingdom's different legal system to that of the United States, Dennis Nilsen was serving life as the country no longer carries out a death sentence.

Nilsen would request parole hearings for immediate release up until his death in 2018 when he died of natural causes. He reached out from within his cell with now banned autobiographies and interviews to sate the appetite of the curious public.

He murdered 15 young men in London over a five year period and kept the victims' bodies for a certain amount of time after he had killed. Then he dissected them and either burned the remains or flushed them down the toilet.

In his life he worked as a military chef, police officer and civil servant. Not the usual career progression to serial killer. To stand in such esteemed positions in work and life and then go on to kill is one that has produced conflicting reports from psychologists and experts alike.

His early life consisted of his parents divorcing because of his father becoming an alcoholic. Nilsen was only four-years-old when it happened and his mother remarried soon afterwards. The disruption in the British Isles after the dust of World War Two had settled was felt throughout the nation, more so on the children born into that era.

As previously noted, World War Two could have been one of the reasons for the rise of the serial killer heading towards 1978. For Nilsen, the break-up of his family at a time of national hardship was crippling.

In his trial and subsequent interviews, Nilsen claimed there was an event in his life, at the age of six-years-old, that was to shape him for many years to come. After his mother remarried, she sent him to live with his grandparents. It was there that he found a kinship with his grandfather, *Andrew Whyte*, but after a couple of years he was returned to his mother in 1951. In the Autumn of that year, Nilsen's grandfather died of a heart attack.

Some serial killers have attributed the death of a grandparent as a turning point in their lives. Alexander Pichushkin, the *Russian Chessboard Killer*, confirmed that after the death of his grandfather he turned to vodka, and then to murder.

What didn't help Nilsen's fragile tendencies at the time was that his mother made him view the body of his grandfather due to her strong religious beliefs. Some psychologists have suggested that this was one of the markers that put Nilsen onto a different path. He later stated that the first time he knew of his grandfather's death was when he saw the corpse.

"It caused a sort of emotional death inside me."

Dennis Nilsen, relating to his grandfather's death.

Two years later, when he was eight-years-old, Nilsen almost drowned in the seas close to his hometown. An older boy who was on the coast at the time, saw what was happening and went in to rescue him. Nilsen later claimed that the boy masturbated over his body. He awoke from his experience with near death to find ejaculate on his stomach.

Afterwards he withdrew into himself, hiding away from the world. He was a loner and kept himself to himself but he was never disliked and had many friends at the time. Yet, he preferred to be with his own company.

He had never killed small animals or exhibited a cruel streak towards living things. He was never aggressive or violent towards his peers. He was for all intents and purposes, a good and well-loved child. He was the opposite of what a potential serial killer was supposed to have been.

On one occasion he helped in the search of a local man who had gone missing. As fate would have it, it was a young Nilsen and a friend who found the man's body on a riverbank. He later said it had reminded him of seeing the body of his grandfather and upon coming across the corpse he had felt no emotion towards it.

He never had a sexual encounter, nor suffered abuse during his childhood or teenage years. It would be almost two decades later when Nilsen would record his first kill.

He joined the British Army at 17-years-old and lasted 11 years. During his military years he said he carried with him a huge weight of loneliness. When he was allowed a private room he would lay down in front of a mirror so he couldn't see his own head in the reflection. He would then masturbate to the sight of what he felt was an unconscious body.

This might in some part have been carried over from his experience on the beach. In 1972 he left the military of his own accord and returned to civilian life. He went on to join the *Metropolitan Police* in London but only served eight months as an officer before once again leaving of his own accord.

He often witnessed autopsied bodies in close proximity. It fascinated him and he revelled in that part of the job but he left because he felt the job didn't fit him well, having come from the military. In 1974 he went on to work as a civil servant in a job centre in London and became active in trade unions. Then the fantasies he'd long held started to seep into his reality.

There are infamous addresses where killers and murderers have carried out their crimes and lived but none more so than *195 Melrose Avenue*. The address in the London area of Cricklewood, would claim 12 victims. He had access to a large garden and was able to burn many of the remains in bonfires. Some of the entrails were thrown over the fence so that local wildlife would consume them.

Nilsen moved into 195 Melrose Avenue, sometimes listed mistakenly as Melrose Place, with a man named *David Gallichan*. It was said to have been purely a platonic relationship. Nilsen wanted more however, he wanted real commitment and after a series of casual sexual encounters, his bizarre corpse fantasies started to become more prominent.

When he positioned himself in front of a mirror so that his head appeared as missing, he would start to add fake blood to his *corpse* to look as though he had been killed. He fantasised someone would take him away and bury him and he started to believe that his *corpse* was the perfect state of his human body. There was nothing more emotionally and physically pleasing to him than fantasising about his own dead body.

After a rough and stressful relationship with Gallichan, Nilsen forced him to leave but was aware of the consequences of being alone.

"Loneliness," he wrote, *"is a long unbearable pain."*

A day before New Year's Eve, in 1978, Nilsen took his first victim. 14-year-old Stephen Holmes had been refused alcohol at a local pub. Nilsen took the opportunity to invite him to his flat on Melrose Avenue to drink alcohol with him.

"He was to stay with me over the New Year period whether he wanted to or not."

Nilsen, regarding his first victim.

After going to bed together, Nilsen woke at dawn and became aroused at the sight of his new friend's sleeping body. Holmes was sleeping on his front when Nilsen straddled him and slipped a tie under his neck. He subsequently drowned the young boy in a bucket of water by resting his head over the edge of a chair.

After the bubbles stopped rising from the water, Nilsen rested him on the floor realising that he had just killed a man whose name he did not know. He was also suddenly fearful of the consequences of his actions. Again, a trait not carried by most serial killers.

Nilsen said later that he just sat there staring at the boy's fresh corpse, shaking with the fear and stress of the situation. He made himself a coffee and smoked some cigarettes to ease his nerves. After washing the corpse in the bathroom he returned Holmes to the bed and was fascinated by the limpness of the corpse.

"It was the beginning of the end of my life as I had known it, I had started down the avenue of death and possession of a new kind of flat-mate."

Nilsen, as quoted from his autobiography.

The concept of keeping corpses as flat-mates was now embedded into Nilsen's psyche. He thought the sight of the corpse was beautiful and not appalling in anyway whatsoever. He hid the body under the floorboards but after a week had gone by curiosity had got the better of him. He wanted to see whether the body had changed in anyway.

As he was carrying the body back to the living room, he felt himself becoming aroused and subsequently masturbated onto the corpse's stomach. He even trussed him up by the ankles for an undisclosed amount of time before putting the corpse back under the floorboards. It would be almost eight months later when Nilsen removed the body to burn it in a bonfire in his garden. He burned rubber to hide the smell and raked the ashes into his garden.

Most of his victims were homeless or homosexual men who he would lure to his home with offers of food, alcohol or a place to rest their heads. His victims were normally killed by strangulation or drowning during the course of the night. He then proceeded to use his butchering skills, learned in the British Army, to help him get rid of the bodies.

He would keep them in various different locations around his home but usually under the floorboards and would constantly engage in sexual activity with the corpses. Over the next three years, Nilsen would murder another 11 men in the ground floor apartment at Melrose Avenue. Of these 11, only four were ever identified.

Kenneth Ockendon was a Canadian tourist he had met at a local pub for lunch in 1979. Nilsen claimed he enjoyed the company of Ockendon and it was the thought of him leaving that drove him to kill again. He strangled him with a headphone cord before washing the body and taking it to bed with him.

Nilsen said he never had sexual intercourse with the corpses but that he did carry out sexual acts with them. He enjoyed masturbating on the corpses and pleasuring himself on certain parts of their bodies. He placed Ockendon under the floorboards and would take the corpse out several times to watch the television with him.

Nilsen said he would sometimes go into a *killing trance* and didn't always remember the act of murder. The feeling of control over the corpses of his *flatmates* thrilled him and he held a certain fascination with how their corpses deteriorated over time. He believed he was appreciating them more dead than alive. When the investigation started after Nilsen's arrest, police investigators found over 1000 bone fragments in the garden of 195 Melrose Avenue. He had used the small garden as his own personal burial ground.

Through his butchering career in the British Army he learned the art of butchery so well he would use this skill to rid the house piece by piece of the corpses that remained. He would strip to his underwear and cut them up on the stone floor of his kitchen. He would then place the organs in a plastic bag.

His fantasy progressed to removing the head and then heating it in a large pan of water to boil off the flesh of the skull. He would burn the rest of the remains over time, sometimes close to the garden fence. He was constantly amazed that he was never caught or that no one ever questioned him and his strange activities.

Nilsen one day decided to leave Melrose Avenue and move into a new place in the city. In some part to leave the murderous part of his life behind and in others to escape from the torment he had inflicted. Before Fred and Rose West's *25 Cromwell Street* was known to the public, *195 Melrose Avenue* was the darkest *house of horrors* in the British Isles.

In 1981, Nilsen moved to *23 Cranley Gardens* and it proved to be his undoing. He found it difficult to get rid of the bodies in his new home and ended up with black bin-liners full of human organs in his wardrobe. He would kill three more at Cranley Gardens over the coming year and a half.

The last victim was dissected in the same way as the previous ones. The head was boiled and the limbs and organs were placed into bags, ready for disposal. But without access to a garden, Nilsen had to come up with different methods of disposal. He would boil the flesh off the bones and start flushing pieces of the bodies down the toilet.

One of the other five tenants who lived in the block complained to the landlord the toilet was not flushing properly. Nilsen had apparently tried to clear the blockage with acid and it mostly worked but it didn't clear the blockage in the external drain.

A local plumber called in a specialist team to get a second opinion and 48 hours later they arrived. One of the technicians, *Michael Cattran,* went into the drains beneath the house.

He found a sludge blocking a part of the sewer coming from a pipe linked to the house. It appeared to be various pieces of animal flesh and so he immediately reported it to his superiors. When the sewer team left, Nilsen went down into the sewers and started removing the lumps of flesh that had congealed together. But some of the other tenants noticed his movements and strange actions and reported it to the police.

At the same time, the results came back from the analysis of what was assumed to be animal remains. The results were unquestionable; it was human remains. Detectives paid a visit to the house the following evening.

DCI Peter Jay waited at the scene with two officers for Nilsen to return from work, they followed him into the block of flats and they immediately smelled rotting flesh. Nilsen asked why the police were interested in the drains. They told him they had found human remains.

"Good grief, how awful," Nilsen said.

"Don't mess about, son, where's the rest of the body?" DCI Jay responded.

Nilsen remained relaxed and calmly said that the remains of the bodies were in two plastic bags in the wardrobe. When they drove him to the police station, they asked him how many bodies he was actually talking about.

"Fifteen or sixteen since 1978."

He pleaded guilty with diminished responsibility but on November 4th, 1983, he was sentenced to life imprisonment. He was convicted of six murders and two attempted murders. The Home Secretary later imposed a whole life tariff, which meant that he would never be released and would subsequently be denied any requests for parole. He died of natural causes in 2018.

Born **November 23rd 1945**.

Active from **1978-1983**.

Arrested on **February 9th 1983**.

Country: **United Kingdom**.

Victims: **12+**.

AKA: **The Muswell Hill Murderer**.

Sentence: **Life imprisonment**.

Current whereabouts: **Died of natural causes in 2018**.

CRANLEY GARDENS, MUSWELL HILL, WHERE NILSEN KILLED AND DISMEMBERED SOME OF HIS VICTIMS

IMAGE ATTRIBUTIONS
(ATTRIB A35) (ATTRIB A36)

DENNIS NILSEN

BITSEVSKY FOREST IN BITSA PARK WHERE PICHUSHKIN KILLED SOME OF HIS VICTIMS

IMAGE ATTRIBUTIONS
(ATTRIB A11) (ATTRIB A38)

ALEXANDER PICHUSHKIN

Onoprienki, Anatoly: The Beast of the Ukraine (Extended Case File)

On April 16th 1996, Ukrainian serial killer *Anatoly Onoprienko, AKA: The Beast of the Ukraine*, was arrested at his girlfriend's house in Zhitomir. The arrest came after an estimated 2,000 police officers and 3,000 military troops were involved in the investigation. The Beast had already killed at least 52 people.

He was born in the Summer of 1959, in what was then called the Ukrainian SSR, part of the Soviet Union. His mother died when he was just four-years-old, and he was handed off to his grandparents. Their father was a decorated World War Two veteran who had been suffering mental trauma from the effects of the war but he decided to *keep* Onoprienko's older brother at his home.

Onoprienki grew to hate his father for leaving him alone with others. There was a time, shortly after, when his grandparents handed him over to an orphanage where he saw a side of life that his brother did not see. Onoprienko later claimed that being raised partially in an orphanage put him on a pre-defined route of violence. He would later claim that voices had tipped him over the edge and he listened to their commands to kill others.

The first confirmed murders happened in 1989, when Onoprienko was 30-years-old. He had been a regular at a gym in his local area and met a man there who would become his short-term accomplice. Together they robbed a house in the middle of the night but the family who lived there woke up and a fight ensued.

By the end of the night, the two parents and all eight of their children had been murdered by the pair of burglars. They would both later claim it was in self-defence. Later in 1989, five more people, including a young boy, were shot dead while sleeping in a car before their bodies were burned on the side of the road. Onoprienko acted alone and again stated that he only intended to rob them.

After committing multiple crimes there came a five year gap where he was said to have been silent. Yet, as he lived mostly off the grid, there could have been many more crimes attributed to him. It was 1996, when Onoprienko began to take lives on an epidemic level. Over a three month period, he slaughtered entire families.

On January 5th 1996, four people became victims of the Beast of the Ukraine. In Oblast, two businessmen named *Odintsov* and *Dolinin* were shot dead as they sat in their broken-down vehicle. A couple of hours later, just down the road from the double murder, a pedestrian and a police officer were shot dead. Onoprienko would later claim the death of the latter two was to kill off any witnesses to the prior murders.

Just one day later on January 6th, on a nearby highway, four more people are shot dead in individual incidents. The victims were a Navy officer, a taxi driver, a chef, and an unidentified man. One of the cars was already stationary while the other cars had been flagged down by Onoprienko before he shot them dead. The rampage struck fear into the hearts of the Ukrainian public at the time. But Onoprienko was only getting started.

"I just shot them. It's not that it gave me pleasure, but I felt this urge. From then on, it was almost like some game from outer space."

Onoprienko, in his confession.

On January 17th, the entire Pilat family were slaughtered and their bodies burned. All five members were shot dead when Onoprienko entered the home in the early morning. He then set fire to the house, burning the bodies within. Two witnesses saw him committing the crime and he went after them. The witnesses; a female rail worker and a train passenger were shot dead as they walked down a nearby street.

On January 30th, four more people died at the hands of Onoprienko. Again, in the Oblast region of the country, Onoprienko used a shotgun to shoot dead a female nurse and her two sons. In a separate incident, he also pulled over another car and shot dead a 32-year-old visitor to the area.

On February 19th 1996, he killed all four members of the Dubchak family. He stormed into their home and immediately shot dead Mr. Dubchak and his son. Then he took a hammer and beat Mrs Dubchak to death in front of her daughter. Onoprienko ordered the daughter to give him money and expensive belongings. According to his later confession, she had refused, and so he also beat her to death with a hammer.

On February 27th, the entire Bodnarchuk family were killed in their home in Malina, Oblast. Upon entering the home, he shot dead both parents and took their seven-year-old and eight-year-old daughters to one side before hacking them to death with an axe. Just one hour later, one of the family's neighbours, wandered too near to the house, and Onoprienko charged outside and killed him with the same axe. He then proceeded to chop him into pieces.

On March 22nd, the final confirmed victims were killed. The Novosad family were killed in their own home. All four members were shot dead and then he set the house on fire to supposedly eliminate any traces of evidence.

"To me it was like hunting. Hunting people down. I would be sitting, bored, with nothing to do. And then suddenly this idea would get into my head. I would do everything to get it out of my mind, but I couldn't. It was stronger than me. So I would get in the car or catch a train and go out to kill."

Onoprienko, in his confession.

In April of 1996, Onoprienko moved in with one of his cousins, Pyotr Onoprienko. Pyotr discovered a large number of weapons, and suddenly realised they were similar to the ones used in the massacres that were bringing the country to its knees. After kicking him out of his home, Pyotr immediately called the police.

A few months before Onoprienko's April 1996 arrest, the investigation had been focused on another man named Yury Mozola. Due to the mounting pressure and public outcry, the Ukrainian Security Service (USS) tortured Mozola for a confession. All the time, Mozola maintained his innocence but the torture continued and after a few days, he died from the injuries of his ordeal. Seven members of the USS were subsequently convicted on his death.

After one of the largest investigations in Ukrainian history, involving thousands of police and military, Onoprienko was finally arrested on April 16th 1996, where upon he confessed to the murders.

His trial was also one of the largest in the country's history, where an estimated 100 volumes of evidence was compiled, along with 400 witnesses. Public reaction was understandably violent and full of anger. Hundreds of people were outside the court room every day and would spit and throw things at the very mention of his name.

Onoprienko was sentenced to life in prison which caused further outrage. Ukraine had just entered the EU treaty of abolishing the death penalty and so Onoprienko could not be sentenced to death. The resulting sentencing caused a further debate in the country regarding the abolishment of capital punishment.

On August 27th 2013, Onoprienko died of a heart attack in his prison cell.

Born **July 25th 1959.**

Active from **1989-1996.**

Arrested on **April 16th 1996.**

Country: **Ukraine.**

Victims: **52+.**

AKA: **The Beast of the Ukraine / Terminator.**

Sentence: **Life imprisonment.**

Current whereabouts: **Died of a heart attack on August 27th 2013.**

Pandy, Andras

The Belgian-Hungarian serial killer *András Pándy, AKA: Father Bluebeard* was convicted for the murder of six family members in Brussels between 1986 and 1990. He has since been linked to at least another eight murders. His two former wives and two children disappeared mysteriously and it has long been suspected that Pandy had killed them and disposed of the bodied.

It is claimed that he killed them all with the help of another daughter named Agnes. He had been involved in a violent incestuous relationship with Agnes since she was a youngster and it had continued into adulthood. In 1984, he began another incestuous relationship with another of his daughters and had Agnes beat her in the basement when she didn't comply. The other girl later escaped to live a new life elsewhere in Hungary.

From 1986 to 1990, multiple children of both his daughters also disappeared, when family members returned from holiday, Pandy told them their siblings had gone to live elsewhere. In reality, Pandy had killed them and disposed of their bodies.

In 1997, both Pandy and Ágnes were arrested. It was the confession of Ágnes that sealed both their fates. She claimed she had helped her father kill most of her disappeared relatives but was solely complicit in the murder of her own mother. They both killed the family members by shooting or hitting them in the head with a sledgehammer.

The bodies were cut into pieces and taken to a bathtub in the basement of their home where they dissolved them with acid and other chemicals. Any remaining bones were taking to a local slaughterhouse for disposal.

In 2002, Pandy was convicted of six murders and the rape of three of his daughters and sentenced to life without parole. Ágnes was sentenced to 21 years for being an accomplice in five murders and one attempted murder. She later claimed to be completely under her father's control and had no way to get out of the situation she found herself in.

In 2013 András Pándy died from natural causes in a Bruges prison. As of 2021, Ágnes remains incarcerated awaiting parole.

Born **June 1st 1927**.

Active from **1986-1992**.

Arrested on **October 20th 1997**.

Country: **Belgium**,

Victims: **6-14+**.

AKA: **Father Bluebeard / The Family Killer**.

Sentence: **András received life imprisonment. Ágnes received 21 years.**

Current whereabouts: **András Pándy died of natural causes in 2013. Ágnes remains in prison.**

Parker, Gerald

On December 1st 1978 in California, American serial Killer *Gerald Parker*, AKA: *The Bedroom Basher*, claimed his first victim. 17-year-old *Sandra Fry* was discovered by her flat-mate in Anaheim late at night. She was nude from the waist down and her blouse was pulled up, exposing her bra.

She had been raped and then hit in the face and head with a blunt object, fracturing her skull. She was barely alive when found and died shortly after in the emergency room.

A sixth woman survived but she was pregnant at the time and her unborn child died. The women were killed by being beaten to death with wooden poles, a hammer or a baseball bat. The husband of the sixth woman was *Kevin Lee Green*, who was convicted of the unborn child's murder and spent 16 years in prison as an innocent man.

He was only exonerated when improvements in DNA forensics proved that Parker was involved. Parker was already in prison at the time and when confronted with the evidence, he confessed to the attack.

Parker brutally murdered six people from 1978 to 1979. He was convicted in February of 1999 and sentenced to death.

As of 2021 he remains on death row.

Born in **1955**.

Active from **1978-1979**.

Country: **USA**.

Victims: **6**.

AKA: **The Bedroom Basher**.

Sentence: **Death penalty**.

Current whereabouts: **Death row**.

Paulin, Thierry

On November 25th 1987, French serial killer *Thierry Paulin* brutally murdered 79-year-old *Rachel Cohen*. She would become one of his 18 accused murders. Later on the same day he brutally attacked 87-year-old *Berthe Finalteri* but she would go on to survive and give a description that would result in the capture of Paulin. The killing of *Genevieve Germont* on November 27th 1987 would be his final victim.

Thierry Paulin had contracted HIV in the years prior and then AIDS. His killings sped up as he realised he was under a biological death sentence and set out to cause as much carnage and chaos as possible. He organised large and expensive parties that were all paid for with stolen credit cards along with the financial gains from his murders.

He was arrested on December 1st 1987 and accused of the 18 murders. He confessed to 21 killings. Just over a month later, Paulin fell ill as AIDS set in. He was subsequently hospitalised and died on April 16th 1989.

Born **November 28th 1963.**

Active from **1984-1987.**

Arrested on **December 1st 1987.**

Country: **France.**

Victims: **18-21.**

AKA: **The monster of Montmartre.**

Current whereabouts: **Died from AIDS on April 16th 1989.**

Peiry, Michel

In Switzerland, *Michel Peiry,* AKA*: the Sadist of Romont*, killed 11 hitchhikers between 1981 and 1987. The Swiss serial killer is said to be the worst in the country since World War Two.

He would abduct or lure teenage hitchhikers then tie them up and rape or abuse them. Afterwards he would violently murder them and burn the corpses. In April of 1987, he claimed two victims. His ninth victim was on April 16th in the now popular Lake Como region of Italy. Eight days later, he attacked a young man in a similar fashion but the man survived. A week later, on May 1st 1987, Peiry was arrested.

Peiry was raised in an unhappy home and his father was violent to both him and his mother. He grew up to lead a relatively normal life until he began to repress his homosexuality. Out of this, he leaned towards violent sexual fantasies which he acquired through a love of bondage. He claimed that sexuality and violence became inseparable.

He was sentenced to life in prison, where he remains as of 2021.

Born **February 28th 1959**.

Active from **1981-1987**.

Arrested on **May 1st 1987**.

Country: **Switzerland / Italy**.

Victims: **5-11**.

AKA: **The Sadist of Romont**.

Sentence: **Life imprisonment**.

Current whereabouts: **In prison**.

Pennell, Steven Brian

American serial killer *Steven Brian Pennell,* AKA*: The Route 40 Killer*, killed five people in the State of Delaware. He is infamous for being Delaware's only known serial killer.

He victims mostly consisted of hitchhikers who he picked up in his work van along Route 40 in Delaware. The carpet of the van proved to be a vital piece of evidence in his capture as small fibres from the carpet were found on the body of the first victim.

The carpet fibres were removed from the van by an undercover policewoman who was posing as a prostitute. She managed to pull some from it when she pretended to admire his carpet, before deciding not to go with him. While the fibres were being forensically tested, he was placed under surveillance.

On November 29th 1987, *Shirley Ellis* was picked up by Pennell, with the promise of money for sex in his van. He then tied Ellis up, then brutally raped, beat and mutilated her. Her body was dumped near Route 40.

He was arrested in 1988 and convicted of two murders. He pleaded no contest on three more murders on the condition that he be executed as a preference. There was another murder in 1988 that he was also linked to but not proven.

He claimed that is would be easier to execute him rather than have his family see him in jail for the rest of his life. In 1992, Pennell was executed by lethal injection, the first to be executed in Delaware since 1946, almost 50 years later.

Born in **1957**.

Active from **1987-1988**.

Arrested on **November 29th 1988**.

Country: **USA**.

Victims: **5+**.

AKA: **The Route 40 Killer**.

Sentence: **Death penalty**.

Current whereabouts: **Executed by lethal injection in 1992**.

Pichushkin, Alexander: The Chessboard Killer (Extended Case File)

Born in Russia on April 9th 1974, *Alexander Pichushkin* would go on to be convicted of 49 murders. He then asked if he could have another eleven added to his body count, bringing it up to 60. After his arrest, officials discovered a chessboard with specific dates on 62 of the 64 squares. Pichushkin would claim that he was aiming for 64 murders, to complete his chessboard, and that if he wasn't caught then he would have succeeded in his macabre mission.

When Pichushkin was a child, he fell off a park swing, and the edge of the seat hit him hard in the forehead. From that moment, he turned from a well-liked child with a bubbly personality to a withdrawn individual who was known to have been anti-social. Brain damage was a term thrown around during his trial, used by media outlets and his lawyers as a soft defence of his crimes.

They suggested that the event may have damaged the frontal cortex of Pichushkin's brain. Damage to the brain in that area is well known to produce poor impulse regulation, along with an aggressive nature that may or may not have been evident before. But the very nature of the brain damage has never been proven and remains conjecture to this day.

After the accident, and because of his change in nature and emotion, his mother chose to remove him from his school. She transferred him from his public school to a special facility for children with learning disabilities. Because the facility was in the same area as his previous school and because of the social climate at the time, Pichushkin was bullied both physically and verbally.

Later, Pichushkin claimed he had learned to hold back his anger at being bullied, he internalised his quiet rage until it materialised in the most of heinous of ways just a few years later. Pichushkin's grandfather became frustrated with the new school, as they didn't push the children to grow beyond their means. And so he introduced Pichushkin to the game of chess, to increase his intelligence.

Pichushkin's grandfather was a chess player himself and knew that the game would be able to focus his grandson's emotions. Little did he know that the mundane action of introducing him to the game of chess would be used for an entirely different purpose. It didn't take long for Pichushkin to be shown the public exhibition games in *Bitsa Park*, also known as *Bitsevski Park*.

Bitsa Park is set in over 18 square kilometres of land with a stretch of 10 kilometres from North to South. It is one of the largest natural parks in Moscow and has extensive trails running through the forests, alongside the *Bitsa* and *Chertanovka River*. This area of beauty was to become synonymous with one of the most notorious serial killers of recent times.

Pichushkin claimed he enjoyed living with his grandfather, as his intellect was respected and he was allowed to progress where others had held him back. It was then fate that his grandfather suddenly died and Alexander had to return to live with his mother. Almost as soon as he returned to his mother's, he was bullied again by the locals. Even as he grew into a young man, he was still being bullied whenever he was outside and this only led to a larger build-up of anger and aggression.

He subsequently turned to drinking vodka in large quantities. Over the years, he became so dependent on vodka that others suggested he had become immune to its effects. He would sometimes drink huge amounts of alcohol and then go and play chess in Bitsa Park. He would still win a majority of his chess games and he found the ability to focus through the veil of alcohol. This was to play a part in his murders as he was often intoxicated when he killed.

It has also been alleged but never proven that his one aim was to outdo the body count of *Andrei Chikatilo,* AKA*: The Red Ripper*, who had recently been convicted for the murders of 53 children and women. The media furore around Chikatilo's case was one that might have influenced Pichushkin's decision to kill.

When Chikatilo was on trial in 1992, Pichushkin at the age of 18-years-old, claimed his first victim. When he was still a student, he pushed another boy out of a window, who fell to his death. It has never been clear whether the other boy had bullied or was bullying him at the time but the death was recorded as suicide. However, Pichushkin spoke of the murder in detail at his trial.

"This first murder, it's like first love, it's unforgettable."

Pichushkin in an interview with police.

It wouldn't be for almost another decade until he would kill again. During this time, his murderous tendencies remained hidden from view and he learned to control his anger and conceal the rage within.

In 2001, Pichushkin began a campaign of murder that would strike fear into the heart of Moscow. He would kill those who were said to be on the fringe of civilised society. His victims consisted of homeless men, runaways, prostitutes and lonely alcoholics.

It started with elderly homeless men who resided in or around the vicinity of Bitsa Park. He would lure them away from their troubles with offers of free vodka. He would befriend and drink with them until they were intoxicated, then he would hit them on the back of the head with a hammer, to avoid spilling blood on his clothes. Many of his victims were unidentifiable, because of their wounds or because they had been off the grid for far too long.

As Pichushkin gained confidence in his killing blueprint, he began increasing the intensity of his crimes. He would push a vodka bottle into the open wound of his victim's heads, through the skull and into the brain itself. His obsession with murder slowly moved him away from elderly homeless men to younger men, women, and children.

"In all cases I killed for only one reason. I killed in order to live, because when you kill, you want to live. For me, life without murder is like life without food. I felt like the father of all these people, since it was I who opened the door for them to see another world."

Pichushkin's confession.

When he began his campaign of murder, he would crudely hide the bodies by dropping them down into the many sewers inside the park. But as the killings increased, he would leave his victims in the open, in the exact location he killed them. This led to a frenzy within the city, and a knowledge that a serial killer was on the loose.

Around 2003, Moscow's citizens began to fear a killer the media had described as the *Bitsevsky Maniac* or *The Bitsa Beast*. It was only in 2003 that the investigation really started to take hold. Pichushkin wouldn't be a suspect for another three years.

In the Spring of 2006, the body of his final victim, 36-year-old *Maria Moskalyova* was found in Bitsa Park, with a bottle of vodka sticking out of her head. Detectives found a Moscow Metro train ticket on her person and traced her on surveillance footage. After following her route through the CCTV, they discovered that Pichushkin was accompanying her a few hours before she died.

While they were hunting Pichushkin, another body was found. Pichushkin had murdered one of his colleagues from a supermarket where he worked. She had left a note for her son, that said she was going for a walk with Pichushkin. Unaware of the letter in her home, he killed her and left the body in the park.

It wasn't until his arrest that police discovered the now infamous chessboard with dates on all but two of its squares. At his trial, Pichushkin's confession was aired on Russian TV stations.

"For me, a life without murder is like a life without food for you."

Pichushkin – in his confession.

In October 2007, it took a jury only three hours to find him guilty of 49 counts of murder and three counts of attempted murder. The death penalty in Russia had recently been ended and so he was sentenced to life in prison with the first 15 years in solitary confinement. The debate surrounding a return of the death penalty in Russia is still debated to this day.

Pichushkin has been interviewed on many occasions and has offered an incredible insight to the mind of a killer. His thoughts on the very nature of human life comes from that of a man obsessed with belittlement and appearing as a higher form of human.

"Human life is not too long. It is cheaper than a sausage. My lawyer: I would cut him open like a fish. I would have killed him like an insect, and I would receive much pleasure from the process. I would cut him up and make belts out of his flesh. But as for remembering everyone I killed, who and when and where, that, I don't remember. I don't even care to remember."

His nonchalance for human life is characteristic of a sociopathic personality, believing that he is better off and more powerful than everyone around him. The feeling of *playing god* is a trait of a serial killer that often shows up.

He later revealed that he did have a dog and the dog's death hit him harder than he could have imagined.

"She died. It was my fault. I treated it, how to say, not very well. She could have been saved. It was a bad situation, it left something in my subconscious."

The feeling of something being left in his subconscious, his dreams at night, could have been the only strand of guilt that Alexander ever felt. He blamed himself for his dog's death and felt bad about it. Yet the multiple destruction of human life was not as important as the loss of that which was close to him.

Alexander Pichushkin has gone on record many times to say that he does not regret anything he ever did.

"No, I do not regret it. So much strength and time spent. Repent? I do not repent, this is again a dull formality. It will not change my sentence. Since I was very young, I dreamed. Everything was different back then. And it all turned out the way I wanted it to."

Like Ted Bundy before him, Pichushkin sometimes spoke of himself in the third person, whether to remove himself of the guilt of the crimes, or to look upon his crimes from an outsider's perspective.

"Even someone wrote: Pichushkin himself doesn't know yet that the history of criminology is changed, that it didn't account for someone such as him, that he will go down in history, forever."

Pichushkin was baptised when he was three-months-old, he would later claim that he did not want it. When speaking of religion he is on record as saying that he does not think that anyone is there.

"I will not either read the Bible or write an autobiography. I have never prayed to God, never will. This is a beautiful fairy tale for the weak."

Various quotes from Pichushkin taken from confessions and interviews:

"I didn't take anything else of value from them. Money, jewellery, I didn't need it. I felt like God."

"I tried to collect their spirits, their souls, I felt no emotion when I killed them."

"I felt like the father of all these people, since it was I who opened the door for them to see another world."

As of 2021, Pichushkin remains in solitary confinement.

Born **April 9**th **1974.**

Active from **1992-2006**.

Arrested on **June 14th 2006**.

Country: **Russia**.

Victims: **49-62**.

AKA: **The Chessboard Killer / Bitsevsky Maniac / The Bitsa Beast**.

Sentence: **Life imprisonment**.

Current whereabouts: **In prison, in solitary confinement**.

Pickton, Robert: The Pig Farmer Killer (Extended Case File)

One of Canada's worst cases of serial killing began in 1983 and continued for 19 years until 2002. *Robert Pickton, AKA: The Pig Farmer Killer,* was responsible for at least 49 murders. Even though he was only convicted on six of them. He was arrested in 2002 and charged with the deaths of another twenty women.

Forensic detection proved difficult because most of the bodies had either been decomposing for a long time or had been consumed by insects and pigs on the farm. The investigation included heavy equipment and even had 15-metre-long conveyor belts and soil sifters to find evidence of human remains.

In 2004, the *Canadian Government* confirmed that Pickton may have ground up human flesh and mixed it with pork to be sold to the public and to the wholesale trade. In conjunction with the *Health Authority*, they issued a warning about meat that had originated from the region.

Almost all of Pickton's victims were prostitutes from the Vancouver area, and in some cases it was suggested that he fed the bodies to his pigs. He was sentenced in 2010 to 25 years in prison without the possibility of parole in what was the maximum sentence for murder under Canadian law. He confessed to 49 murders but wished to kill another to make it a round fifty.

During the trial, laboratory workers confirmed that 80 unidentified DNA profiles had been detected on the evidence provided to them.

Excavations at the farm continued for a year and cost upwards of $70million CAD. The area is now fenced off and all properties belonging to the farm have now been destroyed.

Born in 1949, Robert Pickton came from a family of pig farmers based in Port Coquitlam, British Columbia, just 17 miles east of Vancouver. Pickton and his two brothers grew up on the farm and inherited it from their family. In the mid-1990s, they sold parts of the farm for a few million dollars.

A worker at the farm named *Bill Hiscox* described the remaining part of the farm as a creepy-looking place. He described Pickton as a bizarre individual who would draw attention to himself through any means possible. By 1996, Pickton had already murdered an unknown number of victims. It was in 1996 that things took an even greater turn for the worse.

After selling off parts of the farm, the Pickton brothers neglected the farming operations and looked at events as a way to bring in money. They registered a non-profit company called the *Piggy Palace Good Times Society*. The operation involved the running and managing of events, including functions, dances, shows, and exhibitions on behalf of service and sports organisations.

Mostly it was a way to host raves and mega parties in a converted slaughterhouse on the farm, which sometimes attracted upwards of 2,000 people a night. Clientele included Hells Angels and Vancouver sex workers. The set-up provided all the victims that Pickton needed.

The raves were against the law as they would sell illegal drugs and alcohol without a license to party-goers, they also charged an entrance fee. It has been suggested that the *Piggy Palace Good Times Society* was merely a front for their illegal operations.

Pickton had been linked with missing people and murders all the way back to 1978 but was only convicted of murders that took place between 1997 and 2001. A total of 65 women had disappeared in the area from 1978 to 2001. After the largest investigation in Canadian history, investigators are still unsure as to which missing person was the first of his murders.

Prostitutes on the *Downtown Eastside* area of Vancouver were plentiful in the time that Pickton was killing. The red-light district was known for drug users, prostitutes and crime. Pickton had his pick of victims and it was reported that almost all of his victims were involved in drug use or prostitution. That a murdered prostitute is difficult to investigate, Pickton went unnoticed for two decades.

Before the illegal raves brought a raft of potential victims his way, he would lure the women to his pig farm where no one would hear them scream. He either strangled them with ligatures or shot them dead – before feeding them to the pigs.

Pigs can eat through a human body with ease, it is known that feeding a body to pigs was also used by the *Italian Mafia* at one point in their history. Because the farm processed the meat on site, Pickton had an easy method of disposal at his hands. It is also unclear whether he fed his victims to the pigs whilst they were dead or alive.

By 2001, Bill Hiscox began to notice that women would be seen entering the farm and never leaving. He finally raised his concerns to police and Pickton was arrested after women's items were found on the farm. In 2006, he pleaded not-guilty to 27 counts of murder. It is also claimed he attached a dildo to the end of his gun in order to use it as a silencer. It was then suggested that he inserted the dildo into one of the women before shooting them through it.

One of Pickton's friends, *Scott Chubb*, claimed that Pickton spoke to him about the best ways to kill hookers. He said that if she was a heroin addict then you could inject her with windscreen washer fluid. He even told Chubb that he killed prostitutes by handcuffing them and strangling them. He claimed he would bleed and gut them dry before feeding them to the pigs.

Pickton was convicted of six murders and the rest were discontinued. The court said that even if the rest were convicted then it wouldn't change the sentence Pickton had received. The difficult lack of evidence in most cases was hard to convict him on. Even though he claimed a total of 49 murders.

After his arrest, a witness named *Lynn Ellingsen* came forward to claim she had seen Pickton skinning a small woman hanging from a meat hook on his farm. She didn't tell anyone at the time as she had been blackmailing Pickton about it ever since.

In 2010, Pickton was sentenced to life with no parole for 25 years, which is the longest possible sentence under Canadian law.

Born **October 26th 1949.**

Active from **1983-2002.**

Arrested on **February 2nd 2002.**

Country: **Canada.**

Victims: **26-60+.**

AKA: **The Pig Farmer Killer / Willie.**

Sentence: **Life sentence of 25 years.**

Current whereabouts: **In prison.**

The Monstrous Book of Serial Killers (2nd edition)

ARIAL VIEW OF THE PICKTON FARM IN PORT COQUITLAM

INTERIOR OF PICKTON'S SLAUGHTERHOUSE

IMAGE ATTRIBUTIONS
(ATTRIB A9) (ATTRIB A10)
(ATTRIB A75) (ATTRIB A76)
(ATTRIB A77)

ROBERT PICKTON

Pintaric, Vinko

A Croatian serial killer who murdered five people over a 17-year period between prison escapes and police stakeouts. He spent a lot of the time hiding in the northern regions and as such was considered an outlaw who engaged in various crimes.

He was born in 1941 during World War Two when his father was out fighting with the Partisan resistance. At one point, Vinko's father was beaten in front of his family, then killed not too long after. Vinko's mother remarried and his new stepfather physically and emotionally abused him. From then on, Vinko spoke about avenging his father.

On April 26th 1973, he killed his first victim after drinking heavily in a local bar. When he arrived home, he got into an argument with his neighbour before shooting him dead and injuring his neighbour's tenant. He turned himself into the police 18 days afterwards. He was subsequently committed to a psychiatric institute but escaped and went into hiding, then he killed his wife in a drunken rage on October 24th 1973.

Police surrounded the house on January 20th 1974 and arrested him without resistance. He admitted to all his crimes but pleaded not guilty due to intoxication by alcohol when committing the crimes. He was sentenced to death with was later commuted to 20 years in prison.

After multiple escapes and subsequent prison time, he was later killed in 1991 during a police shoot out.

Born **April 3rd 1941**.

Active from **1973-1990**.

Arrested on **20th January 1974**.

Country: **Yugoslavia**.

Victims: **5.**

AKA: **Čaruga of Zagorje.**

Current whereabouts: **Killed before capture during a police shoot out in 1991.**

Popkov, Mikhail: The Werewolf (Extended Case File)

Mikhail Popkov, AKA: The Werewolf, is Russia's worst ever serial killer. For many years, researchers have assumed that *Andrei Chikatilo* or *Alexander Pichushkin* were the worst, but as of 2021, Popkov is suggested to be linked to over 200 murders. He has already been found guilty and convicted on 78 counts of murder.

In 2015, Popkov was convicted on 22 counts of murder. In 2018, he was convicted of another 56 counts of murder.

Born on March 7th 1964, it is claimed that Popkov was abused by his mother, although not much information on his childhood is known at the present time. He became a police officer in the Irkutsk region of Russia and also worked as a security guard at the Angarsk Oil and Chemical Company, along with private contracts.

His wife and daughter claim to this day that he is innocent of the crimes that he has been found guilty for, and stand by him, protesting his innocence at every turn. However, Popkov has been with investigators when he explicitly showed them how he killed some of his victims and where their remains were buried.

Almost all of his victims were women between the ages of 15-years-old and 50-years-old. He also killed a fellow male police officer but the motive has never been forthcoming. Most of the victims were prostitutes, homeless or drunk. They were people that Popkov considered immoral and of a lower social standing than himself. He chose himself to be judge, jury, and executioner.

While pretending to be on-the-clock in his police uniform, he would lure his victims into his car before killing them in the vehicle or in remote locations around the region. He used knives, axes and baseball bats to kill them. His axe, in particular, had been used to kill at least 17 women.

He killed one of his victims by stabbing her over 170 times. The brutality of his murders and the way in which he completely ripped his victims apart, earned him the moniker of *The Werewolf*. The bodies appeared to have been ripped apart by a vicious animal.

One victim was beheaded and another victim had her heart ripped out of her chest and thrown to the side of her body. Some people who knew Popkov claimed that a lot of the victims had a similar look to his own mother, and it has been suggested that he may have been taking revenge on his own mother by killing those who looked like her.

Ever since 1992, Popkov had been taking victims in a similar manner. The Russian police force was involved in the case from 1994, investigating murders of women across a large region of the country.

This was at a time when the trial of fellow Russian serial killer, Andrei Chikatilo, had infested the national psyche. At the same time, Alexander Pichushkin, a Russian serial killer said to be influenced by Chikatilo, had already claimed a victim, and was building up to a campaign of terror in the Russian Capital.

After two decades, the investigation found patterns in the vehicle tracks near to the remains of some victims. They were the same as the off-road vehicles used by the police force and similar authorities. In 2012, DNA testing of 3,500 current police officers and former police officers in the Irkutsk region, resulted in Popkov's arrest.

"I had a double-life. In one life I was an ordinary person, I was in the service in the police, having positive feedback on my work. I had a family. My wife and daughter considered me a good husband and father, which corresponded to reality. In my other life I committed murders, which I carefully concealed from everyone, realising that this was a criminal offence. My wife and daughter never knew about the crimes I committed and did not even suspect this."

Popkov, in his confession to police.

There were also two survivors, and one of them would speak in detail about her experience. One survivor was attacked, left for dead, and subsequently awoke in a morgue. She had been raped, beaten and repeatedly thrown into a tree. When her battered body crumpled to the ground in a pool of her own blood, Popkov left her, assuming she had died. It remains unclear how she came to awake in a morgue.

In October of 1998, two more victims were discovered by shepherds. 19-year-old Yulia Kuprikova was found next to her friend, 20-year-old Tatiana Martynova. They had attended a concert in the area and then went out for a drink afterwards. After Tatiana failed to return home, her husband, Igor, called the police and a search was undertaken.

Both Yulia and Tatiana had been raped, beaten and mutilated. Popkov was also accused of engaging in necrophilia with the corpses. Tatiana's eldest brother flew from Moscow to the region, to identify his sister's corpse. It is claimed that when he exited the coroner's room, he became sick and could not speak as to what he had seen.

In January of 2015, Popkov was sentenced to life in prison on 22 counts of murder, alongside two attempted murders. At the time, a Russian investigator claimed that Popkov could have murdered up to 200 people. As of 2021, 14 of the victims remain unidentified due to their personal histories or the way in which the bodies had been mutilated.

On December 10th 2018, Popkov was convicted of another 56 counts of murder. There were three more that he confessed to but due to a lack of evidence, they were not pursued in the courts. The convictions only added to his life sentences. At that time, another investigator also claimed that there could be an additional 122 victims, bringing the total body count to the already suggested number of 200.

During his trial, he referred to himself as a cleaner. He claimed to be punishing young women for immoral actions and behaviour.

"They left their husbands and children at home and went out drinking as if for the last time. Of course nobody is without sin. But one must not hurt one's dearest."

Popkov interview in the Russian newspaper *Komsomolskaya Pravda*. (2015).

Psychiatrists' reports list the motive of the murders as purely psychopathic. Medical workers claimed he simply had an irresistible urge to kill and got away with it for so long due to his connections with law enforcement.

Popkov was sent to the *Black Dolphin* facility to serve his sentence. The Black Dolphin is a high-security prison to Russia's East, on the border of Kazakhstan. After the end of the death penalty in 1996, the high-security prison holds Russia's most brutal and heinous criminals.

In July 2020, Popkov confessed to more killings, bringing the total number of admitted victims to 83. As of 2021, Popkov is the country's worst known serial killer by brutality and body count.

Born March 7th **1964.**

Active from **1992-2010.**

Arrested on **June 23rd 2012.**

Country: **Russia.**

Victims: **83-200+**

AKA: **The Werewolf.**

Sentence: **Life imprisonment.**

Current whereabouts: **In prison.**

(Research Article #18) The Vietnam War Divide

It is one of the longest campaigns by the United States, at over 17 years long, from 1955 to the American military withdrawing in 1973. There are said to be more than 35,000 books written about the Vietnam War, mostly from an American perspective.

Over 58,000 Americans were killed during the war but it pales in comparison to the estimated 3.8million Vietnamese. But what most of these books forget to mention beyond the action of the war, is the millions of lives affected by it.

We've already discussed the effects that World War Two had on families. Mostly, it was Europeans that had felt the brunt of the war but the Vietnam War was almost exclusively American.

The displacement of families caused by the removal of young males was the first step to creating a generation of lost and damaged men. FBI reports show that murders in the United States increased amongst all age-groups during the Vietnam Conflict.

The war was unique within the United States as it split opinion and caused divide between the political parties and indeed most families across the country. The rise of violent crime after the country had pulled out of Vietnam, rose to a greater level than before. The link between the Vietnam Conflict and subsequent violent crime is well evidenced.

Sanctioned killing during a war can have a subsequent effect on the level of violent crime and murder beyond the end of such a war. Although you won't find many books on the crimes committed by American military, more data is starting to come out from that lost time.

Because the killing of the enemy was sanctioned, the activities of some military personnel were brushed under the carpet. Many Vietnamese women were raped and murdered by serving American personnel. Many more Vietnamese civilians were murdered in cold blood. Yet, mostly it was simply passed over as an act during war. Only a few cases ever reached military court and it didn't have the effect needed to stop the activities.

The resulting failure of the Vietnam War infected the national psyche like a plague. Personal failure, wasted lives, national failure and a divide that reached the political parties.

For some soldiers, the psychological aspect of surviving the Vietnam War was too much to bear and the country didn't seem to care. There was no soldier kissing a nurse like at the end of World War Two, there were no welcome home parades.

The following is taken from Kenrick Thompson's *Photographic imagery and the Vietnam War: an unexamined perspective*. It describes the mood of the soldiers and the nation in its own painful way.

"Imagine if you had just graduated out of high school and were sent to a guerrilla warfare far away from your home. During the war, you were exposed to a lot of stress, confusion, anxiety, pain, and hatred. Then you were sent back home with no readjustment to the lifestyle in the states, no deprogramming of what you learned from the military, and no "welcome home" parades. You are portrayed to the public as a crazed psychopathic killer with no morals or control over your aggression.

"You find that there's nobody you can talk to or who can understand what you've been through, not even your family. As you re-emerge into civilization, you struggle to establish a personal identity or a place in society because you lack the proper education and job skills. In addition, there are no supportive groups to help you find your way, which makes you feel even more isolated, unappreciated, and exploited for serving your country."

Most of those descriptors point towards causes and some consequences of mental illness. Isolation, feeling unwanted, lack of identity, lack of belonging, deteriorating social skills and being portrayed as a violent criminal. They are indeed as similar to the causes of mental illness as any other reasons.

These men were coming home to a nation that had failed. They were heading back to their families, withdrawn and depressed. There, they would struggle to raise their own children or cope with their own nightmares. A darkness that might have infected them from the experiences in the war.

Most of the American military were drinking lots of alcohol or doing drugs. Some took part in violent rapes and senseless murders. Most were psychologically affected by their experiences. They all came back to the United States and brought their psychological disturbances with them.

The fact that PTSD was not really taken seriously until the early 1980s, meant that many suffered needlessly. Or they might have taken it out on their children or other people. The deadly combination of their own society rejecting them, the government ignoring their pleas, and their families not understanding them, caused Vietnam veterans to suffer both mentally and physically.

World War Two and the Vietnam Conflict gave rise to higher instances of violent crime in the years during and the years that followed. This was due to the returning soldiers themselves, the effects on them, *and* the effects on their families and children. Some of those who served in wars and went on to become serial killers are listed below.

David Berkowitz, *The Son of Sam.* Served with the US Army in South Korea.

Gary Ridgeway, *The Green River Killer.* Served in the Navy and was sent for a tour in Vietnam.

Leonard Lake. Serial killer suspected of killing up to 25 people in the early 1980s served as a Marine in Vietnam.

Arthur Shawcross, *The Monster of the Rivers.* Killed 14 people between 1972 to 1989, including raping and killing a 10-year-old boy. He served in Vietnam.

Roy Norris, one half of *The Toolbox Killers* was deployed to Vietnam.

Howard Unruh, a spree killer who killed 13 people as he walked through his neighbourhood in 1949 was a US Army veteran of World War Two.

Rudy Bladel, *The Railway Sniper.* Killed up to seven people between 1963 to 1978. He served in the Korean War.

William Bonin, *The Freeway Killer.* Killed at least 21 young men and boys from 1979 to 1980. He served in the Vietnam War.

Only a tiny percentage of those who served in active wars go on to become serial killers. Most would go on to have happy lives but some would be psychologically affected from their experiences during wartime.

No conclusive studies have been completed on the effect of war within the countries where the wars have taken place. But it is suggested that millions more have been irreversibly affected by war.

(Research Article #19) The Afghanistan War Divide

Afghanistan divided people, not quite as much as the Vietnam Conflict, but divided, nonetheless. The West had just come out of the Iraq War and the people back home were tired of wars that seemingly served no real purpose.

The main issue with psychological effects of war is that they are never given as much attention as physical issues. Families experience loss and grief caused by the death of their loved one, people their loved ones knew, or those from the country of conflict itself.

People learn to suppress war time anxiety and develop PTSD quicker than they may think.

If we link the Afghanistan War to the Vietnam War then the two are not quite as different as we might think. For starters both are on the border of China. This always raises the notion that China might be protecting their own borders by not allowing the United States to get a foothold in a neighbouring country.

Every war fought by the United States or NATO on the Chinese border has never ended well; The Vietnam War, Afghanistan War and Korean War. And for the British; the Opium War. Although the Opium War was seen as a victory where it really wasn't. It resulted in Britain maintaining control of Hong Kong for 100 years.

Drugs were rife in both wars and reports of drugs at Afghan bases were more telling than not. The public didn't want more war after Iraq and petitioned in their millions against the Afghanistan War but to no avail.

This kind of belittling effect on the war itself and in turn on the soldiers was similar to the fallout of the Vietnam War. Soldiers suddenly didn't know what they were fighting for and many were coming back traumatised over what they had seen.

If the Iraq War was a swap-in for World War Two, then the Afghanistan War could be seen as a similar conflict to the Vietnam War. The public were divided on both and they came shortly after a larger war had been fought.

There is a psychological circle of depression, PTSD and violence that permeates through military families and circles of friends. Even now, some do not see their depression as a mental disorder and thus go under the radar, not even close to appearing on any data lists. The true number affected could be immense.

We talk about the children of war and the soldiers themselves but not about the women or partners that end up having to look after their children and their husbands or partners. The effect on all is dangerous, damaging and worthy of much more statistical gathering.

War shape's individual experience in ways that cannot be easily tabled or listed. Not everything should be labelled under PTSD or depression. The danger is that many are going undiagnosed and for those who end up homeless or removed from society then there's no telling what happens to them after that.

Price, Craig Chandler

On July 27th 1987, in Rhode Island, serial killer *Craig Chandler Price* claimed his first victim, and he was only 13-years-old at the time. He would be arrested before he even reached his 16th birthday and by then he had already murdered four people.

On the evening of July 27th, he broke into a house only two doors away from his family home. He took a knife from the kitchen and killed the occupant; 27-year-old Rebecca Spencer, by stabbing her an astonishing 58 times. He would kill his victims usually when high on marijuana and LSD.

His murders were so violent that the handles would break off the knives with the blades still embedded in the victims. He killed one of his neighbour's eight-year-old daughter by crushing her skull and stabbing her over 30 times. He was arrested in 1989 when he was just 15-years-old and sentenced to life in prison.

He continues to be violent in prison, having stabbed a prison officer in 2009 and another inmate in 2017. He has never shown any remorse for his crimes and remains incarcerated for at least another 25 years.

Born in **1974**.

Active from **1987-1989**.

Arrested in **1989**.

Country: **USA**.

Victims: **4**.

AKA: **The Warwick Slasher**.

Sentence: **Life imprisonment**.

Current whereabouts: **In prison**.

Profit, Mark Antonio

In Minneapolis, Minnesota, serial murderer *Mark Antonio Profit*, AKA: *The Wirth Park Killer*, would be convicted of one murder, with three more confirmed. Since he was 15-years-old, Profit had been outside of prison for a total of only one year. Then over three months in 1996, he killed three women and one man who was a transvestite.

Just 17 days after his release from a halfway-house in Minneapolis, he killed his first victim, and the one he was convicted for. On May 23rd 1996, the nude body of 30-year-old prostitute *Renee Bell* was found floating face down in a creek in Theodore Wirth Park. She had been dead for a couple of days before her discovery.

She had been gagged, raped and strangled to death with a ligature. The material would prove instrumental in Profit's conviction, as fibres from it were found in his vehicle upon his arrest. Profit had gone as far as packing mud onto and into her body in a supposed failed method to see the body decompose quicker.

Then on June 3rd 1996, the burned nude body of 43-year-old *Deborah LaVoie* was found in the same park. On June 19th 1996, the body of 36-year-old *Avis Warfield* was discovered nearby Wirth Park, she had been stabbed and the body and been burned. And then on July 29th 1996, the body of 21-year-old *Keooudorn Photisane* was discovered in bushes near the park's golf course and bike trail.

A year later on June 2nd 1997, Profit was sentenced to two life terms for the murder of Renee Bell and the rape of another woman. For the murder of Avis Warfield, Profit claimed to have been in a County Jail when the murder happened, but authorities confirmed that he had not yet been arrested by that point. He was also placed at the scene of the crime.

In August 2001, while at the start of his sentence, he attempted to kill a prison guard and was charged with attempted murder. Just two months later in early October, Profit was found dead in his cell at the Minnesota Correctional Facility. No cause of death was given.

Born in **1964**.

Active during **1996**.

Arrested on **October 3rd 1996**.

Country: **USA**.

Victims: **4**.

AKA: **The Wirth Park Killer.**

Sentence: **Two life sentences.**

Current whereabouts: **Died of natural causes in October 2001.**

Psicopata, El (The Psychopath)

On July 14th 1987, prostitute *Ligia Camacho Bermudez* was murdered in her home as she was laying on her bed reading a book. She had been shot from outside her house, through the window.

When ballistics were run, it showed the murder was carried out by a notorious Costa Rican serial killer known as *The Psychopath* (El Psicopata). Between 1986 and 1996, The Psychopath was responsible for the murders of at least 19 people in major cities across the country.

The last known murders of El Psicopata were on October 26th, 1996. A young couple were parked beside a road near San José. The killer forced them at gunpoint to get out and leave their car behind, he then marched them away from the road and show them both in the head. It was never clear what happened to the killer after the final murders.

In 1996, the suspect was identified by the Civil Police but never found. Due to the Costa Rican statute of limitations having passed, even if a suspect was found today, he could not be tried for the murders. This effective mean that the culprit would get off scot-free.

Active from **1986-1996**.

Country: **Costa Rica**.

Victims: **19+**.

AKA: **The Psychopath**.

Current whereabouts: **Unidentified killer. Status unknown.**

Quansah, Charles

A rare serial killer from Ghana, *Charles 'Papa' Kwabena Ebo Quansah*, AKA: *The Accra Strangler*, strangled to death at least nine women from 1993 to 2000.

On January 19th 1996, the body of *Akua Serwaa* was discovered just outside the Kumasi Sport Stadium. She had been strangled to death by Quansah. He would be convicted of her murder when he was in custody for killing his girlfriend, *Joyce Boateng*, in 2000.

From 1993, the bodies of multiple women began turning up across Accra, the capital city of Ghana. A serial killer was suspected but the investigation was getting nowhere and Quansah carried on killing. He was a mechanic who lived in the Adenta region of the city.

Quansah was already under suspicion due to previous convictions and prison time for rape in the 1980s. He was under police surveillance as a suspect in some of the murders. When he was arrested in 2000, 34 victims had been attributed to the unknown serial killer. Although Quansah would be convicted on nine murders, he was strongly linked to the other 25.

In July of 2002, Quansah was convicted of the nine killings and sentenced to death by hanging. Quansah claimed he was coerced into a confession by police who tortured him. Until his death shortly after, he proclaimed his innocence at every turn.

Born in **1964**.

Active from **1993-2000**.

Arrested in **July 2000**.

Country: **Ghana**.

Victims: **9+**.

AKA: **Charles 'Papa' Kwabena Ebo Quansah / The Accra Strangler**.

Current whereabouts: **Executed by hanging in 2002**.

Quick, Thomas

Born *Sture Ragnar Bergwall* in Sweden, he is more commonly known as *Thomas Quick*. He is suspected of having killed up to 30 people over various periods of time between 1964 and 1996. He killed in various Scandinavian countries including Sweden, Finland, Denmark, and Norway.

While he was sectioned in mental institutions, he confessed to his murders but claimed it was different parts of his personality that had killed them. He then withdrew his confessions at a later date and the case has since been under the scrutiny of the Swedish press and public. It has been claimed that a cult of psychologists had led Quick to give false confessions.

He took his mother's surname of Quick when he was 14-years-old and went on to a life of crime involving the sexual abuse of children and various assaults on other people. He would ultimately be convicted of eight murders over different trials in a seven year period from 1994 to 2001.

On March 30th 1996, Quick confessed to abducting and killing nine-year-old schoolgirl *Therese Johannessen* in 1988. He gave instructions to police that would lead them to her remains, and even went as far as describing her wristwatch in great detail. Investigators then found bone fragments in the exact place where Quick claimed to have buried her.

Then came the outrage as Quick claimed that his confessions were false and forced upon him. He publicly took back his confessions in 2008. Bizarrely, because each trial had rested on his confession alone, each conviction was quashed, with the last conviction finally overturned on appeal in 2013. There was even no evidence beyond a confession in the murder of *Johannessen*.

What is clear, is that Quick was a criminal in his younger years, and that he did originally confess to the murders of 30 people. What is unclear, is the exact nature of his mental state before, during, and after the murders. Quick has since been released from psychiatric care and is suspected of living a free life somewhere in Sweden.

His treatment plan has been wrapped up in secrecy and cannot be revealed to the press or researchers. Interestingly, from the uncensored portions of his files, it seems that Quick is no longer taking medication and hasn't been since his release. Even though he had been on medication for most of his life.

As of 2021, Quick's whereabouts are known only to a few. He is the only known serial killer to have all of his murder convictions quashed due to failures in the legal system.

Born **April 26th 1950.**

Active from **1964-1996.**

Arrested in **March 1996.**

Country: **Sweden / Finland / Denmark / Norway.**

Victims: **8-30+.**

AKA: **Sture Ragnar Bergwall.**

Sentence: **Convictions quashed due to legal system failures.**

Current whereabouts: **Status unknown.**

Radar, Denis: The BTK Killer (Extended Case File)

Born on March 9th 1945, Denis Radar grew up in a normal household and went on to a happy marriage with children and a dream job at a security company. But Radar had been dreaming and having thoughts about restraining women so he could abuse and torture them. He killed from 1974 to 1991 and had claimed at least ten victims within that period.

His knowledge provided from the security job at ADT made it easier for him to cut the phone lines of his victim's homes. Around the time of the last murder in 1991, technology was on the rise. Computers were becoming more popular and more was known about technology,.

Denis Radar was one of the rare serial killers who it seemed wanted to become famous and it was Radar himself who created his own serial killing moniker. He would write letters to police and goad them constantly. He referred to himself as *The BTK Killer.* BTK standing for; 'Bind. Torture. Kill'.

On January 15th 1974, Radar murdered four members of the *Otero* family in Wichita, Kansas. The parents and two children were murdered, the girl was 11-years-old and the boy was nine-years-old. Their bodies were discovered by the family's eldest child, *Charlie Otero*, as he returned home from school. It wasn't until Radar's arrest in 2005 when he would confess to the murders.

He claims that in October 1974, he wrote a letter that he stashed inside a book in the *Wichita Public Library*. It detailed the killing of the family. It was to be the start of his demand for media attention.

The following is a copy of a letter sent to a television station in 1978, it is displayed here as written with no editing. As such, the grammatical and spelling errors remain and are the style of Denis Radar.

"How many do I have to Kill before I get a name in the paper or some national attention. Does the cop think that all those deaths are not related? Golly -gee, yes, the M.O. is different in each, but look a pattern is developing. The victims are tie up-most have been women-phone cut- bring some bondage mater sadist tendencies-no struggle, outside the death spot-no witness except the Vain's Kids.

They were very lucky; a phone call save them. I was go-ng to tape the boys and put plastics bag over there head like I did Joseph, and Shirley. And then hang the girl.

"God-oh God what a beautiful sexual relief that would been. Josephine, when I hung her really turn me on; her pleading for mercy then the rope took whole, she helpless; staring at me with wide terror fill eyes the rope getting tighter-tighter. You don't understand these things because you're not under the influence of factor x). The same thing that made Son of Sam, Jack the Ripper, Havery Glatman, Boston Strangler, Dr. H.H. Holmes Panty Hose Strangler OF Florida, Hillside Strangler, Ted of the West Coast, and many more infamous characters kill. Which seem s senseless, but we can't help it.

"There is no help, no cure, except death or being caught and put away. It a terrible nightmare but, you see I don't lose any sleep over it. After a thing like Fox, I come home and go about life like anyone else. And I will be like that until the urge hit me again. It not continuous and I don't have a lot of time. It takes time to set a kill, one mistake and it all over. Since I about blew it on the phone-handwriting is out-letter guide is too long and typewriter can be traced to, my short poem of death and maybe a drawing, later real picture and maybe a tape of the sound will come your way. How will you know me? Before a murder or murders you will receive a copy of the initials BTK, you keep that copy the original will show up some day on guess who?

"May you not be the unluck one! P.S. How about some name for me, it's time: 7 down and many more to go. I like the following How about you?

"THE B.T.K. STRANGLER', WICHITA STRANGLER', 'POETIC STRANGLER', 'THE BOND AGE STRANGLER' OR PSYCHO' THE WICHITA HANGMAN THE WICHITA EXECUTIONER, 'THE GAROTE PHATHOM', 'THE ASPHIXIATER'. B.T.K"

Radar was the perfect family man between murders, alluded to in a book written by his daughter, *Kerri Rawson*. She says that he was perceived as a pillar in the community and a family man who had a positive outlook on life with his wife and children.

We already know with *Ted Bundy* that some serial killers are capable of great love for women they hold in high esteem and yet capable of such violence towards those they do not.

Internally, Radar was holding off the desire to kill for months and sometimes years at a time. He would engage in autoerotic fantasies until the desire to kill became too strong.

The statement in the letter above proves that above all else, Radar was a narcissist and showed how much he craved attention. It is then assumed that he was fully aware of people's fascination with serial killers and the macabre, due in some part to the media putting serial killers in the limelight.

Radar confirmed later he knew the public would want to know more about him and they would want to know how he did it and what his motivations were. He was deliberately appealing to society's macabre appetite for murder.

In another letter to authorities, he claimed he could not stop killing and society should be thankful to him for holding back the monster. In doing so, he suggested he should be thanked for holding back. He fantasised more and more about killing and held off by using the trophies of his victims in a sexual manner and masturbating.

He claimed to be seeking victims all the way through the late 1970s to the 1980s. His crimes became sexual in nature. In the killing of the Otero family, he used many methods. He strangled the father by putting a cord around his neck then he put a bag over nine-year-old Joseph Otero's head. He strangled the mother but she '*came back to life*' and so he strangled her harder than before.

He killed the daughter, 11-year-old Josephine Otero last. He dragged her into the basement and tied a noose around her neck. Then he hung her, and he watched her die in front of him all the while saying that she would be joining her family in heaven. Then he ripped off some of her clothing and masturbated over the girl's legs. He took many trophies from the scene.

The last murder was in January of 1991 when he murdered 62-year-old Dolores Davis. He claimed that as he had aged – he was 45 years old when he killed Dolores – he had become weaker and as such needed weaker victims to kill.

He stalked Dolores before realising that she lived alone and seemed like a perfect victim. He was on a boy scout trip at the time and had left the campsite to kill her. He went to his parent's house and got changed into his *'killing clothes'* then drove to a church parking lot. He then walked to her house and broke in by smashing the window on the back door.

She came down and saw Radar waiting for her. He claimed Dolores said she was waiting for someone to arrive at her house shortly, but it didn't stop him. He killed her and then used her own car to drive to a lake where he dumped her body. He then cleaned down the car, left it back at her house, returned home to get changed and went back to the boy scout camp as if nothing had happened.

In a twist of fate, it was Radar's obsession with himself and his desired celebrity status that caught him.

In one of his final letters to police, he asked if a floppy disk could be traced if he put confessions and writings onto one and sent it to them. The police answered in a newspaper ad in the *Wichita Eagle* stating that it would be safe and couldn't be traced. In 2005, he sent it in, along with an item of a victim's jewellery and a letter.

Police found some metadata in a deleted *Microsoft Word* document that included reference to a *'Dennis'* and *'Christ Lutheran Church'*. An internet search linked them as Radar was on the church council and along with other evidence compiled, he was subsequently arrested. He finally got his wish as the Wichita Police announced that the BTK Killer had been caught.

He is currently serving ten consecutive life sentences at *El Dorado Correctional Facility* in Kansas.

Born **March 9th 1945.**

Active from **1974-1991.**

Arrested on **February 25th 2005.**

Country: **USA.**

Victims: **10.**

AKA: **The BTK Killer.**

Sentence: **10 life sentences.**

Current whereabouts: **In prison.**

Rand, Andre

Suspected American serial killer *Andre Rand*, AKA*: The Pied Piper of Staten Island*, kidnapped and killed children from 1972 to 1987. It is claimed that he kidnapped them to be used in Satanic rituals. He was convicted of the kidnapping and murder of a 12-year-old girl in 1987.

On July 9th 1987, 12-year-old *Jennifer Schweiger* went missing. After an intense and widespread search that lasted 35 days, her body was found in a shallow grave in an area of woodland. She had been raped and brutally killed.

Rand was arrested in August of 1987 and was sentenced to 25 years to life in prison. Due to the statute of limitations he couldn't be tried for the murder of his earlier victims and was due for release in 2008. However he was convicted on further kidnapping charges, which are not restricted by the statute.

As of 2021, he remains incarcerated and is now due for paroled release in 2037.

Born **March 11th 1944.**

Active from **1972-1987.**

Arrested in **July 1987.**

Country: **USA.**

Victims: **1-5+.**

AKA: **The Pied Piper of Staten Island.**

Sentence: **25 years to life in prison.**

Current whereabouts: **In prison, due for release in 2037.**

Randall, James Michael

American murderer and suspected serial killer, *James Michael Randall*, was active in Massachusetts and Florida from 1984 to 1996. He raped numerous women and killed at least two in the Tampa Bay area.

The first murder he was linked with was the 1984 death of *Holly Cote*, who was strangled to death. She had been a friend of the family and was last seen alive close to where Randall resided at the time. Randall also alluded to the murder in numerous interviews with psychiatrists, however he was never charged with the murder.

In 1986, he beat his wife, *Linda Randall*, so badly that he was arrested and sentenced to a minimum of five years for assault. He was released in 1992 and moved to Florida, where his blood lust only grew. The two confirmed victims were in 1995 and 1996.

Randall developed a fascination with erotic asphyxiation, which meant that he enjoyed choking his sexual partners during sex. Some of his former girlfriends and former wife confirmed that he would hit them and take enjoyment from it. He was also known to have visited prostitutes regularly, and when he did, he choked and beat them too.

On October 20th 1995, Florida prostitute *Wendy Evans*, was strangled to death. Her nude body was discovered on the side of a road by a delivery driver. Three months later on January 18th 1996, another Florida prostitute, *Cynthia Pugh*, was strangled and her body dumped on the side of the road.

Immediately, Randall became a suspect, due to his previous convictions and that his tire marks matched his vehicle. On June 27th 1996, police went to interview Randall at his house. Shortly after, he sped off in his vehicle, causing police to go after him. After a high-speed chase, Randall jumped out of his car and ran off. He was arrested and charged four days later on July 1st 1996.

Less than a year later, in April of 1997, Randall was convicted on two charges of murder and given two death sentences. After an appeal in 2000, the death sentences were commuted to life in prison.

Randall has long been suspected of killing more prostitutes and continues to be a suspect in various cold cases across Florida. Though none have been proven, as of yet, investigators believe he may be responsible for at least four more murders. When charges of two murders were laid at his feet, he looked at the detectives and said; "is that all?"

Born **August 28th 1954**.

Active from **1984-1996**.

Arrested on **July 1st 1996**.

Country: **USA**.

Victims: **2+**.

Sentence: **Death penalty later commuted to life imprisonment.**

Current whereabouts: **In prison.**

Rasmussen, Terrence Peder

AKA: *The Chameleon killer*, Rasmussen was an American serial killer who took the lives of at least six people. He was known for having used multiple aliases for at least 20 years across many States.

Born in 1943, he joined the *U.S. Navy* at a young age and was discharged for unknown reasons in 1967, when he was 24-years-old. After getting married and having four children, Rasmussen suddenly eloped in Christmas of 1974. He moved around the country and lived in at least seven different States, from Virginia to Hawaii.

He used multiple identities to remain off-the-grid and take work under different names. *Curtis Mayo Kimball, Gordon Jensen, Larry Vanner* and *Gerry Mockerman*, were among some of his more used names. Because of recent genetic genealogy testing, we know more about what Rasmussen did in the early years. A lot of the following information was discovered in 2019, nine years after his death.

In 1978, Rasmussen's then girlfriend, *Marlyse Honeychurch*, her six-year-old daughter and her one-year-old daughter went missing on Thanksgiving. In 1985, their decomposed bodies were found in two barrels, along with two other victims, they become known as the *Bear Brook murders*, and wouldn't be identified until 2019. The one-year-old couldn't be identified, but DNA testing proved it to be the child of Rasmussen. He had murdered them all in cold blood.

On Thanksgiving of 1981, while under the name of *Bob Evans*, Rasmussen is suspected of having murdered his then girlfriend *Denise Beaudin*. As of 2021, her body has never been discovered. He claimed that she had run off due to financial reasons. He then took custody of their six-month-old daughter, who he abandoned shortly after.

He was sentenced in 1986 for child abandonment, served four years, and then vanished again in 1990. Another known murder came in 2002 when he killed and dismembered his then wife; *Eunsoon Jun*. He was arrested in 2002 and confessed to the murder.

Under the name of *Larry Vanner*, he was sentenced to 15 years to life. Fingerprint and DNA then began matching him to other names in different States, and a new investigation began drawing up a much larger map of his crimes.

But in 2010, Rasmussen died in prison of natural causes, taking his secrets to the grave. Or so he thought. Genetic genealogy testing of cold cases and suspected murders linked him to at least five more murders across multiple states.

Rasmussen was considered unique in that he generally killed those who were close to him, rather than strangers. It went against the usual victim selection type for serial killers. He was known as *The Chameleon Killer* due to his multiple aliases and ability to remain hidden from investigations.

Born **December 23rd 1943.**

Active from **1978-2002.**

Arrested in **November 2002.**

Country: **USA**.

Victims: **6+**.

AKA: **The Chameleon killer / Larry Vanner.**

Sentence: **15 years in prison.**

Current whereabouts: **Died of natural causes in 2010.**

Ray, David Parker: The Toy Box Killer (Extended Case File)

From the 1950s to 1999, American serial killer and torturer *David Parker Ray,* AKA: *The Toy-Box Killer* was suspected to have killed up to 60 people. Astonishingly, no bodies have ever been found, but his accomplices statements combined with missing persons reports assured police that Ray was potentially one of America's worst serial killers.

He soundproofed and kitted out a truck trailer with instruments of torture and sexual devices and called it his *toy box*. By the end of the trial in 2001, Ray had been convicted of kidnapping and torture but was never convicted of murder. In recent years, due to the advancements in DNA technology and investigatory procedures, he has been positively linked to 14 murders.

For the victims he raped and tortured but didn't kill, he used drugs and brainwashing techniques so the victims wouldn't remember what happened to them. The FBI later stated that the true extent of his crimes might have been stratospheric.

In the mid-1950s when he was just a teenager, he developed a fascination with bondage and BDSM. When his violent alcoholic father left him and his sister with their elderly grandfather, Ray was known to have had secret fantasies about tying people up and murdering them.

His father would supply him with pornographic magazines depicting bondage and BDSM which carved out an image of women he took into his adult years. He was also bullied by other school children for his shyness around girls. When he was in his late teens, he abducted a woman and tied her to a tree, then he tortured, mutilated, and killed her before dumping the body in the woods.

He married shortly after to a woman named *Peggy*. She claimed she knew of his fantasies but not that he was acting on them. At the time he was married, Ray became addicted to using prostitutes and took part in BDSM relationships with them.

His sole child, a daughter from the marriage, *Glenda Jean Ray*, had previously reported him to the FBI in 1986. She said that her father was kidnapping women and selling them to buyers in Mexico. The FBI didn't believe her story, saying it was too far-fetched with not enough details. It would be another 13 years before Ray was finally arrested. The FBI never commented on their mistake in not following up on the report.

The town he lived in was called *Elephant Butte* which is a small town in New Mexico. He had positioned the toy box trailer in a static location for many years, next to a large lake and area of New Mexico parkland. It has been suggested that bodies could easily be dumped in the area, due to its remoteness. But the area has never been excavated.

Ray also had extensive knowledge of the parkland, due to his position as a maintenance man for the *New Mexico Parks Department*. It is claimed that his knowledge of the land allowed him to hide bodies all over the place.

The toy box was his life's work and he spent all his earnings on it. Inside, there were detailed and intricate torture devices and machines designed to maximise pain and keep his victims restrained with minimal movement.

He would source his victims from rundown bars in the area, prostitutes, or drifters and runaways. Then he would torture his victims by using sexual instruments and industrial items. These included saws, blades, straps, clamps, whips and chains. He also had multiple accomplices, some of whom have never been named. Together they raped tens of women.

He also kept detailed illustrations regarding his various techniques for torture and restraint. He even had an electrical generator that he used to torture his victims. He would put them in large contraptions that kept them bent over in one position and placed a mirror in front of them. Then he would bring in dogs to rape them.

Ray kept a detailed journal which contain information on his victims with dates of abductions and murders. It is claimed that without it, there wouldn't have been any prosecution. However, the FBI had built up a large case against him and three trials took place for the kidnap and torture of three victims. He was subsequently sentenced to 224 years.

In 2002, as part of his plea agreement, he agreed to show investigators where the bodies were buried. Just before he was about to, he died of a heart attack. In doing so, he took the locations of the bodies to his grave.

As of 2021, no bodies have ever been discovered.

Born **November 6th 1939.**

Active from **mid-1950s-1999**.

Arrested on **March 22nd 1999**.

Country: **USA**.

Victims: **14-60+**.

AKA: **The Toy-Box Killer**.

Sentence: **224 years in prison**.

Current whereabouts: **Died of a heart attack in 2002**.

The Monstrous Book of Serial Killers (2nd edition)

THE TOY BOX TORTURE TRAILER WHERE PARKER RAY TORTURED HIS VICTIMS

DAVID PARKER RAY

IMAGE ATTRIBUTIONS
(ATTRIB A87) (ATTRIB A88)
(ATTRIB A5)

GARY RIDGWAY

LOREN HERZOG

HERZOG, L
T-38513

SAN QUENTIN STATE PRISON
SHERMANTINE, W.
T-18128
CONDEMNED

WESLEY SHERMANTINE

IMAGE ATTRIBUTIONS
(ATTRIB A47A) (ATTRIB A47B)

SPEED FREAK KILLERS

Recco, Tommy

Born *Joseph-Thomas Recco*, he was a French serial killer also known as Geronimo. He was sentenced in 1962 for killing his godfather. Released in 1977, he went on to kill at least another six people and was captured in 1980 before being sentenced to life in prison.

In 1979, he killed three cashiers at a *Mammoth Shop*, near Marseille. He had lined them up and shot them in the base of the neck. He would go on to murder again just three weeks later at the beginning of 1980. He shot three people including an 11-year-old girl. He was arrested shortly after and has been incarcerated ever since.

He remains one of the longest serving prisoners in the French system.

Born in **1934**.

Active from **1962-1980**.

Arrested in **1980**.

Country: **France**.

Victims: **7-10**.

AKA: **Joseph-Thomas Recco / Geronimo**.

Sentence: **Life imprisonment**.

Current whereabouts: **In prison**.

Reddy, Umesh

Umesh Reddy is an Indian serial killer and rapist who was convicted of killing nine females. He confessed to 18 but police suspected he had been involved in the deaths of at least 20 women across various states in the country. He began his crimes in 1996.

In November 1996, Reddy attempted to rape a high school girl in the state Chitradurga. The girl escaped his clutches by hitting him in the head with a stone. It is claimed he tried to rape her after escaping from Kashmir.

On December 6th 1996, Reddy raped, beat, and murdered a 16-year-old girl known as *Rupa.* She lived in the same area as the previous victim and she was attacked as she was returning home. Reddy would be arrested and would escape custody an astonishing four times until 2002, when he was arrested and convicted of nine counts of murder and rape.

In 2007, he was sentenced to death for raping a 37-year-old woman in front of her son. As of 2021, he remains on death row in India.

Born in **1969**.

Active from **1996-2002**.

Arrested on **March 2nd 1998**.

Country: **India**.

Victims: **9-20+**.

AKA: **The Bangalore Serial Killer**.

Sentence: **Death penalty**.

Current whereabouts: **Death row**.

Reinstrom, Lutz

German killer *Lutz Reinstrom,* AKA: *The Acid Killer*, murdered at least two people in his underground bunker from 1986 to 1988. He built the bunker in the grounds of his terraced house in Rahlstedt.

In 1986, he abducted a 61-year-old lady who was known to him as the wife of his teacher. He took her belongings and cleared her accounts. Then he raped, tortured and dismembered her over the course of a week.

The other known victim was in 1988 when he abducted a 31-year-old female. He emptied her bank accounts before raping and torturing her. The four-week torture was recorded by Reinstrom and he took multiple photos of her ordeal. He ended her life four weeks after her abduction by dismembering her.

He made his victims write farewell letters and postcards to their relatives claiming they wanted to begin a new life in another country. Reinstrom would then travel to the countries and post the letters.

Another kidnapping in 1991 was botched when his wife came home from vacation early. He let his 53-year-old victim go and she became instrumental in his arrest. During the search of Reinstrom's property, five canisters of hydrochloric acid were found, along with a barrel full of human remains.

Born **March 29th 1949.**

Active from **1986-1991.**

Arrested on **September 17th 1991.**

Country: **Germany.**

Victims: **2+.**

AKA: **The Acid Killer.**

Sentence: **Life imprisonment.**

Current whereabouts: **In prison.**

Resendiz, Angel Maturino

Mexican serial killer and lifetime criminal *Angel Maturino Resendiz, AKA: The Railroad Killer* was suspected to have killed at least 23 people across Mexico and the United States between 1986 and 1999.

Most of the murders were committed near railway tracks, which is where he gained his moniker. He first killed in 1986 by shooting dead an unidentified female in Texas. He claimed that he killed her because she had disrespected him when he picked her up to join him on a road trip.

"Evil contained in human form, a creature without a soul, no conscience, no sense of remorse, no regard for the sanctity of human life."

From the wife of one of his victims. (2006).

On June 15th 1999, his final victims were killed. He robbed and ransacked a house near to a railway track in Illinois. There, he shot dead an 80-year-old man in the head. Later that day he beat to death a 52-year-old woman in the same area. Investigators later found the house owners vehicle 60 miles away and found DNA linking Resendiz to the murder.

He subsequently surrendered to police in July 1999 and was convicted of a murder in 1998. He was sentenced to death and executed by lethal injection, in Texas in 2006.

Born **August 1st 1959.**

Active from **1986-1999.**

Arrested on **July 12th 1999.**

Country: **USA / Mexico.**

Victims: **16-23+.**

AKA: **The Railroad Killer.**

Sentence: **Death penalty.**

Current whereabouts: **Executed by lethal injection in 2006.**

Retunsky, Vladimir

The Soviet-Russian serial killer *Vladimir Nikolaevich Retunsky,* AKA*: The Povorino Maniac*, killed at least eight women between 1990 and 1996. He was also heavily linked to four more but they could not be proven at the time.

In 1990, aged 30-years-old, he claimed his first victim. Retunsky was a truck driver who picked up hitchhikers, or lured women into his truck with drink or drugs. Once they were in the passenger side, they couldn't get out due to the passenger door having no handle.

He raped and beat his victims before murdering them. He would dump their bodies on the roadside or in shallow graves. Some of the victims had body parts removed and it remained unclear why he did this or if he consumed some of them.

In 1996, he claimed his final confirmed victim. When he picked her up, she had a puppy Rottweiler with her. After raping and killing her, he decided to keep the dog and took it back home with him. Suspicions were raised when reports of a women going missing with her dog, ran on the news. When neighbours saw that Retunsky had a similar dog where he had no dog before, a search warrant for his house was issued.

Inside, the investigators found a large collection of pornographic VHS and images, along with notebooks detailing the murders of each of his victims. He called the murders, his '*work*'.

The hatred towards him grew in the public domain, and there were reports that he had to be guarded by multiple security teams so that he wasn't attacked by angry mobs. The trial was held in a closed court and he was sentenced to death for eight murders.

Unbelievably, the sentence was commuted to only 15 years, after an appeal. At the time there were no life sentences in Russia, and 15 years was the maximum.

In 2012, Retunsky was released from prison to live with his sister and remained under a strict curfew from 10pm until 6am every day. He was arrested later in 2012 for stealing cash and sentenced to five years in prison.

On July 22nd 2015, Retunsky was released from prison for a second time and now lives amongst us. His whereabouts are currently unknown.

Born in **1950**.

Active from **1990-1996**.

Arrested in **February 1997**.

Country: **Russia**.

Victims: **8-12+**.

AKA: **The Povorino Maniac**.

Sentence: **Death penalty later commuted to 15 years**.

Current whereabouts: **Released on July 22nd 2015. Status unknown.**

(Research Article #20) Exposure to Lead

When this particular reason was researched as a reason for the abundance of serial killers in the 20th Century, it was approached with dubious nonchalance. How could lead make someone want to kill? It turns out the evidence was overwhelming.

From the 1850s, many American cities built water systems using lead or iron piping. The water improved public health but was offset by the damaging effects of lead. Lead water pipes exposed entire city populations to much higher doses of lead than ever before and it was about to get much worse.

It was already suggested that lead service pipes increased the homicide levels of cities across the United States. Lead is a naturally occurring metal that is soft and pliable as well as being corrosion-resistant. It has been noted since the tenth century that exposure to lead may have health consequences.

Despite the hazards evident in all the centuries since, lead has been used more and more in glass, paints and then gasoline and it was this that led to an increase in crime. The use of lead in paint and gasoline has resulted in higher levels of lead in the air and earth around us.

Most cases of lead poisoning occur through inhaling or ingesting. As of the early 21st Century, there is no agreed-upon safe level of lead in the human bloodstream. However, any amount of lead in the blood can contribute to a huge number of health problems.

Studies have shown that lead can interfere with many neurotransmitters in the brain, most likely because lead can mimic calcium. It is said that exposure to lead can alter brain structure and function. Shockingly, exposure to lead can cause increases in impulsivity and aggression. It is considered to be one of the factors in the development of ADHD (Attention Deficit Hyperactivity Disorder).

Being overly impulsive and aggressive, combined with mild mental disorders can result in abnormal behavioural decisions. The increase of the use of lead in gasoline up until the 1960s was never truly seen as being hazardous. The two world wars from the turn of the century had put the evidence on the back burner.

It wasn't until the 1970s that senate hearings would be held to talk about phasing out leaded gasoline and lead-based paint. It wasn't until later in the decade that blood-lead levels (BLL) would notably drop.

The various acts of the 1970s and the commissions that were set up to monitor lead in the industry were starting to have an effect. But it wouldn't be until the late Twentieth Century that lead was really starting to be phased out.

Lead poisoning can lead to anorexia, anaemia, tremors and stomach problems. In developing brains, lead exposure can be particularly damaging. Lead exposure in children can result in limited brain activity and stunted development of physical and mental faculties.

In males, the human brain reaches its peak at the age of around 22-years-old, in females it is much younger at 19-years-old. Exposure up until those ages are still likely to have further damaging effects.

In the United States, lead was finally phased out in 1996. Australia didn't phase it out until 2002. In a 2017 report, 120,000 children born between 1990 and 2004 were studied for the effects of lead poisoning and its relation to behaviour. Links were made between pre-school lead levels and later behavioural negativity in schools.

The researchers studied children who lived near busy roads because the soil near these roads was heavily contaminated with lead. They reported the effects of lead on those children and children who lived in quieter roads. Their conclusion was that the switch from leaded to unleaded gasoline played a big role in the reduction of crime seen in the 1990s and beyond.

No study has yet confirmed how much lead is needed in the bloodstream for someone to turn to crime but links have been made. Lead exposure can lead to reduced control of impulses and reaction times. It can also heighten aggression and disassociation. People who have these behavioural factors are more likely to commit a crime. Some are then likely to go on and kill.

Increased exposure to lead in childhood is linked to reduced brain activity in later years. It affects the prefrontal and anterior cortices of the brain. This is part of the brain that controls function, mood and most importantly; decision making.

The lead-crime hypothesis still to this day remains a theory but it is one that is still being researched as of 2021. No scientist or researcher has come forward to state matter-of-factly that lead is one of the main causes of crime and serial killing. It would be difficult to prove as the studies only consider the levels of lead and not the cultural differences, poverty division, family life, any trauma in an individual's life.

This is why there are 12 possible reasons in this book as to why serial killing increased dramatically from the late 1970s. There will never be just one reason why a serial killer kills. But a combination of some of these reasons might play a major part in the creation of a serial killer.

Rhoades, Robert Ben

American serial killer *Robert Ben Rhoades,* AKA: *The Truck Stop Killer,* is suspected of killing at least 50 women. He was convicted of three murders and was due to be convicted of more until the victims' families dropped the charges to save them the pain and also because he had already been convicted on the others.

It is suggested that he rapes, tortured and murdered more than 50 women over a 15 year period. The investigation deduced that number due to the routes his truck-driving job took him on with the correlations of missing people around the same time as he was in the location.

Rhoades had created a torture chamber in the sleeping area of the truck. He would keep women tied up in there for days and sometimes weeks, as he tortured and raped them before dumping their bodies. Upon his arrest in 1990, it was discovered he was heavily into the BDSM lifestyle and had been killing for at least 15 years.

He also took many photos of his victims. The most famous is the disturbing photo of 14-year-old *Regina Kay Walters*, who was his last known victim. She had run away with her boyfriend before Rhoades picked them up. The investigation found that Rhoades had killed the boyfriend and kept Walters as his sex slave for up to a month before killing her. The last photo of her was only a few minutes before her death.

In 1994, he was convicted of the murder of Walters and sentenced to life without parole. In the past few years he has been extradited to various States across America to be charged in separate murder cases.

As of 2021, he remains incarcerated and is said to be assisting cold case investigators with missing persons cases.

Born **November 22nd 1945.**

Active from **1975-1990.**

Arrested on **April 1st 1990.**

Country: **USA.**

Victims: **3-50+.**

AKA: **The Truck Stop Killer.**

Sentence: **Life imprisonment.**

Current whereabouts: **In prison.**

Gary Ridgway: The Green River Killer (Extended Case File)

Gary Ridgway, AKA: *The Green River Killer*, was an American serial killer who was convicted of 48 murders and has been linked to many more since. He is one of the country's most prolific killers who killed teenage girls and women in Washington State.

Born *Gary Leon Ridgway* in 1949, a few years after the end of World War Two. He was raised in a home of violent arguments and hatred for a mother who had a dominant personality. His father was a bus driver, and it is claimed he constantly moaned about the large number of sex workers he would see on any given shift.

Ridgway later claimed that he felt a sexual attraction to his mother and as such often fantasised about killing her. Up until the age of 13-years-old, Ridgway was a regular bed-wetter. The humiliation only continued as his mother would make a point of washing his genitals afterwards.

Bed-wetting is one of the elements of the *Macdonald Triad*, which cites three factors during childhood that may be markers to violence later on in life. These include bed-wetting, harm to animals, and setting fires. First proposed by psychiatrist *J.M. Macdonald* in 1963, it has since evolved to various different factors associated with childhood behaviour and later violence.

When Ridgway was 16-years-old, after being held back for a year in school, he lured another pupil into the woods and stabbed him. The boy survived and Ridgway went unpunished. In 1969 he married his 19-year-old girlfriend and then joined the *U.S. Navy*. He was subsequently sent to Vietnam where he was involved in combat. While he was in Vietnam, his wife cheated on him and their marriage ended within 12 months.

But Ridgway wasn't any less innocent at the time, he had encounters with various prostitutes while in the military. The resulting under-achievement of the Vietnam

War infected the national psyche like a plague. Personal failure, wasted lives, national failure, and a divide that reached the political parties.

Most of the American military were drinking lots of alcohol or doing drugs. Some took part in violent rapes and senseless murders. Most were psychologically affected by their experiences. They all came back to the United States and brought their psychological disturbances with them.

Ridgway's second marriage ended in a similar manner with his wife cheating on him. During that time, he found God and fell into religion in a big way, taking part in sermons and reading the bible daily. Regardless of his religion, he continued to use the services of sex workers, due to an insatiable appetite for sexual contact.

There was a noticeably clear paradox at work; Ridgway hated the presence of prostitutes in his area but would use their services more and more as time went on. Soon he began to hate them so much that he refused to pay them.

"I picked prostitutes as my victims because I hate most prostitutes and I did not want to pay them for sex."

His first victim was in 1982, 16-year-old *Wendy Lee Coffield*. Ridgway would earn the trust of a prostitute by showing a picture of his son, before either taking them home, to his truck, or to a secluded area. Then he would rape them and strangle them from behind. For a while he used his hands to kill them but moved to using a ligature to prevent any bruising to himself.

From 1982 to 1998, and possibly a little after, he had killed at least 71 teenage girls and women. In the early 1980s, the *King County Sheriff's Office* created the *Green River Task Force* to investigate the murders.

Two task force members; *Robert Keppel* and Dave *Reichert*, had famously interviewed *Ted Bundy* in 1984. And it was Bundy himself who offered a profile on The Green River Killer. He suggested the killer was revisiting the burial or dumping sites to have sex with his victims. He said that if police found a fresh grave, then they should stake it out and wait for him to come back.

Astonishingly, Ridgway *would* return to the places where he dumped the bodies. He dumped the bodies in '*clusters*', mostly in wooded areas. He would return to the bodies to engage in acts of necrophilia with the corpses. He later claimed that having sex with a corpse stopped him from killing someone else at that very moment.

"I placed most of the bodies in groups which I call clusters. I did this because I wanted to keep track of all the women I killed. I liked to drive by the clusters around the county and think about the women I placed there."

He married again in 1988 and claimed to have loved her more than anything. In the time after his third marriage, he only killed a suspected three more victims until his final arrest in 2001. DNA samples collected in 1987 proved to be vital to his arrest.

At his trial in 2003, he entered a plea bargain to plead guilty to 48 charges of murder instead of the seven he was originally charged with. This allowed the families of 41 more victims to find resolution. He claimed more murders and is linked to at least 71 in total. He was sentenced to life in prison, and as of 2021 is currently incarcerated at the *High Security Federal Prison* in Florence, Colorado.

He is constantly being made available for information relating to open murder investigations and remains one of the most notorious serial killers in the United States.

Born **February 18th 1949**.

Active from **1982-2001**.

Arrested on **November 30th 2001**.

Country: **USA**.

Victims: **49-71**.

AKA: **The Green River Killer.**

Sentence: **Life imprisonment.**

Current whereabouts: **In prison.**

Robinson, John Edward: The First Internet Serial Killer (Extended Case File)

In Kansas, American serial killer *John Edward Robinson,* AKA*: Slave Master*, becomes known for being the first Internet serial killer. He was a life-time criminal who was involved in kidnapping, forgery, assaults and murder. All of his post-1993 victims came from online chatrooms, leading him to be the first serial killer who used the Internet as a means to select victims.

Born in Illinois, he and his four siblings were raised by an alcoholic father and strict mother. In 1957 he was enrolled at a private boy's school for those wishing to become priests. He was removed after a year due to behaviour issues. He then enrolled in medical school but dropped out there after two years.

He was first arrested in 1969 after forging over $30,000 from a medical practice where he worked as an X-ray technician. He was convicted of embezzlement and given a three-year suspended sentence. Up until 1975, he was connected with two more frauds in different companies in different States, with a fraudulent company he had set up.

By 1980, he was becoming well-known around his Kansas City community by involving himself in every possible way. He became a local baseball coach, a Sunday School teacher, and a director of a charity. While working with the charity, he forged letters to the Kansas City Mayor and named himself Man of the Year within the charity. His desire for power was becoming all too evident.

In 1982, he was sentenced to 60 days in jail for another fraud, along with cheque forging. When he was released, he set up another fake company and swindled people out of their money. He claimed it was for his wife's medical care as she was seriously ill – which she wasn't.

In the mid-1980s he claimed to have joined a cult called the *International Council of Masters*. It was a secret S&M cult whose mission was to lure young women to be tortured and raped by the cult members. In 1984, he set up another company and hired 19-year-old *Paula Godfrey*, to work in sales. He then sent her away for 'training'.

After a few days, her parents reported her missing and Robinson claimed he had no idea what had happened to her. A few days later, her parents received a letter from their daughter claiming that she was okay but did not want to see anyone again. The police stopped their investigation as the letter was believed. Godfrey was never seen again, and it is suspected that she was Robinson's first murder victim.

In 1985, he met *Lisa Stasi* at a women's refuge. He offered her a job and took her away. Stasi had a four-month-old daughter and so Robinson contacted his brother who had been unable to adopt a baby. He forged documents and solicited over $5,000 USD for legal fees and gave her the child. Stasi had vanished and was never seen again. She too became a victim of Robinson's.

In 2000, the child was tested, and DNA confirmed that she was the daughter of Stasi. Then in 1987, he hired 27-year-old *Catherine Clampitt* for a fake job. She vanished a few weeks later and was never seen again.

After breaking his probation and being arrested again for multiple fraud incidents, he was sentenced to various prison sentences in Kansas and Missouri. From 1987 to 1993, he remained incarcerated on various charges.

Upon his release, he discovered something that changed the way he selected his victims – the Internet. He used the burgeoning chatroom culture to look for women who enjoyed submissive sex. He went by the name of *Slavemaster* and found a 45-

year-old woman named *Sheila Faith*. He pretended to be a wealthy businessman and offered to help pay for her disabled daughter's healthcare.

In 1994, Sheila Faith and her 15-year-old wheelchair-bound daughter, vanished from the face of the earth. Robinson carried on forging their documents and received pension cheques for another seven years.

By 1999, he was well-known within the growing online BDSM community. In the same year he solicited 21-year-old Polish immigrant *Izabela Lewicka*, after meeting her in the chatroom. She claimed she wanted a BDSM relationship and the Slavemaster obliged. He married her under false pretences and got her to sign a slave contract that listed over 100 elements she had to do. Later that year, she too vanished without a trace.

About the same time, nurse *Suzette Trouten*, gave up her life to travel the world as a submissive sex slave to Robinson. But she too vanished without a trace. Letters that were sent to her family after her disappearance were supposed to have come from various foreign countries but instead had the Kansas City postal stamps.

Although he was becoming known to police, there wasn't enough evidence against him and without a body or a crime scene, it became impossible to link him. It wasn't until an unnamed woman accused him of stealing her sex toys in 2000, that Robinson would be arrested.

Much to the investigators delight, it was enough for a warrant to search Robinson's large farm and farmhouse. The team discovered two decomposed bodies within two chemical drums. It was the remains of Polish immigrant Lewicka, and nurse Trouten.

They then searched his storage properties in Missouri, where they discovered three more decomposed corpses in similar looking chemical drums. The bodies were that of Sheila Faith and her 15-year-old daughter, along with 49-year-old Beverly Bonner, who had been the prison librarian at the same prison where he had been incarcerated. The five victims had been killed with a powerful blow to the back of the head.

The other three missing women have never been found but Robinson was the only suspect in their disappearances. In 2002, after the longest criminal trial in Kansas history, Robinson was found guilty of three murders and sentenced to death.

In Missouri, he pleaded guilty by way of a statement and was convicted of five murders there. For each of the five murders, he received additional life sentences. Missouri was known at the time to actively pursue death sentences, whereas Kansas was not. By pleading guilty in Missouri, Robinson avoided the death penalty there.

Four years later in 2006, while Robinson was on death row, the decomposed body of a young woman was found in a chemical barrel in Iowa. Even with DNA testing, the victim has never been identified and may have been inside the barrel for two decades or more. Investigators then claimed that Robinson's whereabouts for many years was unknown and he had set up businesses all over the country.

But Robinson has long remained tight-lipped and silent on the murders and his involvement. It led one investigator to claim that it was the only control he had left.

"He's maintained the secrets about what he's done with the women, he won't ever tell, it's the last control that he's got. There are other barrels waiting to be opened, other bodies waiting to be found."

An investigator in a 2010 interview with Cold Case Files.

As of 2021, Robinson remains on death row in Kansas.

Born **December 27th 1943**.

Active from **1984-1999**.

Arrested on **June 2nd 2000**.

Country: **USA**.

Victims: **8+**.

AKA: **First Internet Serial Killer / Slave Master.**

Sentence: **Death penalty.**

Current whereabouts: **Death row.**

Rogers, Ramon Jay

On February 18th 1996, in California, actor and heavy-metal drummer *Ramon Jay Rogers*, claims his third victim. He brutally murdered his Polish ex-girlfriend, 32-year-old *Beatrice Toronczak*, when she visited him at the apartment complex that he managed. It is claimed she had threatened Rogers with taking their son back to Poland.

Rogers, who appeared in an episode of *'Renegade'* was arrested in March of 1996, and it led investigators to reopen two other missing persons cases of his former girlfriends and friends. Rogers would also play roles in Crime Stoppers TV shows, where he played all manner of criminals, including murderers.

Previously, the limbs and jaw of one of his previous partners had been discovered but no evidence was found to make an arrest. After his arrest on suspicion of murder, body parts were discovered in a storage locker. Teeth and fingers were identified as Toronczak's, and Rogers was charged with her murder.

In 1997, Rogers was convicted of three murders and sentenced to death. It has long been claimed that he may have killed more.

Born in **1959**.

Active from **1996-1996.**

Arrested on **March 13th 1996.**

Country: **USA.**

Victims: **3.**

Sentence: **Death penalty.**

Current whereabouts: **Death row.**

Romanov, Vladimir

In Russia, serial killer and paedophile *Vladimir Ivanovich Romanov*, AKA: *The Kaliningrad Maniac*, killed at least 12 people from 1991 to 2005, but is suspected of killing at least 20 and raping numerous more.

In 1991, he killed two teenage girls and buried their bodies in shallow graves. They were listed as missing persons until Romanov's confession in 2006. In the same year he raped a 12-year-old girl who survived the attack. She gave a description that led to his first arrest in 1991. He was convicted of raping her and sentenced to 10 years in prison. It was claimed he was raped by another inmate whilst in prison.

For ten years, Romanov had been dreaming of killing again, and in 2001 he was released with a plan in mind. From 2001 to 2005, he killed at least 10 more young girls between the ages of 12-years-old to 19-years-old. He raped all of them before burying their bodies in forests or burning their remains.

In 2006, he attempted to rape a young-looking 24-year-old, who fought him off and escaped. Two days later he was arrested, where he confessed to 13 murders in total, with hints that he had killed more.

While in solitary confinement, awaiting trial in 2006, Romanov hung himself with his bed sheets, shortly after leaving an apologetic suicide note to his own family. He denied families of the victim's true justice for his crimes.

Born in **1950.**

Active from **1991-2005**.

Arrested in **September 2006**.

Country: **Russia**.

Victims: **12-20+**.

AKA: **The Kaliningrad Maniac / Taxi Driver**.

Current whereabouts: **Committed suicide in 2006**.

Rose, Lindsey Robert

On January 19th 1987, Australian serial killer *Lindsey Robert Rose* broke into a house in the West Ryde area of New South Wales. It was the home of *William Graf*, a known businessman. Rose had intended to rob the property of some of the pricier belongings but he was caught in the act by Graf's partner *Reynette Holford*.

Rose then stabbed Reynette multiple times with a screwdriver and a vegetable knife. He tied her up after he had attacked her before running from the property, she was left to die of her injuries. Rose was caught ten years later in 1997 and was convicted of five murders between 1984 and 1994.

The first murder was in 1984, when he shot dead *Edward John Cavanagh* and Cavanagh's girlfriend, *Carmelita Lee*, in their home in Sydney. He claimed it was out of revenge for Cavanagh beating up one of his friends a few years before. He killed Carmelita Lee as he did not want any witnesses to the murder.

As of 2021, he remains in prison serving five consecutive life sentences.

Born in **1955**.

Active from **1984-1994**.

Arrested in **1994**.

Country: **Australia**.

Victims: **5**.

Sentence: **Five life sentences**.

Current whereabouts: **In prison**.

(Research Article #21) The Renfield Syndrome

Renfield's Syndrome, also known as *clinical vampirism*, is a rare psychiatric disorder in which the sufferer feels a compulsion to consume blood by drinking or eating organs. The disorder is classified as some types of *schizophrenia* or *paraphilia*.

The condition is named after the infamous character of *Renfield* in Bram Stoker's novel *Dracula*. Renfield is a mental patient who consumes insects in the belief that he will absorb their life force. Eventually, he begins feeding flies to spiders and spiders to birds, then consuming the birds to obtain a greater concentration of life force.

People who suffer from this illness commonly believe they obtain some sort of power or strength through the consumption of another organism's blood or brain matter.

Sufferers of Renfield's Syndrome are usually male. The disorder is typically sparked by an event in childhood in which the sufferer associates the sight or taste of blood with excitement. During puberty, the feelings of attraction to blood become sexual in nature.

The condition typically follows three stages.

Auto vampirism or Autohemophagia.

The sufferer drinks his own blood, often cutting himself in order to do so.

Zoophagia.

This consists of eating live animals or drinking their blood. Obtaining animal blood from a butcher or slaughterhouse for consumption also falls into this stage.

Vampirism.

The sufferer's attention turns to other human beings. He may steal blood from hospitals or blood-banks, or drink blood directly from a living person.

After entering this stage, some individuals commit violent crimes, including murder. Richard Trenton Chase is one case of a known serial killer who clearly had this disorder. But even today, it is not fully recognised or understood by medical professions around the world and as such it is largely ignored. It will, however, be synonymous with the crimes carried out by the Vampire of Sacramento.

Rylkov, Oleg

Over a five year period in the city of Tolyatti in Russia, *Olga Rylkov*, AKA: *The Tolyatti Ripper*, raped 39 young girls and killed four people. All of his victims were between the ages of six-years-old to 13-years-old, and the victims would mostly be attacked in their own homes. He waited for the parents or adults to leave before knocking on the door, raping the victim and robbing the home.

The first confirmed murder came on February 7th 1996, when he killed a seven-year-old boy named Ruslan Tkachev. He lured the boy to a small village on the outskirts of the city and violently stabbed him to death multiple times. When the body was discovered, the boy's genitals, eyes, ears, tongue and fingers had been cut off. The body had been so badly mutilated that the gender of the corpse couldn't be identified at first.

On July 20th 1996, Rylkov lured a young girl from the streets and brutally raped and murdered her. He left her body in an abandoned military bunker near the city. When he abducted the girl, there were witnesses who gave his description to police. When they went to arrest him, Rylkov pretended to be someone else – and the police believed him, so he escaped arrest.

At around the same time, in October 1996, another Russian serial killer named Alexander Spesivtsev was arrested for the murder and rape of at least 20 people. For a while, police believed Rylkov to be the culprit of the murders but in reality, Rylkov had remained in Tolyatti.

In 1997, Rylkov then murdered a 40-year-old woman with an axe, which led to his arrest as the two had often been seen together. He went to trial and was found guilty of all his crimes. In 1998, he was sentenced to death which was commuted to life because of a change in the death penalty in Russia at the time.

He is currently an inmate at the infamous *Black Dolphin Prison* on the border of Kazakhstan, where he continues to confess to further murders and rapes.

Born **December 21st 1966.**

Active from **1992-1997.**

Arrested on **July 1st 1997.**

Country: **Russia.**

Victims: **4+.**

AKA: **The Tolyatti Ripper.**

Sentence: **Death penalty later commuted to life.**

Current whereabouts: **In prison.**

Sakharov, Nikolay Alexandrovich

In February 1979 in Vologda Oblast, Soviet Union, Nikolay Alexandrovich Sakharov, AKA: The Vologda Ripper, was executed by firing squad for the murders of three people. In 1977, he brutally raped three young girls, before beating them to death with a hammer.

He went on to burn the bodies and shatter the skulls into smaller pieces, before wrapping their remains in cloth and discarding of them in a local river. He even kept trophies of some of the victims and handed them out to his various mistresses. Despite killing three young girls, at least five in total had gone missing from the region in 1977. The figures weren't helped by locals who exaggerated the number of missing girls. At one point it was claimed that dozens of girls had fallen victim to the ripper.

On December 15th, 1977, Sakharov was arrested after witness statements led to police tracking his vehicle. In January 1978, Sakharov confessed to the murders of Tatyana Svetina, Natalia Vinogradova and Marina Mukhina. He claimed he would dress up as a police officer in order to lure girls into his car.

Then he would take them to a remote location, usually a forest, where he raped them before beating them to death. His trial during 1978 was one of the largest the region had ever seen, leading to a massive police presence in the area for fear that lynch mobs would overrun the courts. Sakharov was sentenced to death and executed by firing squad on February 5th 1979.

Born in **1954.**

Active during **1977**

Arrested in **December 1977.**

Country: **Soviet Union.**

Victims: **3.**

AKA: **The Vologda Ripper.**

Current whereabouts: **Executed by firing squad on February 5th 1979.**

Saldivar, Efren

In California, American *'Angel of Death'* serial killer, *Efren Saldivar*, murdered at least six of his patients, but confessed to 50. It was suspected by investigators that he may have been responsible for at least 200 deaths in total.

He killed his victims by administering a paralytic drug which would lead to respiratory or cardiac arrest. Most of the time, he used an overdose of morphine to end their lives. He chose victims who were already close to death, which made catching him even more difficult.

In 1988, he quit his job and made a voluntary confession in which he claimed he had killed 50 patients under his care. The resulting investigation exhumed 20 bodies and found six that had unusually high levels of the drug that Saldivar said he had used.

In 2002 he was convicted on six counts of murder and sentenced to six consecutive life sentences, without the possibility of parole. An internal investigation at some of the hospitals where Saldivar had worked, disclosed that it might have been likely that 200 patients died at his hands. The deaths couldn't be proven because most of the victims had been cremated, leaving no physical evidence behind.

Born **September 30th 1969**.

Active from **1988-1998**.

Arrested on **January 10th 2001**.

Country: **USA**.

Victims: **6-50+**.

AKA: **Angel of Death**.

Sentence: **Six life sentences.**

Current whereabouts: **In prison.**

Sanchez, Altemio: The Bike Path Killer (Extended Case File)

An American serial killer, also known as *The Bike Path Rapist/Killer*, who was active over a 25 year period. He was confirmed to have killed at least three women and raped at least 10 girls and women in the Buffalo region of New York.

Sanchez was born in Puerto Rico and moved with his family a couple of years after his birth to Florida. After his father died young and his mother married again, Sanchez moved to Buffalo to be a factory worker. There was nothing untoward in Sanchez's childhood that suggested he would go on to become a serial killer.

In 1980, when he was 19-years-old, he married and had two sons. His wife had no idea of what he was doing and divorced shortly after his conviction. Sanchez had embedded himself into the local community, being a baseball coach, gardener, and even joined a fun-run in memory of one of his own murder victims.

All in all, he was a well-liked individual, but somewhere along the line he developed a hatred for women. From the mid-1980s, he had begun stalking and raping women. In the early 1990s, Sanchez began using prostitutes on regular occasions and was arrested in 1991 and 1999 for the solicitation of prostitution.

His first known murder victim came on September 28th 1990. 22-year-old University student *Linda Yalem* was raped and strangled to death by Sanchez. The attack happened on the Ellicott Creek Bike Path, one of many cycleways and public paths that Sanchez would use as hunting grounds.

In November 1992, 32-year-old prostitute *Majane Mazur*, was murdered near rail tracks. Sanchez had grabbed her from behind, raped her then strangled her to death. The last known murder victim was on September 29th 2006, when Sanchez murdered 45-year-old *Joan Diver*.

Sanchez would patiently wait for the right moment to attack and chose secluded areas of bike or pathways that were close to wooded areas. He would then attack them from behind and drag them into the wooded area where he raped them. He would use a ligature or his own hands to strangle them into submission.

He then used duct tape or medical tape to cover his victim's eyes, nose and mouth. All of the attacks took place from May to November and all of his victims were of slim build, between the ages of 14-years-old to 45-years-old. His 14-year-old victim came in October of 1994, when he grabbed the schoolgirl from behind a junk yard.

While Sanchez was still raping victims from the 1990s, a special *Bike Path Task Force* was set up by the Erie County Sheriff's Office, with assistance from the FBI. Sanchez was a suspect from the early 2000s but there was no evidence against him. While he was under surveillance, police watched him eat at a Latin restaurant, when he had finished, they covertly took his glass, cutlery and a napkin to obtain DNA.

Immediately, the DNA retrieved matched eight victims of rape or murder. While they were still investigating Sanchez, they connected him to another six rape victims in the area. On January 15th 2007, Sanchez was arrested and confessed to three murders.

Due to the absurdity of the Statute of Limitations, which sets out time limits on how long after a crime a person can be prosecuted, Sanchez escaped many of the rape charges. Murder, however, was not time-limited by the same statute, and Sanchez was convicted of three murders.

In August 2007, convicted of three murders, Sanchez was sentenced to 75 years to life in prison. It has long been claimed by investigators that he may have killed more but has never confessed. Sanchez's crimes would go on to be infamous for more than just his convictions.

Back in 1985, *Anthony Capozzi*, a man suffering from schizophrenia, was convicted of the rapes of two women. After Sanchez was convicted, police looked at rapes with similar circumstances and noticed Capozzi's crimes that he had been convicted for. DNA from Sanchez matched Capozzi's two victims, it appeared that they had convicted the wrong man.

Capozzi, who had maintained his innocence for over two decades, was released after 22 years in prison. He later won a $4.25million USD lawsuit for wrongful conviction and imprisonment. After this, new laws were introduced that would speed up similar lawsuits, and the legislation became known as Anthony's Law, named after Capozzi.

The fact that New York had to create a new law to speed up lawsuits for those who have been wrongfully convicted, is disturbing enough. It is also a damning indictment for the absurdity of the Statute of Limitations.

As of 2021, Sanchez remains incarcerated at a New York prison.

Born **January 19th 1958.**

Active from **1990-2006.**

Arrested on **January 15th 2007.**

Country: **USA**.

Victims: **3+**.

AKA: **The Bike Path Rapist / The Bike Path Killer.**

Sentence: **75 years to life in prison.**

Current whereabouts: **In prison.**

Satish

In Bahadurgarh, Haryana, India, a serial killer known as *Satish*, killed at least 10 young girls between the ages of five-years-old to nine-years-old, from 1995 to 1998. He was suspected of abducting and raping another four children. He is sometimes known as the *Bahadurgarh Baby Killer*.

During Satish's reign of terror, the local communities lived in fear but also claimed the police were not doing enough to find the killer of children. The police force came under immense pressure to arrest the culprit and get a conviction. This resulted in riots cause by the local residents. In order to placate the growing anger, the police arrested and convicted three innocent men.

Each man was arrested one after the other as another murder took place while the previous one had been convicted. Satish wasn't arrested in connection with the murders until 1998, when he was only 25-years-old.

On January 9th 1996, six-year-old *Sweta* left her home with her sister to meet her friends and play with other children. Her sister ran back home shortly after, in a panic, and told her mother that a man on a bicycle had kidnapped Sweta. The man had been wearing a shawl and couldn't be identified. Sweta was raped and murdered and her body was found a day later on January 10th.

On June 12th 1996, seven-year-old *Janno* was abducted from the front of her house, as she slept. Her sleeping parents were only a few metres away from her when she was taken. Just a few hours later, her body was discovered in a ditch, she had been raped and murdered by Satish.

In 1998, one of his victims was left for dead in a wooded area. When the young girl was found in a delirious state two days later, she led police to the house where she was being kept, where Satish was subsequently arrested. A $10,000 USD reward for the capture of the killer, put up by the Delhi Police Force, was later given to the young girl in recognition of her bravery and information that led to Satish's capture.

As of 2021, Satish remains incarcerated at an Indian prison, despite calls of replacing his life sentence with a death sentence.

Born in **1972**.

Active from **1995-1998**.

Arrested on **December 29th 2006**.

Country: **India**.

Victims: **10-14**.

AKA: **Bahadurgarh Baby Killer / Surender Koli**.

Sentence: **Life imprisonment**.

Current whereabouts: **In prison**.

Schaefer, Gary Lee

On December 13th 1979, in Springfield, Vermont, the skeletal remains of 13-year-old **Sherry Nastasia** were discovered in a shallow grave in a remote area. She had been a victim of serial killer **Gary Lee Schaefer** who killed three people between 1979 and 1983. Nastasia had been abducted near to an apartment complex where she lived with her parents. The same apartment complex that Schaefer's brother was managing.

In 1981, he killed Theresa Fenton, whose body was discovered in a similar fashion. In 1982, 17-year-old Deana Buxton survived an assault by Schaefer. Her victim statement pinpointed Schaefer as the attacker but police found there was minimal other evidence against him.

On April 9th 1983, Schaefer abducted Catherine Richards before driving her to a remote location, raping her and crushing her skull with a rock. The body was discovered the next day. Witness reports also pointed towards Schaefer and he was finally arrested in September 1983 and pled guilty in December of the same year. He was later sentenced to 30 years to life in prison.

Born in **1951.**

Active from **1979-1983.**

Arrested in **September 1983.**

Country: **USA.**

Victims: **3**

Current whereabouts: **In prison.**

Scheanette, Dale Devon

In Texas, *Dale Devon Scheanette,* AKA: *The Bathtub Killer,* killed at least two people in 1996 alone. In her Arlington apartment on September 17th 1996, the nude body of 26-year-old *Christine Vu* was discovered lying face down in her bathtub.

She had been tied up with duct tape, raped, strangled, and then drowned. Scheanette had left his fingerprints at the scene and DNA on Vu's body but it didn't show up any suspects on the system. And so Scheanette was free to kill again.

On December 24th 1996, another murder happened in the exact same apartment block where Vu lived, and in the exact same manner. The body of 20-year-old *Wendie Prescott* was discovered face down in her bathtub. She too had been restrained with duct tape, raped and strangled to death.

The murders became referred to in the media as the *Bathtub Killings*. But no suspect was found and the murders remained unsolved for another four years. In 2000, the Arlington Police Department, ran the fingerprint through the system again and this time they found a match.

Scheanette was arrested shortly after and then linked to another four rapes of four other women in their own homes. In 2003, Scheanette was sentenced to death for the murder of Wendie Prescott. On February 10th 2009, Scheanette was executed.

His final meal consisted of two spicy chicken legs, two spicy fried pork chops, and French fries. He refused to acknowledge the witnesses to his death.

Born **May 7th 1973.**

Active during **1996.**

Arrested in **2000.**

Country: **USA.**

Victims: **2.**

AKA: **The Bathtub Killer.**

Sentence: **Death penalty.**

Current whereabouts: **Executed on February 10th 2009.**

Schiffer, Egidius

German serial killer, *Leo Egidius Schiffer*, AKA: *The Strangler of Aachen*, killed five young women between 1983 and 1990. In Germany, his crimes became known as the *Disco-Murders* or *Hitchhiker Killings*.

He first killed in 1983 when he was 27-years-old. In Alsdorf, 18-year-old Marion Gerecht was waiting at a bus stop when Schiffer approached her and attacked her. She fought him and broke his windscreen but she was eventually strangled, stripped naked and her body was dumped in a fishing pond.

Then in 1984, Schiffer killed 15-year-old *Andrea Wernicke* after she was walking home alone from a nightclub. He raped her before strangling her and dumping her body near a dirt track. In the same year he murdered 17-year-old hitchhiker *Angelika Sehl* who was walking from a different nightclub. Her partially clothed body was found in a forest shortly after.

In 1985, he abducted 18-year-old *Marion Lauven* from a bus stop, before raping and killing her. Schiffer drove across the country with Lauven's body in the trunk until he found a suitable forest to dump her corpse. It is unclear if Schiffer killed again before his next victim in 1990.

He was finally arrested in 2007 while he was trying to steal scrap metal. He voluntarily gave a saliva sample which was subsequently linked with five murders. He confessed to the five murders and claimed he received a massive amount of sexual pleasure in killing the girls. He was sentenced in 2008 to life in prison.

On July 22nd 2018, Schiffer was found dead in his cell. He had been using electrical cables in a sexual manner and had accidentally electrocuted himself to death.

Born in **1956**.

Active from **1983-1990**.

Arrested in **March 2007**.

Country: **Germany**.

Victims: **5+**.

AKA: **The Strangler of Aachen / Disco-Murders / Hitchhiker Killings.**

Sentence: **Life imprisonment.**

Current whereabouts: **Died by self-electrocution on July 22nd 2018.**

Seel, Manfred

A German serial killer, known as '*Jack the Ripper of Scwalbach*', he is suspected of killing five people and linked to another four. He also died of cancer in 2014 before the full extent of his killings were uncovered. He killed his victims by using '*harsh violence in sexually relevant zones*'.

He would remove organs from each body or other body parts such as genitals, arms or legs and keep them as trophies. It is suspected he returned to their corpses for sexual gratification.

Shockingly, the victims all had different body parts removed. An investigator told a press conference that '*if you put the missing parts together, you could actually make a new body by doing it*'. Police discovered over five terabytes of violent porn in images and videos on his various hard drives.

He would perceive his victims as objects for his sadistic fantasies. German investigators called it the most inexplicable and unfathomable case known to them.

Born **September 30th 1946.**

Active from **1971-2004.**

Country: **Germany**.

Victims: **5-9.**

AKA: **Jack the Ripper of Scwalbach.**

Current whereabouts: **Died of cancer in 2014 before capture.**

Segundo, Juan

On October 6th 1987, in Fort Worth, Texas, an unnamed woman awoke in the middle of a sexual attack by American serial killer *Juan Segundo*. He carried on the attack and then physically assaulted her before fleeing the property.

The unnamed victim survived the ordeal but at least four others died at the hands of Segundo. He was sentenced for the burglary of the house to ten years in prison but was released only one year later. It wasn't until 2005 when he was arrested by using DNA detection on cold cases.

He was sentenced to death for the 1986 rape and murder of 11-year-old *Vanessa Villa*, who he strangled to death. She was living in Fort Worth with her mother and siblings when she was killed. On that fateful Sunday, she went to help out at a Dallas flea market and returned home claiming that she wasn't hungry. It was unclear at this point whether Segundo had contacted the girl whilst still in the market.

That same night, Segundo broke into her home and raped her before strangling her to death. Segundo was known to be a family friend and was never suspected until DNA evidence linked him to the murder. It is also claimed that he even attended the funeral of the girl. Vanessa's mother even defended him when he became a suspect, informing the investigation that he was not the type to kill people.

He was also linked by DNA evidence to three more murders between 1994 and 1995. Segundo is currently on death row awaiting execution by lethal injection.

Born **January 25th 1963.**

Active from **1986-1995**.

Arrested on **April 19th 2005**.

Country: **USA**.

Victims: **4+**.

Sentence: **Death penalty**.

Current whereabouts: **Death row**.

Sells, Tommy Lynn

On November 18th 1987, in Illinois, police descend on a mobile home in the village of Ina. Inside they find an entire family has been slaughtered. 29-year-old *Russell Keith Dardeen* was found in a nearby field he had been shot and his genitals were mutilated. His pregnant wife and son who were in the mobile home were beaten to death. *Ruby Elaine Dardeen* was so savagely beaten that she went into labour. Shockingly, the new-born was also beaten to death.

Convicted serial killer *Tommy Lynn Sells* who was on death row for separate murders confessed to the killing of the Dardeen family. He had been convicted of two murders but was suspected of at least another ten.

His first killed in 1980, when he was just 15-years-old. He had broken into a house to discover an adult man performing oral sex on a little boy. Sells then killed the man in a haze of anger and violence.

His last murder was on New Year's Eve, 1999, in Del Rio, Texas. He lured and raped two small girls. 13-year-old *Kaylene Harris* and 10-year-old *Krystal Surles*. He stabbed to death Harris and cut the throat of Surles. Miraculously, Surles survived and stumbled 500 metres along a road to her house while holding her throat in place.

She then gave a description to the police and Sells was finally arrested just a few days later on January 2nd 2000. Surles went on to make a full recovery and was instrumental in the capture of one of America's most prolific serial killers.

Police connected Sells to at least 22 murders but he himself claimed over 70 victims. He was executed by lethal injection on April 3rd 2014.

Born **June 28th 1964.**

Active from **1980-1999.**

Arrested on **January 2nd 2000.**

Country: **USA.**

Victims: **10-70+.**

AKA: **The Cross-country Killer.**

Sentence: **Death penalty.**

Current whereabouts: **Executed by lethal injection on April 3rd 2014.**

Sewage Plant Killer, The

The *Sewage Plant Killings* were an unexplained series of murders in Frankfurt during the late 1970s and early 1980s. To this day, no one had been caught for the murders. All victims were male aged between 11 and 18-years-old. They were handcuffed or tied with roped and then killed.

Most drowned in the sewage of the sewer tunnels. Only one victim could be autopsied due to the putrefaction of the discovered bodies. Some had been naturally mummified in the sewage over time.

Active from **1976-1989**.

Country: **Germany**.

Victims: **7+**.

Current whereabouts: **Unidentified killer. Status unknown.**

(Research Article #22) Movies that Influenced Killers

The influence of movies inspiring crime is still debated and argued over to this day. Most people who watch violent movies do not go on to re-enact what they might have seen. But there are some people that do. Before we look at some examples, let's take a closer look at the truth of it.

"*Pornography and violence poison our music and movies and TV and video games. The Virginia Tech shooter, like the Columbine shooters before him, had drunk from this cesspool.*"

Mitt Romney, during his presidential campaign.

Romney sat on the extreme side of the fence and was in effect blaming entertainment for the reasons behind violent crime. Is the death of Simba's father in *The Lion King* any more violent than John McClane taking out bad guys in *Die Hard*?

Apparently it's only one's opinion on things that makes a difference. The assertions that violent movies cause people to become violent has been around for quite some time and a lot of research has been written on the subject. The fear has always been that watching a violent movie will make someone violent in real life. The same has always been said about gaming.

However, in an article in the *Washington Post* by *Fareed Zakaria*, he claims that people should look to Japan as a counter-argument for any claims of entertainment influencing violence. The Japanese are the biggest gaming-country in the world, when player and population ratio is looked at, yet the murder rate in Japan is close to zero. He put forward the argument that the main difference is the restrictions on firearms in Japan.

Many people want violent movies to be banned or at least restricted to a certain age group, which mostly they are. But some have claimed that it would mean censorship should reach all areas of entertainment, right down to fairy tales, which arguably have more written violence in them than most films.

On the flip-side, it has been proven that violent movies and games have more benefits than they do negatives. Researchers found that watching any type of movie, violent or not, can help people cope with their emotions. It can help people overcome challenging situations, expand their imagination, and relieve stress.

There is of course a bigger argument *against* the influence of movies on normal people. The people who go on to kill or commit crime after seeing a film were more likely to have been aggressive in the first instance. Those who commit violent crime, including murder, already exhibited aggressive traits. Such attributes were predictive of criminal behaviour, and not the viewing of movies themselves. Movies might validate one's own beliefs, rather than changing them.

The Collector (1965)

This 1965 British film is said to have directly influenced a number of cases. Serial killer *Robert Andrew Berdella Jr.* AKA: *The Kansas City Butcher* remains one of the evilest killers in the modern era. His case was one of the first known instances of a movie directly impacting the thought processes of someone who had the potential to kill *and* would go on to kill.

The plot of *The Collector* is about a man who abducts women and holds them captive in his basement to add to his *collection*. It is a direct correlation to the exact process used by Berdella in his future murders. Except that he chose men instead of women. Berdella directly cited the film as an influence of how he could kill.

The Collector was also said to have influenced the serial killing duo *Leonard Lake* and *Charles Ng*. who together in the mid-1980s killed at least 11 people but was suspected to be 25. The pair built a bunker to imprison two of their female victims. They were planning on using them as sex slaves and housemaids. They documented some of their interactions on tapes but decided to murder them instead.

They had a self-built torture-chamber in a secluded area of forest which was home to a number of elaborate torture machines on the walls and all around. They had even built a dentist's chair used for restraining their victims.

Basketball Diaries (1995)

The film featured *Leonardo DiCaprio* as a basketball player who succumbs to heroin addiction. In a dream sequence he walks into his school wearing a black trench coat and carrying a shotgun. Then he massacres his classmates.

The 1996 school shooting carried out by *Barry Loukaitis*, was a virtual mirror to the scene in the film. He killed three people and injured more while walking through his school wearing a black trench coat. He was heard quoting lines from the film. In school shootings over the years that followed, many more would wear black trench coats.

It is suggested that these people would have done what they did anyhow, but they used certain entertainment mediums to provide the final inspiration.

Scream (1996)

In Belgium in 2001, *Thierry Jaradin*, a 24-year-old lorry driver lured and killed his 15-year-old neighbour, *Alisson Cambier*. She had visited Jaradin's house to swap some videotapes and have a chat. She then rejected his sexual advances and he excused himself shortly after.

He returned wearing a black robe and the *'ghostface'* mask from the movie. He had two large kitchen knives in his hands as he lunged at Cambier. He stabbed her 30 times, and in doing so had ripped open the entire left side of her body. He then carried the mutilated corpse to his bed, slipped a rose into one of her hands, then called his father to confess.

In the 2006 murder of 16-year-old *Cassie Jo Stoddart*, Scream was cited yet again as a direct inspiration of the killing. After her boyfriend had left her home, two of her high school classmates went to her house and cut the power to the property. They then broke in and stabbed her at least 30 times. They had both planned the murder ahead of time and cited *Scream* and the *Columbine Massacre* as direct inspirations.

The Matrix (1999)

Unbelievably, the *'Matrix defence'* has become a real thing. The premise of the film is that our reality is not real, instead we live in a giant computer program that we only perceive to be real. Several killers used the logic that people who were killed were not real people.

In Sweden, exchange student *Vadim Mieseges* killed and dismembered his landlady. Upon his arrest he told police that he had been sucked into the Matrix. In 2002, murderer *Tonda Lynn Ansley* of Ohio, also killed her landlady by shooting her in the head. She was found not guilty by reason of insanity as she had used the Matrix defence.

Robocop 2 (1990)

American serial killer *Nathaniel White* from New York killed six females from 1991 to 1992. He beat and stabbed them to death while on parole. White already had an aggressive personality but claimed it was *Robocop 2* that inspired him to kill his first victim.

In the film, a victim's throat was cut and the knife slit down the chest to the stomach. White copied the exact same style of murder and then left the body in the same position as it had been left in the scene of the film. He was sentenced to 150 years in prison.

Interview with the Vampire (1994)

A day after *Daniel Sterling* had watched *Interview with the Vampire* at the cinema, he took on Vampiric tendencies. *Lisa Stellwagen* had seen the film with him and visited him again the next day at his home.

He told her that he was going to kill her and savour her blood. Then he stabbed her seven times and drank her blood for several minutes. Stellwagen survived and her testimony sent Sterling to prison. Sterling later claimed that he enjoyed the movie but wouldn't blame his attack on it.

Shankariya, Kampatimar

On May 16th 1979, in Jaipur, India, one of the country's most notorious serial killers was executed by hanging. **Kampatimar Shankariya** killed at least 70 women and men from 1977 to 1978 by beating them to death with a hammer. He usually hit them on the side of the head just under the ear because he found it to be more effective at killing.

He later told investigators that he killed purely because he took great pleasure in doing so. He also claimed that there were probably more than 70 victims but he could not remember them all. Just before his execution he said that he had murdered in vain and that no one should become like him.

Born in **1952**.

Active from **1977-1978**.

Arrested in **1978**.

Country: **India**.

Victims: **70+**

Current whereabouts: **Executed on May 16th 1979.**

Shawcross, Arthur

Also known as the *Monster of the Rivers* or the *Genesee River Killer*, he would kill 14 victims in New York. He first killed a young boy and girl in Watertown, in 1972. He raped and killed 10-year-old Jack Blake after luring the boy to a local wooded area. Four months later he raped and killed eight-year-old Karen Ann Hill.

He was swiftly caught and sentenced to 25 years. After an early release, he went on to kill 12 more women, mostly prostitutes in Munroe County. He claimed that his mother performed oral sex on him when he was nine-years-old and that he had a sexual relationship with his sister.

In a later interview, he bragged about removing and eating the vulvas of three of his victims. He died in prison in 2008.

Born **June 6th 1945.**

Active from **1972-1989.**

Arrested on **January 5th 1990.**

Country: **USA**.

Victims: **14**.

AKA: **Monster of the Rivers / The Genesee River Killer.**

Sentence: **250 years in prison.**

Current whereabouts: **Died of natural causes in 2008.**

Shermantine, Wesley & Herzog, Loren: The Speed Freak Killers (Extended Case File)

The Speed Freak Killers is the moniker attributed to serial killing duo *Loren Herzog* and *Wesley Shermantine*. They were suspected to have been involved in as many as 72 murders in California from 1984 to 1999. The pair disposed of bodies in old mine shafts, remote hills, and some beneath a trailer park.

Herzog and Shermantine became friends when they were children. They were born and lived in the small town of Linden, California. They quickly became addicted to amphetamines and methamphetamine's and made their first kill together when they were only 19-years-old.

They were arrested separately in 1999, when they were both 33-years-old. Herzog was charged with the 1998 abduction and murder of 25-year-old *Cyndi Vanderheiden*, along with four other murders dating back to 1984. It appeared that the investigation had only scratched the surface of the terror that the pair had inflicted in the region.

Shermantine was also charged with her murder. Together they were convicted of the murder of two drifter killings in 1984. 31-year-old *Paul Raymond Cavanaugh* and 35-year-old *Howard King* were found shot dead in their car on a remote area of road. Both Herzog and Shermantine would have been only 19-years-old at the time.

Herzog was also linked to and charged with the 1984 murder of 41-year-old *Henry Howell*, who had been shot dead near *Highway 88*. Another victim was the 1985 murder of 24-year-old *Robin Armtrout*. His naked body had been discovered near a creek and he had been stabbed more than 10 times.

Shermantine was charged individually for the murder of 16-year-old *Chevelle Wheeler*. The schoolgirl had decided to skip school for the day but never returned home. DNA in her home was linked to Shermantine, but her remains are still undiscovered.

The investigation believed that Shermantine alone killed at least 20 people, with bodies scattered in old mine shafts and his own trailer park. Multiple witnesses testified against his character.

Five women came forward and stated that he had violently raped and abused them. One of them was a babysitter who had visited him to collect money that he owed her. A former wife of Shermantine claimed that he beat her for years, even while she held children in her arms.

"Listen to the heartbeats of people I've buried here. Listen to the heartbeats of families I've buried here."

Shermantine – to a woman in his trailer park.

It was their heavy amphetamine use, that birthed the moniker of the Speed Freak Killers. They killed for the thrill of killing and it was claimed that they killed for sport. Shermantine stated that he hunted humans as the ultimate thrill kill.

During the trial, both men pointed the blame at each other and implicated one another in further killings. FBI also seized over $40,000 worth of firearms from Shermantine's parents' house. A large number of technicians and forensics experts studied the weapons to see if they could link them to further murders.

In 2004, an appeals court overturned the convictions of Herzog due to the fact that his confessions were coerced. A retrial was ordered but never took place. Herzog instead pleaded guilty to manslaughter in the death of Cyndi Vanderheiden.

Herzog had his life sentence commuted to 14 years. He was paroled in 2010, causing an outcry in California. There was so much opposition that no county in the

State would house him and so he was paroled to a trailer at the gates of the *High Desert State Prison* in Susanville.

In Linden, California, in February of 2010, investigators were led to a well where over 1000 bone fragments were unearthed. Shermantine had been writing letters to his sister while waiting on death row and explained where the abandoned well was. The owner of the property at the time stated that the well had been sealed up long before the murders.

It took another two years for the site to be excavated and the amount of bone fragments shocked even the hardened investigators. In March of 2012, the FBI's *Evidence Recovery Team* was drafted into the investigation, mostly because of the way the excavation of the well was actioned.

In the same year, before more victims were found, Herzog committed suicide by hanging himself inside the trailer.

The identity of some of the remains were found to be that of two Californian teenage girls who disappeared in 1984 and 1985. Another unidentified victim was found along with the remains of a foetus. More bodies were discovered in the same year at a property owned by Shermantine's parents.

Later in 2012, Shermantine was allowed into police custody to show them four more abandoned well sites where he claimed more bodies would be found. No remains were unearthed but wild animals in the area may have consumed the bodies, had they been there in the first instance.

In 2018, the *San Joaquin County Police Department* re-opened the case of the Speed Freak Killers. In the hope that a new investigation with modern technology would link the killers to more bodies and give families of certain missing people a greater sense of closure.

As of 2021, Shermantine is on death row at *San Quentin State Prison*.

Born **December 8th 1965 (Herzog), February 24th 1966 (Shermantine).**

Active from **1984-1999.**

Arrested on **March 17th 1999.**

Country: **USA.**

Victims: **4-70+.**

AKA: **The Speed Freak Killers.**

Sentence: **Shermantine received a death penalty. Herzog received life imprisonment which was later commuted to 14 years.**

Current whereabouts: **Shermantine remains on death row. Herzog committed suicide in 2012.**

Shemyakov, Eduard

Ukrainian-born, Russian serial killer *Eduard Vasilyevich Shemyakov*, killed at least 10 people over a two year period from 1996 to 1998. Also known as The Resort Maniac, he claimed he was ordered to kill by the voices in his head.

It is claimed he was bullied in the army for living with his parents and being awkward around girls. He left shortly after and watched a 1972 Russian film called *'The Dawns Here Are Quiet'*. It was an anti-war film that focused on a regiment of women in the Russian Army. He became enraged after watching it, and combined with the growing voices in his head, he wanted to kill women.

He carried out his crimes in St. Petersburg, and would rape his victims, decapitate them and dismember their corpses. On at least one occasion, he ate a part of his victim. His youngest victim was only 11-years-old. Shemyakov killed his sister's girlfriend, at the same time as his mother found a half-eaten piece of human flesh in the fridge. He was arrested without trouble, later the same day.

In 2002, due to the nature of his crimes, he was deemed insane and detained in a psychiatric hospital. Despite appeals from the victim's families, he currently remains within the hospital's walls.

Born **September 30th 1975.**

Active from **1996-1998.**

Arrested in **1998.**

Country: **Russia.**

Victims: **10.**

AKA: **Eduard Vasilyevich Shemyakov / The Resort Maniac.**

Sentence: **Committed to psychiatric institution.**

Current whereabouts: **High-security psychiatric hospital.**

Shipilov, Sergey

Sergey Aleksandrovich Shipilov, AKA: The Velsk Chikatilo, is a Russian serial killer who took the lives of at least 14 people, mostly in his hometown of Velsk. Shipilov first killed in 1995, he claimed he robbed and then stabbed to death an unknown female. He confessed to it in 2016.

In 1996, he killed at least three more people. In April 1996, he murdered a female hitchhiker after raping her. He made no effort to hide her corpse and dumped her near a fence on an industrial estate. She had been stabbed so hard in the heart, that the knife broke inside of her. The DNA he left in and on her body would be crucial in bringing him to justice in 1999.

Over the Summer of 1996, he killed two more women in a similar fashion and buried them in shallow graves around the Primorsky District. One victim escaped from him after he had raped her and she went straight to the police. He was arrested on rape charges and sentenced to eight years in a regime colony. At the time, he was never suspected of the murders until that point.

At the colony, some prisoners were allowed outside the walls on special leave. Shipilov killed again in 1998 and covered the woman's body with branches instead of burying her in a shallow grave. He continued to rape and kill in this fashion for another year, and in 1999 he killed four people in 16 days.

He was held on suspicion of murder in late 1999, and in 2000 was convicted of 12 murders and an additional nine rapes. In 2016, he confessed to further murders.

As of 2021, he remains incarcerated in isolation at Arkhangelsk Central Prison in Northern Russia.

Born **May 17th 1959**.

Active from **1995-1999**.

Arrested on **October 10th 1999**.

Country: **Russia**.

Victims: **14+**.

AKA: **The Velsk Chikatilo**.

Sentence: **Life imprisonment**.

Current whereabouts: **In prison**.

Shipman, Harold: Doctor Death (Extended Case File)

On August 7th 1978, *Harold Shipman*, killed *Sarah Hannah Marsland*, one of his patients. It was one of four confirmed murders in 1978. It was also one of 215 convicted murders and he was suspected of killing over 250. He would kill three more times in 1978, again in August and two more in December.

On New Year's Day, 2000, a jury found Harold Shipman, who became known as *Doctor Death*, guilty of the murder of 215 patients under his care. It is the highest convicted murder count in the world with claims that more victims were attributed to him. Although Pedro Lopez claimed 310 victims, not all of them were confirmed and most were suspected or by using his own claims.

Because the United Kingdom does not have a death penalty, Shipman was sentenced to life in prison but hung himself in 2004.

He killed his first victim in March of 1975, *Eva Lyons*, she was one day shy of her seventy-first birthday. Then in February 1976, he was convicted of obtaining the drug; *pethidine*, by deception to feed his drug addiction. Later he managed to obtain enough morphine to kill an estimated 360 people. He received treatment in York before appearing as a GP in the Manchester area of Hyde.

He would kill his victims by injecting them with diamorphine which is a medical version of heroin. He managed to get away with killing 71 patients at the *Donnebrook Medical Practice* in the town. He killed the rest of his victims, mostly at his surgery in Market Street.

He killed 171 women and 44 men. The youngest was 41-years-old and the oldest was 93-years-old. There was suspicion in later investigations that some of his victims were children but this has never been substantiated.

When we think of serial killers, we generally don't think of medical practitioners. At least not in the way that Harold Shipman was. Our likely belief of a serial killing doctor tends to look like *Jack The Ripper*, were he of course to have been a doctor.

Shipman wasn't killing out of sexual perversity, he wasn't mutilating his victims and he wasn't having to worry about hiding corpses. But he still murdered 250 people.

"The police complain I'm boring. No mistresses, home abroad, money in Swiss banks, I'm normal. If that is boring then I am."

Harold Shipman, in letters to a friend from prison.

Because Shipman killed himself in prison in 2004, he robbed the world of understanding how he could have killed so many. Some people suggest that he was avenging the death of his mother as medical practitioners were unable to save her.

Whereas some considered that he was even easing the burden on the National Health Service (NHS). Though this might have been the case in his early murders, it would have changed as he continued at such a prolific rate.

Some psychiatrists have suggested that he killed simply because it gave him control and this goes back to one of the reasons in this book about controlling behaviour. Although he wouldn't physically dominant or *possess* his victims as Ted Bundy would have done, he did control their life and death. Possibly, he just couldn't resist playing God.

It wasn't until the case of Harold Shipman that British medical law was reviewed and majorly changed in the wake of his killings. What he got away with from the 1970s to the late 1990s would not be possible in the medical world beyond his conviction.

He was fired from *Todmorden Practice* for forging prescriptions. He got a fine but was not struck off the medical register. Instead, the General Medical Council (GMC) sent him a warning letter, and that was it.

It wasn't until 1998 that *Hyde Undertakers* became suspicious at the large number of his patients that were dying under his care. Another medical practice in the town learned that Shipman's death rates were almost ten times higher than their own. Concerns were raised with a coroner and then the *Greater Manchester Police* became involved.

An investigation followed but the police failed to run even basic checks. It might have been because the image of a general practitioner in the 1990s was linked with someone of high-esteem within the community. The police did not check his criminal record or contract the GMC at all. They didn't even contact Shipman himself or the family of his patients.

It wasn't until he forged the will of one of his victims, *Kathleen Grundy*, that he would be caught. Shipman had become greedy. He killed her on June 24th, 1998 and ticked the cremation box but she was fortunately buried instead. A local solicitor informed her children of the will and the doubts of its authenticity. It had apparently been made by Kathleen Grundy herself but it voided her children from the will and instead left £386,000 to Shipman.

Her body was exhumed and was found to contain traces of diamorphine. Shipman claimed she was an addict but a police search on his computer showed that he falsified hers and others medical records.

The subsequent review into the Shipman murders saw changes sweep across the medical industry in the UK. The British Government even changed the constitution of the General Medical Council. This was to ensure that the previously independent body was no longer dominated by its elected medical practitioners and instead would be made directly accountable to parliament.

Harold Shipman's legacy is alive to this very day. His giant victim count stands as one of the largest in recorded history for a serial killer. For a relatively small geographical country such as the United Kingdom, Doctor Death continues to dominate documentaries, books, and historical records.

Born **January 14th 1946**.

Active from **1975-1998**.

Arrested on **September 7th 1998**.

Country: **United Kingdom**.

Victims: **215-250+**.

AKA: **Doctor Death**.

Sentence: **Life imprisonment**.

Current whereabouts: **Committed suicide by hanging in 2004**.

Shulman, Robert Yale

Robert Yale Shulman was an American serial killer who was arrested on April 6th 1996. He was a postal worker from Long Island, New York, who was convicted of the murder of five prostitutes between 1991 and 1996. He has also been a suspect in numerous other cold cases.

His first known victim came in 1991 when he murdered 24-year-old *Lori Vasquez*. Her dismembered body was later discovered in a trash can. Another dismembered body of an unidentified woman was discovered in a similar trash can in 1992.

Three more victims followed in 1994 and 1995. All victims had been dismembered. The final victim on December 8th 1995, had her hands sliced off and had been discovered wrapped in a sleeping bag. While investigators went door to door, they discovered that hotel managers had seen a man in a blue Cadillac canvassing the streets on various occasions.

Shulman became a suspect and was arrested in 1996, with evidence from the sleeping bag and his car. A search of his bedroom resulted in hundreds of bloodstains that hadn't been cleaned properly. It was suggested then that Shulman had killed them in his home before dumping their bodies around the city.

The Monstrous Book of Serial Killers (2nd edition)

HAROLD SHIPMAN

IMAGE ATTRIB. A46

JOSEPH MICHAEL SWANGO

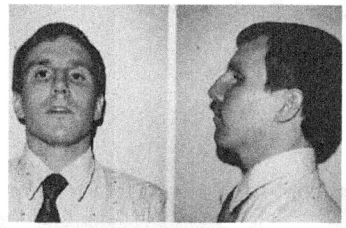

IMAGE ATTRIB. A40

GERALD STANO

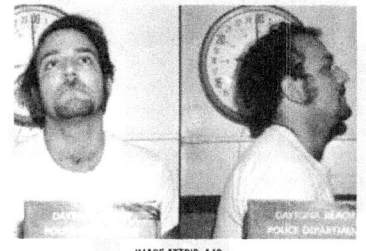

IMAGE ATTRIB. A42

ANATOLY SLIVKO

IMAGE ATTRIB. A43

Shulman was sentenced to death for one of the murders and life in prison for the other four. His death sentence was later reduced to life after an appeal in 2004. Shulman's attorney had stated that Shulman suffered from depression and a 'weak grasp of reality'.

On April 13th 2006, Shulman died in prison of natural causes.

Born **March 28th 1954.**

Active from **1991-1996.**

Arrested on **April 6th 1996.**

Country: **USA.**

Victims: **5+.**

Sentence: **Death penalty later commuted to life imprisonment.**

Current whereabouts: **Died of natural causes on April 13th 2006.**

Sikder, Ershad

Bangladeshi serial killer *Ershad Sikder* killed at least seven people and committed numerous other crimes over an eight period in the 1990s. After moving to the Khulna District in his teens, he became a railway worker and began robbing trains. After a few run-ins with local gangs, he went on to form his own gang.

His gang life saw him become involved in terrorism, theft and violent assaults. Amazingly, beyond that he entered the world of politics, and in 1988 was elected as Commissioner of Ward 8 of the Jatiya Party. With more power at his fingertips, he began to take possession of various properties and criminal activities.

He purchased an ice factory and went on to use it as his own personal torture facility. After a large investigation, Sikder was arrested in 1999 on the suspicion of up to 70 murders in the region from 1991 onwards. He was convicted of seven murders and sentenced to death, along with an additional four life sentences.

Sikder was executed on May 10th 2004.

Active from **1991-1999**.

Arrested on **August 11th 1999**.

Country: **Bangladesh**.

Victims: **7-70**.

AKA: **Ranga Chora**.

Sentence: **Death penalty**.

Current whereabouts: **Executed on May 10th 2004**.

Silveria Jr., Robert Joseph

American serial killer *Robert Joseph Silveria Jr.* AKA: *The Boxcar Killer,* murdered between nine and 28 victims. Over a period of 15 years from 1981 to 1996, Silveria rode the freight train routes and claimed to have killed 28 people.

Silveria was part of the Freight Train Riders of America (*FTRA*) who were suspected to be a criminal group that committed crimes by moving between freight trains all over the United States and Canada. Some of them were thought to have been involved in train derailments.

The FTRA was claimed to have been created by a group of Vietnam War veterans who were distraught at their treatment by the United States government. They slept in box cars, under bridges, and train yards.

Silveria was linked to the murders of homeless people and runaways along the freight rail routes. He would shoot or stab them before leaving their bodies in the open. He was also known as '*Boxcar Bob*'. Because of these murders, the FTRA received nationwide attention and a large investigation began.

Another FTRA members, named *Michael Elijah Adams*, was also eventually caught and was linked to 17 murders. Another recent FTRA member, *Robert James LeCou*, was convicted of killing three people in Montana, he was subsequently sentenced to 300 years in prison.

Silveria was arrested in 1996 and was sentenced to double life sentences without parole. He was also convicted in Wyoming, Florida, and Kansas, but remains imprisoned in a Medium Correctional Institution in Wyoming.

Born **March 3rd 1959.**

Active from **1981-1996.**

Arrested on **March 2nd 1996.**

Country: **USA.**

Victims: **9-28.**

AKA: **The Boxcar Killer / Boxcar Bob.**

Sentence: **Two life sentences.**

Current whereabouts: **In prison.**

Simons, Norman: The Station Strangler (Extended Case File)

South African serial killer *Norman Avzal Simons* killed at least 22 young boys between 1986 and 1994. He was convicted on one of the murders and is part of an ongoing court process to this day. By 1994, the residents of *Mitchell's Plain* were haunted by the plague of a serial killer known as *The Station Strangler*.

South Africa in 1994 was going through a process of rebirth and struggle. Apartheid had fallen and the country was about to celebrate the news by holding its first democratic elections. For a large number of families, the new freedom meant little because their children were dead, and the killer was still walking their streets.

During his childhood, Simons was deemed to be an intelligent boy who played classical instruments such as the piano. He also learned and spoke seven languages and went on to a career in teaching. He taught Grade-five students, which is generally children aged between 10-years-old to 11-years-old. It is no surprise then that most of his victims were around that age group.

He is known to be South Africa's *Andrei Chikatilo* and was even inspired by the stories coming out of Russia. Chikatilo was a Russian serial killer who killed young boys and girls by mostly luring them away from train stations. Simons utilised the same method and thus became known as *The Station Strangler*. He is to this day, one of South Africa's most notorious serial killers.

Simons claimed that during his formative years, his older stepbrother raped him on many occasions. His brother was an alcoholic Rastafarian who was murdered in 1991 in a separate incident. Simons also claimed that he heard his brother's voice in his head, ordering him to kill others.

His brother then moved from voices to possession. His spirit jumped into Simons body and lived inside him, ordering him to kill. He claims that the voices and delusions began when his brother started to rape him. He refrained from acting on the voices until 1986.

He claimed his first victim in that year when he was just 19-years-old. He lured 14-

year-old *Jonathan Claasen* away from *Modderdam Station*, before raping and killing him. Claasen's body was discovered on October 3rd 1986. Generally, Simons would tie their hands behind their backs and strangle them with their own underwear. He would dump the bodies near to the stations in shallow graves with the corpses lying face down.

The area of Mitchell's Plain is 20 miles from Cape Town and is one of South Africa's largest suburbs. It was a large housing area that quickly became an urban ghetto. The transition from housing projects to ghetto came about because of poverty, drugs and a rising criminal underclass. Children were still free to roam and play around until the bodies began to pile up.

On January 7th 1987, the body of 10-year-old *Yussuf Hoffmann* was discovered. He had been killed in the exact same manner. Hoffman had been raped and strangled to death with a piece of his own clothing. His hands were tied behind his back and his face had been pushed into the sand in the area of Rocklands.

On January 23rd 1987, the body of 13-year-old *Mario Thomas* was discovered in Kuilsriver, less than 20 miles away from the location of Hoffman's body. It was already becoming clear that a perverse serial killer was stalking the streets of Mitchell's Plain.

In June 1987, 12-year-old *Freddie Cleaves* was discovered near *Belhar Train Station*, just six miles away from the body of Mario Thomas. In August 1987, the body of 14-year-old *Samuel Ngaba* was discovered at the exact same station as Cleave's body.

On October 1st 1987, the seventh victim was discovered almost a year to the day of the discovery of the first victim. The unnamed boy was found in exactly the same location as Simons very first victim, at Modderdam Railway Station.

By the beginning of 1988, nine young boys had been found murdered in the same fashion and the community of Mitchell's Plain was in a state of panic and fear. Serial killers were and are rare in South Africa, despite the huge amount of crime in the country. And so the local detective assigned to the case had no experience or training in how to solve serial killing cases.

Because of the public knowledge of the killings, the murders ceased for a number of years until 1992 when The Station Strangler returned to his old stomping ground of Mitchell's Plain and began killing again. The body of an 11-year-old boy was found in October of 1992, face down on a local beach.

It wasn't until January 1994 that he would kill again in what came to be known as the *month of horror*. It began on January 13th, when the body of an unidentified young boy was discovered in the remote *Weltevrede Dunes* outside of Cape Town. The dunes were considered remote enough that bodies would be hard to find.

Like the *Texas Killing Fields* in the United States, the Weltevrede Dunes became The Station Strangler's killing fields. Every victim from then onwards would be found in the dunes. Even up until 2021, they have become synonymous with the murders.

Once the first body had been found, more bodies began turning up on the dunes. The community was in shock and demanded action, so the police began searching the dunes themselves. Over the month of January 1994, in conjunction with the *South African Army*, the police discovered a total of 11 bodies on the Weltevrede Dunes.

On January 27th alone, six bodies were uncovered on the dunes. One was an adult male killed in the same fashion and the other 10 were of young boys. In February 1994, a special task team consisting of 14 men was set up, called the *Station Strangler Squad*. The task team was given every resource available and even had help from FBI serial killer profiler *Robert Ressler*.

Ressler was set on heading to South Africa to assist the team but the political unrest in the country at the time put him off and in the end he remained in the States. Ressler reviewed some of the profiles drawn up about The Station Strangler and mostly agreed with what had been written. He would later go to a South African press conference where he would praise the investigatory team on their work.

On April 13th 1994, Norman Simons was arrested in connection with another murdered boy who had been discovered on the Weltevrede Dunes in March. He would go on to confess that he had been killing young boys since 1986. An officer with no knowledge of the case was brought in to accompany Simons as they undertook a walk-through of the dunes.

Simons pointed out where the bodies had been found and even showed him areas where other bodies should have been. He pointed out an area in the dunes where he stated he killed another boy. No body was found there but items of clothing were recovered. It was also known that wild animals would come to the dunes to hunt and it was suggested that more bodies may have been consumed by them.

"I am nothing. I am dirty. I am filthy and not worthy. I am sorry for letting you down. Don't get caught in the same thing. I really regret everything. It's hard to be possessed by unknown forces. These forces cannot be explained by medication."

Norman Simons – from his confession.

The trial began in 1995 and lasted three months. Because of lack of evidence due to decomposition of the bodies, they were only able to convict him on the final victim in March of 1994 based on eye-witness reports. He was sentenced to life and is currently incarcerated at the *Drakenstein Maximum Correctional Facility* in Paarl, the same prison were Nelson Mandela was imprisoned.

Further prosecutions were ruled out and Simons repeatedly appealed his conviction but the sentence was upheld at every juncture. An inquest in 2005, led Simons defence team to claim his innocence in the crimes. There is now a public perception that the wrong killer may have been caught and that Simons was merely a copycat killer.

It was alleged that even during his trial, more boys had gone missing and more bodies were found. Although this is in hearsay, there is a huge belief in it and also in the conspiracy that authorities covered up the subsequent murders to not look inept in the eyes of the community. However in 2008, the inquest ended and it was suggested there was sufficient evidence for Simons being the killer in at least some of the murders.

In 2014, a man who testified to being a surviving victim of *The Station Strangler*, claimed that *Norman Simons* was not the man who had attacked him. He and a friend were lured to a remote area and raped with an attempt to strangle them. When the man had fallen asleep, they both managed to escape.

Because their friends knew Norman Simons, they were sure that he was not the man who attacked them. The man who attacked them was apparently known to police but was never questioned in the investigation for the murders.

A short while later, a radio station in Cape Town was debating the case live on air when they received a phone call from one of the prosecutors, *Mike Stowe*, who was involved in the original trial. He claimed live on air that he was sure they had convicted the wrong man.

He claimed that witness statements didn't add up and that no one had seen Simons near the train stations when the boys had gone missing. He also cited further information that he felt was inconclusive.

Stowe's conversation and admission of possible innocence sent shock waves through the country and especially the area of Mitchell's Plains. Family members of the victims were in uproar and suddenly the entire Station Strangler story was thrown into confusion.

In 2016, 58-year-old *Brian Shofer* killed himself in his police cell. Shofer was a convicted South African paedophile who had been arrested just two days prior for the rape of a 17-year-old boy. The boy in question had been living with Shofer since he was 12-years-old. Shofer spent a lifetime surrounding himself with children and taught children in his home, or theirs, under a private tutorship.

Shofer was a resident in Mitchell's Plain at the same time that the Station Strangler was active. Shofer claimed that he was violently abused as a child and that his uncle raped him on numerous occasions. His father knew of the abuse and allowed it to happen. He also claimed that from this abuse, he grew to prefer children as sexual contacts.

Shortly after a 2010 conviction for sexual assault, he began working at a primary school in the Cape Town area. He left shortly after when his landlords claimed that Shofer had been in a relationship with a 16-year-old girl. Both of them happened to believe that he was the real strangler. Even as far back as 1994, Shofer had been found guilty of multiple rapes on young boys under the age of 15-years-old.

Before he killed himself, Shofer was about to be charged with 18 cases of sexual assault involving homeless children and runaways. After his death, some criminal profilers came forward who suggested there were two serial killers, who had exactly the same process of killing young boys.

The inquest into Norman Simons concluded that there was sufficient evidence to link him to at least six of the murders but not good enough evidence to link him to the rest. But because he had pointed out the murder scenes and one other where clothes were found, then it is generally assumed that Simons *is* The Station Strangler, regardless of the minimal evidence that convicted him.

If there was a second strangler or an accomplice then it is also generally assumed to be Shofer. However, he now takes his secrets to the grave and the end of the story remains solely with Norman Simons – The Station Strangler.

Born in **1956**.

Active from **1986-1994**.

Arrested in **1994**.

Country: **South Africa**.

Victims: **22+**.

AKA: **The Station Strangler / Norman Avzal Simons**.

Sentence: **Life imprisonment**.

Current whereabouts: **In prison**.

Sinclair, Angus: The World's End Murderer (Extended Case File)

On November 20th 1978, the body of 17-year-old *Mary Gallacher* was found on waste ground near a footbridge at *Barnhill Railway Station*, in Glasgow, Scotland. She would come to be known as a victim of one of Scotland's worst serial killers.

The judge who first sentenced him, called Sinclair; "a dangerous predator capable of sinking to the depths of depravity."

In 1961 at the age of just 16-years-old, Angus Sinclair was convicted of murdering his seven-year-old neighbour *Catherine Reehill*. He was subsequently sentenced to ten years in prison but served only six behind bars. Upon his release, in his early twenties, he got married and had a son, nothing was seemingly untoward.

However, his inability to control his urges would lead him to the 1978 killing of Mary Gallacher. He would not be convicted of that particular murder until 2001, when DNA matching cold cases connected him to the crime. It had remained until then, one of Scotland's most mysterious murders.

During 1977, six young women had disappeared after nights out across the central belt of Scotland which is generally referred to as a fifty mile stretch from Glasgow to Edinburgh. Their bodies were found dumped on farmland or waste ground.

On October 15th 1977, two teenagers named *Helen Scott* and *Christine Eadie* were seen leaving the *World's End Pub* on Edinburgh's Royal Mile. They would later become known as the World's End Murders, and Sinclair; The World's End Murderer.

The next day, Christine's naked body was discovered by hikers in East Lothian. Helens' body was found over six miles away from Christine's in a corn field. Both of the victims had been savagely beaten, gagged and tied. They had been raped, abused and strangled to death and their bodies left in the open without any attempt to hide them.

Due to the media running with the story in a big way, some witnesses suggested they had seen the girls with two men that night. This claim was backed up by police who said that both girls had been tied with different knotting methods.

As the possible link between two men was given, the investigation garnered widespread attention and over 13,000 witness statements were given. In May of 1978, they scaled down the investigation. The World's End murders, at least for a while, fell into dark Scottish legend. The scaling down of the investigation surely led to Sinclair killing again in November of 1978.

At the time of the World's End murders, the police had failed to make a connection with four other women who had been found and killed in a similar fashion throughout the same year.

This deepened the divide between Glasgow and Edinburgh. It was assumed by some that murders in Glasgow were not deemed as important as those in Edinburgh, due to the poverty and cultural divide between Scotland's two largest cities.

The death of Mary Gallacher in 1978 led him to change the way he killed. Gallacher had been raped and beaten before having her throat slit. There had been a witness to her abduction and the police were closing in. It was this, psychologists believe, that led Sinclair to devise different tactics. Unfortunately, it led him to start preying on children.

Between 1978 to 1982, Sinclair would rape, sexually abuse, or assault tens of children in the Glasgow area. In 1982, he pleaded guilty to the rape and sexual assault of 11 children between the ages of six to 14-years-old.

The cold case review of Mary Gallacher in 2000 led to his conviction of her murder in 2001. In 2007, the World's End murders had been attributed to him but the trial collapsed in an extraordinary miscarriage of justice.

Sinclair's lawyers had put forward two special defences, one that included the belief that the two girls had consented to sexual intercourse with Sinclair. The second being that anything that happened after that was the actions of Sinclair's late brother. Because there was insufficient evidence to prove that any sexual encounter had not been consensual then the judge dismissed the case.

The news of the verdict caused mass outcry in Scotland and widespread criticism of the police and justice system. The resulting shift in Scottish Law was felt internationally as the Scottish Parliament pretty much managed to legally circumnavigate the double jeopardy law. A law which used to mean that one couldn't be tried for the same crime.

In 2011, the Scottish Parliament passed the *Double Jeopardy Act 2011*. It had made various provisions for circumstances when a person convicted or acquitted of an offence could be newly prosecuted.

As such, in 2014, there was a controversial retrial of the World's End murders, which involved the jury visiting the sites where the bodies were found. Sinclair was then found guilty in November 2014 and sentenced to life imprisonment. He was the first person in Scotland to be given a retrial of the same crimes under the new law.

Angus Sinclair died in *HM Prison Glenochil* on March 11th 2019.

Born in **1945**.

Active from **1961-2005**.

Country: **United Kingdom.**

Victims: **4+**.

AKA: **The World's End Murderer.**

Sentence: **Life imprisonment.**

Current whereabouts: **Died of natural causes on March 11th 2019.**

Sinclair, Charles Thurman

On July 14th 1987, in Spokane, Washington, coin shop owner *Leo Cashatt* was shot dead and his coin shop was robbed. He was one of the victims of *Charles Thurman Sinclair*, AKA: *The Coin Shop Killer*.

Sinclair was an armed robber, murderer and rapist of women and was active from the early 1980s. He left a trail of bodies across Western states of America and parts of Canada. Investigators followed his crimes across the country and he was arrested in August of 1990.

Police officers in Alaska arrested Sinclair for the suspected connection of eight murders. When the investigation searched a storage shed owned by him they found the evidence they needed. Maps, false ID machines, C-4 explosives, land-mines and an entire stash of rare coins were the tip of the iceberg.

He was subsequently linked to at least **11** murders and two rapes. He would specifically target coin shops to rob, before killing the owners to hide any witnesses. In October 1990, while in custody, he died of a heart attack, leaving the investigation at a standstill.

Born in **1946**.

Active from **1980-1990**.

Arrested on **August 13th 1990**.

Country: **USA**.

Victims: **11+**.

AKA: **The Coin Shop Killer**.

Current whereabouts: **Died of a heart attack before trial.**

Sleepy Hollow Killer

In South Africa, an unidentified serial killer known as the *Sleepy Hollow Killer*, raped and killed at least 13 prostitutes, from the early 1990s to at least 2007. The killer would strangle his victims using their own underwear, and it was this method where three victims were linked in 2007.

Before that date, the killings supposedly stopped in 2001, leading some to believe that they belonged to a copycat killer. As all murders are still open and active cases, the three from 2007 have been attributed to the Sleepy Hollow Killer.

All victims had been raped and their bodies were discovered along the N3 Highway in Pietermaritzburg. It wasn't until 2001, that an investigation was opened, and seven of the unidentified victims were exhumed from their graves, to see if modern technology could help identify them. No matches or new evidence was found and the investigation shut down in the same year.

The three 2007 victims were found on the same stretch of highway, with the same murder method, over a six month period. Around the same time, more victims were discovered further away from the region, all had the same methods of killing. A special task force was set up to look for connections and examine the evidence, in order to catch the killer.

As of 2021, the investigation is still ongoing and no charges have been brought to any one person. The Sleepy Hollow Killer remains unidentified.

Active from **1990-2007.**

Country: **South Africa.**

Victims: **13+.**

Current whereabouts: **Unidentified killer. Status unknown.**

Slivko, Anatoly

The Russian serial killer murdered seven people over a 19-year period. Slivko witnessed a violent automobile death of a teenage boy in 1961 and it acted as a catalyst for his own murders. He would kill young boys in an attempt to recreate what he had witnessed as it had sexually aroused him.

When Slivko worked at a children's club, once or twice a year he would befriend a young boy and lure them into an experiment. Whereby he would hang them in a controlled environment to stretch the spine. But when they passed out he would strip them naked and sexually abuse them.

Over a period of many years, he persuaded 43 boys to take part in the experiment. Seven of them he would kill, dismembering their bodies and pouring gasoline over the remains, to remind him of the death he had witnessed in childhood.

He was caught in 1985 and executed by firing squad in 1989.

Born **December 28th 1938.**

Active from **1964-1985.**

Arrested in **December 1985.**

Country: **Soviet Union.**

Victims: **7.**

Sentence: **Death penalty.**

Current whereabouts: **Executed by firing squad in 1989.**

Slovak, Jozef

A Slovakian serial killer who killed at least five women. On August 22nd 1978, Slovak killed his first victim he'd met on a train. They went into the Bratislava Woods together and he tried unsuccessfully to have sex with her. She refused and fought back so he choked her to death.

He then dragged her body deeper into the forest and covered it in light foliage and branches. He burned some of her clothing within the woods but disturbingly gave some of her belongings as gifts to his girlfriend.

In 1982 he was sentenced to 15 years but released in 1990. He then went on to kill four more women. His second murder was only two months after his release.

He was arrested again and sentenced to life. Psychologists found him to have a high IQ, and noted he was the holder of several electronic patents. They also found him to be a narcissistic psychopath.

Born **April 7th 1951.**

Active from **1978-1991.**

Arrested on **July 18th 1991.**

Country: **Czech Republic / Slovakia.**

Victims: **5+.**

AKA: **The Bratislava Strangler.**

Sentence: **Life imprisonment.**

Current whereabouts: **In prison.**

Smith, Lemuel

He was already in prison for the murders of five people when he murdered a female prison guard in Green Haven Correctional Facility, in New York. In 1958, he robbed and beat to death *Dorothy Waterstreet*, he was only 16-years-old at the time. The following year, after being arrested for a different offence, he was charged for the murder and would serve almost 20 years in prison.

In 1976 he was released. In the same year he brutally murdered two people the day before thanksgiving. In December of the same year, a 24-year-old woman was raped, murdered and mutilated in her car at the car park of the *Colonie Center Mall*.

He went on to kill two more people in the coming years. After the murder of the prison guard he was transferred to isolation at Five Points Correctional Facility in New York.

As of 2021, Smith is still considered one of the most dangerous prisoners in the city and is held in isolation for 23 hours a day.

Born **July 23rd 1941**.

Active from **1958-1991**.

Arrested on **August 19th 1977**.

Country: **USA**.

Victims: **6**.

Sentence: **Life imprisonment**.

Current whereabouts: **In prison, in isolation**.

Smithers, Samuel

In Florida, on May 12th 1996, *Samuel Smithers,* AKA: *The Deacon of Death,* murders his first victim, prostitute *Denise Roach*. He killed her at the vacant Whitehurst estate, that he was taking care off.

Smithers claimed that Roach had been loitering around the property on at least two occasions. On May 12th, he asked her to leave but she had refused. She had apparently hit Smithers in the arm and threw a potted plant at his vehicle. He claimed that he pushed her into a wall and a small plank of wood fell from a shelf and hit her head, killing her.

He returned the next day and hid the body in the pond. Unfortunately for Smithers, his story didn't match up with the subsequent coroner's report. Roach had been hit at least 16 times in the head, most likely with an axe. She had fractures to her face and injuries consistent with strangulation.

On May 28th 1996, he murdered his second known victim, prostitute *Cristy Cowan*. He killed her at the same vacant Whitehurst estate. Smithers told varying stories of how he had come to kill her. In an attempt to cover his own back, he claimed that he saw a car parked on the side of the road and went to help. He then drove Cowan to a nearby store where she demanded money or she would accuse him of rape.

He took her to Whitehurst and gave her all his money but she was angered at the amount and she threw a drink over him. Smithers claims he reacted badly, picked up an axe and smashed it into the side of her head. He then dragged her to the estate's pond. A coroner's report later confirmed she had died of strangulation combined with massive head trauma.

At the same time, the owner of the property, Mr. Whitehurst, dropped by to check on the house and saw Smithers cleaning an axe over a pool of blood on the carpet. Smithers claimed someone had killed an animal in the house. Whitehurst contacted the local police department, who went to the property later that day.

The blood had gone but the drag marks remained. They followed them to the pond where they found Cowan's body floating. After a further search, they found the decomposed body Denise Roach. Evidence found at the scene and on CCTV in the local area, led to Smithers' arrest.

After the arrest, the true nature of a the *'kind-hearted'* Baptist deacon, came to light. Other prostitutes in the area recognised Smithers as a previous customer of theirs. Smithers claimed he was innocent through all the initial interviews but failed a polygraph test. He later subsequently confessed to the two murders but changed his story every time he could.

He was convicted of two murders and sentenced to death. As the years passed, various cold cases have been linked to Smithers, including the unsolved murder of *Roslin Kruse*, who had lived with Smithers at the time. Some investigators have stated that Smithers may have killed many more and hid their bodies in various parts of the country.

He was convicted of two murders and sentenced to death. As of 2021, he remains on death row.

Born **January 30th 1953**.

Active during **1996**.

Arrested on **May 28th 1996**.

Country: **USA**.

Victims: **2+**.

AKA: **The Deacon of Death**.

Sentence: **Death penalty**.

Current whereabouts: **Death row**.

Snowtown Murders: The Bodies in the Barrels (Extended Case File)

In Snowtown, Australia, *The Snowtown Murders*, AKA*: The Bodies in the Barrels*, was a series of killings carried out by three serial killers, operating as part of a gang.

John Bunting, Robert Wagner and *James Vlassakis* killed at least 12 people between 1992 and 1999. A fourth member named *Mark Haydon*, was convicted on conspiracy to murder as he had helped dispose of the bodies. The Snowtown Murders are one of the most infamous cases in Australian history.

In 1999, Police in Snowtown, Adelaide, discovered eight bodies in barrels in an abandoned bank vault. Each of the victims had been dismembered and left to rot. Most of the victims were their own family members or acquaintances that one of them knew. The discovery and resulting trial made Snowtown famous for all the wrong reasons.

John Bunting claimed that each of the victims were either paedophiles, gay men, or simply considered inferior. He made the others believe that murder was the right way to do things, to rid the world of true evil, as he saw it. Before they killed their victims, they subjected each of them to horrific torture. All the victim's identities were stolen, and their bank accounts were emptied.

Bunting was the ring-leader of the serial killing gang and instigated all of the killings. When he was eight-years-old, he was violently beaten and raped by a family member of one of his friend's. It has been suggested since that it was this abuse that led to him wishing to kill those who attacked children.

On August 31st 1992, Bunting claimed his first victim, 20-year-old *Clinton Trezise*. He invited him over for a drink and accused him of being a paedophile. After an argument, Bunting beat Trezise to death with a shovel, and buried the body in a shallow grave. His body was discovered in 1994, and it had never been proven that he had abused children.

In Australia, the slang for a paedophile is *Rock Spider*. In one of the rooms in his home, he created a *Rock Spider Wall* of information, where he stuck the names and photos of people he suspected to be paedophiles or gay men. He bundled gay men under the same Rock Spider banner as he saw them as immoral and dirty.

Bunting was known to be socially active and easy to talk to, this allowed him to bring people in close and empower others. He would become known as a master manipulator. This gave him some control over others who wanted to help him out or do things for him, but his darker side would shine through more often than not.

He once killed a friend's dog simply because he wanted to see how the body functioned, claiming he was curious about the anatomy of animals and humans. He also told others that he skinned cats alive and enjoyed slaughtering animals whenever he could.

When the investigation discovered where most of the victims had died they found a veritable horror house of tools and implements used to torture people. This included knives, rope, gloves, pliers, a shotgun, metal rods and an electric shock tool, which was used on the genitals of the men they killed.

On some of their victims, they crushed the toes with pliers, shoved lit sparklers into their genitals, burned their ears and nose with cigarettes, and beat them with clubs and metal rods. The killers ordered their victims to refer to them by many controlling names, including; *Master, God,* or *Lord*.

Their final victim was 24-year-old David Johnson, who was James Vlassakis's stepbrother. Vlassakis lured him to an empty bank building where the others were waiting. They tied him down and told him to read from a pre-defined script, which included fake crimes and fake confessions of things that Johnson had never done. They went to empty Johnson's bank account and when they returned, he had died from his injuries.

This upset Robert Wagner, who claimed they hadn't made the most of their time torturing him. They all dismembered Johnson's body and sliced off parts of him, then they fried the flesh and sat down to feast on them.

Some of the victims were killed in their own homes, the gang would rampage through their houses, smashing things up before killing their victims. They would also trash the homes of those people they believed to be gay. Most victims however were lured to Bunting's home, where they were tortured before being dismembered.

Eight of the bodies were found in giant plastic barrels that were full of acid. Two of the bodies had been pushed into just one of the barrels. They stored the barrels in an old bank vault, and Bunting would return to the barrels on regular occasions to see how well they were being dissolved in the acid.

"They're rotting very nicely."

Bunting to his gang, when remarking on the first victim to be put in a barrel.

Bunting enjoyed watching the bodies dissolve and made notes on how long it took each body part to rot away. He kept his last victim, Johnson, in two separate barrels. They were finally caught not long after they killed the wife of Mark Haydon, 37-year-old *Elizabeth Haydon*, without Mark knowing. When he was shown the body in the barrel, Haydon reportedly huffed and smiled to himself.

She had been killed because Bunting claimed she had made sexual advances towards him and he saw this as immoral and dirty – thus she needed to die. She died in November 1998 and was found in May of 1999. It was the police investigation into her disappearance that led police to the old bank where they found the eight victims in the barrels.

Police suspected that the perpetrators moved the barrels around to avoid detection, mostly because they knew they were being investigated. When police searched the homes of the suspects, they found two more bodies in Bunting's garden. On May 21st 1999, Bunting, Wagner, Vlassakis and Haydon were arrested on suspicion of murder.

The subsequent trials were amongst the lengthiest and most expensive in Australia's history. Bunting showed no remorse for his crimes and spoke about the torture of the victims in such an open manner that three of the jury members had to walk out at one point, with their hands to their mouths. Bunting would also ignore the trial, instead he would read a book and not listen to what was going on around him.

They were all sentenced in 2003. Bunting received eleven life sentences without the possibility of parole. Wagner got life without the possibility of parole. Vlassakis was sentenced to life with a 26 year minimum term, due to spilling the beans on the others. And Haydon got 25 years in jail with a minimum term of 18 years.

Snowtown, in Adelaide, is now synonymous with the murders, and at one point the community had voted to change the name to Rosetown, but for whatever reason, it didn't change. However the murders gained such infamy that tourist shops in the area began selling Snowtown Murder souvenirs.

As of 2021, all four of the killers remain incarcerated in prisons in Australia.

Active from **1992-1999.**

Arrested on **May 21st 1999.**

Country: **Australia.**

Victims: **12+.**

AKA: **Bodies in the Barrels.**

Sentence: **25 years to multiple life sentences.**

Current whereabouts: **All four remain in prison.**

Solomon Jr., Morris

On March 19th 1987, In Sacramento, the body of 18-year-old prostitute *Maria Apodaca* was discovered. She had been bound, wrapped up in bedding and then buried. She had been raped and killed by American serial killer, *Morris Solomon Jr. AKA: The Sacramento Slayer.*

Solomon had been raised in rural Georgia by an abusive grandmother. She would beat him and his brother daily for if they wet the bed, spoke with bad grammar or cried during a beating from the day before. There were times when she beat them for no other reason than it had become a normal routine.

She also made Solomon remove all his clothing and stand on a stool in the corner. She would beat his naked body until he bled, and on one occasion she tied him to a pole so he couldn't escape her violence, before whipping him with electrical cord.

On April 20th 1987, the body of 26-year-old prostitute and drug-user *Cherie Washington* was uncovered on Solomon's property. He had given police permission to search the car in his yard. Upon doing so they noticed a depression in the ground.

They borrowed a shovel, excavated and discovered Washington's body. She had been raped and killed by Solomon, before being bound, wrapped in bedding and then buried. This method became his modus operandi.

On April 22nd, Police discovered two more bodies on the property. 24-year-old *Linda Vitela* and 17-year-old *Sheila Jacox* were unearthed, they had been tied up and buried in bedding. Both victims were prostitutes and drug-users, their bodies had been in the ground for a year before being uncovered.

On April 29th, another body was discovered on the property. 29-year-old *Sharon Massey* was discovered buried and wrapped in bedding near to the site of previous victim; Maria Apodaca. Massey had been raped and murdered by Solomon and had been dead for approximately six months before her body was unearthed.

Solomon is currently on death row at San Quentin, after being convicted of six murders. He is linked to at least one more.

Born in **1944**.

Active from **1986-1987**.

Arrested on **April 22nd 1987**.

Country: **USA**.

Victims: **7+**.

AKA: **The Sacramento Slayer**.

Sentence: **Death penalty**.

Current whereabouts: **Death row**.

Spencer, Timothy Wilson: The Southside Strangler (Extended Case File)

On November 22nd 1987, 15-year-old high school student *Diane Cho*, was found dead in her family's, in Chesterfield County. She had been raped and strangled by serial killer *Timothy Wilson Spencer*, AKA: *The Southside Strangler*. Spencer would be convicted of five murders from 1984 to 1987 and was the first serial killer in the United States to be convicted on DNA evidence.

His case also involved the first person to be found innocent of a crime they had previously been convicted for, all because of the advances in DNA technology.

Born in 1962, Spencer was raised in the Green Valley area of Arlington, Virginia. At the time, it was generally a black neighbourhood and known as a lower-income region area prone to violence.

In 1984, Spencer claimed his first victim, *Carolyn Hamm*, from Virginia. Her body was discovered face down near the door to her garage. She had been raped, tied up and hung with a cord from a Venetian blind. Her murder was in an area where violent crime was considered rare, and due to media attention, an arrest was made quickly. A confession was obtained and charges were brought to *David Vasquez*.

Vazquez was wrongly convicted and served five years of a 35 year prison sentence before the conviction was overturned in 1989. He was the first person to have his conviction overturned due to advancements in DNA technology.

On November 27th 1987, Spencer murdered 44-year-old *Susan Tucker* who was strangled to death in her condominium. The body wasn't discovered until December 1st. In a similar fashion to the 1984 murder, a cord had been taken from a nearby Venetian blind and used to strangled her. She had also been raped and her body had been found nude, partially covered by a sleeping bag.

In both cases, the killer had entered the properties through a first floor window and it was suggested that due to the prevalence of semen stains that Spencer had masturbated over the bodies. An investigation then linked three more murders that were carried out in 1987, over a hundred miles away in Richmond

On September 19th 1987, in Richmond, *Debbie Davis* was found dead in her first floor apartment which she lived in alone. She had been strangled with a sock that had been tied around her neck and twisted tight with a small section of pipe. Spencer had left multiple semen stains on Davis as well.

Just two weeks later and less than a mile away from the Davis crime scene, *Dr. Susan Hellams* was found dead in her bedroom closet. She had been killed in a remarkably similar fashion to Davis and the other victims.

And then 15-year-old high school student *Diane Cho* was raped and strangled by Spencer. She had been killed in her bedroom while her family slept nearby in the other rooms. Duct tape had been put across her mouth to stop her from crying out. She too had been strangled with a ligature and semen stains were found on the body and the sheets.

It took a large effort by lead investigators to convince different departments that the murders were linked. This is referred to as *linkage blindness* and makes serial killing cases difficult to investigate. The lead investigator, *Joe Horgas*, then connected various rape and burglary cases in the region.

In one incident of burglary, Spencer had climbed through a basement window of a woman's apartment and left porn magazines in the house along with a cord from a Venetian blind on her bed. It was suggested that Spencer was waiting for her to come home but for some reason decided to leave.

After following up the burglary and rape cases, Horgas determined that Spencer's methods had been perfected over many years. Beginning with burglaries then rape and then finally moving onto murder. The pattern was becoming obvious as the crime scenes were starting to look remarkably similar.

Spencer was arrested in 1988 and subsequently convicted of murder and rape. He was sentenced to death and executed in the electric chair on April 27th 1994. He was known to have killed five people and raped many more.

Born in **1962**.

Active from **1984-1988**.

Arrested on **January 20th 1988**.

Country: **USA**.

Victims: **5**.

AKA: **The Southside Strangler**.

Sentence: **Death penalty**.

Current whereabouts: **Executed in the electric chair on April 27th 1994.**

Spesivtsev, Alexander: The Siberian Ripper (Extended Case File)

Russian serial killer *Alexander Nikolayevich Spesivtsev, AKA: The Siberian Ripper*, would be convicted for the murders of four people in Novokuznetsk in 1996. He has been accused of killing up to 19 people but police evidence recently suggested he may have killed as many as 80.

Astonishingly, Spesivtsev was assisted by his mother, who helped him abduct homeless children and young women across the region. The victims would be lured into the apartment they shared, where they would be brutally murdered. It was also proven that Spesivtsev ate some of his victims.

Born in 1970, he was constantly ill as a child after having been born premature. As he grew up, he remained unsociable and isolated, preferring his own company instead of making friends. He was bullied by school pupils and returned home to an abusive alcoholic father.

It has been suggested that his mother may have persuaded Spesivtsev to kill in the first instance. As he was growing up, and at an influential time of his life, she would share a bed with him and show him pictures of dead bodies and autopsies from true crime books and magazines.

He did get a girlfriend in his late teens but he would often show an aggressive streak and she broke up with him. Spesivtsev didn't take it too kindly and kidnapped his ex-girlfriend. He took her to his apartment where he proceeded to abuse and torture her for an entire month. He was arrested and sent to a secure psychiatric unit in the area.

He was discharged three years later, in 1991, and fell down a rabbit hole of hatred and paranoia. He developed a hatred of homeless children and began associating with street people in order to get close to the younger ones. He then began luring victims to the apartment, and shortly after, his mother began luring victims for him.

All of his victims were street children, runaways, or those from poor areas. The collapse of the Soviet Union meant that construction sites and abandoned industrial factories were left to rot. Many children played in those areas and Spesivtsev began selecting his victims from there.

In the apartment, he would torture the children and then slaughter them. Most of the victims would be cannibalised to some degree. Any remaining body parts were put into buckets by his mother, who would dispose of them in a local river, in the middle of the night.

As time passed by and cases of missing children began to rise, more and more body parts were being discovered in the area. These ranged from severed heads, torsos, arms and legs of small children. Most of the remains had been washed up onto the banks of the river his mother had been dumping them in.

It took a while for the authorities to believe they were dealing with a serial killer. At first, investigators believed they were dealing with organ smugglers who sometimes operated on the city's boundaries. They had police officers searching baggage on outward flights and infiltrating criminal gangs in the region.

Pressure from local communities and the amount of body parts being found, pushed the investigation forward and then they realised that it could be the work of a single serial killer.

Witnesses had spotted Spesivtsev's mother with some of the victims before their disappearances, and police managed to track her down. She claimed that her son was still under psychiatric care at a hospital outside of the city but she was arrested anyway and questioned for three days. While she was under arrest, a neighbourhood officer and a maintenance man contacted the police, and the investigation turned a corner.

They claimed that they had visited a communal apartment block to unclog the drainpipes and needed access to the Spesivtsev apartment. Alexander Spesivtsev had answered the door and claimed that he was a mental patient who was being forced to remain in the apartment.

When the two men caught wind of a putrid smell coming from the apartment, they forced their way in. Spesivtsev ran to the building's roof and disappeared. The two men were left in the apartment, and they found a place of horrors.

15-year-old *Olga Galtseva* was laying on the floor, bleeding from a single deep stab wound to the chest, fighting for her life. In the bathroom, a decapitated body was found in the bathtub with its arms and legs missing. Various blood stains and the smell of rotted flesh adorned the entire apartment.

Spesivtsev was arrested a week later on October 30th 1996. He was found on the streets, suffering from cold and hunger. He kept a detailed journal of the murders and it was this that partially led to his conviction. When the apartment was searched, 82 items of blood-stained clothing was found, along with various other souvenirs, including jewellery and photos of the victims.

It was too late for 15-year-old Olga Galtseva, who died the following day from the stab wound to her chest.

On October 5th 1999, Spesivtsev was declared insane and committed to a mental hospital by a court for the rape and killing of four young girls. His mother was sentenced to just 13 years in prison for being an accomplice in the murders.

As of 2021, Spesivtsev remains committed at the Kamyshin Regional Hospital, which is a locked neuropsychiatric specialised hospital.

Born **March 1st 1970.**

Active from **1991-1996.**

Arrested on **October 30th 1996.**

Country: **Russia.**

Victims: **4-80+.**

AKA: **The Siberian Ripper / The Cannibal of Siberia.**

Sentence: **Committed to psychiatric institute.**

Current whereabouts: **High-security psychiatric hospital.**

Stafford, Roger Dale

On June 22nd 1978, serial killer *Roger Dale Stafford*, along with his wife and brother, flagged down a vehicle on the side of Interstate 35 in Oklahoma. Stafford then robbed and murdered the entire Lorenz family; Melvin, Linda and their 12-year-old son.

He began killing in 1974 when he shot dead an assistant manager working at a *McDonald's* in Alabama. In July 1978, he would kill six employees at a *Sirloin Stockade* restaurant in Oklahoma City during a robbery.

He was quickly arrested and then convicted in 1979 before his execution in 1995 by lethal injection. Stafford's wife would later implicate him in the killing of 34 people.

Born in **1951**.

Active from **1974-1978**.

Arrested on **March 13th 1979**.

Country: **USA**.

Victims: **9-34**.

Sentence: **Death penalty**.

Current whereabouts: **Executed by lethal injection in 1995.**

Stano, Gerald Eugene: The Boardwalk Serial Killer (Extended Case File)

On August 5th 1978, *Sandra DeBose* was found shot to death in West Cocoa, Florida. She is one of many victims of a horrific serial killer named *Gerald Stano*. If ever there was a case of nature versus nurture and nature winning out then Stano is it. He is Florida's worst serial killer and has been linked with up to 90 murders.

His beginnings were more than brutal. He was born *Paul Zeininger* in 1951, in New York, his mother already had four other children, three of whom she had given up for adoption. Paul was also then put up for adoption. He was adopted by Eugene and Norma Stano whose hearts went out to the malnourished and neglected boy.

When he was just 13-months old, a team of psychologists and social workers examined him and determined that he would be unable to be adopted due to severe neglect. According to psychologists at the time, the 13-month-old was functioning with animalistic behaviour.

It was written that he would remove his own diaper and play with his own excrement. Clearly, the neglect from his birth mother had been so bad, that the boy had been dehumanised from birth.

Undeterred, the Stano's adopted him six months later. We do know that many serial killers suffer abuse during childhood, but not much research has been carried out on abuse on babies and the psychological effects on their development. Being adopted comes with its own dangers, with the FBI claiming that 16% of all serial killers had been adopted at some point in their childhood.

The *lost identity* in being adopted sometimes leads to the child questioning who their parents actually were and then they might paint a morbid picture of their parents in their heads. There is also very few studies on the impact of adoption in serial killer cases.

Fitting into the *McDonald Triad,* Stano was a bed wetter up until the age of ten-years-old and was emotionally distant from everyone. During his teens, he was isolated, preferring to be alone which made him a target for bullies in school. Teenage girls, specifically, would make fun of him and use him as the basis for belittlement and emotional bullying.

In 1967, the family moved to Pennsylvania in the hope that Stano's behaviour might get better but it worsened. His adoptive parents were still sure that they could give him the life he deserved and the love he never received.

They still believed there was good in him.

Stano had killed his first two victims in 1969, in Pennsylvania. The rest of his alleged 33 victims were between 1973 and 1980, in the Florida region.

After a graduation when he was 21-years-old, he moved into a motel and then got a job at a hospital but was fired for stealing money again. He then moved with his parents to Florida and found himself moving from job to job, mostly because of being fired for theft, or lack of attendance.

He married a local woman in 1975 and for a while things were going well. However, he began drinking heavily and only a few months after being married he started abusing his wife, physically and emotionally. She quickly filed for divorce and he moved back in with his parents again.

He would later receive the death penalty for stabbing to death 17-year-old *Cathy Lee Scharf* in Brevard County, in 1973. Stano preyed on prostitutes and hitchhikers whose ages ranged from 13 to 35-years-old.

They were killed either by shooting, stabbing, or strangulation. Because none of his discovered victims were raped, it was concluded by psychiatrists that his motives arose from simply enjoying the act of killing.

"I can't stand a bitchy chick."

Stano's reply to an officer when asked his reason for the murders.

In April 1980, he was arrested after an intended victim managed to escape from him. She had fallen into a police station with stab wounds, dripping in blood, but later surviving the attack. Her evidence was vital in catching him, it is said that if she had not managed to escape then many more lives would have been lost.

In his confession, Stano directed the investigation to the buried remains of 24 identifiable victims and two Jane Does. There is a theory that officers were feeding him information about the murders. But it doesn't quite stack up because if they knew where the bodies were, then they wouldn't have waited for Stano to tell them. He also described wound details that would only later become known in coroner's reports.

By December 1983, he had provided details of 41 victims and had already been sentenced to eight life terms before the death sentence received for his 1973 killing of Cathy Lee Scharf.

It is suggested that he may have killed more than 41 people and even as many as 90. It's also suggested that he was coerced into confessing crimes he didn't commit. An investigation into his murders and other crimes in the area at the time is still being undertaken.

The evidence was stacked against him and he was finally executed in the electric chair in 1998.

Born **September 12th 1951**.

Active from **1974-1986**.

Arrested on **April 1st 1980**.

Country: **USA**.

Victims: **22-41**.

AKA: **The Boardwalk Serial Killer**.

Sentence: **Death penalty**.

Current whereabouts: **Executed in electric chair in 1998**.

(Research Article #23) The Rise of True Crime Pornography

The influence of violent sexual images is still debated and argued over to this day. Although almost all men who see such images do not go on to sexually assault or even murder women, there are a small amount of men who do. Violent pornography is not a main cause of serial killing but it is attributed as one of the factors than can inspire someone to want to kill.

True crime pornography is vastly different from actual pornography as we perceive it to be in the 21st Century. In 1989, *Ted Bundy* claimed it was an overbearing exposure to the *True Detective* magazine that opened his eyes to what could be. Before his execution, he met with *Dr. James Dobson*, who was a campaigner against pornography and a religious psychologist.

He told Dobson when he was growing up, he had become addicted to *True Detective* magazine and other magazines similar to its type. The front covers of some of the magazines contain images that in this day and age would be considered exploitative and sexually explicit. They generally showed images of sexual violence against women.

True Police Cases, *October 1971.*

Front cover is of a woman in her bra showing cleavage and bare legs hidden only by small shorts. Her wrists are tied and her arms are hoisted above her head with rope. With the following headline; Before dying, the stabbed girl cried; "Please untie me, I've been raped."

Real Detective, *April 1980.*

Cover is of a scared woman, bound and gagged, her top has been ripped down the front and her cleavage is showing, barely protected by her bra. An unseen man behind her is leaning over her with a length of rope, ready to strangle her. Headline; "Now no one else can save her!"

True Detective, *June 1959.*

A man crouches behind a terrified women as she is on the floor. Her hands are tied behind her back and he is wrapping a cloth around her mouth to gag and silence her. Headline; "The frightened blonde who saw murder." At the bottom left corner is a smaller piece of text that says; "Girls for sale."

True Police Cases, *October 1978.*

A screaming woman is fighting with a man who has a gun in his hand, he has his arm around her neck. Her denim jacket is thrown open and she is not wearing a bra, her breasts are close to being exposed. Headline; "Playboy bunnies held as sex slaves! Drugged and defiled!"

Detective Cases, *October 1976.*

A naked women, barely covered by her bedsheets, tan-lines obvious, is sprawled out as if she has just been murdered. Headline; "It looks like a wild animal mauled her in bed." At the top line of the front cover; "Can you rape... a whore?"

Inside Detective, *August 1976.*

A topless man is holding a knife to a terrified woman's neck as she is laying on a bed. A mirror reflection shows her legs to be open, she is wearing a small pink top and her mouth is wide open. Headline; "An orgy of blood at the massage parlour."

Best True Fact Detective, *September 1980.*

A woman is laying on her front on the floor of a dark room, she has been tied with rope in a way associated with bondage and has duct tape over her mouth. She is looking at the supposed photographer with fear in her eyes. She appears to be topless and is wearing small pink panties that accentuate her rear. Headline; "Let's rape the girl next door."

That last one would be heavily censored, if not moved to the adult section of the shelves. The image is heavily comparable with BDSM and is just like those found in hardcore porn and fetish sites today. Images described in the previous examples with those types of headlines were all the rage in the middle to the end of the Twentieth Century. People couldn't get enough of it.

Generally, the images didn't have much to do with the inner pages of the magazine but offer a tantalising entry into a world of true crime, murder and serial killers of the day. For the likes of Bundy and others, it had launched their addiction to violence

"Pornography can reach in and snatch the kid out of any house today. It snatched me out of my home."

Ted Bundy to Dobson.

True crime magazines could be bought by incredibly young children with no age restrictions. Having reviewed a lot of the front covers of these types of magazines I would argue that some of them are borderline, if not clearly pornographic. Or at least they insinuate something else quite entirely.

It is in this insinuation that can lead one to use their own imagination and fill in the gaps. These types of teasing images can allow one to create their own story, their own fantasy around them. For those who already have a predilection towards violence or sexual perversity, it can give them opportunity to amplify their thoughts.

Hundreds of millions of people today view porn or sexual images, they might do so healthily and are not influenced to act upon any dark thoughts which may arise. But then most people have good moral boundaries and ethical ways in which they live their lives. Some do not and so porn or true crime exploitation fuels their already existing desires further.

Because so many serial killers have cited porn as one of their factors of killing, then it simply cannot be ignored. We can't blame true crime magazines, but we can look at the influence they might have had on allowing people to revel in their own fantasies. In some instances it might be the first stepping-stone to seeking out harsher and more sexually explicit images.

A study put forward a four-step syndrome of how porn can affect a person viewing such images.

Addiction to viewing images.

Increased appetite to seek more images.

Desensitisation to the images.

Acting out the images.

In the 1970s and earlier decades, sex education was not something that was generally taught in schools. Children would learn either through their family members, peers or exploratory methods. For some, true crime magazines had become their sex education. The publications put out a violent understanding of sexual encounters and were generally focused on domination and control.

There are other pop culture elements such as horror films, horror stories, thriller books, satanic music, and various other publications which might coerce one's view on violence and sex. Yet we cannot deny the availability of true crime magazines on the youth of the mid-Twentieth Century.

According to other killers like *Denis Radar,* he claimed that the magazines inspired him to practice new ways of restraining his victims and got him in the *mood to kill.*

Melvin Rees, Jr. killed seven people in the 1950s and blamed it on true crime magazines.

In the modern era, far more shocking images and videos are accessible from just a few clicks on the internet. Children can find a world of the most degrading sexual images at the click of a button. We could be headed for another violent crime epidemic if we're not already in the midst of one.

(Research Article #24) The Rise of Violent Pornography

In the *True Crime Pornography* research article, we discussed the effect of images of women under duress on fragile minds. That people like Ted Bundy claimed porn was an influence and motivation for his own desires is scary enough. That the type of porn available in today's world is more disturbing than ever is even scarier.

In the 1970s, porn was a relatively new thing, at least to the mainstream masses. Amateur photography was on the increase and VHS was about to make its mark on history. It wouldn't have been easy to find porn back in the 1970s.

The likes of Bundy and Dennis Radar said it had influenced their outlooks on women and was a contributing factor in both of their cases.

In 2020 and leading up to 2028, porn is at an unprecedented level of accessibility. It is one of the biggest industries in the world and one of the most searched for terms on the internet. Just a few clicks and every kind of porn is available to everyone.

It was relatively mild images that influenced the likes of Bundy and other serial killers. They used their own imagination to fuel their fantasies, using certain images only as a marker in their mind's eye.

Today, there is no need for imagination. Every type of porn; bizarre or degrading, is instantly available to every age group on any device, anywhere in the world. Some countries have banned some elements of the internet but it doesn't stop people using proxy servers to navigate their way around a firewall to the entire World Wide Web.

Because of the type of images now readily available to everyone, the rise of the serial killer in 2028, fifty years after 1978, is inevitable. As is the rise in mental health issues amongst young people who are witness to such images and who use them as a basis for a normal relationship.

The days of soft-core true detective magazines are still with us. But they pale in comparison to the vast amount of violent pornography that fills over half of the known internet.

Internet anonymity has afforded people with dark thoughts to talk to others about their fantasies or use social media to spark up dehumanising conversations. Some comments underneath degrading images might leave one struggling to see any resemblance of the ethical and moral society we believed we lived in.

This stuff is easily accessible by children, who's developing brains can and will be affected by what they see. It in essence changes their outlook on other people, sexual relations, and the way they perceive the world.

Steinwegs, Kurt-Friedhelm

A German serial killer convicted of six murders in a seven-year period, he is also known as '*The Monster from Lower Rhine*'. In 1978, he killed 13-year-old *Andrew Robinson*, whilst Steinwegs was living with his father after a divorce.

Shortly after, he was committed to a psychiatric hospital where he killed another four people. He would take great care in removing the genitalia of his victims.

When he was arrested in 1984 he confessed to six murders but may have killed more. Upon his arrest he was named '*The Beast*' due to the viciousness of his murders. As of 2021, he remains imprisoned in a forensic clinic in Germany.

Being sent to a forensic clinic in Germany means the patient has been found unfit to be detained in a prison or mental health facility.

Born **December 5th 1960**.

Active from **1974-1983**.

Arrested in **1984**.

Country: **Germany**.

Victims: **6+**.

AKA: **The Monster from Lower Rhine / The Beast**.

Sentence: **Committed to a high-security psychiatric institute**.

Current whereabouts: **High-security psychiatric institute**.

Stoneman, The

In India, over a four year period, at least 13 homeless people were killed during their sleep. They were killed by an unidentified killer known only as The Stoneman.

The murders took place in Calcutta but at the same time, another 13 homeless people were killed in a similar fashion in Mumbai, two cities over 1,200 miles apart. The same moniker was also given to the Mumbai killer whose victims were killed during 1985 to 1988.

It has since been suggested that the killings were committed by the same person, which meant that The Stoneman was responsible for at least 26 murders. It still remains unclear why the homeless people were killed, or if they were murdered by one individual or a group.

The victims were all killed in the same fashion. The killer or killers found a homeless person sleeping alone in a dark area of the city. Then they would crush the victims head with a single stone that weighed as much as 30 kilograms. Almost all of the victims remain unidentified and it wasn't until the sixth murder that the police began to see the connections.

As of 2021, all the murders remain unsolved and no one has ever been linked with the killings.

Active from **1985-1989**.

Country: **India**.

Victims: **13-26+**.

Current whereabouts: **Unidentified killer. Status Unknown.**

Storozhenko, Vladimir

He was a soviet serial killer also known as '*The Smolensky Strangler*' who killed 13 people from 1978 to 1981. His crimes were carried out in the city of Smolensk in Russia. In that time period, there were more than 20 violent sexual attacks on women and girls in the city, 13 of them resulted in murder.

Although he was called a '*strangler*' he would always brutally torture his victims before killing them. One of his younger victims, a 12-year-old student from a local school, was discovered in a sand pit and she had been tortured before her death.

His final victim managed to escape and recognised a tattoo when shown photos of suspects. Storozhenko was sentenced to death by firing squad in 1984.

Born in **1953**.

Active from **1978-1981**.

Arrested on **July 21st 1981**.

Country: **Soviet Union**.

Victims: **13**.

AKA: **The Smolensky Strangler**.

Sentence: **Death penalty**.

Current whereabouts: **Executed by firing squad in 1984**.

Suradji, Ahmad: The Black Magic Killer (Extended Case File)

In Indonesia, *Ahmad Suradji, AKA: The Black Magic Killer*, killed at least 42 young girls and women between 1986 and 1997. He became known by many names, including *Dukan AS, Nasib Kelewang, Datuk Maringgi,* or *The Sorcerer.*

Suradji's victims were between the ages of 11-years-old to 30-years-old and were part of an ongoing ritual that saw him requiring 70 victims. He strangled them and buried them in the ground up to their waists, on his sugar cane plantation. He *planted* them in such a way that their heads were facing his house, believing their positions imbibed him with extra powers.

He lived in Medan, in the North Sumatran region of Indonesia, where he worked as a cattle-breeder. He claimed to be a *dukun*, which is a class of shaman who are supposed to hold supernatural powers. He assisted local women on how to find fortune and how to keep their beauty.

In 1986, Suradji's deceased father visited him in a dream and commanded him to murder 70 females as part of a larger black magic ritual. Believing it to be a real commandment, he began his campaign of murder. He married three sisters, who lived with him on the plantation and appeased his every need. Upon his arrest, they were also arrested on conspiracy to murder as accomplices.

He told them of the visitation from his father and what needed to be done. He claimed that by killing 70 women, he would become even more powerful and be able to perform more elaborate and compelling acts of supernatural magic, including becoming a mystical healer. Although he was linked to 42 murders, there were reports at the time that over 80 people had gone missing in the area and that he may have reached his target of 70.

In 1997, a 21-year-old girl named *Sri Kemala Dewi*, was dropped off by a rickshaw driver at the home of the datuk healer. Three days later, her naked body was discovered in a sugar cane field. The rickshaw driver told police that he had dropped her off at the home of Suradji. Upon visiting the property, they found items belonging to the victim, including her handbag.

On April 30th 1997, Suradji was arrested. He confessed to her murder and the murders of at least 42 other females in the same manner. When the investigation turned to excavating the sugar cane plantation, 42 bodies were found with some so far along the decomposition process that they could not be identified.

He claimed his father's ghost told him to drink the saliva of 70 dead women to reach the level of power that he wanted to have. He said it would have taken too many lifetimes to encounter 70 dead women and so he decided to kill in order to drink their saliva and speed up the process of gaining more magical powers.

"My father did not specifically advise me to kill people. So I was thinking, it will take ages if I have to wait to get seventy women. I was trying to get to it as fast as possible, I took my own initiative to kill."

He chose victims from the women that came to visit him for spiritual guidance and magical assistance. Enough women were coming to him but when he had a gap with no victims, he purposely went out to seek prostitutes and homeless women. Word spread around local villages of his healing powers, so more and more people came his way to gain advice or assistance.

Before he would give guidance, or healing, he charged each of his victims the going rate for the ritual which was approximately $200 USD. For those who wanted to be more sexually attractive to men, he would charge more. Once he had the money in hand, he led them to the deaths.

He took them into the nearby sugar cane fields where he had the victims dig their own graves before burying them up to their waist. They believed it was all part of a magical healing ritual. When they couldn't move out of the mud, he then strangled them until they were dead and drank the saliva from their mouths. Then he removed the clothes of the victims and buried them back in the ground with their heads facing his house.

Suradji's three wives were investigated after the murders were discovered but only one was charged as his accomplice. *Tumini* went on trial at the same time as Suradji. She received the death penalty but it was later commuted to life in prison. His other two wives had no knowledge of the murders or ritual.

"The black magic came from God. I don't have it anymore, I have repented. I hope I have a chance to live."

Suradji – in a final interview.

Suradji was sentenced to death and was executed by firing squad on July 10th 2008. He was allowed one last liaison with his convicted wife, Tumini, before he was led out to the firing range.

Born **January 10th 1949**.

Active from **1986-1997**.

Arrested on **April 30th 1997**.

Country: **Indonesia**.

Victims: **42+**.

AKA: **The Black Magic Killer**.

Sentence: **Death penalty**.

Current whereabouts: **Executed by firing squad on July 10th 2008**.

Sutcliffe, Peter: The Yorkshire Ripper (Extended Case File)

On January 21st 1978 *Yvonne Pearson*, a 21-year-old prostitute from Bradford, UK, was bludgeoned to death by *The Yorkshire Ripper*. Her body would not be found for another two months.

After appearing at Peter Sutcliffe's car window, they had quickly agreed a price of only £5 for her services. They ended up at a waste ground where Sutcliffe hit her over the head with a hammer. But the story itself was to have more twists and turns than expected.

The following details are from Peter Sutcliffe's confession in 1981. Regarding the murder of Yvonne Pearson. The interview was recorded on January 5th, 1981 from 9:50am to 3:15pm.

"She stepped straight up to the car as I stopped and tapped on the window. She asked me if I wanted business. This was one time when I was genuinely going home as it happened, but I still had a hammer in the car on the floor, under my seat. I told her to get in. She suggested that I turn the car round and she told me where to drive.

"I drove back along Lumb Lane, past Drummond Mill, turned right down a road onto White Abbey Road, and I was directed to turn by Yvonne left into a street behind Silvios Bakery. I drove to the very end of this street where there was a large open space like a parking space and parked the car.

"I asked her how much she wanted. She said, 'It depends how much you can afford.' 'A good time £5, more than a good time £10.' She had very few words to say after that, the last words she said was, 'Shall we get into the back?' We both got out and she went round to the back door of the car on the nearside, she tried to open it but it was locked. I opened the front passenger door, reached in, and opened the rear door catch.

"As she opened the door, I hit her from behind twice on the head with the hammer. She fell down and started to moan loudly. I dragged her by the feet on her back about 20 yards or so to where there was an old settee lying on its back on some spare land. When I got her to the settee she was still moaning loudly. At that moment, a car drove up and parked next to my car.

"I saw there was a blond woman in the car and a man driving. To stop her moaning, I took some filling from the settee, I held her nose and shoved the straw into her mouth, then I shoved it down her throat. I was kneeling behind the settee, hiding from the motor car, keeping hold of her nose.

"I let go after a while to see if she was still making a noise through her nose, but when I did, she started again, so I took hold of her nose again. The car seemed to be there for ages before it drove away. I stayed still, petrified with fear while the car was there.

"When the car had gone I was seething with rage. Her jeans were nearly off, because she had undone them at the car, and when I was pulling her by the feet I nearly pulled them off. I pulled her jeans right off. I think I kicked her hard to the head and body. I was senseless with rage and I was kicking away furiously at her.

"After this, I remember acting very strangely, I talked to her and apologised for what I had done, but she was dead. I put the settee on top of her. I was very distraught and I was in tears when I left her. This was the first time I had apologised to someone I had killed. I drove home, I cannot recall the time, but it was after 9:00pm. I can't remember if Sonja was in the house or not.

"I remember stopping on the way home and I just sat in the car trying to work out why I had done this killing. My mind was in a turmoil."

He ended this section of his confession with an important line:

"...I didn't dare go back to where she lay, there was no reason to go back."

There is a mystery regarding Peter Sutcliffe and the Ripper murders and it's as mysterious as those of *Jack The Ripper*.

On March 26th, Easter Sunday in 1978, Yvonne Pearson's body was discovered under the sofa where Sutcliffe had left her. Her body had been putrefying for two months and had started to rot. She was spotted by a passer-by because her arm was sticking out from under the sofa.

Police were shocked that her body had not been found earlier in such an obvious position. There was also a copy of the *Daily Mirror* wedged underneath one of her arms, it appeared as though it had been deliberately positioned there. The newspaper was dated February 21st, exactly one month after the murder but Sutcliffe confirmed that he never returned to the body's location.

Regarding the body of Yvonne Pearson, *Professor David Gee's* examination of her led him to believe an alternative theory. He claimed that the injuries to her head were caused by a large rock or boulder and not a hammer. He concluded that it *wasn't* a victim of The Yorkshire Ripper.

Of course, this goes against Peter Sutcliffe's own confession. In stating that he apologised to Yvonne's corpse, it would seem pointless to lie about not going back to the body and so it remains a mystery to this day, although Sutcliffe was charged with her death.

As the murders escalated from 1977 until 1980, over 350 detectives from three counties had been involved at some point. The Ripper murders had cost the British taxpayer over £4million throughout the investigation.

There has been a theory put forward by *Noel O'Gara*, that Peter Sutcliffe was a *copycat* Yorkshire Ripper and the real Yorkshire Ripper was killing around the same time *and* after Sutcliffe's imprisonment. He went on to state that subsequent murders were covered up by the police as they couldn't risk the public knowing that the Ripper was still out there. Again, this is a theory and the evidence surrounding it is rather thin but it remains out there in the public domain.

Yet, Sutcliffe was convicted for killing 13 people and the attempted murder of seven others over a period of five years. He later claimed the voice of God had sent him on a mission to kill prostitutes. He was sentenced to life in prison without the possibility of parole.

In 2017, further investigations were underway looking at unsolved murders from 1964. Sutcliffe was a lorry driver who regularly went to Europe with his work. The investigation spread to Northern Europe and looked at possible links with the unsolved murders of sex workers in the region.

As of 2021, he remains incarcerated at *HM Prison Frankland* in County Durham, England.

Born **June 2nd 1946.**

Active from **1975-1980.**

Arrested on **January 2nd 1981.**

Country: **United Kingdom.**

Victims: **13+.**

AKA: **The Yorkshire Ripper.**

Sentence: **Life imprisonment.**

Current whereabouts: **In prison.**

IMAGE ATTRIBUTIONS
(ATTRIB A41) (ATTRIB A78)

PETER SUTCLIFFE

WORLD'S END PUB, HIGH STREET, EDINBURGH, WHERE SINCLAIR'S VICTIMS WERE LAST SEEN ALIVE

ANGUS SINCLAIR

IMAGE ATTRIBUTIONS
(ATTRIB A41) (ATTRIB A78)

Swango, Joseph Michael

American physician and serial killer Joseph Michael Swango is estimated to have killed at least 60 people through poisoning of patients and some of his colleagues. He admitted to four deaths but the investigation linked him to dozens more.

Swango joined the Marine Corps but received a discharge in 1976 for an unknown reason. He went to train at a medical school at Southern Illinois University School of Medicine (SIU). While there he went through a strict regime of physical training and was known to punish himself with push ups and jogging if he got something wrong.

From the moment he got a surgical internship, patients began mysteriously dying around him. He would kill by injecting them with drug overdoses. His crimes didn't stop at patients and he would drug his colleagues by preparing the food for them and lacing them with overdoses of sedatives.

By 1994, the medical community and an investigation was on to him so he changed his name and moved to Zimbabwe of all places. There he got a job in a hospital and continued to kill patients and colleagues. He was arrested in 1997 while boarding a flight to Saudi Arabia. First sentenced in Zimbabwe, he was subsequently extradited to the United States to be sentenced to three life terms with no parole.

As of 2021, he remains incarcerated at the ADX Florence supermax prison near Florence, Colorado.

Born **October 21st 1954.**

Active from **1981-1997.**

Arrested in **June 1997.**

Country: **USA / Zimbabwe.**

Victims: **4-60+.**

AKA: **David J. Adams / Michael Kirk / Jack Kirk / Michael Swan.**

Sentence: **Three life sentences.**

Current whereabouts: **In prison.**

Thwala, Sipho

Sipho Mandla Agmatir Thwala is a South African rapist and serial killer who murdered at least 16 women and raped an additional 10. He began his killing spree in 1996, in South Africa's KwaZulu-Natal province.

He would lure young local women into the sugar cane fields just outside of the town of Phoenix, with the offer of employment. He would then attack them from behind, tie them up with their own underwear and rape them. Afterwards he would strangle or beat them to death and leave them to be burned in the sugar cane fields.

He was arrested a year later in 1997 after DNA from one of his victims matched his from a previous arrest. In 1999, he was found guilty of 16 murders and 10 rapes and sentenced to 506 years in prison. As of 2021, he is incarcerated at a prison in Pretoria, South Africa.

Born in **1968**.

Active from **1996-1997**.

Arrested on **August 14th 1997**.

Country: **South Africa.**

Victims: **16-20+.**

AKA: **Sipho Mandla Agmatir Thwala / Phoenix Strangler / Cane field Killer.**

Sentence: **506 years in prison.**

Current whereabouts: **In prison.**

Tinning, Marybeth

Nine children would die under American serial killer, *Marybeth Roe Tinning's* care, during a 14 year period from 1971. She was convicted of only one murder, that of her ninth child, four-month-old *Tami Lynne*, in 1985. She was suspected of being involved in the deaths of her eight previous children.

Six autopsies were carried out on most of the children and their causes of death varied from natural to unnatural. She was released on parole in August 2018 and vehemently denied all the murders except that of her daughter in 1985.

Her husband believed Marybeth to be innocent and stood by her all the time she was incarcerated. He was there to meet her at the gates of the prison upon her release.

Born **September 11th 1942**.

Active from **1971-1985**.

Arrested on **February 4th 1986**.

Country: **USA**.

Victims: **1-9**.

Sentence: **20 years to life in prison**.

Current whereabouts: **Released in August 2018**.

Tkach, Serhiy Fedorovich

Over a 25 year period, from 1980 to 2005, Ukrainian serial killer *Serhiy Fedorovich Tkach* killed at least 37 women and girls. He confessed to over 100 more murders at his trial.

Tkach targeted young female victims between the ages of 8-years-old and 18-years-old. He would rape them before suffocating or strangling them. He would engage in sexual acts with their corpses, before leaving their bodies at random locations throughout the country.

In a chilling comparison with fellow Soviet serial killer, *Andrei Chikatilo*, Tkach chose victims near railway lines and especially those that had recently been installed. The tar of the tracks covered the scent of some of the bodies, meaning that police dogs were thrown off course.

In 2005, Tkach had the gumption to attend the funeral of one of his victims. It was other children at the funeral who raised the alarm as they had seen Tkach with the dead girl shortly before her abduction and death. He was arrested shortly after and confessed to over 100 murders.

In 2008, he was sentenced to life without parole for the murder of 37 victims. Ten years later on November 4th 2018, Tkach died of natural causes and was buried by prison staff. Thus ending the life of one of Ukraine's most notorious serial killers.

Born **September 15th 1952.**

Active from **1980-2005.**

Arrested in **August 2005.**

Country: **Soviet Union / Ukraine.**

Victims: **37-100+.**

AKA: **Pavlohrad Maniac / Polohy Maniac.**

Sentence: **Life imprisonment.**

Current whereabouts: **Died of natural causes on November 4th 2018.**

Tobin, Peter: Bible John (Extended Case File)

Scottish serial killer and rapist *Peter Britton Tobin* killed three women over an extended period of time and raped many others. In 1991, he killed two teenage girls and hid their bodies in the flat he had at the time, in Kent, England.

On February 10th 1991, 15-year-old schoolgirl *Vicky Hamilton* vanished from a bus stop in Falkirk, Scotland. Tobin fled Scotland to a new flat in Kent, shortly after he had killed her. He took her body with him. Six months later, in Essex, England, 18-year-old student *Dinah McNicol* vanished while hitchhiking with her boyfriend. The boyfriend was dropped off where he wanted to go but McNicol stayed in the car.

Over the coming months, regular withdrawals of £250, were taken from ATM's using her card. It was the maximum one could withdraw from a cash machine at the time. The withdrawals were out of character for McNicol and so it was later suspected that Tobin had forced her to give him her PIN, in order to take money out. Both of the 1991 victims were not discovered until late 2007, when a forensic search of the house turned up their remains.

In 1993, he raped two 14-year-old-girls at his flat in England. Leigh Park in Havant is a large residential area just north of Portsmouth. The two girls went to visit a neighbour who wasn't in so asked to wait in Tobin's flat.

He then held them at knifepoint, forced alcohol down their throats and then raped them. He stabbed one of them and turned the gas on in the house to kill them. Somehow they survived the attack and went straight to the police. Tobin went on the run. To avoid police he joined a religious sect in Coventry, England, named the *Jesus Fellowship*. He was arrested shortly after in Brighton, on the southern coast of the country.

In 1994, he was sentenced to 14 years in prison but only served 10. He was released in 2004 and sent back to Scotland, where he disappeared from the authorities by exploiting open-door policies at churches and religious groups. He went under many different names in order to remain '*off-the-grid*' and hid the fact he was on the sex offenders' register.

In September 2006, he attacked and killed 23-year-old Polish student *Angelika Kluk*, who was staying in the accommodation building of a church that Tobin was working at. She was raped, beaten and stabbed to death. He hid her body under the floor of the church, near to the confessional booth.

A few days later, her body was discovered and Tobin was arrested. He had gone to Accident and Emergency under a false name with a false ailment, simply to avoid detection. Tobin was charged and went to trial in 2007, where he was found guilty of the rape and murder of Kluk. Tobin was sentenced to a minimum of 21 years in prison.

Shortly after, Tobin was connected to other crimes, and an investigation looked at older cases. Due to the number of properties that Tobin was known to have lived in, forensic searches of numerous houses and flats were undertaken across the country, including one at the seaside town of Southsea, Hampshire.

On November 14th 2007, police confirmed that human remains had been unearthed at a former residence of Tobin's, in Margate, Kent. The first remains to be discovered was that of 15-year-old Hamilton. At the same time, Essex Police opened a cold case for Dinah McNicol and linked up with the Tobin investigation. A few days after Hamilton's remains were discovered, McNicol's remains were discovered in the grounds of the same house.

In November 2008, Tobin was transferred to a court in Dundee, Scotland, where he was convicted for the murder of Hamilton. After a trial which lasted a month, Tobin had his 21-year sentence increased to a 30 years minimum.

"Yet again you have shown yourself to be unfit to live in a decent society. It is hard for me to convey the loathing and revulsion that ordinary people will feel for what you have done."

The judge in Hamilton's murder trial.

For McNicol's murder, Tobin went to trial in 2009, in an Essex court. His defence offered no evidence in Tobin's favour. It took less than 15 minutes for the jury to find him guilty, and he was sentenced to an additional life term. On the same day that Tobin was convicted for the third murder, police reopened what they called *Operation Anagram*.

Investigators came to believe that Tobin may have been involved in at least 13 more murders. He was also linked to the *Bible John Murders* in Glasgow, which remain unsolved to this day. The three murders were similar in style to Tobin's method of murder, and he would have been in and around the area at the time.

The artist photofit of Bible John matched photos of how Tobin looked at the time. Eyewitnesses claimed that the suspect had one tooth missing on the right-hand side of his mouth. Tobin had one tooth removed in the late 1960s, in the same place that matched eyewitness accounts. He got the name of Bible John because it was suspected that he went to rape his victims but found them in the middle of their menstrual cycle, so he killed them instead

He also left Glasgow just a few weeks after the final known Bible John murder. Unfortunately, police recently confirmed that DNA evidence from the three Bible John murders had deteriorated due to incorrect storage of the samples. This means that if Tobin was Bible John, then without a confession, it would be difficult to now prove.

Operation Anagram went into full speed in 2010. Police forces across the United Kingdom checked DNA against cold cases and followed up on missing people that would have been connected with Tobin. In the end, multiple murder cases of teenage girls and women were reopened.

During interviews with Tobin, psychiatrists and profilers suggested that he most likely had killed many more, beyond the three he had been convicted for. The operation diminished in 2011 when they failed to positively link any more victims to Tobin. Since then, many investigators have suggested that he would have killed more.

While in prison, Tobin boasted to a psychiatrist that he had ended the lives of 48 people. He then leaned in with a smile and said;

"*Prove it.*"

There was even a connection to the infamous 'Babes in the Woods' murders in Brighton, England. 10-year-old *Karen Hadaway*, and nine-year-old *Nicola Fellows*, had been raped and strangled to death, with their bodies dumped in an open field. Currently, no positive connection has been made.

As of 2021, Peter Tobin remains alive and incarcerated at an Edinburgh prison. He has recently suffered a heart attack and is also suffering from cancer. Family members of the victims wish him to live as long as possible, so that he can suffer before he finally dies.

Born **August 27th 1946.**

Active from **1991-2006.**

Arrested on **October 3rd 2006.**

Country: **United Kingdom.**

Victims: **3-13+.**

AKA: **Bible John.**

Sentence: **Life sentence plus 30 years.**

Current whereabouts: **In prison.**

The Monstrous Book of Serial Killers (2nd edition)

PETER TOBIN

IMAGE ATTRIB. A39

METOD TROBEC

IMAGE ATTRIB. A90

GWENDOLYN GRAHAM

IMAGE ATTRIB. A18A/A18B

CATHERINE WOOD

Trobec, Metod

Trobec was a Slovenian serial killer. Slovenia was one of the surviving states of former Yugoslavia and he was born a Yugoslavian. He began his crimes at an early age, mostly involving arson or theft. In a two year period from 1976 to 1978, he raped, killed and cremated at least five women.

His body count might have been higher but suggested victims have never been officially linked to him.

He was the last person to be sentenced to death in Slovenia but he killed himself in 1996.

Born **July 6th 1948**.

Active from **1976-1978**.

Country: **Yugoslavia / Slovenia**.

Victims: **5+**.

AKA: **The Monster of Gorejne Vasi**.

Sentence: **Death penalty**.

Current whereabouts: **Committed suicide in 1996**.

Trudeau, Yves

'The Mad Bumper' killed 43 people. *Yves 'Apache' Trudeau* was a member of the Hells Angels North Chapter outlaw motorcycle gang in Quebec. He was labelled a psychopathic killer and killing machine by those who knew him and interviewed him afterwards.

He became anxious through copious use of cocaine and suspected his fellow gang members were plotting to kill him. So he became a government informant and received a lenient sentence in exchange for supplying information. He was given life in prison but was paroled after seven years.

He was arrested again in 2004 and sentenced to four years for sexually assaulting a young boy. In 2007 he was transferred to a medical centre where he died of cancer shortly after.

Born **February 4th 1946**.

Active from **1973-1985**.

Country: **Canada**.

Victims: **43**.

AKA: **The Mad Bumper / Apache**.

Sentence: **Life sentence**.

Current whereabouts: **Died of cancer in 2007**.

Tuchlin, Pawel

The Polish serial killer was also known as the 'Scorpion'. He was convicted of killing nine women and the attempted killing of another 11 people. He attacked a total of 20 women and killed his victims with a bloody hammer.

The hammer was carefully wrapped up with a bandage because it made his stomach cold when he wore his pants looking for victims.

After his sentencing he believed the authorities would release him from prison in order to hunt down the real murderer.

He was hung in 1987 for his crimes.

Born **April 28th 1946.**

Active from **1975-1983.**

Country: **Poland.**

Victims: **9.**

AKA: **The Scorpion.**

Sentence: **Death penalty.**

Current whereabouts: **Executed by hanging in 1987.**

Ture, Joseph Donald Jr.

In Washington County, Minnesota on May 10th 1979, 18-year-old **Marlys Wohlenhaus** died of injuries sustained in a brutal axe attack two days earlier. She had been found by her mother on the floor of their basement. A $50,000 (USD) reward for information was offered which led to the arrest of a wanted serial killer.

Joseph Donald Ture Jr. was later convicted of her murder. He would kill at least six people by shooting or beating them with an axe. He was arrested and charged with the Wohlenhaus murder. In 1981, he was sentenced to life in prison. But it was the tip of the iceberg.

In 1978, Alice Huling and three of her four children were shot dead with a shotgun at their home near Clearwater. The fourth child played dead to escape being shot. Their murders remained unsolved until a 2000 trial found Ture guilty of their slayings. He was given a life sentence for each murder.

Born in **1951.**

Active from **1978-1979.**

Arrested in **1979.**

Country: **USA.**

Victims: **6+**

Current whereabouts: **Serving a life sentence in Minnesota jail.**

Turner, Chester Dewayne

On March 9th 1987, in Los Angeles, 21-year-old *Diane Johnson* was murdered by American serial killer, *Chester Dewayne Turner,* AKA: *The Southside Slayer*. The victims was confirmed by DNA evidence provided by police and he was finally arrested in 2003.

On October 29th 1987, 26-year-old *Annette Ernest* was found dead along the hard shoulder near Grand Avenue and 106th Street in Vermont Vista. She had been raped and strangled to death by Turner.

Chester DeWayne Turner was sentenced to death in 2007 for the murder of Ernest and nine other women. Authorities believe he was tied to another seven killings.

In 2007, he was first convicted of killing 10 women from 1987 to 1998, in addition to the death of an unborn child. By 2014 he was convicted of another four murders, bringing his total to 15 victims, and suspected of many more. He is suspected to be one of the most prolific serial killers in the city of Los Angeles.

He received death sentences in both trials, and as of 2021 he remains on death row.

Born **November 5th 1966.**

Active from **1987-1998.**

Arrested in **September 2003.**

Country: **USA.**

Victims: **15+.**

AKA: **The Southside Slayer.**

Sentence: **Death penalty.**

Current whereabouts: **Death row.**

Unterweger, Jack

An Austrian serial killer who would go on to kill at least ten victims. He was convicted first in Austria of a single murder in 1974. Believing him to be rehabilitated, he was released on parole in 1990. He became a popular playwright and journalist but ended up secretly killing women.

He was then convicted of another nine murders in 1994 and he killed himself in prison by hanging in the same year. Unterweger would usually kill prostitutes or sex-industry workers by beating them, raping them with tree branches, and strangling them with their own underwear.

Born **August 16th 1951.**

Active from **1974-1992.**

Arrested on **February 27th 1992.**

Country: **Austria / USA.**

Victims: **10+.**

AKA: **Vienna Woods Killer.**

Sentence: **Life imprisonment.**

Current whereabouts: **Committed suicide by hanging.**

Urdiales, Andrew: The Monster in the Desert (Extended Case File)

American serial killer *Andrew Urdiales*, sometimes referred to as *The Monster in the Desert*, was convicted on two counts of murder in 2002 and another five counts of murder in 2018. He is known to have killed eight women but may have killed at least two more.

He was said to have been raised in a happy home but when he was 11-years-old, he took a baseball bat and bludgeoned his family's dog to death. He told his parents that the dog had been injured after falling from a wall. After he completed school, he enrolled in the Marine Corps, served in Desert Storm in Iraq, and was stationed at Pendleton, California, until 1991.

He committed his first murder in January of 1986. He chose his victim deliberately and followed her on numerous occasions, to know her routine. He then stabbed 23-year-old student, *Robin Brandley*, 41 times. Her body was discovered the next day in the spot where she had died. Urdiales was a serving Marine at the time. While he was a Marine, he would kill five women.

He killed three more women, two of them prostitutes, in 1988 and 1989. Most of the time, he didn't hide the bodies but left them where he had killed them. In 1992, a year after his discharge from the Marine Corp, he met 19-year-old *Jennifer Asbenson*, in California, while on holiday.

He lured her into his car, drove her out to the desert then raped her before dumping her in the trunk of his rental car. She managed to escape but her story wasn't believed by local police. It wouldn't be for many years until Jennifer's story finally rang true with police and with the public.

Out of fear he would be caught, Urdiales didn't kill again until 1995 when the urge became too strong to resist. Upon a brief return to California, he raped and murdered 32-year-old prostitute *Denise Maney*, before dumping her body in the desert. Urdiales would usually cross State lines in order to kill.

A forensic psychiatrist named Dr. Park Dietz, stated that Urdiales was motivated by a misplaced revenge on the world, he wanted to kill women who rejected him or didn't serve him as he wished. Another stated that he was a monster masquerading as a respectable member of the military.

On April 14th 1996, the body of 25-year-old *Laura Ulyaki* was discovered in Wolf Lake, on the border of Chicago and Indiana. She had been raped and murdered just days earlier.

On July 14th 1996, the body of 21-year-old *Cassandra Corum* was discovered in the Vermilion River Mountains in Illinois. He pleaded not guilty to her murder and tried to claim mental incapacity. On the advice of his lawyers, he changed his plea to guilty.

On August 2nd 1996, the body of 22-year-old *Lynn Huber* was discovered in Wolf Lake. She too had been raped and murdered and was his last confirmed victim.

He was arrested for a second time in April of 1997, after an attack on a prostitute. They checked his weapon against the outstanding murders, but before the results came back he confessed to eight murders. Because the murders were in multiple States, it wasn't until 2002, after a lengthy trial that he would be found guilty of two murders and sentenced to death.

His death sentence was commuted to life in 2011, when Illinois Governor, Pat Quinn, signed an order to abolish the death penalty in the State. But the trials didn't stop. In California, on May 23rd 2018, Urdiales was convicted of five murders, and a few months later he was also sentenced to death in California.

On November 2nd 2018, while on death row at San Quentin State Prison in California, Urdiales killed himself in his cell. Just one hour earlier, another death row inmate was found dead of a suspected suicide.

51-year-old Virendra Govin was sentenced to death in 2004 for the murders of four people. He and his brother had attacked four members of a family who owned the neighbouring motel. They strangled and beat them to death, before burning the bodies.

San Quentin State Prison confirmed that the two suicides were exactly one hour apart and by unknown causes, but some people didn't believe the official line. Some theorists at the time had claimed that something supernatural had stalked the death row cells of the prison and that the apparent suicides were not suicides at all. Still, the official line is that it was coincidence that they killed themselves on the same night.

In 2017, a year before his death, Jennifer Asbenson, who escaped his clutches but was not believed, finally got to testify against her attacker.

"I just tried to go somewhere else in my mind. I wanted to die."

"He's nobody that will ever have a hold of my emotions again."

Jennifer Asbenson.

She took a documentary crew to the location where she had been kidnapped and where she had escaped. She said that as she ran away from the car, Urdiales was chasing after her with a machete.

In October of 2018, Jennifer Asbenson released a book about her life an ordeal and how she went from being a victim to an inspiration to victims all over the world. Her book: *The Girl in the Treehouse: A Memoir*, is available at most international bookstores.

Born **June 4th 1964.**

Active from **1986-1996.**

Arrested on **April 23rd 1997.**

Country: **USA**.

Victims: **8+**.

AKA: **The Monster in the Desert.**

Sentence: **Death penalty.**

Current whereabouts: **Committed suicide on November 2nd 2018.**

Vakrinos, Dimitris

On August 6th 1987, 43-year-old *Panayiotis Gaglias* was murdered by Greek serial killer Dimitris Vakrinos. Gaglias was a guest in Vakrino's house and had threatened to go to the police over a stolen shotgun. Vakrinos killed him as he slept in his bed by hitting him with an iron bar.

He moved the body and dumped it on the side of a highway not too far away from his home. The body was found eight days later. Between 1987 and 1996, Vakrinos was a taxi driver who murdered five people over minor instances of disagreement. He attempted to kill another seven, along with a raft of other crimes including arson and robbery.

Vakrinos was a serial killer who had a bad childhood which led to him associating with sexual oppression, low self-esteem and excessive anger. As he was shorter than the average man, he responded to challenges by using weapons in place of his smaller stature.

Vakrinos was caught and arrested in April of 1997. In May of the same year he committed suicide in the prison's shower rooms by tying shoelaces to the shower head.

Born in **1962.**

Active from **1987-1995.**

Arrested on **April 6th 1997.**

Country: **Greece.**

Victims: **5.**

Current whereabouts: **Committed suicide by hanging in May 1997.**

Vega, Jose Antonio Rodriguez

On August 6th 1987, in Santander, Spain, 82-year-old *Margarita González* was raped and suffocated by Spanish serial killer *José Antonio Rodríguez Vega*, AKA: *The Old Lady Killer*. He forced González to swallow her own false teeth.

Two more victims were named after being murdered in 1988. The names of the other victims were never released publicly. Vega was diagnosed as a psychopath who would ensure he knew his victim's routines inside out. He would then gain their trust until he was invited into their homes. Where he would cold-heartedly kill them.

He also took souvenirs from each of his victims including a television from one of them. Most of the murders were thought to have been caused by natural causes due to the age of the victims. It was only after his capture that police released a video of the items that Vega had collected that other families would come forward claiming they belonged to a deceased family member.

Vega raped and killed at least 16 elderly women from the ages of 61-years-old to 93-years-old over a nine-month period from 1987 to 1988. He was arrested in May 1988, convicted, and sentenced to 440 years in prison.

In October 2002 he was stabbed to death by two other prison inmates.

Born **December 3rd 1957.**

Active from **1987-1988.**

Arrested on **May 19th 1988.**

Country: **Spain.**

Victims: **16+.**

AKA: **The Old Lady Killer.**

Sentence: **440 years in prison.**

Current whereabouts: **Killed in prison in October 2002.**

Watts, Carl 'Coral'

Also known as '*The Sunday Morning Slasher*', Watts body count is suspected to be closer to 100 victims across an eight-year period. He was convicted of two murders but at least 80 more victims have been linked to him. Ever since he was 12-years-old, Watts claimed that he began dreaming of torturing and killing girls and women.

He is suspected to have killed his first victim by 15-years-old. When he was 20-years-old, in 1974, he was kidnapping victims from their home, torturing them and brutally murdering them. His crimes were not thought to be sexually related and it became difficult to link just one person with the murders.

He claimed he killed over 40 but subsequent investigations linked him with closer to 100 murders in total. He died of cancer in 2007.

Born **November 7th 1953.**

Active from **1974-1982.**

Arrested on **May 23rd 1982.**

Country: **USA.**

Victims: **14-100+.**

AKA: **The Sunday Morning Slasher.**

Sentence: **Life imprisonment.**

Current whereabouts: **Died of cancer in 2007.**

Waxin, Denis

Waxin was a French serial killer and child molester who killed three young girls between 1985 and 1999. During that time period he would also rape another girl and two small boys.

Waxin's father was strict while his mother was hard-working and it is claimed the parents never spoke to each other. Waxin was neglected as a child and left alone in isolation, his only solace was his older brother who left the home when Denis was 17-years-old. He became depressed and walked the streets alone for hours at a time.

The same year, in 1985, Waxin lured seven-year-old *Nathalie Hoareau* to an area of wasteland. There he raped and strangled her before stabbing her twice in the heart. Her partially nude body was discovered the same evening by police.

A few years later in 1990, he was confirmed to have killed nine-year-old *Cathy Monchaux* in Wazemmes. He lured her from her garden and took her to an old football field where he raped and then stabbed her fourteen times. Her body was found the next day by a dog-walker.

In 1992, four-year-old *Nadjia Thebib* from Moulins went missing. Waxin lifted her up in his arms as her Aunt ran after him. The Aunt fell to the ground as she pursued him and lost sight of the direction he went in. Waxin raped Nadjia, stabbed her in the neck and choked her with a plastic bag.

On January 6th 1999, a six-year-old girl named *Wendy* was lured to an abandoned factory. He threatened her by telling her that he killed little girls and so she allowed Waxin to undress and rape her. He let her go and followed her to let her know he was watching her. A passing driver saw her and carried her to the police station.

The six-year-old girl gave a facial description to police which subsequently led to Waxin's arrest. He was sentenced to life in prison for the murders and rapes of children. He remains incarcerated as of 2021.

Born in **1969**.

Active from **1985-1999**.

Arrested on **July 13th 1999**.

Country: **France**.

Victims: **3+**.

Sentence: **Life imprisonment**.

Current whereabouts: **In prison**.

West, Fred and Rose: House of Horrors (Extended Case File)

On May 10th 1978, *Shirley Robinson*, a former lodger at 25 Cromwell Street, disappeared. She was murdered by serial killer *Fred West*. Mostly in league with his wife, *Rosemary West*, they would take the lives of at least 12 young women before being arrested in 1994.

Their address of 25 Cromwell Street became synonymous with the murders and became known as the *House of Horrors*. So much hate was subsequently directed towards the House of Horrors, that *Gloucester City Council* intervened. They purchased the property for £40,000 in 1996, in the knowledge that no one would live there. They then unceremoniously destroyed the property, and with it, any physical trace of the horrors that had haunted the building.

Fred West was born in 1941, raised during World War Two, and killed his first victim in 1967. In January 1972, he married *Rosemary Letts*, who was 18-years-old. By that point, during their blossoming relationship, Rose had already murdered Fred's

547

daughter, *Charmaine West*.

It was unclear for a while who exactly had killed her but recent evidence showed that Fred West was serving a small sentence for unrelated crimes at the time of her death. Yet, he had already killed many years before Rose.

Fred would later move the hidden body and bury it at their Midland Road address. Throughout his life, Fred had displayed domineering control to all the women in his life. His violent sexual lust resulted in him abusing most of his children. He would sexually abuse them, beat them, and encourage them into prostitution.

The crossing of dark souls with Fred and Rosemary West was a match made in hell. At least eight of the victims had been raped, tortured, and mutilated. Before being murdered they were used in violent sexual fantasies where bondage played a heavy part of the household.

They would then dismember the bodies and bury them in the cellar and garden of 25 Cromwell Street. Fred killed two on his own and Rosemary killed one; Charmaine. The rest of their victims were killed as a pair. The level of control they asserted over others is as horrific as it is shocking.

Rose worked as a prostitute and used an upstairs room in the house for her clients. She would also engage in casual sex with both male and female lodgers. It was stated that when she had sex with other women, Rose would become more violent as the control slipped. She would partially suffocate them and insert exceptionally large sex objects inside them.

If they cried or showed fear or pain then Rose would become more excited. The room also had a spy-hole where Fred could watch his wife engage in violent encounters with clients and others.

Shockingly, when Rose's father found out about her prostitution, he would regularly visit her to have sex with his own daughter. By 1983, Rose had given birth to eight children, some of them black, but they raised them as their own.

It was clear that both Fred and Rose took to extreme levels of sexual perversity. It was this that resulted in the deaths of so many. Fred West also collected VHS videos that showed bestiality and child abuse. It has always remained unclear how he was sourcing these types of tapes but they were surely a catalyst to even more crimes.

Since the marriage in 1972, the sexual violence would increase. It became shocking to many that these level of crimes were going mostly unseen in what was a busy residential street.

All of the West's children were abused in some form or another. They took 'great care' not to mark the children's faces or hands when they assaulted them. Any admittance to hospitals were explained away as accidents and never reported.

All the children witnessed the abuse inflicted on each other and regular sexual abuse became the norm. Eight-year-old Anna Marie, Fred's daughter from another relationship, was dragged to the cellar of 25 Cromwell Street and had her clothes torn off. She was tied naked to a mattress and gagged before Fred raped her as Rose egged him on.

"Everybody does it to every girl. It's a father's job. Don't say anything to anybody."

Rose West, to Anna Marie.

They would then sexually abuse Anna Marie at any time from then on, by tying her to various items of furniture and forcing her into degrading acts. Fred would rape her regularly and then force her to do her chores while wearing a mini-skirt adorned with adult sexual devices.

When Anna Marie was 13-years-old, she was forced to prostitute herself in 'Rose's Room' with Rose watching every encounter with clients in case Anna Marie revealed her true age. That was only one of the children. Others would suffer even worse at the hands of Fred and Rose.

"I made you, I can do what I like with you."

Fred West, to his daughters.

They killed 12 young women, mostly their daughters, or hitchhikers who ended up at the house. In 1987, they killed their daughter, Heather West, and buried her under the patio of their garden. Fred even put a wooden table over her makeshift grave, a table where he would have family dinners outside in the Summer. The other children didn't know their sister was beneath them as they dined.

It was the excavation of the patio after their arrest that led to multiple bodies and body parts being uncovered. The investigation found remains in the ground floor bathroom, multiple bodies in the cellar and a large number in the garden.

Each body had been heavily mutilated and had been subject to extremely violent sexual abuse before their deaths. They found severed limbs, a skull, knives and various bondage materials. Bizarrely, every one of the human remains were missing some of their bones, most notably; the phalange bones, which are generally considered to be the fingers.

Was this Fred's attempt at hiding their identity or was there something even more macabre at work? As he killed himself in prison on New Year's Day 1995, there is no way to know. Rose West remains alive to this day, incarcerated for the rest of her life. During his interviews, Fred West claimed to have killed 30 people. Since then other crimes have been tentatively linked to him but have not been confirmed.

Rose West receives only one sole visitor; Anna Marie West. In 1999, Anna Marie attempted suicide but failed in her attempt. One of the West's sons; Stephen West, attempted suicide in 2002. Later in 2004, he was jailed for having sex with a 14-year-old girl. The West's horrific legacy continues to this day.

Born **September 29th 1941 (Fred), November 29th 1953 (Rose).**

Active from **1967-1987.**

Arrested on **February 24th 1994 (Fred), April 1994 (Rose).**

Country: **United Kingdom.**

Victims: **12+.**

AKA: **House of Horrors.**

Sentence: **Life imprisonment for both Fred and Rose West.**

Current whereabouts: Fred West committed suicide on New Year's Day 1995. Rose West remains in prison.

IMAGE ATTRIB. A31

JACK UNTERWEGER

IMAGE ATTRIBUTIONS
(ATTRIB A28) (ATTRIB A29A)
(ATTRIB A29B)

FRED AND ROSE WEST

Wilken, Stewart

In Port Elizabeth, in South Africa, serial killer *Stewart Wilken* AKA: *Boetie Boer*, racks up a body count of at least 10 victims over a seven year period from 1990 until 1997. His victims ranged from female prostitutes to young boys.

Wilken also engaged in necrophilia and cannibalism. He murdered the son of his second wife and engaged in sexual acts with the corpse. Another victim had her nipples sliced off, and Wilken ate them. It is unclear whether he cooked them first.

When he was six-months-old, in 1967, Wilken and his two-year-old sister were abandoned by their parents in a telephone booth. They were found by a house maid who took them to the home of her employer. The man then abused Wilken in the most horrific of ways. He burned him with cigarettes, forced him to eat from a bowl on the floor, and then forced him to engage in sexual acts with his dogs. It is unclear what became of Wilken's sister.

On September 29th 1995, Wilken killed his daughter from his first marriage. Wilken claimed that his daughter had suffered sexual abuse from her stepdad, so Wilken had decided to save her soul by killing her, enabling her to go to Heaven.

On May 22nd 1996, the skeletal remains of a young girl was discovered beneath a blue tarpaulin, behind a Holiday Inn. At the time of the discovery, the girl couldn't be identified and it wouldn't be until Wilken showed police where he had hidden the bodies, that an identification could be made. The girl's identity has remained protected.

On May 25th 1996, Wilken picked up 22-year-old prostitute, *Katriena Claassen*. He took her down to the shoreline where she provided him with her services. Afterwards, Wilken shoved a plastic bag down her throat and strangled her. He then raped her, before killing her and dumping her body on the beach.

In 1998, Wilken was convicted on seven counts of murder and sentenced to a life sentence for each of them.

Born **November 11th 1966.**

Active from **1990-1997**.

Arrested on **January 31st 1997**.

Country: **South Africa**.

Victims: **10+**.

AKA: **Boetie Boer**.

Sentence: **Seven life sentences**.

Current whereabouts: **In prison**.

Wood, Gwendolyn Graham & Catherine

American medical serial killer couple *Gwendolyn Gail Graham* and *Catherine May Wood* killed five elderly patients Michigan, in 1987. They worked at as nurse's aides at the Alpine Manor nursing home, where they killed all their victims.

They fell in love in 1986 when they both met at the nursing home. Graham had recently moved from Texas. Wood ended up testifying against Graham in order to gain a reduced plea but it has long been suspected that Wood was the mastermind and instigator off the murders.

In January 1987, an elderly victim was killed when the couple smothered her with a small towel. Until their arrest in 1988, the five deaths later attributed as murders, were considered to have been the result of natural causes. The first murder became a blood pact for the couple which in effect prevented the other partner from leaving due to their joint guilt.

In 1987, a total of five elderly people were killed by the couple, most of the victims suffered from Alzheimer's. Wood portrayed Graham to be sexually and physically dominant and would turn the murders into a game. It was claimed that they took souvenirs from their victims but none were ever recovered.

They split up when Graham cheated on her with another nurse at the nursing home, before moving back to Texas. In 1988, Wood's ex-husband went to the police based on storied he'd heard Wood talking about. Both Graham and Wood were arrested and sent to trial.

Graham had secretly confessed to her new girlfriend, who testified against her. She was convicted of five murders and sentenced to five life sentences without the possibility of parole. As of 2021, Graham remains incarcerated in a Women's Correctional Facility in Michigan.

Wood was charged with second-degree murder and conspiracy to commit murder. She was sentenced to 20 years but remained incarcerated until January 2020. She walked free from prison on January 16th 2020 after being granted parole. It has been claimed that Wood was the mastermind behind all the murders and was a pathological liar who could manipulate people to do her bidding. One claim said that she had set up Graham in revenge for leaving her.

Wood's whereabouts are currently known only to relevant law enforcement agencies.

Born **March 7th 1962 (Wood), August 6th 1963 (Graham).**

Active during **1987.**

Arrested in **December 1988.**

Country: **USA.**

Victims: **5.**

AKA: **The Lethal Lovers.**

Sentence: **Graham received five life sentences. Wood received 20 years.**

Current whereabouts: **Graham remains in prison. Wood was released in 2020, her whereabouts are unknown.**

Woodcock, Peter

He called himself *David Michael Krueger* but was born *Peter Woodcock*. He was a Canadian serial killer, child rapist and psychopath. He killed three young children in the late 1950s and killed again in 1991 on his one-day release from a psychiatric hospital. It is claimed he abused and raped up to 50 children before he murdered the three.

In 1957 he raped and killed four-year-old *Carole Voyce*. The cause of death was a tree branch inserted deep into her vagina. He died in 2010 and claimed to be the 'serial killer they couldn't cure'.

Born **March 5th 1939**.

Active from **1956-1957** then **1991**.

Arrested in **1957**.

Country: **Canada**.

Victims: **4**.

AKA: **David Michael Krueger**.

Sentence: **Committed to psychiatric institute**.

Current whereabouts: **Died of natural causes in 2010**.

Yapicioglu, Yavuz

In Turkey, *Yavuz Yapıcıoğlu,* AKA: *The Screwdriver Killer*, is a serial killer said to hold the highest body count of any serial murderer in the country. Between 1994 and 2002, he killed at least 18 people, mostly by way of arson.

After a troubled childhood, Yapicioglu left home at a young age and dropped out of school shortly after due to an argument he had with his parents. By all accounts,

Yapicioglu was an intelligent child who hit the highest grades in school. After many a failed business, he joined a religious cult in Istanbul, searching for his place in the world. He began to lash out at people and quickly became aggressive towards others.

In 1994, he stabbed three people to death after one of them supposedly wished him a good morning. He was arrested shortly after and committed to a psychiatric hospital. While there, he attacked his fellow patients and nurses, and then set his ward on fire.

After a short while, he was discharged and then killed six more people in a manner of weeks, in the same year. He then burned his brothers shop to the ground for not lending him money, then burned two of his relative's homes to the ground. He then attacked his father and killed his grandmother with an ashtray. His mother had a heart attack upon hearing that her son had killed her mother.

After being arrested again, he was committed to the same hospital where he was discharged *again* after only a year. Upon his discharge, he killed three more people with a screwdriver and then drove to a neighbouring town to murder a night guard with the same screwdriver.

Finally in 2002, he was arrested yet again, and this time was found criminally liable for the murders. This meant he was convicted and sentenced to life in prison. As of 2021, he remains in a Turkish prison without the possibility of parole.

Born in **1967**.

Active from **1994-2002**.

Arrested in **2002**.

Country: **Turkey**.

Victims: **18-40+**.

AKA: **The Screwdriver Killer.**

Sentence: **Life imprisonment.**

Current whereabouts: **In prison.**

Yates, Robert Lee

On June 14th 1996, the body of 39-year-old *Shannon Zielinski* was found Northeast of Spokane. Her body was discovered in a remote location just off from the major roads in the area. She was a victim of serial killer Robert Lee Yates.

Yates would murder at least 13 prostitutes in Washington and would claim another two in Walla Walla and one in Skagit County. Yates would have sex and do drugs with them in his van before killing them and dumping their bodies in rural locations. All of the women died by a gunshot wound to the head.

He wasn't arrested until 2000, and currently remains incarcerated after having his death sentence commuted to life.

Born **May 27th 1952.**

Active from **1975-1998.**

Arrested on **April 18th 2000.**

Country: **USA**.

Victims: **16.**

AKA: **Spokane Washington's Serial Killer.**

Sentence: **Death penalty later commuted to life.**

Current whereabouts: **In prison.**

(Research Article #25) Active Serial Killers

Every decade, criminologists come out with some form of statistic that shows how many serial killers are currently active within the United States or other countries.

Serial Killer and *America* have gone hand in hand for almost a century and it is the country with the most known convicted serial killers. I say *known* because in countries within Africa and some in Asia, it is difficult to get viable information out of their police records. The investigative systems are not as tight as they are in the West.

It is quite possible that in a countries like *Laos* or *Cambodia* there are serial killers who have been active for generations and probably many who have never been caught. Yet, we don't know about them, or information about them has never been made public.

It is a common piece of information that in the United States there are at least 80 serial killers who are currently active within the general population. It is said 20 in the United Kingdom and another 40 across the EU. The given figures are based on historical data.

How does anyone really know how many serial killers are currently at large? The truth is, no one does, but these types of statistics are drawn up by looking at previous convictions and any outstanding victims that have not been attributed to a known killer.

Of course, this does not just apply to the United States but many other countries where serial killers have been prevalent or in the least, known to have been active. Statistics are statistics and it all depends how much of it has been tested or based on fact, and indeed how it is interpreted and presented to you.

If you read that 80,000 people go missing every year, you might just miss the part where it says that 79,000 either return home (runaways) or are found safe and well. Of course, that might mean 1,000 people have actually gone missing but it's not as bad as you might first think.

Simple logic and deduction tell us that there *are* serial killers out there who are actively killing victims in whatever vile way they please. So if we know there are serial killers out there who have never been caught then the next question would be; where are they?

Certain traits within serial killers are used by criminal profiling agencies and authorities across the world but more predominantly within the FBI.

The neighbours of *Dennis Nilsen* would have had no idea that the hard working civil servant employee was boiling heads in his broth pot at night or keeping bags of human organs in his wardrobe.

They only found out when their drains became blocked with human flesh on account of flushing the '*little bits*' down the toilet. They would have spoken to him in the hallways and on the streets and claimed he was a genuinely nice man who wouldn't have hurt a fly.

In larger countries like the United States, Russia, and India, it can be easier for a serial killer to survive in the wild, longer than in smaller countries. Would *Andrei Chikatilo* of Russia have been able to commit as many murders as he did, in a country like Jamaica?

Probably not. So he would have adapted and adaptation is the key. But then he might not have been led to commit the crimes in a country that wasn't torn to bits by the horrors of World War Two.

Serial killers tend to be moulded by their surroundings and their country of birth. If Chikatilo's parents had moved to Jamaica and given birth to him there, would he have grown up to kill?

If you believe that serial killers are born to kill then you believe that it is *nature* that makes them evil. If you believe, as most criminologists do, that serial killers are moulded into killers by their experiences growing up, then you are on the *nurture* fence of the argument.

We do know there are more serial killers in larger countries. But an argument against larger countries making it easier for serial killers to kill is *Harold Shipman,* from the United Kingdom.

Although it is one of the most '*populated per square mile*' countries in the world, it can be famously difficult in the modern era to get away with severe acts of crime. The surveillance '*ring of steel*' around London is an obvious deterrent.

Yet, the investigation into Shipman claimed he had managed to kill a suspected 250 victims during his time as a doctor, despite the United Kingdom's small size.

He adapted to his environment and hid amongst his peers for decades whilst syphoning money from his elderly victims through their wills. Ironically, it was his greed in garnering their wills that got him caught and not the mistakes in which he killed people.

He was respected by his patients and his neighbours knew nothing untoward was happening in the shadows of his mind.

So because we know that there must be serial killers out there, what's to say they don't live in your city? Or maybe your town?

Do you really know your neighbours *that* well?

Appendices

Bibliography

Citations, data, and suggested reading.

A. Nortje, C. G. Tredoux, K. Kempen and A. Vredeveldt. (2013) "Applying Laboratory Techniques to a Real-Life Case: What Insight can we Provide about the Station Strangler Case?" *American Psychology-Law Society*.

Aamodt, M. G. (2016) Serial killer statistics. Retrieved (14/01/2019) from http://maamodt.asp.radford.edu/serial killer information center/projectdescription.htm *Radford University*.

Aamodt, M. G., & Moyse, C. (2003) Researching the multiple murderer: A comprehensive bibliography of books on specific serial, mass, and spree killers. *Journal of Police and Criminal Psychology*, 18(1).

Administration for Children and Families (2001) Victims. Child Maltreatment. http://www.acf.dhhs.gov/programs/cb/publications/cm01/chapterthree.htm. *Childhelp USA*.

Akbulut-Yuksel Mevlude. (2009) Children of the War: The Long-run Effects of Large-scale Physical Destruction and Warfare on Children. *IZA Discussion Paper No. 4407*.

Archer, Dane, and Rosemary Gartner. (1976) "Violent Acts and Violent Times: A Comparative Approach to Postwar Homicide Rates." *American Sociological Review, 41(6)*.

Bale, A. Bolton, J. Gabriel, R. Jackson, M. Lee, H. (2002) Health Status and Clinical Diagnosis of 3000 UK Gulf War Veterans. *Journal of the Royal Society of Medicine. 95*.

Ballingtyne and Hanks. (2000) Lest We Forget: ExServicemen and Homelessness. *Crisis*.

Bartels, K. (1998). Serial Killers: Sublimity to Be Continued. Aesthetics and Criminal History. Amerikastudien / American Studies, 43(3), 497-516.

BBC News. (Jan 2004) "Shipman's 215 Victims." Retrieved from; http://news.bbc.co.uk/go/pr/fr/-/1/hi/uk/2138888.stm. *BBC Article.*

Bingham A, Delap L, Jackson L, & Settle L. (2016) "Historical child sexual abuse in England and Wales: The role of historians." *History of Education, 45(4).*

Branson, Allan. (2013). African American Serial Killers: Over-Represented Yet Under-acknowledged. *The Howard Journal of Criminal Justice. 52.*

Brunt, Martin. Sky News. (2008) "Ex-Detective Held Over Axe Murder".. https://news.sky.com/skynews/Home/Sky-News-Archive/Article/20080641313539 *Sky.com News Archive.*

Carlo, P. (2006) The Iceman: Confessions of a Mafia Contract Killer. New York. *St. Martin's Press.*

Carrabine, Eamonn. (2008) Crime, Culture, and Media. Cambridge, UK. *Polity Publishers.*

CBS Sacramento. (2016). "California Inmate On Death Row Since 1988 Dies In The Hospital" https://sacramento.cbslocal.com/2016/12/14/california-inmate-on-death-row-since-1988-dies-in-the-hospital/. *CBS.*

Central Intelligence Agency. (Retrieved 2019) Research papers and FOIA requests on Project MK-Ultra. https://www.cia.gov/library/readingroom/search/site/mk%20ultra. *CIA.*

Chang, S. (2005) The prodigal "son" returns: An assessment of current "Son of Sam" laws and the reality of the online murderabilia marketplace. *Rutgers Computer and Technology Law Journal.*

Chen, Edwin. Los Angeles Times. (April 27th 1989). "Man Convicted of 4 Murders; 2 Linked to Southside Slayer Case." https://www.latimes.com/archives/la-xpm-1989-04-27-me-1912-story.html. *Latimes.com*

Cohen, M. (1997). Inside the Murderer. Studies in Popular Culture, 19(3), 49-63.

Conrath, R. (1994). The Guys Who Shoot to Thrill: Serial Killers and the American Popular Unconscious. *Revue Française D'études Américaines, (60), 143-152.*

Dahl, G., & DellaVigna, S. (2009). Does Movie Violence Increase Violent Crime? *The Quarterly Journal of Economics, 124(2), 677-734.*

Danziger, Sheldon H, Robert Haveman, eds. (2001) Understanding Poverty. New York: *Russell Sage Foundation.* Cambridge: *Harvard University Press.*

Delap, L. (2018). "Disgusting Details Which Are Best Forgotten": Disclosures of Child Sexual Abuse in Twentieth-Century Britain. *Journal of British Studies, 57(1).*

Disaster Center Crime Data. *(Retrieved 2019)* http://www.disastercenter.com/crime. DCC.

Dodd, Vikram. Guardian, The. (2014). Cherry Groce inquest: officer takes full blame for shot that led to Brixton riots https://www.theguardian.com/uk-news/2014/jul/01/cherry-groce-inquest-officer-takes-blame-shooting-brixton-riots *Guardian.com.*

Donna Youngs, Maria Ioannou. (2013) A Model of Client-Related Violence Against Female Street Sex Workers. *Journal of Forensic Social Work, 3(3).*

Douglas, John E.; Allen G. Burgess, Robert K. Ressler, and Ann W. Burgess. (2006) Crime Classification Manual: A Standard System for Investigating and Classifying Violent Crimes. *Second, Wiley.*

Douglas, John. Mindhunter: Inside the FBI's Elite Serial Crime Unit. (1995) *New York, Scribner.*

Dresser, R. (2011). At law: Families and Forensic DNA Profiles. *The Hastings Center Report, 41(3), 11-12.*

E. G. L. (1919). The Statute of Limitations and the Conflict of Laws. *The Yale Law Journal, 28(5), 492-498.*

Egger, Steven A. (2000) Why Serial Murderers Kill: An Overview. *Contemporary Issues Companion: Serial Killers.*

Federal Bureau of Investigation. (2008) Serial Murder: Multi-disciplinary Perspectives for Investigators. Washington, DC. *U.S. Department of Justice.*

Federal Bureau of Investigation. (2009). Highway serial killing database release. https://archives.fbi.gov/archives/news/stories/2009/april/highwayserial_040609. U.S Department of Justice.

Feigenbaum, JJ, & Muller, C. (2016) Lead exposure and violent crime in the early twentieth century. *Explorations in Economic History.*

Forsyth, C. J. (2015) Posing: The sociological routine of the serial killer. *American Journal of Criminal Justice, 40(4).*

Fox, J. A., & Levin, J. (2015) Extreme killing. Understanding massive serial murder (3rd ed.). Los Angeles. *Sage publications Inc.*

Fox, J., & Levin, J. (1998). Multiple Homicide: Patterns of Serial and Mass Murder. *Crime and Justice, 23, 407-455.*

Foy, D. (1987). Disasters at Sea and their Prevention. *RSA Journal, 136(5377), 13-24.*

Friedrichsen, Gisela. (1995) Criminal Justice. https://www.spiegel.de/spiegel/print/d-9247676.html *Der Spiegel 52/1995.*

Gabriel, R. Neal, L. (2002) Post-Traumatic Stress Disorder following military combat or peace keeping. *British Medical Journal. 324.*

Gagnon, J. (1965) Female Child Victims of Sex Offenses. *Social Problems, 13(2).*

Ganesan, N., & Kim, S. (Eds.). (2013). State Violence in East Asia. *University Press of Kentucky.*

Godwin, M., (2008) (2nd Edition). Hunting Serial Predators. *Jones & Bartlett Publishers, MA.*

Gorman, Anna. (2004). "Ten Murder Charges Filed." Retrieved 2019. *Los Angeles Times.*

Guardian, The. (2012). Terry Waite returns to Lebanon 25 years after kidnapping https://www.theguardian.com/world/2012/dec/09/terry-waite-returns-lebanon-kidnapping?CMP=share_btn_tw. *Theguardian.com*

Gunner and Knott (1997) Homeless on Civvy Street: Survey of Homelessness amongst Ex-Servicemen. *Ex-Service Action Group*

Gurian, E. A. (2013) Explanations of mixed-sex partnered homicide: A review of sociological and psychological theory. *Aggression and Violent Behaviour, 18(5).*

Hacking, Ian. (1991) "The Making and Molding of Child Abuse." *Critical Inquiry, 17(2).*

Hans Gross, (1907, retrieved 2019) Criminal Investigation: A Practical Handbook for Magistrates, Police Officers and Lawyers.

Harrison, Marissa & M. Hughes, Susan & Jordan Gott, Adam. (2019) Sex Differences in Serial Killers. *Evolutionary Behavioral Sciences.*

Hart, Timothy C., Troshynski, Emily I. (2016) Perceptions of Stalking Victimization among Behaviorally Defined Victims. *The Wiley Handbook on the Psychology of Violence.*

Havill, Adrian. (2001). Born Evil: A True Story of Cannibalism and Serial Murder. *New York, N.Y.: St. Martin's Press.* Retrieved 2019.

Hickey, E. W. (2002) Serial murderers and their victims (3rd ed.). *Belmont, Wadsworth.*

Historical Institutional Abuse Inquiry. (2017) http://www.hiainquiry.org/index.htm Inquiry updated at https://www.nidirect.gov.uk/articles/historical-institutional-abuse

Holmes J, Fear N T, Harrison K, Sharpley J, Wessely S. (2013) Suicide among Falkland war veterans. *BMJ 346.*

Jacob Bucher, Michelle Manasse, Jeffrey Milton. (2015) Soliciting strain: examining both sides of street prostitution through General Strain Theory. *Journal of Crime and Justice 38(4).*

Jacquelyn Monroe PhD. (2005) Women in Street Prostitution: The Result of Poverty and the Brunt of Inequity. *Journal of Poverty 9(3).*

Jarvis, C., (March 20th, 1997). "Academic sleuth made startling predictions". NEWS & OBSERVER, RALEIGH, NC.

Jones N, Fear NT, Jones M, Wessely S, Greenberg N. (2010) Long-term military work outcomes in soldiers who become mental health casualties when deployed on operations. *Psychiatry. 73(4).*

Jooyoung Lee, Sasha Reid. (2018) Serial Killers & Their Easy Prey. *Contexts 17(2).*

Joyce Prince and TCN Gibbens, (1963) Child Victims of Sex Offences. *Institute for the Study and Treatment of Delinquency.*

Kandel, Jason, (2011). "Police tie Grim Sleeper suspect to six more killings." https://www.reuters.com/article/us-crime-grimsleeper/police-tie-grim-sleeper-suspect-to-six-more-killings-idUSTRE7A20L120111103. *Reuters.*

Kathryn Ann Farr PhD. (2000) Defeminizing and Dehumanizing Female Murderers. *Women & Criminal Justice 11(2).*

Keenan, Thomas, 'Getting the Dead to Tell Me what Happened: Justice, Prosopopoeia, and Forensic Afterlives', in *Forensic Architecture, ed., Forensic, 35-55.*

Kesternich I, Siflinger B, Smith JP, Winter JK. (2013) The Effects of World War II on Economic and Health Outcomes across Europe. Rev Econ Stat.

LAPD Online. (Retrieved July 2019) Photos of Grim Sleeper Victims. http://www.lapdonline.org/grimsleeper. *Lapdonline.com*

Leskanic, T., (2004) "Inmate indicted in 1995 killing." Retrieved 2019. FAYETTEVILLE OBSERVER.

Lewis, Jack. (May 1985) "Lead Poisoning: A Historical Perspective." *EPA Journal article.*

Lodinews. (2016) "Convicted killer Loren Herzog commits suicide." *Lodinews.com.* http://www.lodinews.com/news/article_64587e42-4122-11e1-b68e-001871e3ce6c.html

Louise A. Jackson. (2000) Child Sexual Abuse in Victorian England. London. *Routledge.*

Love, T., Laier, C., Brand, M., Hatch, L., & Hajela, R. (2015) Neuroscience of Internet Pornography Addiction: A Review and Update. *Behavioral sciences.*

McClellan, Janet. (2007) Animal Cruelty and Violent Behavior: Is There a Connection? *Journal of Security Education.*

McNichol, Dan. (2006) The Roads That Built America: The Incredible Story of the U.S. Interstate System. New York. *Sterling.*

Meija, Brittny. Los Angeles Times. (Nov 9th 2015). Grim Sleeper: Defense backtracks on expert witness https://www.latimes.com/local/lanow/la-me-ln-grim-sleeper-defense-backtracks-expert-witness-20151109-story.htm.l Retrieved 2019. *latimes.com*

Miller, G. (2010). Familial DNA Testing Scores A Win in Serial Killer Case. *Science, 329(5989), new series, 262-262.*

Montgomery, Ben. Zayas, Alexandra. (July 8th 2007). "Valley murder victims." Concord Monitor. Archived from the original in 2015. *Concordmonitor.com.*

Nathan W. Pino. (2005) Serial Offending and the Criminal Events Perspective. *Homicide Studies 9(2).*

Nelson, Harold E. (1987). NIST Interagency/Internal Report *(NISTIR) – 87-3560.* May 29th.

Nesta H Wells. (1958) "Sexual offences as seen by a woman police surgeon". *British Medical Journal.* Dec 6th article.

NSQCCA 327. (1999), Regina v Rose [1999]. New South Wales Criminal Court of Appeal. *No. 60520 of 1998*

Oakley, Ben. Luisa, Marina. (2019) Mentacracy: Living under the Rule of Mental Illness. United Kingdom. *Twelvetrees Publishing.*

Oakley, Ben. (2019) 1978: Year of the Serial Killer. 1987: Year of the Serial Killer Chapter 2. 1996: Year of the Serial Killer Chapter 3. United Kingdom. *Twelvetrees Publishing.*

Panayiotopoulos CP (1999) Typical absence seizures and their treatment. *Archives of Disease in Childhood.*

Parfitt CH, Alleyne E. (Jan 2018) Not the Sum of Its Parts: A Critical Review of the MacDonald Triad. *Trauma Violence Abuse.*

Pelisek, Christine (2007). "Death Penalty for Chester Turner". *LA Weekly. Village Voice Media.* Rtvd 2019. http://www.laweekly.com/2007-05-17/news/death-penalty-for-chester-turner/

Potterat JJ, Brewer DD, Muth SQ, Rothenberg RB, Woodhouse DE, Muth JB, Stites HK, Brody S. (2004) Mortality in a long-term open cohort of prostitute women. *Am J Epidemiol.*

Ram, N. (2011). Fortuity and Forensic Familial Identification. *Stanford Law Review, 63(4),* 751-812.

Randall and Brown (1994) Falling Out: A Research Study of Homeless Ex-Service People. *Crisis.*

Ressler, Robert K., Schachtman, Thomas. (1993) Whoever Fights Monsters: My Twenty Years Tracking Serial Killers for the FBI. New York. *Macmillan/St. Martin's.*

Rijt, Arnout & Song, Hyang-Gi & Shor, Eran & Burroway, Rebekah. (2018) Racial and gender differences in missing children's recovery chances. *PLOS ONE. (13).*

Robinson, Kathleen. (2012). "Puerto Rico fire is the second-deadliest hotel fire in U.S. history." *NFPA Journal,* November/December 2012.

Rosen, Fred (July 1, 2015). Body Dump: Kendall Francois, the Poughkeepsie Serial

Killer. Open Road Media. ISBN 9781504022644.

S. Thompson, Kenrick & C. Clarke, Alfred. (1974) Photographic Imagery and the Vietnam War: An Unexamined Perspective. *The Journal of Psychology.*

Scheanette v. Office of Chief Disciplinary Counsel, Not Reported in F.Supp.2d, 2005 WL 3147874 (N.D.Tex. 2005) (Pro Se).

Schildcrout, J. (2014). Murder Most Queer: The Homicidal Homosexual in the American Theater. Ann Arbor: *University of Michigan Press.*

Schmid, David. (2005) Natural Born Celebrities: Serial Killers in American Culture. Chicago. *University of Chicago Press.*

Scottish Government. (Retrieved 2019) Public Inquiry into Child Abuse in Scotland, http://www.gov.scot/Topics/People/Young-People/protecting/child-protection/historical-child-abuse

Seltzer, M. (1995). Serial Killers (II): The Pathological Public Sphere. *Critical Inquiry, 22(1),* 122-149.

Smith, C., Lobban, G., O'Loughlin, M. (Eds.) (2013). Psychodynamic Psychotherapy in South Africa: Contexts, theories and applications. Johannesburg: *Wits University Press.*

Stevelink, Sharon & Malcolm, Estelle & Mason, C & Jenkins, Sarah & Sundin, Josefin & Fear, N.T. (2014) The prevalence of mental health disorders in (ex-)military personnel with a physical impairment: A systematic review. *Occupational and environmental medicine. 72(10).*

Susan L. Murray PhD, PE, Matthew S. Thimgan PhD, (2016). *"Human Fatigue Risk Management."*

Tallichet, Suzanne & Hensley, Christopher. (2004) Exploring the Link between Recurrent Acts of Childhood and Adolescent Animal Cruelty and Subsequent Violent Crime. *Criminal Justice Review. 29.*

Taylor MP, Forbes MK, Opeskin B, Parr N, Lanphear BP. (2018) Further analysis of the relationship between atmospheric lead emissions and aggressive crime: an ecological study. *Environmental Health. 17(1).*

Times, Los Angeles, (Retrieved 2019). "Guilty verdicts in Grim Sleeper serial killer case." https://www.latimes.com/local/lanow/la-me-ln-grim-sleeper-death-verdict-

20160606-snap-story.html. *latimes.com.*

Trend, David. (2007) The Myth of Media Violence: A Critical Introduction. Malden, MA. Blackwell Publishing.

Trevor A. Kletz DSc, FEng, FIChemE, FRSC, (1990). *Critical Aspects of Safety and Loss Prevention.*

United Nations. (2014) World Urbanization Prospects: The 2014 Revision. *Department of Economic and Social Affairs: Population Division*

Walker, J., (1997). The Traumatic Paradox: Documentary Films, Historical Fictions, and Cataclysmic Past Events. *Signs, 22(4), 803-825.*

Weingroff, Richard F. (1996) "Federal-Aid Highway Act of 1956, Creating the Interstate System". *Public Roads. Article. 60(1).*

Wright, Jeremy & Hensley, Christopher. (2003) From Animal Cruelty to Serial Murder: Applying the Graduation Hypothesis. *International journal of offender therapy and comparative criminology. (47).*

Image Attributions

Attrib 1.) Description: Prison photo of Rodney Alcala. Date September 2nd 1997. Author: San Quentin State Prison, California Department of Corrections and Rehabilitation. Notes: CC BY-ND 2.0

Attrib 2) Photo of Baekuni. Description: Photo of serial killer Baekuni. Notes: *Public domain.*

Attrib 3.) Description: Painting by serial killer John Wayne Gacy. Date: January 1st 2007 release. Author: *The Orchid Club.* Notes: CC BY-ND 2.0

Attrib 4.) Description: Photo of Jeffrey Dahmer as a senior in high school. Date: 1978. Source: Reverie, yearbook of Revere Senior High School, Richfield, Ohio. Notes: *Public domain.*

Attrib 5.) Description: Booking Photo of Gary Ridgway, the Green River Killer. Date: 30 November 2001. Source: Kings County Sheriff's Office. Notes: *Public domain.*

Attrib 6.) Description: Prison Photo of Pedro Lopez. Date: 23 April 1987. Source: Fiscalía General de la Nación. Notes: *Public domain.*

Attrib 7.) Description: Ted Bundy in a courtroom. Date: 1979. Source: Florida Memory Project hosted at the State Archive of Florida. Notes: *Public domain.*

Attrib 8.) Description: Pitkin County Courthouse in Aspen, that the American serial killer Ted Bundy escaped from. Date: circa 2005. Author: *Matthew Trump.* Notes: CC BY-ND 2.0

Attrib 9.) Photo by: Historica Canada. Description: Pickton at work. Accessed via the Canadian Encyclopedia in September 2020. Notes: qualifies as fair use under United States copyright law, where no free equivalent is available or could be created that would adequately give the same information to illustrate the subject in question.

Attrib 10.) Photo by: Historica Canada. Description: Arial view of the Pickton Farm in Port Coquitlam, BC. Accessed via the Canadian Encyclopedia in September 2020. Notes: qualifies as fair use under United States copyright law, where no free equivalent is available or could be created that would adequately give the same information to illustrate the subject in question.

Attrib 11.) Photo by: Stolbovsky. Date: July 2015. Description: Bitsevsky forest in Bitsa Park. Notes: CC BY-ND 2.0/CC BY-SA 4.0

Attrib 12.) Photo by: Mark T. Foley. Date: May 1979. Description: Tallahassee, Florida. Dr. Richard Souviron presents dental evidence at the trial of Ted Bundy for the Chi Omega Murders. Notes: This work is from the Florida Memory Project hosted at the State Archive of Florida and is released to the public domain in the United States under the terms of Section 257.35(6), Florida Statutes.

Attrib 12 (13).) Description: Ted Bundy mug shot. Date: 13 February 1980. Source: Florida Memory Project hosted at the State Archive of Florida. Notes: *Public domain.*

Attrib 14.) Description: Suspect Theodore Bundy after his original arrest. Date: July 1978. Source: Florida Memory Project hosted at the State Archive of Florida. Notes: *Public domain.*

Attrib 15.) Description: Mug Shot of Steven David Catlin in 2007. Date: July 1978. Source: California Department of Corrections and Rehabilitation. Notes: *Public domain.*

Attrib 16.) Source: Image was first published in Russian-language newspapers. Date: April 1992. Description: Andrey Chikatilo in court, intended to illustrate a significant section upon the trial chapter regarding Chikatilo and depicts the subject in question. Notes: qualifies as fair use under United States copyright law, where no free equivalent is available or could be created that would adequately give the same information to illustrate the subject in question.

Attrib 17.) Photo by FBI. Description: Photo of Edward Wayne Edwards. Source: FBI database. Notes: Public domain.

Attrib 18.) Photo of Gwen Graham and Cathy Wood. Mugshots from source. Notes: qualifies as fair use under United States copyright law, where no free equivalent is available or could be created that would adequately give the same information to illustrate the subject in question.

Attrib 19.) Description: Chateau du Sautou, former home of Michel Fourniret. Date: January 2007. Notes: Photo released into public domain.

Attrib 20.) Description: Police search at Chateau du Sautou, former home of Michel Fourniret. Date: Released to public in January 2007. Notes: Photo released into public domain.

Attrib 21.) Description: Mugshots of Monique Olivier & Michel Fourniret. Date: Released to public in 2001. Notes: Photos released into public domain.

Attrib 22.) Photo by: PoughkeepsieNative. Date: December 25th 1998. Description: Kendall Francois' former home taken three months after police searched the house and removed the bodies. Notes: This file is licensed under the Creative Commons Attribution-Share Alike 4.0 International license. *CC BY-SA 4.0*

Attrib 23.) Description: Mugshot of convicted serial killer Kendall Francois. Notes: Photo released into public domain.

Attrib 24.) Photo by Los Angeles Police Department. Date: September 1998.

Description: Lonnie David Franklin Jr., American serial killer inmate photo. Notes: Public domain file released from San Quentin State Prison which also qualifies as fair use.

Attrib 25.) Photo by: White House photographer. Date: May 1978. Description: White House photograph of First Lady Rosalynn Carter with Democratic Party activist and serial killer John Wayne Gacy. Notes: Public domain.

Attrib 26.) Description: John Wayne Gacy in clown suit. Notes: This file is licensed under the Creative Commons Attribution-Share Alike 4.0 International license.

Attrib 27.) Photo by: San Quentin State Prison. Date: June 2007. Description: Mugshot of serial killer Randy Steven Kraft. Notes: qualifies as fair use under United States copyright law, where no free equivalent is available or could be created that would adequately give the same information to illustrate the subject in question.

Attrib 28.) Description: Photo of Fred and Rose West. Notes: qualifies as fair use under United States and United Kingdom copyright law, where no free equivalent is available or could be created that would adequately give the same information to illustrate the subject in question. Used to illustrate and encyclopedic entry.

Attrib 29.) Photos of Fred West and Rose West were released for criminal purposes in the British media. Images are at least 30 years old. Notes: qualifies as fair use under United States copyright law, where no free equivalent is available or could be created that would adequately give the same information to illustrate the subject in question. It is needed to identify Fred West and Rose West for educational purposes in this encyclopedia entry.

Attrib 30.) Photo by: Wise County Police. Date: November 2018. Description: Samuel Little. Notes: Public domain.

Attrib 31.) Photo of Jack Unterweger. Image is at least 30 years old. Notes: qualifies as fair use under United States copyright law, where no free equivalent is available or could be created that would adequately give the same information to illustrate the subject in question. It is needed to identify Jack Unterweger for educational purposes in this encyclopedia entry.

Attrib 32.) Photo of Stefano Baldi and Susanna Cambi, the victims of the fourth crime of the so-called Monster of Florence, killed October 23, 1981. Notes: Public domain.

Attrib 33.) Photo of Horst Wilhelm Meyer and Jens-Uwe Rüsch, the victims of the sixth crime of the so-called Monster of Florence, killed on September 9th 1983 in Giogoli.

Notes: Public domain.

Attrib 34.) Photo of Jean-Michel Kraveichvili and Nadine Mauriot, the victims of the eighth crime of the so-called Monster of Florence, killed between 7th and 8th September 1985 at Scopeti. Notes: Public domain.

Attrib 35.) Photo by Sutton Prison. Description: Dennis Nilsen mugshot. Notes: Public domain.

Attrib 36.) Photo by Chris Whippet. Date: December 2008. Description: Cranley Gardens, Muswell Hill. Notes: Under creative commons fair use license. This file is licensed under the Creative Commons Attribution-Share Alike 4.0 International license.

Attrib 37.) Photo by California Department of Corrections and Rehabilitation, Sacramento, California, United States. Date: June 2007. Description: Inmate photo of American serial killer Gerald Parker. Notes: Public domain.

Attrib 38.) Photo of Alexander pichushkin. Notes: qualifies as fair use under United States copyright law, where no free equivalent is available or could be created that would adequately give the same information to illustrate the subject in question.

Attrib 39.) Description: mugshot of Peter Tobin. Notes: qualifies as fair use under United States and United Kingdom copyright law, where no free equivalent is available or could be created that would adequately give the same information to illustrate the subject in question.

Attrib 40.) Police photo of Joseph Swango. Description: mugshot of Joseph Swango. Notes: Public domain.

Attrib 41.) Photo of Peter Sutcliffe. Notes (1): It is only being used to illustrate the article in question. Notes (2): qualifies as fair use under United States copyright law, where no free equivalent is available or could be created that would adequately give the same information to illustrate the subject in question.

Attrib 42.) Police photo of Gerald Stano. Notes: Public domain with one version. Second version of same photo qualifies as fair use.

Attrib 43.) Photo of Anatoly Slivko. Date: 1986. Description: Image of serial killer Anatoly Slivko. Notes: Public domain.

Attrib 44.) Photo by Kim Traynor. Date: October 2011. Description: World's End pub, High Street Edinburgh. Notes: Under creative commons fair use license. This file is licensed under the Creative Commons Attribution-Share Alike 4.0 International license.

Attrib 45.) Police and court photo of Angus Slnclair. Notes: Public domain with one version. Second version of same photo qualifies as fair use.

Attrib 46.) Photo by Wakefield Prison. Description: Harold Shipman mug shot. Notes: qualifies as fair use under United States and United Kingdom copyright law, where no free equivalent is available or could be created that would adequately give the same information to illustrate the subject in question

Attrib 47.) Photo of Loren Herzog and Wesley Shermantine. Description: Mugshot of serial killer Herzog and mugshot of serial killer Shermantine. Notes: Public domain.

Attrib 48 to Attrib 53.) Selection of photos from the personal collection of Rodney Alcala. Includes unidentified females and identified females. Notes: Released to the public by various law enforcement agencies. Considered public domain due to nature of release.

Attrib 54.) Photo of the rear of Fox Hollow Farm. Description: Location where Herb Baumeister lived and killed some of his victims. Notes: Public domain.

Attrib 55.) Photo of the front of Fox Hollow Farm. Description: Location where Herb Baumeister lived and killed some of his victims. Notes: Public domain.

Attrib 56.) Photo of Herb Baumeister. Description: Mugshot of serial killer Baumeister. Notes: Public domain.

Attrib 57.) Photo of Robert Andrew Berdella. Notes (1): It is only being used to illustrate the article in question. Notes (2): qualifies as fair use under United States copyright law, where no free equivalent is available or could be created that would adequately give the same information to illustrate the subject in question.

Attrib 58.) Photo of David Berkowitz. Notes (1): It is only being used to illustrate the article in question. Notes (2): qualifies as fair use under United States copyright law, where no free equivalent is available or could be created that would adequately give the same information to illustrate the subject in question.

Attrib 59.) Photo of David Berkowitz. Description: Mugshot of serial killer Berkowitz in 2003. Notes: Public domain.

Attrib 58.) Photo of Robert Black. Notes (1): It is only being used to illustrate the article in question. Notes (2): qualifies as fair use under United States copyright law, where no free equivalent is available or could be created that would adequately give the same information to illustrate the subject in question.

Attrib 61.) Photo of Richard Trenton Chase. Description: Mugshot of serial killer Chase. Notes: Public domain.

Attrib 62 to Attrib 69.) Colonial Parkway Murder Victims. Source: High School yearbooks and police releases. Notes: All Public domain.

Attrib 61.) Mug shot of Jeffrey Dahmer. Source: Milwaukee Police Department. Date: July 23, 1991. Notes: qualifies as fair use under United States copyright law, where no free equivalent is available or could be created that would adequately give the same information to illustrate the subject in question.

Attrib 71.) Description: Mugshot taken of John Wayne Gacy, taken following his arrest for murder. Notes: (1): It is only being used to illustrate the article in question. Notes (2): qualifies as fair use under United States copyright law, where no free equivalent is available or could be created that would adequately give the same information to illustrate the subject in question.

Attrib 72.) Description: Mugshot taken of Danny Lee Barber, taken following his arrest for murder. Notes: (1): It is only being used to illustrate the article in question. Notes (2): qualifies as fair use under United States copyright law, where no free equivalent is available or could be created that would adequately give the same information to illustrate the subject in question.

Attrib 72.) Description: Court photo of Velma Barfield. Notes: (1): It is only being used to illustrate the article in question. Notes (2): qualifies as fair use under United States copyright law, where no free equivalent is available or could be created that would adequately give the same information to illustrate the subject in question.

Attrib 75.) Photo by: John Riojas on Unsplash. Description: Close up photography of white and brown pig photo. Small image utilised for the purpose of Robert Pickton.

Attrib 76.) Description: photo of Robert Pickton. (1): It is only being used to illustrate the article in question. Notes (2): qualifies as fair use under United States copyright law, where no free equivalent is available or could be created that would adequately give the same information to illustrate the subject in question.

Attrib 77.) Description: Interior of Pickton's slaughterhouse. (1): It is only being used to illustrate the article in question. Notes (2): qualifies as fair use under United States copyright law, where no free equivalent is available or could be created that would adequately give the same information to illustrate the subject in question.

Attrib 78.) Description: Photo of Peter Sutcliffe. Notes: qualifies as fair use under United States and United Kingdom copyright law, where no free equivalent is available or could be created that would adequately give the same information to illustrate the subject in question

Attrib 79.) Photo of Pedro Rodriguez Filho. Description: Prison photo of serial killer Filho. Notes: Public domain.

Attrib 80.) Photo of Charles Ray Hatcher. Mugshot from source. Notes: qualifies as fair use under United States copyright law, where no free equivalent is available or could be created that would adequately give the same information to illustrate the subject in question.

Attrib 81.) Photo of Archibald Hall. Notes: qualifies as fair use under United States copyright law, where no free equivalent is available or could be created that would adequately give the same information to illustrate the subject in question.

Attrib 82.) Photo of Phillip_CARL Jablonski. Notes: qualifies as fair use under United States copyright law, where no free equivalent is available or could be created that would adequately give the same information to illustrate the subject in question.

Attrib 83.) CP photo of Gilbert Paul Jordan. Notes: qualifies as fair use under United States copyright law, where no free equivalent is available or could be created that would adequately give the same information to illustrate the subject in question.

Attrib 84.) Photo by Jonathan Korner on Unsplash. Description: Cityscape photo of Florence, Italy. Small image utilised for the purpose of the Monster of Florence.

Attrib 85.) Photo of Roger Kibbe. Description: Mugshot photo of serial killer Kibbe. Notes: Public domain.

Attrib 86.) Photo of Timothy Krajcir. Description: Mugshot photo of serial killer Krajcir. Notes: Public domain.

Attrib 87.) Photo of David Parker Ray (mugshot). Notes: qualifies as fair use under United States copyright law, where no free equivalent is available or could be created that would adequately give the same information to illustrate the subject in question.

Attrib 88.) Photo of David Parker Ray'S Toy Box. Notes: qualifies as fair use under United

States copyright law, where no free equivalent is available or could be created that would adequately give the same information to illustrate the subject in question.

Attrib 90.) Police photo of Metod Trobec. Notes: qualifies as fair use under United States copyright law, where no free equivalent is available or could be created that would adequately give the same information to illustrate the subject in question.

FREE SAMPLE AHEAD!

TRUE CRIME 365 IS A SERIES OF BOOKS THAT INCLUDE AT LEAST ONE TRUE CRIME RELATED INCIDENT FOR EVERY SINGLE DAY OF THE YEAR!

IN EVERY EDITION, YOU'LL FIND SERIAL KILLERS, MURDERERS, ARMED ROBBERS, COLD CASES, MISSING PERSONS, MYSTERY DISAPPEARANCES, PROTESTS, INVASIONS, ASSASSINATIONS AND SO MUCH MORE.

LOOK FOR THE TRUE CRIME 365 LOGO

INTRODUCTION

This is your true crime almanac for the year 1980!

True Crime 365 is a series of books that include at least one true crime related incident for EVERY SINGLE DAY OF THE YEAR! Each entry and record have been fact-checked and cross-referenced to ensure you have the best book possible in your hands.

Inside this 1980 edition, you'll find serial killers, murderers, armed robbers, cold cases, missing persons, mystery disappearances, protests, invasions, assassinations and so much more.

At the end of the book, to relax you after all that death and destruction, you'll also find bonus lists, facts and Top 10 round-ups of everything important in 1980. It includes sports, films, music, books, video games and bonus facts like the world population and richest countries in the world circa 1980.

Swap your tea for a Dirty Banana and let's dive into 1980!

JANUARY

MYSTERY DISAPPEARANCE - January 1st

In Marina Del Rey, California, on New Year's Day, 15-year-old Kimberly Ann Kahler vanished without a trace. She had last been seen in the company of an unidentified white male. In recent years, Kahler has been linked to numerous Jane Doe's across the United States but no match has ever been made. A wedding certificate was uncovered a few years later but the age and description of the person did not match. It has long been suspected that Kahler was a victim of foul play but no trace of her has ever been found. Her disappearance remains a cold case to this day.

MURDER - January 2nd

In what kick-started a year of murder and bombings in Northern Ireland, former Ulster Defence Regiment (UDR) soldier, Samuel Lundy, was shot dead. He had been killed at his workplace by the Provisional Irish Republican Army (IRA). No one was ever arrested for the murder but it came about due to the troubles in Northern Ireland in the 1970s and 1980s.

AFRICAN MURDER - January 3rd

In *Shaba National Reserve*, Kenya, 69-year-old naturalist **Friederike Victoria Adamson** was murdered. Her body was found by her assistant, **Pieter Mawson**. Due to their work with lions and other big cats, it was initially assumed that she had been killed by a lion. A later investigation found that her wounds were too sharp to have been caused by an animal. Police were led to former employee of Adamson, **Paul Nakware Ekai**, who was later sentenced to life in prison for the murder. Adamson was well-known in the conservation world because of her book, *Born Free*, which described her experiences looking after a lion cub named *Elsa*. The book, released in 1960, was later turned into a film in 1966.

COLD CASE - January 4th

In Toulouse, France, 24-year-old **Monique Rejembeau** left her workplace in the city to have lunch with her mother in the residence they shared. Somewhere between her workplace and home, she disappeared. The following day, her purse was discovered at the *Garonne Hydroelectric Station*, on the banks of the Garonne river. Her car was found a week later in the *St. Michael* alleys of the city. French police closed the case and listed her as missing, despite an investigation reopening in 1985. In 1996, witnesses claimed to have seen Monique in Barcelona, Spain, in an area of the city known for the sex trade. Despite witnesses and a new investigation, no trace of Monique has ever been found.

RAPE & MURDER - January 5th

In Beaufort County, South Carolina, 18-year-old **David Krulewicz** and his 15-year-old girlfriend were sitting in a van, when **Isaiah Gadson** shot David through the window and then proceeded to rape his girlfriend. Gadson was identified as the killer 36 years later and was charged with the murder. He had shot and killed David purely to remove him as an obstacle for getting to his girlfriend. In May 2018, Gadson was sentenced to 50 years in prison for murder and three 30-year sentences for rape, kidnapping and robbery.

BOMB ATTACK - January 6th

In County Down, Northern Ireland, three *Ulster Defence Regiment* (**UDR**) soldiers were killed in a bomb attack. Private **Richard Wilson**, Private **Roy Smith**, and Private **James Cochrane** died when their *Land Rovers* triggered an explosive device that contained one ton of explosive material. The first vehicle in the two-vehicle convoy took most of the blast, while the second Land Rover drove straight into the 30-foot crater left by the explosion. The bomb had been set by the **IRA** and was triggered by a command wire in a house over 200-metres away. Four other soldiers were injured in the large explosion. The IRA claimed responsibility but no one was ever arrested for the attack.

CHILD MURDER - January 7th

In Tacoma, Washington, 12-year-old **Carla Wright** vanished on the walk to school. Her mother was unable to take her to school due to medication and an early doctor's appointment on the other side of town. Carla had taken a shortcut to **Gray Junior School** but never reached her destination. 12 days later, Carla's body was found near the trail she had taken. She had been raped and strangled to death. Despite links to child killer **David Fischer**, no suspect has ever been arrested. Her murder remains a cold case to this day.

DRUG MURDERS - January 8th

In Dade County, Florida, four men were killed after being beaten, tortured, and then set alight in the trunk of a car. The victims were **John Merino**, **Scott Benett**, **Rudolfo Ayan** and **Nicomedes Hernandez**. They had been killed by **Bernard Bolander** and his two accomplices, **Paul Thompson** and **Joseph Macker**, after a drug deal had gone wrong. An argument had broken out at Macker's residence when two of the victims arrived to settle a drug deal. Bolander and the accomplices, ordered the victims to lay on the floor, and robbed them. Bolander had suspected the victims were hiding 20kg of cocaine.

When they refused to tell Bolander where the drugs were, he beat and stabbed to them death as they were being dragged to an outside car, where they were set alight. The suspects were all arrested five days later. Thompson was sent to a psychiatric hospital but sentenced to 35 years in 1990. Macker testified against Bolander and was sentenced to life in prison. Bolander was sentenced to death and executed in the electric chair on July 18th 1995.

COP KILLER - January 9th

In Henry County, Indiana, *Sergeant* **Ronald L. Lampe** was shot and killed while serving a warrant on a home. He was with five other officers at the time. Two officers in plain clothing had attempted entry to a party at the house but the suspect became nervous and failed to let them in. Lampe then decided to proceed with the warrant himself and went to the back door. While the officers searched the house, the suspect opened fire on them with a rifle. Lampe was hit multiple times and died shortly after. Another officer was also hit in the chest and went on to survive. The suspect was later acquitted during the trial after his defence proved that he had fired in self-defence because the officers had not identified themselves.

MYSTERY DISAPPEARANCE - January 10th

In New South Wales, Australia, 18-year-old **Annette Shirley Briffa** vanished without a trace. She had last been seen hitchhiking on the *Pacific Highway* and getting into an orange *Mazda*. Her disappearance remained a mystery until January 2005 when a New South Wales *Deputy State Coroner* suspected to a strong degree that Briffa has been abducted and murdered. She had been out drinking the night before with **Raymond Nixon** who was later incarcerated for the murder of his wife but the investigation did not consider him a suspect.

There were suggestions that Briffa may have killed by serial killer **Ivan Milat**, who lived in the area and killed at least seven backpackers from 1989 to 1993. Another theory led to Briffa's uncle who owned an orange vehicle that was similar to the witness description. Not long after Briffa disappeared, the uncle dumped his car in remote bushland. Despite many suspects, the murder of Shirley Briffa remains unsolved.

RACIST MURDER - January 11th

In Indianapolis, Indiana, a 19-year-old black man was shot dead while standing in front of a **Church's Fried Chicken** takeaway. He had been murdered by Joseph **Paul Franklin**, AKA: **The Racist Killer**. Franklin took the shot with a 30-calibre rifle from over 400 feet away, in a sniper-style attack. Franklin killed between seven and 21 people with the intention of inciting a race war. He also shot and paralysed magazine publisher and pornographer **Larry Flynt** in 1978. He was arrested in 1980 and confessed to numerous murders including the 'Church's Fried Chicken murder' but he was never indicted due to the lengthy process of extraditing him to Indiana. Franklin was sentenced to death for other murders and executed by lethal injection on November 20th 2013.

COLD CASE - January 12th

In Sacramento, California, State University student 19-year-old **Khymbrly Marcella Scruggs** disappeared without a trace. She lived in an apartment with a roommate who had spent the night with her boyfriend. She returned home to find that

Khymbrly had vanished. Khymbrly had nothing planned and was scheduled to work the next day but never turned up. All her personal belongings and clothes were still in the apartment which led to investigators suspecting foul play. No trace of Khymbrly has ever been found. Her disappearance is an active cold case in the State of California.

MYSTERY DISAPPEARANCE - January 13th

In Arizona, 41-year-old *Ranger* **Paul Braxton Fugate** vanished without a trace from the **Chiricahua National Monument**. After a morning working at the monument's visitor centre, he left to hike a well-known trail but never returned. Despite a large search of the area, no trace of Fugate has ever been found. Investigators have long suspected foul play and as such, the **National Park Service** (*NPS*) has put up a $60,000 (USD) reward to anyone who can provide information that leads to a suspect.

FAMILY MURDERS - January 14th

In Vandenburgh County, Indiana, **Donald Ray Wallace Jr.**, robbed the home of **Ralph Hendricks**, while Hendricks was out for the night. Wallace then became greedy and decided to break into the house next door. He found the Gilligan family inside. **Patrick Gilligan**, his wife **Teresa** and their two children aged four and five, were tied up and shot in the head, killing them all instantly. Wallace then robbed the property of guns, collectables, and other belongings, all of which were traced, leading to Wallace's arrest. Initially, Wallace was found incompetent to stand trial and remained in a psychiatric hospital for two years before his trial. He was later convicted and sentenced to death for the four murders. He was executed by lethal injection in Indiana on March 10th 2005.

COLD CASE - January 15th

In Columbia County, Florida, 36-year-old **Willie Mease Presley** was shot dead at *Presley Place*. She was discovered in the back room of the business, laying on her side. No suspect was ever caught for the murder and no motive was ever found. Despite numerous investigations over the years, Presley's murder remains unsolved. It is an active cold case in Columbia County.

COLD CASE SOLVED WITH BEER MUG - January 16th

In Castle Rock, Colorado, the body of 21-year-old **Helene Pruszynski** was found in a field on *Daniels Park Road*. She had been raped and stabbed to death just hours earlier by an unidentified attacker. She had been returning home from her internship at a radio station when she was abducted from a bus stop nearby. The case went cold for almost 40 years until December 2019, when *Douglas County Sheriff's* detectives arrested **James Curtis Clanton** in Florida.

A few days before his arrest, detectives watched him in a bar and worked with the bar attendant to get hold of the empty beer mug. DNA from it matched the suspect in the Pruszynski murder. They had previously used new genealogy tracking to finger him as the suspect. Clanton, who was 22-years-old at the time, lived near the scene of the crime and had previously been charged with rape in 1975. Clanton was recently charged with Pruszynski's murder.

TRAIN BOMBING - January 17th

In Dunmurry, Belfast, the *Provisional Irish Republican Army* (**IRA**) exploded a bomb on a passenger train travelling from Ballymena to Belfast. The intention had been to explode the device as they neared Belfast but the bomb went off prematurely.

The explosion killed three people, injured five more and destroyed the train. One of the dead was 26-year-old IRA member **Kevin Delaney**. The fire had been so intense that the three dead victims had nearly been burned to ash. One of the injured was IRA member, **Patrick Flynn**, who was severely disfigured in the explosion. He was arrested and convicted of manslaughter and explosive offences.

MACABRE DISCOVERY - January 18th

At Ballinagee Bridge, near the *Turloch Hill power station* in Ireland, the decomposing body of factory worker **Phyllis Murphy** was discovered. On December 22nd 1979, she had spent the day Christmas shopping in Newbridge and was last seen at a bus stop outside the *Keadeen Hotel* in the early evening. She was never seen alive again. Her murder remained a cold case for 23 years, until 2003 when former Army sergeant and father-of-five **John Crerar** was convicted of her murder. He had raped Murphy, before strangling and beating her to death. Crerar was later sentenced to life in prison.

MYSTERY DISAPPEARANCE - January 19th

in New South Wales, Australia, 28-year-old **Barbara Gibson** disappeared without a trace. Gibson had moved to Sydney from Wangi Wangi, just two weeks before and said that she was going flat-hunting with a friend. She was last seen by her aunt in Sydney on this day in 1980. Gibson has packed a bag with the intention of staying with her parents for a few days back in Wangi Wangi but she never arrived. She was reported missing four days later. Despite being a regular hitchhiker, no trace of Gibson has ever been found. Investigators have long suspected that Gibson had been a victim of foul play.

BOMBING - January 20th

In Basque Country, Northern Spain, a bomb planted in a local bar exploded and killed four people with another 10 injured. The attack had been carried out by the *Grupos Armados Españoles* (**GAE**), who were an armed group operating in the Basque Country in the early years of Spanish democracy. The bar had been a target as it was thought to have been a meeting point for *Basque Nationalists*. The bomb was placed in a cardboard box next to the entrance door. The explosion was so powerful that it collapsed the roof of the building and split nearby cars in half. Investigators stated that one of the victim's body had been *'completely destroyed'*. No arrests have ever been made.

MACABRE DISCOVERY - January 21st

In Spokane County, Washington, the body of an unidentified 35 to 45-year-old white male was discovered in a railroad tunnel, east of Spokane city. The man was considered to have been homeless and was found by three other homeless people inside the tunnel, two days after his death. The man had been beaten so forcefully that he had received multiple fractures and broken bones. He was then set on fire and burned to death. The circumstances surrounding the murder and the identity of the victim remain a mystery to this day.

MYSTERY DISAPPEARANCE - January 22nd

In Ashland County, Wisconsin, 22-year-old *U.S Navy Seaman* **Andrew Thomas Viater**, left his home in a blizzard and was never seen again. His father heard the front door slam and looked outside to see footprints in the snow. He followed the footprints toward the nearby railroad tracks where they mysteriously stopped. His father reported him missing two days later. Throughout the years, numerous investigators have looked at the case, even trying to match dental records with various **John Doe's** throughout the country but there has been no match. Despite a suggestion that he had eloped and created a new identity, no trace of Viater has ever been found.

MURDER - January 23rd

In Philadelphia, police officers responded to a call of unrest at an apartment block on *West Logan Street*. When they entered the third-floor apartment, they discovered 51-year-old **Edward Gathright** laying on his bed with a gunshot wound to the head. He was immediately taken to hospital where he died of his wound shortly after. Despite witnesses and leads, no suspect was ever found. Gathright's murder remains unsolved and an active cold case in the city of Philadelphia.

MURDER - January 24th

In Maricopa County, Arizona, 22-year-old **Scott Schwartz** was brutally murdered by three men. **Darrick Leonard Gerlaugh**, **Joseph Encinas**, and **Matthew Leisure**, had decided to hitchhike and the kill whoever offered them a ride. They ordered Schwartz to a remote location where they attacked him. They drove their car over him and positioned the wheel on Schwartz' body before revving it to full power. Gerlaugh and Leisure then stabbed him 40 times with a screwdriver before hiding the body in a nearby field. They were all arrested shortly after and charged with the murder. Encinas and Leisure were sentenced to life in prison. Gerlaugh was sentenced to death and executed by lethal injection on February 3rd 1999.

BANK SIEGE - January 25th

In Pretoria, South Africa, members of *Umkhonto we Sizwe* (**MK**) unit entered the **Silverton Bank** and held the customers hostage. They had been on their way to carry out an unknown mission when police confronted them, so they took over the bank before they could be caught. A shoot-out began that lasted all day between the MK unit and the *Pretorian Police*. By the end of the day, two civilians and all three MK members had been killed. The event became known as the **Silverton Bank Siege**.

MURDER - January 26th

In Derry, Northern Ireland, prison officer **Graham Cox** was shot dead while driving home from work at **Magilligan Prison**. He had been killed in an ambush carried out by the **IRA**, during the troubles in Northern Ireland in the 1970s and 1980s. Many prison officers and ex-prison officers were killed during this period. The IRA were a paramilitary organisation who sought the establishment of a republic, the reunification of Ireland, and more importantly the end of British rule in Northern Ireland. They gave up arms in 2005 with the intention of pursuing peaceful campaigns to meet their objectives.

COIN SHOP KILLER - January 27th

In Everett, Washington, 36-year-old antique shop owner **David Sutton** was found dead. An estimated $80,000 (USD) in silver coins had been robbed from the shop. Sutton was the first victim of serial killer **Charles T. Sinclair**, AKA: **The Coin Shop Killer**. Sinclair was arrested in Alaska in 1990 for the suspected connection of eight murders. When the investigation searched a storage shed owned by him, they found the evidence they needed. Maps, false ID machines, C-4 explosives, land-mines and an entire stash of rare coins were the tip of the iceberg. He was subsequently linked to at least **11** murders and two rapes. He would specifically target coin shops to rob, before killing the owners to hide any witnesses. In October 1990, while in custody, he died of a heart attack, leaving the investigation at a standstill.

KILLED IN THE LINE OF DUTY - January 28th

In New York, police officer **Cecil Frank Sledge** was shot dead while making a routine traffic stop in Brooklyn. Sledge had recognised 22-year-old **Salvatore De Sarno** as being wanted in connection with a robbery. Sledge pulled him over and was approaching the vehicle when De Sarno shot him. Sledge's gun belt became trapped in the car wheel and he was dragged over a quarter of a mile before rolling away. Sledge died of his wounds shortly after. Realising he was the subject of a manhunt, De Sarno broke into the home of an elderly female and held her hostage until police finally arrested him. Despite claiming it was self-defence, De Sarno was sentenced to a minimum of 25 years in prison in 1981. He has since been denied parole twice, once in 2014 and again in 2016.

COLD CASE DISAPPEARANCE - January 29th

In New South Wales, Australia, 20-year-old **Marcus Wayne Allcorn** vanished without a trace. His friends had arranged a birthday party at the **Imperial hotel** where Allcorn worked. He had finished his night shift and was on his way to the gathering. He was last seen in the early hours of the morning but he never arrived at the party and was reported missing shortly after. A lengthy investigation suspected that he had been a victim of foul play. No trace of Allcorn has ever been found. The investigation is now an active cold case but is no closer to solving the mystery.

TAXICAB MURDER - January 30th

Marion County, Indiana, taxi driver **Kenneth Chambers** was killed by **Gary Burris** and robber by two accomplices, **Emmett Merriweather** and **James Thompson**.

Chambers' nude body was found face down in an alley, in the early hours of the morning. He had been tied up and shot in the head. The three of them were caught the next day when investigators read the cab company log and saw that Burris was the last passenger. Merriweather was sentenced to 15 years in prison. Thompson was sentenced to 50 years in prison. Burris was sentenced to death and executed by lethal injection on November 20th 1997.

EMBASSY ATTACK - January 31st

In Guatemala, a group of armed peasants belonging to the work union, **Committee for Peasant Unity**, entered the *Spanish Embassy*. They announced they had arrived at the embassy in peace and wanted a press conference shortly after. Spain was believed to have been sympathetic to the cause of the peasants. Before their press conference could begin, 300 armed police and Guatemalan agents surrounded the building, forcing the group to take hostages and barricade windows.

At some point, a fire started and tore through the building. The intensity of the fire killed 36 people by burning them alive. *SWAT* police chief, **Pedro García Arredondo**, had refused firefighters to combat the fire. In 2015, Arredondo was convicted of murder and crimes against humanity.

FEBRUARY

CONVOY ATTACK - February 1st

In Ispaster, Spain, the Basque separatist organisation **ETA** attacked a convoy of civil guards who were protecting a group of workers and weapons. The guards were moving the weapons from *Esperanza y Cia Arms factory* to an unknown location in Bilbao. Six guards were killed by gunfire and grenade attacks. Two ETA members were also killed by their own grenades. In 1984, **Jaime Rementería Beotegui** was found guilty of participation in the attack and was sentenced to life in prison but released in 2002.

PRISON RIOTS - February 2nd

in Santa Fe County, New Mexico, the **New Mexico State Penitentiary Riot** began and lasted for almost 36 hours. It went on to become one of the most violent prison riots in United States history. Inmates managed to take complete control of the prison and took 12 prison guards' hostage. Seven of the guards were brutally beaten and raped during the takeover. 33 inmates at the prison were murdered by other inmates, including 12 who had been in the *Protective Custody Unit*. Some of them had been mutilated and tortured before being dismembered. Over 200 people were injured in the riots. 36 hours later, heavily armed officers managed to slowly regain control of the prison. Although some inmates with charged with minor felonies, most of the crimes committed during the riots went unpunished.

SERIAL KILLER DOUBLE MURDER - February 3rd

In West Hollywood, 15-year-old **Charles Miranda** was picked up by serial killer **William George Bonin** and accomplice **Gregory Matthew Miley**. Charles was raped, beaten, and strangled to death with his own shirt because Miley was not able to get sexually aroused. His restrained and nude body was discovered the next morning beside an alley in Malibu. On the same evening, after dumping Charles's body, the pair of murderers sought another victim. They picked up 12-year-old **James McCabe** who was on his way to Disneyland with family. Bonin raped McCabe in the back of the van and they both later beat and strangled him to death. McCabe's body was found in a dumpster three days later.

William Bonin became known as **The Freeway Killer**. He was known to dump his victim's bodies on the side of freeways. Bonin killed at least 21 people from 1979 to 1980 and was sentenced to death. He was executed in February 1996. **Miley**, who helped Bonin kill some of his victims, was sentenced to 25 years to life in prison.

DOUBLE MURDER - February 4th

In Belfast, Northern Ireland, 60-year-old ex-prison officer **Patrick Mackin** and his wife, 58-year-old **Violet Mackin**, were shot dead in their own home. The devout Catholics had been assassinated by the *Irish Republican Army* (**IRA**). No one was ever arrested for the murders. Their deaths were linked to the troubles in Northern Ireland in the 1970s and 1980s.

COLD CASE DISAPPEARANCE - February 5th

In Half Moon Bay, California, 23-year-old **William Robert Prescott** disappeared without a trace. He had last been seen driving a white *1964 International Harvester* pickup truck. Despite being well-liked in the community and having no reason to vanish, no trace of Prescott has ever been found. Investigators have long suspected foul play.

ROBBERY/MURDER - February 6th

In Harris County, Texas, 22-year-old **Donna Kate Thomas** was shot dead in her own apartment. **Darryl Elroy Stewart** and an accomplice had broken into her home with the intention of robbing her. When Thomas refused to have sex with him, he shot her at close range, killing her instantly. Both Stewart and his accomplice were caught shortly after. The accomplice received 20 years in prison for pleading guilty to robbery. Stewart was sentenced to death for murder and executed by lethal injection in Texas on May 3rd 1993.

CONVICTIONS OVERTURNED - February 7th

In Brooklyn, New York, a fire broke out at a *Park Slope* townhouse on *Sackett Street*. 27-year-old **Elizabeth Kinsey** and her five children were killed in the ferocious fire. The owner of the building, **Hannah Quick**, told investigators that she heard three men whispering in the hallway shortly before the fire. A fire marshal later testified that an accelerant had been used. Despite only circumstantial evidence, **Raymond Mora**, **William Vasquez**, and **Amaury Villalobos** were convicted of arson and six counts of murder. They were sentenced to 25 years to life in prison.

In 2014, Hannah Quick died of natural causes. Before she died, she told her daughter that she had framed the three men and received a large insurance pay out due to the fire. In 2015, based on the deathbed confession and new evidence that claimed it was not an arson attack, the three men were exonerated. It had come too late for Mora, who died in 1989 while serving his sentence. Vasquez and Villalobos were paroled in 2012 and had their convictions overturned.

CAR THEFT MURDER - February 8th

In Jefferson Parish, Louisiana, **David Vogler Jr.**, was stabbed to death in his car during a robbery gone wrong. He was murdered by career criminal **Johnny Taylor Jr.**, who was attempting to steal Vogler's vehicle. Vogler's body was found in the trunk of his car the following day. Four months later in Alabama, on June 17th, Taylor was caught driving Vogler's wife's car which he had stolen instead. He was charged with the murder and subsequently sentenced to death. Taylor was executed in the electric chair on February 19th 1984.

MURDER - February 9th

In Denver, Colorado, the body of 37-year-old **David Sullivan** was found in an alley behind **Smokey's Bar** on *North Osage Street*. The report had been phoned in by a bartender from the bar. Sullivan worked two jobs, at night he worked at the **Regency Inn** and during the day worked at the **Stop n' Go** in the city. He was found with multiple stab wounds and died a few hours later in the hospital. Despite a murder investigation and multiple leads, the case remains a mystery and no suspect has ever been caught. It has been suggested that the killer may have been a customer in the shop or guest at the Inn.

ROBBERY/MURDER - February 10th

In Galveston County, Texas, career criminal **Warren Eugene Bridge** and accomplice **Robert Joseph Costa**, entered a convenience store with the intention of robbing it.

599

During the robbery, Bridge shot 63-year-old shop worker, **Walter Rose**. Bridge and Costa had eloped with just $24 (USD). Rose had been shot four times and died of his wounds two weeks later. Four days before his death, Bridge and Costa were captured during a raid on their motel room. Costa was sentenced to 13 years for aggravated robbery. Bridge was sentenced to death and executed by lethal injection in Texas on November 22nd 1994.

COLD CASE MURDER - February 11th

In Dundee, Scotland, 20-year-old trainee nursery nurse **Elizabeth McCabe** was reported missing by her parents. She had been out with friends the night before and was last seen in the early hours of the morning near a nightclub in the city. On February 26th, her partially nude body was found in undergrowth at *Templeton Woods*. Her clothing was found a few days later. On March 13th, Tayside police officers attended a séance, held by psychics, to determine what happened to McCabe but didn't come up with any solid evidence. In 2007, after being accused of the murder multiple times, taxi driver **Vincent Simpson** was found not-guilty during a trial and went free. McCabe's murder was linked to that of **Carol Lannen**, whose body was also found in *Templeton Woods* in 1979. Despite links to numerous serial killers, the deaths of both victims have never been solved.

MACABRE DISCOVERY - February 12th

In Volusia County, Florida, the skeletal remains of an unidentified 25 to 40-year-old female were discovered near a roadway. She had died at least one year earlier. Despite having no recognisable features, an investigation suspected she had been the victim of foul play. No missing person in the area was linked to her. The circumstances surrounding her death remain a mystery and she has never been identified.

RADIO STATION BOMBING - February 13th

In San José, Costa Rica, a large explosion ripped through the **Radio Noticias del Continente** (radio news station) causing thousands of dollars' worth of damage. The bombing had been carried out by the **Fifteenth of September Legion** (*Legión Quince de Septiembre*) who were an anti-communist guerrilla group founded in Guatemala. Their mission was to overthrow the **Sandinista National Liberation Front** government. No one was killed in the explosion and no suspects were ever caught.

COLD CASE DISAPPEARANCE - February 14th

In Baldwin, Pennsylvania, 25-year-old **Michael Rosenblum** disappeared under mysterious circumstances. A day earlier, after numerous encounters with drugs, his parents finally banished him from their home. He left with his girlfriend, **Lisa**. During the 14th, after a quick visit to the hospital for a drug hangover, Lisa was driving them home when they stopped at a gas station. Rosenblum suddenly became agitated and drove off in her car, leaving Lisa stranded at the station. He was never seen again.

His father actively searched for him, under the assumption that he could finally get him off drugs for good. Although the car was found two weeks later, it was impounded and remained unidentified for three months. Later investigators claimed that the car fiasco led to a mishandling of the case and had lost them valuable time. In 1990, a skull fragment was found a few miles from where the car was found. A coroner confirmed it was highly likely that it belonged to Rosenblum but couldn't confirm a cause of death. Rosenblum's family believed that the Baldwin police department covered up the disappearance. Despite a large reward and numerous searches, the disappearance remains unsolved.

MURDER - February 15th

In Howard County, Maryland, 70-year-old **Rebecca H. 'Dolly' Davis** was stabbed to death by **Vernon Lee Clark**. He was a handyman who had helped Davis out on numerous occasions and at the time was never considered a suspect. Davis' partially nude and decomposing body was found in the back yard of her home on February 22nd. Over two decades later, new DNA technology linked Clark to the murder. He was already serving a life sentence for the 1989 murder of 23-year-old Kathleen Gouldin, who had been found beaten to death in her own apartment. Clark was also linked to the 1981 murder of **Evelyn Dietrich** and the 1984 death of **Myrtle Watson**. He was sentenced to life in prison without the possibility of parole for the Davis murder.

COLD CASE - February 16th

In Riverside County, California, the body of an unidentified female in her early twenties was discovered in a remote ravine. She had been killed the day before and dumped in the ravine. Her clothes were of a high quality and it was assumed that she belonged to the middle or upper class but no one of her description had been reported missing. The circumstances surrounding her death and her identity remain a mystery. She became known as the **Riverside County Jane Doe**.

MISSING PERSON COLD CASE - February 17th

In Marin County, California, 20-year-old **Jorgen 'Andy' Andersen** missed his plane and was never seen again. He had last been seen leaving his apartment in San Rafael, heading towards **San Francisco International Airport**. He had purchased a flight ticket to visit his parents in Jamaica but was reported missing shortly after. A police investigation found no trace of him in his apartment of near the airport.

They learned that there was a warrant issued for his arrest for an automobile theft but it wasn't so serious that he needed to elope. Despite the case still being open, investigators have long suspected foul play.

SERIAL KILLER - February 18th

Near the *Templin Highway* in California, the decapitated body of 19-year-old Marine, **Mark Alan Marsh**, was discovered. He had last been seen hitchhiking towards *Buena Park*. He had been picked up and killed by serial killer **Randy Steven Kraft**, AKA: **The Southern California Strangler** or **The Scorecard Killer**. The California Strangler was the name that the investigation attributed to Kraft's murders. The Scorecard Killer attribute was given to Kraft after his arrest because he kept coded references to his victims. He had beaten Marsh to death before cutting of his head and hands. Kraft was captured in 1983 and was convicted of 16 murders but it is suggested he may have been responsible for 67 killings during his campaign of terror.

MURDER - February 19th

In Kings County, California, **Nancy Adams** shot dead her friend and lover, **Jerry Lee Pollock**. Adams attempted to get away with it by coming up with a weak cover story. Shortly after she killed him, on a remote roadway, she waited in her van and flashed down a passing car. When the occupants, **David Oliveira** and his wife **Kathy**, approached Adams, she began screaming about two or three men who had ambushed them and killed Pollock. The Oliviera's took Adams to a nearby house and waited with her for the police to arrive. Her father also arrived with police and Adams cried out that they had shot '*her Jerry*', who she claimed was going to marry her the following day.

Within a few days, Adams was the prime suspect. The gun used to kill Pollock, had been fired from Adams own vehicle, even leaving bullet cases on the floor. The bullets were matched to Adams own gun and she was arrested. After numerous interviews she finally confessed to the murder, claiming she had acted out violently after an intense argument. She was later sentenced to 25 years to life in prison.

ROBBERY/MURDER - February 20th

In Grand Rapids, Michigan, in the early hours of the afternoon, **Janice Kahn** was found dead in the back room of the **Prism Shop**. She had been shot execution-style with a bullet to the head. Despite her clothes being ripped and semen found on her thigh, there was no sign of a sexual assault. The murder was deemed to be the result of a robbery. Witness statements and forensics led to the arrest of **Brady Goree** who had been in the shop earlier in the day. He was later sentenced to life in prison without the possibility of parole.

COLD CASE - February 21st

In Brighton, Colorado, the body of 19-year-old **Cynthia Mae Boyd** was discovered near a roadway exiting the city. She had been strangled to death in the early hours of the morning by an unidentified assailant. Despite evidence of murder being found at the scene, no suspect has ever been caught and it remains an open cold case to this day.

HOLLYWOOD MURDER - February 22nd

In New York, American actor and **Dick Kallman** and his partner **Stephen Szladek** were murdered during a home invasion at their Hollywood apartment. Three intruders had broken into the home with the intention of robbing them of their collection of art, antiques, and jewellery. They were later caught and convicted of murder. Kallman was known for playing the title role in the TV sitcom, **Hank**.

MURDER - February 23rd

In Bowie County, Texas, **Leon Calahan** was shot dead outside of a nightclub by brothers **William Kendrick Burns** and **Victor Burns**. That same night, they kidnapped **Bryan Keith Sanders** during a robbery and threatened to kill him. They stopped the car near a lake and threw Sanders out of the car. They were about to kill him when they were interrupted by law enforcement. Believing it was just a fight, the officers let them go. On March 28th 1981, the brothers robbed and killed 18-year-old **Johnny Lynn Hamlett**. They were arrested in April of 1981 and charged with both murders. Victor Burns was sentenced to life in prison without the possibility of parole. William Burns was sentenced to death and executed by lethal injection in Texas on April 11th 2002.

MURDER FOR HIRE - February 24th

In Salt Lake City, Utah, the body of 22-year-old **Timothy Glashien** was discovered by hikers at *Millcreek Canyon*. He had been shot multiple times the day before by hitman-for-hire **Stephen Wayne Anderson**, who later confessed to the murder. He was also convicted of another murder in California and had used the same weapon to kill Glashien. He was later sentenced to death and executed in January 2002. Anderson never told investigators who hired him to kill Glashien, and to this day, their identity remains a mystery.

DOUBLE MURDER - February 25th

In Harris County, Texas, 30-year-old **Robert Banks** and 26-year-old **Bob Skeens** were strangled to death in Banks' apartment. The night before, Banks had picked up three hitchhikers, **James Michael Briddle**, Briddle's ex-wife and their friend, **Pamela Perillo**. The following morning, on the 25th, the three of them robbed and killed Banks and Skeens. They were arrested shortly after and convicted of multiple crimes. Perillo was sentenced to five years for robbery. Briddle's ex-wife was sentenced to death which was commuted to life when she testified against Briddle. Briddle was sentenced to death and executed by lethal injection in Texas on December 12th 1995.

DEATH SENTENCE - February 26th

In Texas, robber and murderer **Cesar Roberto Fierro** was sentenced to death for the murder of taxi driver **Nicolas Castanon** on February 27th 1979. The murder led to a manhunt that lasted five months. The criminal case against Fierro was controversial because Mexican police had apparently arrested his parents and threatened to torture them unless Fierro confessed. Fierro was arrested in the Summer of 1979 and charged with the murder. He was sentenced to death on February 26th 1980. Fierro remained on death row for almost 40 years until December 2019 when his death sentence was commuted to life in prison.

EMBASSY SIEGE - February 27th

In Bogotá, Colombia, 17 members of the **19th of April Movement** (*M-19*) stormed the **Dominican Embassy** in the city and captured 60 hostages. The siege lasted two months until April 27th when all the members orchestrated their escape and fled to Cuba. One member of the group was killed on the first day of the siege by police. M-19 were a Colombian guerrilla organisation movement whose aim was to pave the way for democracy in Colombia. They had been inspired by other South American guerrilla groups, including the **Tupamaros** in Uruguay and the **Montoneros** in Argentina. Aside from the member who had been killed, no other member was caught in relation to the siege.

SERIAL KILLING BABYSITTER - February 28th

In Florida, two-year-old **Cassidy Johnson** died from what was assumed to be encephalitis, after having been rushed to hospital a few days earlier. A later autopsy report showed that Cassidy had suffered a severe skull injury. Unbeknownst to investigators at the time, she had been murdered by serial killing babysitter **Christine Falling**, who was only 16-years-old. Between 1980 and 1982, Falling murdered five children by suffocating them. She later claimed that she was hearing voices telling her to do it. After a lengthy investigation, Falling was arrested in 1982 and later convicted of three of the murders. She was sentenced to life in prison.

COLD CASE MURDER - February 29th

In Denver, Colorado, police officers went to the property of 44-year-old **Ronald Alexander**, after reports of gunshots. They found Alexander on his garage floor. He had been shot by an unidentified assailant. Despite being taken to hospital, he died the following day of his wounds. There seemed to be no motive in the murder. The circumstances surrounding his death and the identity of the shooter have remained a mystery ever since.

—SAMPLE END—

TRUE CRIME 365 BOOKS ARE

AVAILABLE INTERNATIONALLY THROUGH AMAZON

DIGITALLY OR AS A PAPERBACK

www.benoakley.co.uk

'Thank you for reading and coming along for the ride! I hope you had as much fun as I did. If you have time to spare then a short review would be hugely appreciated.'

Visit **Ben Oakley** to discover new stories, find out more about the author and make contact. Make sure to follow Ben Oakley on the book site of your choice.

Printed in Great Britain
by Amazon